BETWEEN WOMEN

WITHDRAWN

BETWEEN WOMEN

Friendship, Desire,
and Marriage in
Victorian England

Sharon Marcus

PRINCETON UNIVERSITY PRESS

PRINCETON AND OXFORD

Published by Princeton University Press, 41 William Street, Princeton,
New Jersey 08540
In the United Kingdom: Princeton University Press, 3 Market Place,
Woodstock, Oxfordshire OX20 1SY

Library of Congress Cataloging-in-Publication Data

Marcus, Sharon, 1966–
Between women : friendship, desire, and marriage in Victorian England /
Sharon Marcus.
    p.   cm.
Includes bibliographical references and index.
ISBN-13: 978-0-691-12820-7 (hardcover : alk. paper)
ISBN-10: 0-691-12820-0 (hardcover : alk. paper)
ISBN-13: 978-0-691-12835-1 (pbk. : alk. paper)
ISBN-10: 0-691-12835-9 (pbk. : alk. paper)
1. Women—England—History. 2. Women—Social networks—England.
3. Lesbians—England—History. 4. Female friendship—England. 5. Women
in Literature. I. Title.
HQ1599.E5M37   2007
306.84′8094209034—dc22   2006020026

British Library Cataloging-in-Publication Data is available

This book has been composed in Sabon

Printed on acid-free paper. ∞

pup.princeton.edu

Printed in the United States of America

10 9 8 7 6 5

Contents

Illustrations

Acknowledgments

FIRST AND FOREMOST I THANK the institutions who generously provided me with the time and support needed to research and write this book: the University of California, Berkeley; Columbia University; the American Council of Learned Societies, through the Frederick Burkhardt Residential Fellowship Program for Recently Tenured Scholars, and the School of Social Science at the Institute for Advanced Study.

I am deeply grateful to a series of brilliant research assistants whom I won't call tireless, since their sheer number suggests I wore them out all too quickly: Simon Stern, Karen Tongson, Susan Zieger, Matthew Lewsadder, Esther Pun, Jami Bartlett, Jill Salmon, Michele Hardesty, Kristi Brecht, Alexis Korman, Christine Leja, Avi Alpert, and Sydney Cochran.

It has been a pleasure to discover over and over again how others often understand what we are trying to say better than we do ourselves. This book would not exist without the help of colleagues who talked with me about my work and invited me to talk about it with others, especially Vanessa Schwartz, Richard Stein, Michael Wood, Deborah Nord, Claudia Johnson, Joan Scott, Judith Butler, Florence Dore, Elizabeth Weed, Ellen Rooney, Didier Eribon, Françoise Gaspard, Deborah Cohen, Masha Belenky, Margaret Cohen, Nancy Ruttenburg, Leah Price, Elaine Hadley, Andrew Miller, Ivan Kreilkamp, Deborah Cohen, Michael Lucey, Karen Tongson, Kate Flint, Martha Howell, Judith Walkowitz, Anne Higonnet, Carolyn Dinshaw, Anne Humpherys, Gerhard Joseph, Heather Fielding, Ruth Leys, Lila Abu-Lughod, Marianne Hirsch, Seth Koven, Jean Howard, and Susan Pedersen. Diana Fuss, Carolyn Dever, and Bonnie Anderson read the manuscript in its entirety and made superb suggestions for revision.

A particularly generous set of friends and colleagues offered help and comments at crucial junctures and on short notice: Ellis Avery, Dori Hale, Richard Halpern, Jeff Knapp, Hermione Lee, John Plotz, Christopher Nealon, Neil Goldberg, Cindy Hanson, Jennifer Callahan, Michael Lucey, Matt Pincus, and Alex Robertson Textor. Others have offered other forms of love and wisdom, especially Beth Biegler, Rena Fogel, Atsumi Hara, Ed Stein, Steve Lin, Anita Parately, and Sid Maskit.

Chapters 3 and 5 include significantly revised material from previously published essays. For permission to reprint material from "Reflections on Victorian Fashion Plates," which appeared in *differences: A Journal of Feminist Cultural Studies* 14.3 (2003), 4–27, I thank Duke University

Press. For permission to use material from "The Queerness of Victorian Marriage Reform," which appeared in Carol R. Berkin, Judith L. Pinch, and Carol Appel, eds., *Exploring Women's Studies: Looking Forward, Looking Back* (2006), 87–106, I thank Pearson Education, Inc., Upper Saddle River, NJ. I also express appreciation to the University Seminars at Columbia University for their help in publication. Material in this book was presented to the University Seminar on British History.

It has been a delight to work with Hanne Winarsky, my incisive and enthusiastic editor at Princeton University Press, and with the expert staff there. A very special thanks as well to Kathy McMillan and Dimitri Karetnikov, who did a meticulous job of preparing the images, and to my wonderful copyeditor, Jennifer Liese.

The greatest pleasure of this project has been sharing it with Ellis Avery: tireless cheerleader, eagle-eyed editor, fabulous girlfriend, supportive partner, all-around sweetheart, and my merry accomplice in crimes against nature.

BETWEEN WOMEN

The Female Relations of Victorian England

IN 1844 A TEN-YEAR-OLD GIRL named Emily Pepys, the daughter of the bishop of Worcester, made the following entry in the journal she had begun to keep that year: "I had the oddest dream last night that I ever dreamt; even the remembrance of it is very extraordinary. There was a very nice pretty young lady, who I (a girl) was going *to be married to!* (the very idea!) I loved her and even now love her very much. It was quite a settled thing and we were going to be married very soon. All of a sudden I thought of Teddy [a boy she liked] and asked Mama several times if I might be let off and after a little time I woke. I remember it all perfectly. A very foggy morning."[1] Emily Pepys found the mere idea of a girl marrying a lady extraordinary ("the very idea!"). We may find it even more surprising that she had the dream at all, then recorded it in a journal that was not private but meant to be read by family and friends. As we read her entry more closely, it may also seem puzzling that Emily's attitude toward her dream is more bemused than revolted, not least because her prospective bride is "a very nice pretty young lady," and marrying her has the pleasant aura of security suggested by the almost Austenian phrase, "It was quite a settled thing." Even Emily's desire to be "let off" so that she can return to Teddy must be ratified by a woman, "Mama."

A proper Victorian girl dreaming about marrying a pretty lady challenges our vision of the Victorians, but this book argues that Emily's dream was in fact typical of a world that made relationships between women central to femininity, marriage, and family life. We are now all too familiar with the Victorian beliefs that women and men were essentially opposite sexes, and that marriage to a man was the chief end of a woman's existence.[2] But a narrow focus on women's status as relative creatures, defined by their difference from and subordination to men, has limited our understanding of gender, kinship, and sexuality. Those concepts cannot be fully understood if we define them only in terms of two related oppositions: men versus women, and homosexuality versus heterosexuality. Our preconceptions have led us to doubt the importance of relationships such as marriage between women, which was not only a Victorian dream but also a Victorian reality; many adults found the idea of two women marrying far less preposterous than little Emily Pepys did. When activist and author Frances Power Cobbe published a widely read autobiography in 1894, for example, she included a photograph of the house she lived in with sculptor Mary Lloyd. Throughout the book, references to joint finances and travels, to "our friends," "our garden," and "our beautiful and beloved home" treated Cobbe's conjugal arrangement with Lloyd as a neutral public fact, one Cobbe expressed even more clearly in letters to friends in which she called Lloyd both her "husband" and her "wife."[3]

Female marriage, however, is not the sole subject of this book, which also examines friendship, mother-daughter dynamics, and women's investment in images of femininity, in order to make a fundamental but curiously overlooked point: even within a single class or generation, there were many different kinds of relationships between women. Often when I would tell people I was writing a book about relationships between women, they would assume that was a timid way of saying I was writing about lesbians. There are lesbians in this book, if by that we mean women who had sexual relationships with other women, but this book is not only about lesbians; nor is it about the lesbian potential of all relationships between women. Indeed, if we take "lesbian" to connote deviance, gender inversion, a refusal to objectify women, or a rejection of marriage as an institution, then none of the relationships discussed here was lesbian. Women like Frances Power Cobbe embraced marriage as a model for their sexual partnerships with women even as they sought to reform marriage as a legal institution. Female friendships peaceably coexisted with heterosexual marriages and moreover, helped to promote them. The hyperfeminine activities of looking at fashion plates and playing with dolls encouraged women to desire feminine objects, and mother-daughter relationships were rife with the same eroticized power struggles as those between male and female kin.

OVERVIEW

The first section of this book is about friendship. Chapter 1 uses lifewriting (memoirs, autobiographies, letters, and diaries) to show the importance of female friendship in middle-class women's lives. Friendship between women reinforced femininity, but at the same time it licensed forms of agency women were discouraged from exercising with men. As friends, women could compete for one another, enjoy multiple attachments, and share religious fervor. This chapter also distinguishes female friendship from female marriage, as well as from unrequited love and infatuation between women. Chapter 2 surveys the Victorian novel and shows the paradigmatic importance of female friendship in courtship narratives, including *David Copperfield*, *Aurora Leigh*, and *Shirley*. It concludes with a reading of Charlotte Brontë's *Villette* as an exception that proves the rule, since its heroine rejects female friendship but also never marries. In these readings, I depart from theories of the novel that emphasize how homosexuality and female friendship have been repressed by heterosexual plots and can be retrieved only through symptomatic reading, which seeks to reconstruct what a text excludes. Rather than focus on what texts do not or cannot say, I use a method I call "just reading," which attends to what texts make manifest on their surface, in this case the crucial role female friendship plays in courtship narratives. Female friendship functions as a narrative matrix that generates closure without being shattered by the storms and stresses of plot. A series of detailed analyses shows that female friendship was neither a static auxiliary to the marriage plot nor a symptomatic exclusion from it, but instead a transmission mechanism that kept narrative energies on track.

The second section focuses on femininity as an object of desire for women. In chapter 3, I show that hyperfeminine discourses about fashion and dolls shared with pornography a preoccupation with voyeurism, exhibitionism, punishment, humiliation, domination, and submission. The connections could be astonishingly literal, as when pornographic literature reprinted fashion-magazine correspondence debating the propriety of adult women birching adolescent girls. Fashion imagery and doll tales depicted women and girls in erotic dynamics with feminine objects; both represented those impulses as especially strong between mothers and daughters. The chapter makes a theoretical distinction between the sexual and the erotic in order to show that mainstream femininity was not secretly lesbian, but openly homoerotic. Within the realm of domestic consumer culture, Victorian women were as licensed to objectify women as were Victorian men. Chapter 4 is a close reading of Charles Dickens's *Great Expectations* in light of the argument in chapter 3. For Victorians, femininity depended as much on homoerotic as on heteroerotic desire, and Dickens explores what that might mean for men who desired women. His novel presents an older woman's obsessive, objectifying desire for her adopted daughter as a primal scene for the hero, who learns to equate social status and erotic desire with being a woman's pampered, fashionable doll. The female dyad's overt contempt for him as a working-class boy leads him to reject his male body by using fashion to become feminine—that is, to become a woman's object of desire.

The third and final section addresses marriage. Chapter 5 focuses on debates about marriage that followed the legalization of civil divorce in 1857. I show that many involved in those discussions were either women in female marriages or knew women in female marriages. Familiarity with those conjugal partnerships shaped feminist reformers' vision of marriage as a plastic institution that could be reformed into a dissoluble contract based on equality, rather than an irrevocable vow that created a hierarchy.

The notion of marriage as contract made it possible for some social think-ers to define marriage in nonheterosexual terms and to posit increasing equality and similarity between spouses as progress towards modernity. I turn to early anthropologists such as Henry Maine, Johann Bachofen, and Friedrich Engels to show how their histories of the family accommodated forms of kinship that depended neither on sexual difference nor on biolog-ical reproduction. Chapter 6 is a close reading of Anthony Trollope's novel *Can You Forgive Her?* The chapter opens by establishing that Trol-lope knew women in female marriages, then shows how he gave that knowledge narrative form. Like the anthropologists, Trollope associated female marriage with egalitarian contracts between husbands and wives, but unlike most of them, he branded both contract and female marriage as primitive. Even so, he remained eminently Victorian in the value he accorded intimacy between women, for female amity remains the basis of all the successful marriages in his novel.

Each of this book's sections provides evidence that relationships be-tween women were a constitutive element of Victorian gender and sexual-ity, and the force of that argument derives from the variety of relationships addressed. One could say that the first section is about the homosocial, the second about the homoerotic, and the third about the homosexual, but that terminology might falsely imply that the homoerotic and the homosexual lay outside the realm of the social. Instead, I address how each social bond differed from the other by virtue of its content, structure, status, and degree of flexibility.

The first section establishes that as an ideal, friendship was defined by altruism, generosity, mutual indebtedness, and a perfect balance of power. In a capitalist society deeply ambivalent about competition, female friend-ship offered a vision of perfect reciprocity for those who could afford not to worry about daily survival. In a liberal society that idealized self-development and sifting opinion through argument, female friendship epitomized John Stuart Mill's dream of subjectivity as dialogue.[4] The ob-ject that epitomized friendship was the gift, which could represent the giver's body (a lock of hair), merge with the recipient's body (a ring), or be a body (a man bestowed by one friend on another). Novelists and deeply religious women articulated that reciprocal ideal most forcefully, while worldly women highlighted the ways that friendship introduced an element of play into the gender system, licensing women to be more assert-ive and spontaneous with their female peers than they were with men. Friendship thus had an elastic relationship to the Victorian gender system: it could temporarily confer a new shape on femininity without altering its basic structure.

The second section of the book focuses on desire—not as an antisocial force but as a deeply regulated and regulating hierarchical structure of longing.[5] The female worlds of the fashion magazine and the doll tale revolved around differences in rank and power between image and viewer, woman and girl, punisher and punished, fashionable and lowly, mistress and doll. At stake in this section are erotic bonds between women and objects: images, toys, girls, and femininity itself. Where the ideal of friendship equated femininity with an ethic of spiritual coalescence and balance, fashion magazines and doll tales depicted femininity as a set of violent fantasies about the female body: its containment, explosion, display, or magical transformation. Female objectification was invested in binary divisions, but ironically, it was also the most mobile type of bond between women. The definition of fixed poles—object and owner, viewer and viewed, arrogant and abject—promoted the desire to shuttle back and forth between them. Dolls come to life, women become captives, and girls and boys change into ladies. Gayle Rubin famously identified men's traffic in female objects as the central dynamic of patriarchal culture; this chapter identifies an equally strong current in Victorian consumer culture, a female traffic in feminine objects displayed and sold for women's enjoyment and exploitation.[6]

The third and final section focuses on marriage as an institution that was mutating in the Victorian present, inspiring competing visions of what it had been in the past and might be in the future. Reform exposed the contradictions within the norm of happy hierarchical marriages, and divorce trials revealed the differences between the ideals embedded in the law and the complex reality of marriage as a lived institution. Those familiar with female marriages and their contractual principles of formation and dissolution had an extra-legal vantage point from which to reform marriage law. As social thinkers registered that marriage could accommodate variations such as divorce and same-sex unions, they became aware of the institution's plasticity, its ability to change without undergoing the kind of radical ruptures that yield completely new forms.

HISTORICAL AND DISCIPLINARY BORDERS

Why focus on England from 1830 to 1880? Those decades lie at the core of the Victorian period, which continues to be a touchstone for thinking about gender and sexuality, not least because the Victorian era has the remarkable capacity to seem both starkly different from the present and uncannily similar to it. The general public continues to see Victorians as terribly repressed, while specialists have by and large accepted Foucault's assertion that our own contemporary obsession with sex originates with the Victorians.[7] Having selected Victorian England for its canonical status in the history of sexuality, I stayed within the years from 1830 to 1880 because those years constitute a distinct period, especially with regard to gender, the family, and same-sex bonds between women. During those decades, the belief that men and women were opposite sexes, different in kind rather than degree, took hold in almost every class, and the previous era's concerns about female sexual voracity shifted to a view of women as either inherently domestic, maternal, and self-restrained, or susceptible to training in how to be so.[8] Marriage and family underwent corresponding changes. Historians of kinship argue endlessly about exactly when it first became common to think of marriage as the union of soulmates, but most agree that by 1830 that ideal had become a norm. Before the 1830s, certain classes of people did not valorize companionate marriage: workers often did not legally marry; aristocrats were openly adulterous; and Romantics and revolutionaries challenged the very bases of marriage. By the 1830s, companionate marriage was the standard for measuring alliances in all classes. Finally, the lesbian was not a distinct social type during the years 1830 to 1880, although male sodomy was a public and private obsession.[9] In the eighteenth century, it was possible to name the sapphist or tribade as an explicit object of satire, but by the 1830s new codes of propriety meant that only doctors and pornographers wrote directly about sex between women.[10] The figure of the sapphist came to seem less and less embedded in the social world of domestic conjugality, and therefore less and less related to women who lived in couples and adopted features of legal marriage.

Women, sexuality, and marriage began to change dramatically in the 1880s. Eugenics shifted the meaning of marriage from a spiritual union to a reproductive one that depended on heterosexual fertility and promoted racial purity. New Woman fiction and doctrine criticized men's oppression of women in ways that sexualized marriage, or rather heterosexualized it, by comparing it to prostitution and rape.[11] A new sense of heterosexuality, as a distinct sexual orientation formed in diametrical opposition to homosexuality, made marriage and the family the province of male-female unions.[12] In the 1890s, a discourse of lesbianism began to emerge in Edward Carpenter's homophile writings, Havelock Ellis's sexological studies, and women's responses to them.[13] Awareness of sex between women also increased after two well-publicized trials raised issues of sapphism and female inversion: the Maud Allan trial of 1919 and the Radclyffe Hall trial of 1929.[14] Women in female couples continued to use marriage as a model for their relationships—think of Gertrude Stein and Alice Toklas—but many female couples began to identify either with an ideal of pure, sexless love, or with a bohemian modernism that rejected marriage and monogamy as patriarchal institutions.[15]

I have chosen 1830 and 1880 as my temporal borders because they constitute a distinct period in the history of marriage and sexuality, but

I also recognize that much of what we consider Victorian can be traced back to the eighteenth century and persisted long after 1880. The Victorian era was neither the first nor last to value a variety of bonds between women. What was historically specific were its ways of doing so. At the same time, it is also notable that four of this book's six chapters concentrate on one decade within that broader time span—the 1860s. It is not surprising that a "fast" decade of feminist activism, avid consumerism, and obsession with the bold and showy "Girl of the Period" coincided with debates about marriage and with a rising number of publications revolving around feminine display and aggressive female fantasies.[16] Nevertheless, the broader temporal framework still holds. Throughout the period, society encouraged women to cultivate female friendships, and a variety of people acknowledged female marriages without demonizing them. The conventions of fashion imagery and doll tales remained more or less the same from the 1840s through the 1870s. The liberal feminist agenda of marriage reform that coalesced in 1857 first took shape among utilitarians and Unitarians in the 1830s and retained the same basic contours until Socialists and New Women radicalized the issues in the 1880s. Though the anthropological texts and individual novels I discuss are pinpointed very precisely in time, their scope extends well beyond the years in which they were composed and published. Dickens's novel of the early 1860s reflected back on the Regency period, and Trollope and the anthropologists looked to the primitive past in order to define the present.

As in my previous book, *Apartment Stories: City and Home in Nineteenth-Century Paris and London,* I have here combined the practices of several disciplines without making any one method the key to all mythologies. If one can identify the core method of any discipline, then the method of theory is the critique of existing assumptions; the method of history is generalization based on immersion in the largest number and widest range of sources possible; and the method of literary and visual criticism is interpretation based on close reading. Each chapter in *Between Women* uses theory to identify and examine the often unstated assumptions of previous scholarship. My training in literary studies is evident in my drive to unpack the meaning of linguistic and visual details, but I do not believe that one can exclusively use literary critical methods and fictional texts to make historical arguments. For that reason, only two chapters focus on a single novel. The majority of the chapters in this book use a large number of sources to make generalized claims for their place and era and to outline the parameters within which many individual lives took shape and from which a smaller number took flight. Rather than concentrate on change over time, *Between Women* follows the model of historical studies that delimit a period and then explore its internal complexities. I have made every effort to ground my claims in sources that recorded daily life (journals, letters, memoirs, biographies) or texts that aimed to mold it (conduct books, fashion magazines, children's literature). I draw on popular sources, written by men and women, and read in large numbers (conduct books, fashion magazines, novels), as well as on texts that were less widely read but reflected on laws and policies that affected many people (legal arguments, anthropological studies, debates in the periodical press).

Why focus on literature at all, and why on the texts that I do? The nineteenth-century novel was one of the most important cultural sites for representing and shaping desire, affect, and ideas about gender and the family. Since nineteenth-century novels consist almost entirely of accounts of social relationships—bonds between individuals and the ways that communities respond to those bonds—novels have an important place in this study. The second chapter draws on numerous texts to argue that the formal properties of the marriage plot defined the novel as a genre during the middle decades of the nineteenth century. The fourth and sixth chapters are devoted to close readings of individual novels, not because I consider novels more valuable than other sources, but because carefully composed, formally intricate, and technically complex works require and reward closer attention than brief children's tales and hastily written journals that yield more meaning in the aggregate. I have chosen *Great Expectations* because it is one of the most widely read, taught, and discussed Victorian novels and one of fiction's most sustained explorations of how bonds between women affect men. Although Trollope was and remains a widely read author, and *Can You Forgive Her?* is recognized as one of his major works, it is included here less for its representativeness than for its uniqueness: it is one of the few Victorian novels to coordinate female marriage, female friendship, egalitarian marriage, and hierarchical marriage within a single narrative.

Between Women makes historical claims that can be best assessed by specialists in Victorian studies, but it also makes broadly applicable theoretical interventions in queer studies, women's studies, and the theory of the novel. Those who approach this book expecting to learn about Victorian lesbians may initially be puzzled by the extended discussions of fashion, dolls, and marriage between men and women; those who pick it up to learn about "women" implicitly defined as heterosexual may find the pages devoted to female marriage and homoerotic desire between women irrelevant. I hope, however, that by the end of this book, both sets of readers will be convinced that lesbian lives are best studied as part of the general history of women and the family, and that heterosexual women's lives can only be fully understood if we attend to their friendships with women and their relationships to female objects of desire.

HOW THIS BOOK ENGAGES SCHOLARLY DEBATES

Studies of Victorian women have focused on how they both accepted and contested belief systems that defined women in terms of male standards, desires, and power, but have paid relatively little attention to how relationships between women defined normative gender. Scholars have dismissed nineteenth-century dolls and fashion as mere tools for teaching women to become objects for men. Writing on contemporary fashion photography and Barbie dolls has drawn attention to their lesbian dynamics and queer erotics, but no one has used that work to explore how Victorian dolls and fashion iconography encouraged girls and women to desire images of femininity, without marking such desires as queer or lesbian.[17] Studies of nineteenth-century marriage, particularly by literary critics, have explained how it was never only a bond between men and women, but the focus has been on how marriage formed alliances between men, often at the cost of ties between women.[18] Women are at the center of histories of the nineteenth-century family, but primarily in relation to husbands, fathers, and brothers. The links between women within the middle class have thus been remarkably ignored in some of the most important scholarship on gender. Consider *Family Fortunes: Men and Women of the English Middle Class, 1780–1850*, a major work by Leonore Davidoff and Catherine Hall that continues to be a reference point for nineteenth-century studies. Under the category of "femininity," the index lists "brothers' influence," and its "see also" rubric directs the reader to "division of labour by gender," "domesticity," and "motherhood." "Femininity," however, does not include friendship, sisters, or even mother-daughter relationships. The entry for "family" directs us to "see also friendship," but friendship between women takes up only a few sentences in the book. The authors note the "passionate" language used between female friends, then throw up their hands: "There is no way of speculating the exact emotional, much less physical meaning of such relationships." They briefly mention male "homosexuality" on the same page, remarking that it was regarded with "outraged horror," but the concept has no place in their index.[19]

The implicit theory here defines family and marriage as institutions that govern relationships between men, and between men and women, but not between women. The massive increase in scholarship about the history of same-sex relations since the publication of *Family Fortunes* has done little to challenge its view of the family, for much of that research has similarly assumed a basic opposition between lesbians and gay men on one side and marriage and the family on another. Studies of the family and femininity do not consider bonds between women to lie within the purview of their analyses, while work on female bonds situates them either outside the family or in a separate compartment within the family.[20] Female friendship and lesbian love, the two relationships between women that have received the most attention, are conflated as essentially feminist alliances that helped women to subvert gender norms and rebel against the strictures marriage placed on women, or that flourished only because they were sequestered within what Carroll Smith-Rosenberg called "the female world of love and ritual."

In 1975 Smith-Rosenberg contended that before the invention of homosexuality as a pathological form of deviance, sensual and emotional intimacy between women were accepted elements of domestic family life.[21] A few years later, Adrienne Rich proposed the idea of a lesbian continuum in which all forms of female intimacy would be related by their common rejection of "compulsory heterosexuality."[22] In contrast to Smith-Rosenberg, who characterized the female world as secure and serene, Rich underscored that women who placed women at the center of their lives risked stigma, ostracism, and violence. In the late 1980s and early 1990s, Esther Newton, Lisa Duggan, Terry Castle, and others mounted powerful critiques of the continuum theory and the concept of the female world.[23] They cited evidence that some nineteenth-century Americans and Europeans did see women's bonds as deviant or pathological.[24] They showed that both paradigms desexualized lesbianism by equating it with asexual friendships and with mother-daughter bonds purged of the alienation, exploitation, and conflicts inherent in male-female relations. They argued that to define lesbianism as a repudiation of men and masculinity left no room for mannish lesbians and the women attracted to them.

As many readers will recognize, my title alludes to Eve Kosofsky Sedgwick's *Between Men: English Literature and Male Homosocial Desire* (1985), which drew on Rich's notion of a lesbian continuum to speculate briefly that women might not have experienced the panic around boundaries between homo- and heterosexuality that men did (2–3). My response on first reading that suggestive proposition, and on rereading it many times in later years, has always been, "Yes, but . . ." Yes, homophobia was less powerful between women than between men, but was that because all forms of love between women were essentially interchangeable, as the continuum theory suggests? Yes, women's relations were less violently policed than men's, but are they therefore less interesting? Yes, women had more latitude with one another, but aren't we beginning to see that some relationships between Victorian men enjoyed the fluidity Sedgwick considered the monopoly of women? Yes, relationships between women were different, but don't we need at least an entire book to explore that—a book that engages Sedgwick's wise insight that homo– and hetero– are inherently interrelated? Without presuming to have succeeded, I have aimed to provide that book—one that will interest those who answer the last question in the affirmative, and one that takes to heart Sedgwick's powerful precept that to understand any particular aspect of gender and sexuality we must draw equally on feminist and queer theories and histories.

In feminist and lesbian studies, the turn to queer theory inaugurated with the publication of Judith Butler's *Gender Trouble* in 1990 led many to abandon the female world of the lesbian continuum for the project of undoing gender and sexuality categories altogether.[25] But few studies that address Victorian women's bonds have incorporated the insights of queer theory, and most still argue either that women's relationships were asexual or that women in the past anticipated current definitions of lesbians. Those seeking to restore lesbians to history portray their subjects as an outlawed minority defined by their exceptional sexual desire for women, their transgressive identification with masculinity, and their exclusion from the institutions of marriage and family.[26] Ironically, what all of these arguments share is an assumption that the opposition between men and women governs relationships between women, which take shape only as reactions against, retreats from, or appropriations of masculinity. The ongoing dominance of the continuum and minority paradigms is illustrated in the similarities between Lillian Faderman's *Surpassing the Love of Men* (1981) and Martha Vicinus's *Intimate Friends: Women Who Loved Women* (2004), the latter a set of case studies that revisits many of the women Faderman first grouped together. Faderman argued that romantic friendships between women were accepted because they were asexual relationships.[27] Vicinus shows that many of the relationships Faderman studied were in fact sexual, but her decision to use the word "friends" in the title of a book about lesbians indicates her adherence to the continuum theory. Vicinus advances the continuum thesis by using the terms "women's friendships" and "women's erotic friendships" interchangeably and by arguing that both were "consistently marginalized as 'second best' to heterosexual marriage."[28] She defines "intimate friendship" broadly, as "an emotional, erotically charged relationship between two women" (xxiv). But she makes that point in a section whose title, "Defining the Lesbian," evokes the minority thesis, and argues throughout that lesbians posed a "threat to [the] social norms" (59) followed by most women, who are thus implicitly removed from the only nominally inclusive category of "women who loved women." The minority thesis also surfaces in Vicinus's claim that "gender inversion was the most important signifier of same-sex desire" (xxix). Although *Intimate Friends* shows that women in lesbian relationships "created metaphoric versions of the heterosexual nuclear family," she emphasizes that such metaphors "failed when subjected to literal interpretation" (xxvii), thus reasserting a distinction between the lesbian minority and the heterosexual norm.

Because histories of gender, family, and marriage have focused on how women were defined relative to men, bonds between women have been analyzed primarily within lesbian studies. Lesbian studies put relationships between women on the scholarly agenda and produced exponential increases in knowledge, but its premises suggested that bonds between women mattered only to the history of women's resistance to heterosexuality, which to date has been far less common than their participation in it. The use of lesbian theory as a master discourse for understanding all relationships between women has thus made it difficult to conceptualize friendships between women who embodied feminine norms; to see the differences between female friendship, female marriage, and unrequited love between women; and to understand how friendship extended well beyond an isolated "female world." Literary-critical frameworks have also blinded us to the ways in which Victorian marriage plots depended on friendship between women. As my second chapter demonstrates, novels by men and women assigned female friendship so much agency that many narratives represented it as both a cause and effect of marriage between women and men. Idealized versions of the mother-daughter bond, which both Smith-Rosenberg and Rich posit as the origin of all bonds between women, have made it almost taboo to mention the eroticized aggression between mothers and daughters addressed in chapters 3 and 4. To understand how femininity was objectified and displayed for women as well as for men, the other topic of those chapters, we need to abandon the persistent assumption that erotic interest in femininity can only be masculine. Finally, in order to see that sexual relationships between women have been part of the history of the family and marriage since at least the nineteenth century, we need to abandon continuum and minority theories that define kinship as exclusively heterosexual and frame female couples in terms of their rejection of marriage or their failed appropriation of it. Many nineteenth-century women in what some Victorians called "female marriages" were not seen as challenging the conventions of kinship. Instead they saw themselves, and their friends, neighbors, and colleagues saw them, as a variation on the married couple. Even a traditionalist like Trollope was able to articulate the ground that female marriage shared with modern forms of marriage between women and men.

In the course of writing this book I have been asked certain questions over and over again. Weren't Victorians too invested in female sexual purity to admit that lesbians existed?[29] Didn't the conviction that women had no sexual desire run so deep that in fact women couldn't have ever had sex with each other? Granted that a handful of women were able to take the plunge—weren't they anomalies, cut off from mainstream society or so privileged they didn't have to worry about what people thought?

Didn't most people think of women who had sex with other women as deviants, almost a third sex, who had little in common with women who became wives and mothers? Weren't most women's lives totally governed by heterosexuality—by biological reproduction and by a sense of opposite sexes powerfully drawn to each other but also perpetually in conflict? As is already clear, my answer to these questions is "no"—not because I do not believe that Victorian women were deeply invested in men, nor because I think that secretly all Victorian women were really lesbians, but because I came to see the basic premises of these questions as anachronistic and misguided.

My belief that we should pose different questions comes in part from my engagement with contemporary queer theory. Queer theory led me to ask what social formations swim into focus once we abandon the preconception of strict divisions between men and women, homosexuality and heterosexuality, same-sex bonds and those of family and marriage. That skepticism about the transhistorical truth of gender and sexual categories owes a great deal to Denise Riley, Joan Wallach Scott, Eve Kosofsky Sedgwick, and Judith Butler, who have all argued that woman, desire, sexuality, and kinship are not fixed essences.[30] *Between Women* makes a historical point about the particular indifference of Victorians to a homo/hetero divide for women; this is also a theoretical claim that can reorient gender and sexuality studies in general. Queer theory often accentuates the subversive dimensions of lesbian, gay, and transgender acts and identities. The focus on secrecy, shame, oppression, and transgression in queer studies has led theorists, historians, and literary critics alike to downplay or refuse the equally powerful ways that same-sex bonds have been acknowledged by the bourgeois liberal public sphere.[31] Studies of same-sex practices of kinship and reproduction have undone the idea that the family must be heterosexual, but continue to detect and in some cases advocate for a basic conflict between the heterosexual family and its queer variants.[32] *Between Women* shows, by contrast, that in Victorian England, female marriage, gender mobility, and women's erotic fantasies about women were at the heart of normative institutions and discourses, even for those who made a religion of the family, marriage, and sexual difference.

This book makes new arguments because it brings fresh perspectives to bear on familiar materials, but also because it draws on sources that have been relatively neglected in sexuality studies. The history of sexuality has depended disproportionately on trial records and medical sources that foregrounded pathology and deviance. Women were not included in the legal definition of sodomy and were less likely than men to be arrested for public sex acts, and thus have faded from view in work based on police reports and state records. Studies that adopt Foucault's foundational account of sexuality as the production of desires, bodies, races, and classes through generative prohibitions and the manufacture of sexual identities have defined homosexuality in terms of deviance, secrecy, and subcultures. Women have appeared in those studies only to the extent that they illustrate the reach of medical discourses of difference. In reading over one hundred examples of women's lifewriting, however, I found almost no evidence that women incorporated medical definitions of femininity or sexual inversion into their understanding of their bodies or desires. In lieu of marginal and subversive identities, this book offers an alternative concept that makes it easier to place women in history, and that women themselves used to define their place in the world: the social relationship, which is not reducible to sex, power, or difference. Social relationships are the stuff of everyday life, and of historical documents such as women's letters, diaries, memoirs, and biographies, as well as of novels, fashion magazines, and children's literature. Historians of women and lesbians have studied those sources before, but they have almost always assumed the dominance of a heterosexuality whose evidence stems from the fact that it is all we have been trained to see. A different theory allows us to use these sources to make new distinctions—for example, between how women wrote about friends and lovers. It also establishes new connections—for example, between femininity and homoeroticism, or between female marriages and marriages between men and women.

How I Came to Write this Book

Having summarized this book's conclusions, I would like to end this introduction by recounting the process that led me to them. At many points in this book I show how other scholars have failed to realize that relationships between women are central to the history of gender, sexuality, marriage, and the family. I am not surprised that they did not see a fact supported by abundant evidence, because I had difficulty seeing it myself. Although this book focuses almost exclusively on England, it began with a comparative observation. Like many before me, I was struck by how differently French and British literature represented lesbians. French poets, novelists, painters, and social investigators were notoriously interested in sex between women. Baudelaire wrote about it, as did Zola, Gautier, and Balzac; Courbet and Toulouse-Lautrec painted it; and Parent-Duchâtelet wrote about its prevalence among prostitutes. By contrast, the only British discourse to portray explicit sex between women was pornography, although occasional references also appeared in medical texts. In researching an essay called "Comparative Sapphism," I found that British reviews of French literature about lesbians proved that Victorians were capable of deciphering even very coded allusions to sex between women. At the same time, however, they dismissed sapphic characters as morbid, diseased, perverse, exotic, and abnormal, and linked lesbianism to adultery, sodomy, and incest, all unnatural realities too degraded to mention.[33]

The horror that British readers expressed at French literature about lesbianism initially puzzled me, because British literature was so much more invested than its French counterpart in representing intimacy between women. Steeped as I was in the theory of the lesbian continuum, I did not yet see that there was simply no reason to assume that female friendship or love between female kin had anything to do with lesbian sex. The intense physicality of British representations of female friendship and kinship only intensified my confusion. Here is Jane Eyre befriending schoolmate and moral paragon Helen Burns: "Resting my head on Helen's shoulder, I put my arms round her waist; she drew me to her, and we reposed in silence."[34] Dying of consumption, Helen invites Jane into bed with her: "[Y]our little feet are bare; lie down and cover yourself with my quilt" (113). Jane "nestle[s] close to her" in bed and before Helen dies, "clasp[s]" her "arms closer round" her as the girls exchange a last kiss (113–14). Half-sisters Marian and Laura in Wilkie Collins's *The Woman in White* (1860) offer another example of passionate devotion when one declares of the other, "I won't live without her, and she can't live without me. . . . I . . . love her better than my own life." The night before Laura weds, she creeps into Marian's bed, announcing, "I shall lose you so soon, Marian. . . . I must make the most of you while I can."[35] In Christina Rossetti's poem *Goblin Market* (1862), one character tells another, "Did you miss me? / Come and kiss me. / Never mind my bruises, / Hug me, kiss me, suck my juices / . . . / Eat me, drink me, love me; / Laura, make much of me."[36] The fact that the speaker of these lines is a woman addressing her sister did not faze Victorian readers. Though in the twentieth century the poem has inspired lesbian tableaux in softcore pornography, Victorians included the poem in an anthology for schoolgirls.[37]

As I thought about those examples, I realized that one clear difference between them and the characters in French sapphic literature was that in the British cases, a woman's emotional and sensual connection to another woman helped unite her to a beloved husband, whereas the French lesbian canon highlighted the antagonisms between sapphism and bourgeois ideals of marriage. Even so, I wondered if such idealization of ardent bonds between women in England was confined to literature. Having combined historical and literary methods while researching and writing my first book about cities and domestic architecture, I welcomed a chance to delve into the archive again and turned to women's diaries, letters, biographies, and autobiographies. Some were manuscripts, some printed for private circulation only, others produced for the general public. Victorian women's lifewriting followed strict conventions, and putting friendship between women at the core of a life story was one of them. Women wrote to friends daily and kept in touch their entire lives. Whether writing about one another to third parties or directly addressing each other, their language was as romantic and gushing as that in any novel or poem. Prescriptive conduct literature presented a similar picture. When I reread texts by Sarah Ellis, whose publications set the tone for decades of Victorian domesticity, I found that she, too, made friendship a rule in women's lives. Although scholars who cite her today rarely remark on it, her works included entire chapters on female friendship. Calling on "woman to be true to woman," Ellis announced that friendship was as important an aspect of femininity as being a daughter, wife, and mother.[38]

I then began to wonder whether the British focus on women's bonds might be an effect of literacy and writing. Perhaps the abstractness of language made it an acceptable medium for discussing bodily actions and sensations that were not socially approved. Perhaps the ways in which British novels and lifewriting emphasized sentiment and sympathy, or letters depended on distance, neutralized the intensity and the physicality of the relationships described. This was an easy hypothesis to test, since the Victorians were as prolific in their production of images as they were in their generation of texts. Paintings, photographs, and illustrated magazines showed, however, that female and male artists also treated the female twosome as a ubiquitous compositional convention. Portraits of women together usually focused on sisters, but friends often had themselves photographed together, and British fashion magazines portrayed women gazing at each other and touching, without identifying the relationship between them.

As I leafed through the magazine articles that surrounded those fashion plates, I was surprised to see that for several years in the 1860s, letters to the editor of the *Englishwoman's Domestic Magazine* focused on topics like forcing young women's unruly pubescent bodies into corsets, or the rectitude of adult women using corporal punishment to discipline daughters, wards, or pupils. It is well known that Victorian pornographers were obsessed with flagellation, but the scholarship I had read insisted that birching was a strictly masculine affair, that only men wrote or read about such things and that men were always the central figures in beating scenarios. Here, however, were women engaging in precisely the same fantasies; indeed, many of the letters published in women's magazines resurfaced in pornography, either reprinted verbatim or cited in Victorian bibliographies of erotic literature. In a magazine directed at middle-class housewives, interspersed with recipes, household hints, and news about the latest Paris fashions, were dozens of letters like this one from an "English Mamma": "I made her take off her trousers [underpants] in order that she might feel the chastisement properly. I then put her across my knee in 'the old-fashioned style,' and gave her about twenty sound strokes with the birch."[39] Some correspondents accused women who punished girls of prurient motives; others wrote in asking where they could buy a birch rod or recommending slippers as a more ladylike instrument for punishing disobedient daughters.

Mothers in fashion magazines were a far cry from the dead maternal angels of Victorian novels or the idealized figures of conduct literature and lifewriting.[40] Annie Besant, commenting in her autobiography on the "idolatry" she felt for her mother, generalized that "[a]ll girls have in them the germ of passion. . . . I had but two ideals in my childhood and youth, round whom twined these budding tendrils of passion: they were my mother and the Christ."[41] Besant's adoration for her mother was echoed across the century in the lifewriting of women such as Edith Simcox, Frances Power Cobbe, Ethel Smyth, and Augusta Becher.[42] The diverse sexual lives of these women as adults (Besant was a sexual radical, Simcox lived for her unrequited love for a woman, Cobbe married a woman, Smyth had numerous affairs with women and a few men, and Becher married a man) shows that the homoeroticism of the mother-daughter bond did not have any fixed relationship to what we would now call sexual orientation. Nor did interactions between mothers and daughters always take the idyllic form typically found in women's memoirs. Fashion magazines presented mothers and daughters as *objects* for one another and showed women indulging with remarkable freedom in public fantasies about exposing, humiliating, and punishing girls.

Fashion necessarily draws attention to bodies, however, and so even though the fashion magazines were family publications that reproduced middle-class values, it seemed important to see whether their interest in cross-generational objectification and aggression was unique. I turned to children's literature, reasoning that it was defined by its integration into family life. Rather than focus on canonical works, I decided to cast a wider net and concentrate on literature written mostly by women for girls. During the period I was examining—the 1830s to the 1880s—school stories were not the dominant form they became later in the century, but dolls were a remarkably popular topic in literature for children and young adults. The dynamic between women and girls found in fashion magazines turned out also to structure stories about girls and their dolls, who could represent beautiful ladies for girls to worship, or disobedient subordinates for them to punish. Lady Seraphina, the doll who narrates *The Doll and Her Friends* (1852), declares: "I belong to a race the sole end of whose existence is to give pleasure to others [of] the female sex." She underscores the power the female sex exercises over dolls who are "mere dependents; some might even call us slaves . . . . forced to submit to every caprice of our possessors."[43] Tale after tale described dolls as the love objects of girls who were both adoring paramours and harsh, fickle mistresses.

I had begun by wondering why the British were so hesitant to discuss lesbianism in print, and so hostile to it when they did, given how interested they were in other forms of intimacy between women. The more I read, the more I realized that although I saw a necessary relationship between lesbianism and other types of bonds between women, Victorians did not share my assumption. The issue was certainly not that they could not imagine sex between women or even girls. British pornographers represented a full range of sexual acts between women, and like the nineteenth-century medical writers studied by Thomas Laqueur, recognized the importance of the clitoris to female sexual pleasure.[44] In *The Romance of Lust*, for example, a woman writes a letter to another woman, a former lover, bragging about her "clitoris. You know, by experience, what an excitable one it is."[45] In 1846, feminist and art historian Anna Jameson warned that letting a girl share a bedroom with her governess might result in "mischief," and doctors cautioned mothers that girls who slept together or with teachers or servants ran the risk of "exciting the passions."[46]

Scholars had written about Victorian women's friendships, about fashion images and the corporal punishment debates, and about the importance of doll play for girls, but none grasped how typical each was of a normative femininity that could not be understood solely in terms of women's submission to men.[47] Historians and literary critics viewed female friendship either as an education in chaste passivity or as a rebellion against marriage and men. But Victorian narratives took a wider view of female friendships, and in fact considered them crucial to realizing marriages between men and women. Women's lifewriting showed that wives preserved the friends of their youth and made new ones, often with the approval of their husbands, parents, and ministers. Interpretations of nineteenth-century fashion imagery assert that it objectified women for men, but nineteenth-century fashion imagery was all about women's beauty being displayed for women's enjoyment. Most studies of dolls celebrated or denounced them for teaching girls to be passive playthings for men, but Victorian children's books depicted girls having their way with dolls and actively subjecting these literal playthings to their wills.

As I mused over the gaps between contemporary paradigms and the evidence of the past, the problem became more and more clear: contemporary definitions of femininity presume that heterosexuality and lesbianism are opposed and mutually exclusive positions. Judith Butler has shown how psychoanalytic theories of desire and kinship depend on what she calls the "heterosexual matrix of gender," in which to be feminine is to be the opposite of masculine and to desire to be desired by the masculine.[48] According to the logic of this matrix, any relationship between women that is not confined to pure identification lacks psychic and cultural coherence; it exists outside the bounds of femininity, the family, and the social, in the shadowy, denigrated realm to which the middle decades of the twentieth century relegated lesbians and gay men. This clarified why scholars were so intent on placing female friends in a separate, parallel universe: a conceptual system that posits women as the opposites of men also assumes that women's relationships with one another must oppose those they have with men. It also explained why so many argued that fashion imagery required the women who made and viewed it to assume a masculine perspective. They had assumed that desire for women was exclusive to men and to lesbians, which made it impossible to see that women who were not lesbians could also eagerly consume images of desirable femininity.

Like many others, even as I sought to go beyond the heterosexual matrix of gender, I had remained caught in its terms when I thought that British commentary on French sapphism was the relevant context for understanding relationships between women. Without meaning to, I had assumed that all relationships between women had to refer to lesbianism and be external to male-female desire. As a result, I sought to define relationships between women solely in relation to sexual desire, the glue that binds masculine to feminine in the heterosexual matrix. My assumption that relationships between women must oppose dominant heterosexuality had made it seem like a contradiction that people who were repulsed by lesbian sex in French literature encouraged and praised other intimate bonds between women. There was really no reason to think, however, that one had anything to do with the other, once I let go of the notion that all bonds between women functioned as the antithesis of heterosexual relations. Heterosexual gender itself no longer seemed an adequate concept for understanding the Victorian past. The sole thread connecting sapphic characters to magazines for housewives, lifewritings about female friendship, and girls' books about dolls was the term "woman," and only an unduly impoverished definition of the term could posit it as meaning the same thing in each instance.

This realization raised a final question, however, and answering it helped me to clarify my argument. I now grasped that our contemporary opposition between hetero- and homosexuality did not exist for Victorians, and that Victorians were thus able to see relationships between women as central to lives also organized around men. It seemed unlikely that the middle-class female majority who wrote adoringly of their friends or enjoyed reading about adult women whipping teenage girls were actively engaged in sex with women. But what of the small but real number of Victorian women who did have sexual relationships with other women? Did Victorians who were not themselves in such relationships see them as nothing but chaste friends or recognize them as sexual, and if so, how did they characterize them? Did they treat women in same-sex couples with the fear and contempt that British reviewers directed at the sapphic characters they saw less as women and more as diseased monsters? Or did they accord them the same respect, admiration, and encouragement as female friends? Did they consider women in female couples to be masculine, hyperfeminine, or divided into male and female roles?

In pursuing answers to these questions, I was assisted by recent studies that have advanced lesbian history beyond endless debates about whether women in the nineteenth century ever had sex with other women. It is a ridiculous controversy, since if it were true that no women had sex with women in the nineteenth century, that era would turn out to be the only lesbian-free zone in recorded history. Preposterous as that may sound, it is a belief that people articulate all the time, either as a global proposition or on a case-by-case basis. By the time I wrote this book, however, Terry Castle, Lisa Merrill, Julia Markus, and Martha Vicinus had established that women such as Anne Lister, Charlotte Cushman, Rosa Bonheur, Harriet Hosmer, Emily Faithfull, Minnie Benson, Ethel Smyth, and Frances Power Cobbe all had sexual relationships with other women, after the eighteenth-century tribade had faded from polite discourse and before nineteenth-century sexology invented the invert.[49] As I read about those women and their lovers, I was struck that several were married to men, and even more by how many defined their longterm relationships with women as marriages. Furthermore, often both women in a couple identified interchangeably with the roles of husband and wife. They called each other "sposa," "hubby," "wedded wife," "my other and better half," described themselves as "married," and were recognized as couples by men and women leading far more orthodox lives.[50]

The question of whether or not women in female couples actually had sex became less important than the fact that they themselves and many in their social networks perceived them as married. The mere fact of both members of a conjugal unit being women was not sufficient to discount their relationship as a socially recognized form of kinship. British reviewers saw fictional sapphists like Nana and Paquita in terms of a reality too carnal, raw, and lawless to be countenanced, not simply because of their sexual acts with women, but because of their disregard for wedlock: Nana and her female lover are both prostitutes, and Paquita has sex with a man because he resembles her married female lover. Women who established longterm relationships with other women, by contrast, saw themselves, and were seen by others, as placid embodiments of the middle-class ideal of marriage: a bond defined by sex that also had the power to sanctify sex. The French sapphist was an antisocial threat to family life, but women in female marriages had a place in the social order, as variations on its domestic ideal.

The ease with which women in female marriages were assimilated to conjugality helped me to refine the place of sex in what I now saw was my central preoccupation: the different forms of socially valued relationships between Victorian women. Friendship, infatuation, marriage, and women's objectification of women had to be differentiated, not measured in terms of a single sexual standard. Work in queer studies on same-sex families helped me to understand how, especially in the nineteenth century, marriage signified not only a private sexual bond but also a host of other relations: integration into social networks, the sharing of household labor, physical and spiritual caretaking, and the transmission of property.[51] Having developed a definition of the erotic that helped to explain how important objectifying women was to the constitution of normative femininity, I now saw the importance of understanding how marriage was legitimated by activities other than sex.

CONCLUSION

Between Women offers a history of sexuality and gender that does not focus on power differences or oppositions between polarized genders and antithetical sexualities. Instead it explores what remains to be seen if we proceed without Oedipus, without castration, without the male traffic in women, without homophobia and homosexual panic. Unsettling commonalities emerge. Egalitarian affection turns out to be common to female friendships and marriages between women and men. Matrons, housewives, and ladies of fashion act in ways usually identified with heterosexual masculinity. Aggression, hierarchy, objectification, and voyeurism dominate representations of mothers and daughters, girls and dolls, and images of femininity designed for female consumers. Positing the existence of more than one kind of relationship between women leads us to recognize that many of those relationships worked in tandem with heterosexual exchange and patriarchal gender norms.

To find a fit between marriage, the family, and bonds between women is not to accuse women of complicity with gender and sexual oppression. Nor do my points about the elasticity, mobility, and plasticity of norms and institutions suggest that they were equitable in the past or offer models for the present. Rather, my aim is to demonstrate their variability. Past theories and histories have seen the bonds between women as either the quintessence of femininity or its defiant inversion. *Between Women* shows that even in the past, in a society that insisted strenuously on the differences between men and women, there existed institutions, customs, and relationships whose elasticity, mobility, and plasticity undid even the most cherished and foundational oppositions.

So much of what Victorians had to say about conventional women exceeded the sexual difference model, yet so little of what we have detected in the Victorian past goes beyond the limits of our present-day belief that heterosexual norms dominate all lives, even those of people who self-consciously exist outside them. Gender and sexuality as defined by marriage and the family have been opposed to gender and sexuality as defined by same-sex bonds. This book proposes that we try to understand how they were intertwined in ways that make homosexuality and heterosexuality less than useful categories for dividing up the Victorian world. The power of men to define women's lives and the centrality of men in women's lives were both real and important aspects of Victorian society, and it is not my intention to demonstrate otherwise here. Our mistake has been to assume that those structural forces precluded the strong, complex, and socially acknowledged bonds between women that are the subject of this book.

PART ONE

Elastic Ideals: Female Friendship

CHAPTER 1

Friendship and the Play of the System

IN THE MOST INFLUENTIAL conduct book of the nineteenth century, Sarah Stickney Ellis identified *The Women of England* (1839) as daughters, wives, and mothers ensconced in a familial, domestic sphere. She also assigned women another obligatory role we may now be surprised to find so prominent in a guide to correct feminine behavior: friend.[1] Ellis returned to friendship between women in *The Daughters of England* (1842), where a chapter on "Friendship and Flirtation" affirmed the importance of a woman's "circle of . . . private friends" as the site where "she learns what constitutes the happiness and the misery of woman." Just as Ellis had established codes of behavior for daughters, wives, and mothers, she set out rules of conduct for female friends, stating that flirtation with men should never set women asunder: "I cannot see why [male attentions] should ever be so much the subject of envy amongst women, as to cast a shade upon their intercourse with each other."[2] Ellis assigned equal value to female friends and male suitors, making friendship between women as essential to proper femininity as a woman's obedience to her parents, subservience to her husband, and devotion to her children. Yet despite the prominence and complexity of friendship in Ellis's works, contemporary scholars who cite her as representative of Victorian gender ideology consistently overlook her articulation of female friendship as a basic element of a middle class organized around marriage, family, and Christian belief.

I begin this book with friendship for two reasons. First, female friendship is an excellent test of the arguments that women's relationships were central to Victorian society, that women were not defined only in relation to men, and that they formed legible and legitimate bonds with one another. Second, understanding the divergent uses of the term "friend" among Victorian women allows us to distinguish between two distinct relationships that often went under the same name: sexual and nonsexual intimacies between women. It is a common misconception that Victorians were confused about the differences between sexual and nonsexual bonds between women, not least because of an ambiguity embedded in the word "friend" itself, which in Old English meant both "a near relation" and "a person joined by affection and intimacy to another, independently of sexual or family love." By the time of late Middle English, "friend" could mean a beloved who was neither kin nor lover, but also a relative or "a romantic or sexual partner."[3] Before the nineteenth century, "friend" was a capacious term that included kin, patrons, neighbors, and spouses, along with freely chosen confidants to whom one was not bound by blood, political obligations, physical proximity, or sexual intimacy.[4] Twentieth-century Western societies define friendship more narrowly, but the term remains ambiguous: "friend" still refers to a sexual partner, an acquaintance with whom one shares a relatively indiscriminate sociability, and a close connection with whom one forms a dyad based on exclusivity, disclosure, and commitment.[5] Likewise for Victorians, a friend was first and foremost an emotional intimate who was not a relative or a sexual partner, but the term could also be a euphemism for a lover. Only through a discreet but marked rhetoric did Victorians qualify that some "friends" were not friends, but special friends, life friends, and particular companions who in private communications could as easily be called wife or husband.

Victorians accepted friendship between women because they believed it cultivated the feminine virtues of sympathy and altruism that made women into good helpmates. But the embrace of friendships that trained women for family and marriage was not simply, as one might darkly conjecture, an attempt to press women's bonds into patriarchal service. It also indicated a shift in the spiritual and emotional definition of marriage from a hierarchical bond dictating that inferior wives obey their superior husbands to a more egalitarian conception modeled on friendship. A society that defined the social bond between husband and wife in terms of affection, companionship, and equality—alongside the persisting economic, legal, and political dependence of wives on husbands—easily made room for friendship. Female friends were integrated into the domestic realm as marriage brokers who helped facilitate courtship, but female friendship was defined in terms of affection and pleasure, not instrumental utility. Female friendship reinforced gender roles and consolidated class status, but it also provided women with socially permissible opportunities to engage in behavior commonly seen as the monopoly of men: competition, active choice, appreciation of female beauty, and struggles with religious belief. As friends, women could comport themselves with one another in ways forbidden with men, without compromising the respectability so prized by the middle class.

The complexity of friendship supports this book's central claim that Victorian society, in which marriage between men and women was a supreme value, did not suppress bonds between women but actively promoted them. Neither a celebration nor a rebuke, my argument takes the history of women and sexuality beyond models of subversion and containment to explore the complexity of systems in which constraint was inseparable from liberty, action, and recreation, from a degree of give built into social rules, offering those who lived by them flexibility, if not utter freedom. I call this give "the play of the system," adopting a term from Roland Barthes. In *Sade/Fourier/Loyola*, a study of three writers obsessed with social structures, Barthes contrasted logically fixed, closed, orthodox "systems" with infinitely open, destabilizing, ambiguous "systematics," which he defined as "the play of the system."[6] For Barthes, the play of the system is external to the system, a utopian alternative to the oppressive, self-contained structure from which systematics take flight. Unlike Barthes, I use "the play of the system" to conceptualize the yield built *into* systems. Play signifies the *elasticity* of systems, their ability to be stretched without permanent alteration to their size or shape; it thus differs from *plasticity*, which refers to a pliability that allows a system or structure to acquire a new shape and be permanently changed without fracture or rupture. The Victorian gender system, however strict its constraints, provided women latitude through female friendships, giving them room to roam without radically changing the normative rules governing gender difference.

To understand what Victorians meant by the word "friend," and to explore how women negotiated the rules that governed them, I turn to lifewriting, a genre that includes manuscript diaries, published diaries, correspondence, biographies, and autobiographies. Female friendship, utterly absent from the philosophical discourse on amity, was the very stuff of lifewriting: women wrote about friends in their diaries, regularly addressed letters to female friends, and were memorialized in print by friends as well as relatives and spouses. This chapter is based on over one hundred published and unpublished sources, many by or about women so ordinary they left no other historical traces. A few were authors, actresses, activists, nurses, or teachers; two-thirds were married at some point in their lives. Almost all were alive between the 1830s and the 1880s. The corpus includes women from all classes and all denominations, though the majority cited were middle-class Anglicans. Around ten were working-class women, who remain drastically underrepresented relative to men in the current archive of working-class lifewriting from the middle decades of the century.[7] The rest of the sample includes the daughters and wives of shopkeepers, professionals, clerics, industrialists, gentry, rentiers, politicians, and aristocrats; girls educated at home, at day schools, and at boarding schools; and girls raised within families small and large, in London, other urban centers, and every provincial nook and cranny of the United Kingdom. I draw on unpublished sources, primarily manuscript diaries, and on published books, some intended for sale, some printed for private circulation. Because lifewriting tends to appear in print years after its subject has died, roughly 70 percent of the works discussed here were published between the 1870s and the 1940s (about ten in each decade).

The period I focus on here, 1830 to 1880, was not homogeneous: The 1830s and 1840s were more politically and economically uncertain than the prosperous and stable 1850s; the Evangelical piety, fervor, and introspection of the 1830s gave way in the 1860s to a more athletic and irreverent generation of girls who had professional and educational options their mothers had lacked. Lifewriting reflects those changes: one finds more Evangelical anxiety about sin, salvation, and duty in the 1840s and 1850s, while in the 1860s and 1870s, women of all ages expressed themselves more through socializing, education, and aesthetic practices—visiting, reading, writing, studying visual and musical arts, attending to dress and interior decoration, frequenting theaters and galleries, instructing children, or pursuing knowledge in their own right. Writing in the 1860s about smoking, cross-dressing, flirting with men, and the bodily transformations of adolescence, Laura Troubridge (1853–1929) exhibited a boisterous playfulness rarely seen since the Regency, when Anne Lister (1791–1840) recorded her seductions of numerous women in Parisian boarding houses and English country homes.[8] But lifewriting also frustrates the impulse to view individual lives as exemplifying historical trends and social position, because the genre emphasizes idiosyncrasy. For instance, missionary Caroline Head (1852–1904) was far more religious in the relatively secular 1870s than the young Anne Noel King (1837–1917) in the 1850s, despite the fact that King was raised by a grandmother devoted to Evangelical philanthropy.

Varied as the women who left records of their lives between 1830 and 1880 were, they nevertheless had an understanding of friendship not shared with those who came before and after them. The relatively unchanged discourse of amity between 1830 and 1880 identifies those decades as a coherent period within the history of friendship. Female friendship existed as a social category and practice before and after this period, of course, but the era from 1830 to 1880 was the heyday of sentimental friendships legitimated in terms of affection, attraction, and pleasure and federated into marriage and family ties. In the eighteenth century, aristocratic women viewed friendship as an alternative to marriage and justified it as the cultivation of reason, equality, and taste; in the wake of Romanticism and Evangelicalism, nineteenth-century women defined friendship as the expression of emotion, affinity, personal inclination, and religious faith.[9] In the 1880s, friendship merged with altruistic activism and became a model for bridging class differences to forge a better world.[10] By the twentieth century, the increasing importance of school, the emergence of adolescence as a life stage, anxiety about lesbian deviance, and the popularity of developmental models that equated maturity with heterosexuality made it almost inevitable that same-sex friendship would come to be defined as antithetical to the family and the married couple.

FEMALE FRIENDSHIP IN FEMINIST STUDIES

Victorians recognized women's friendship as a social bond comparable to kinship and conjugal love, but the last several decades of scholarship on marriage and the family have defined female friendship as external to family life. Studies of family and marriage place friendship outside the purview of their analysis or define it as a social relationship at odds with the isolated nuclear family. Leonore Davidoff and Catherine Hall dismiss female friendships as irrelevant to their study of familial gender politics, and John Gillis argues that by the nineteenth century, the married couple existed in opposition to the collective world of friends.[11] Lesbian studies place women's friendships on a continuum with lesbian relationships and equate both with resistance to the family and marriage. As Adrienne Rich influentially argued, women's friendships and lesbian sexual bonds both defy "compulsory heterosexuality."[12] The move to valorize women's friendships as a subset of lesbianism and as a subversion of gender norms continues to be the dominant paradigm. In *Intimate Friends: Women Who Loved Women, 1778–1928*, a series of richly documented case studies in lesbian history, Martha Vicinus identifies "heterosexual marriage" as a "strong impediment to same-sex intimacy" and argues that an "undefined continuum" linked "erotic friendships" in particular with "women's friendships" in general. Rich's continuum becomes the apposition in Vicinus's title: "intimate friends" are "women who loved women," and both terms stand for lesbians who risked "social ostracism" and posed "an unnamable threat to social norms."[13]

The concept of a lesbian continuum, once a powerful means of drawing attention to overlooked bonds between women, has ironically obscured everything that female friendship and lesbianism did not share and hidden the important differences between female friends and female lovers. Female friends and female lovers alike expressed affection, shared confidences, and idealized one another's physical and spiritual qualities. But friends differed significantly from female lovers who threw themselves into obsessive passions or lived together, functioned socially as a couple, merged finances, and bequeathed property to each other. Indeed, although the lesbian continuum posits female friends and lesbian lovers as united in their opposition to patriarchal marriage, many nineteenth-century lesbian relationships resembled marriages more than friendships—and as a result shared with friendship a high degree of acceptance by respectable society.

Rather than valorize an invisibility or transgressiveness that all women's relationships share, or define women's relationships in terms of an intrinsic ambiguity that blurs the line between friendship and sexual partnership, we need distinctions that allow us to chart how different social bonds overlap without becoming identical. The question of how to conceptualize friends in relation to same-sex lovers is not unique to women, and it has haunted modern gay discourse since its inception. At the outset of the twentieth century, Edward Carpenter advocated expanding gay and lesbian history by incorporating the history of friendship, while Magnus Hirschfeld insisted on "drawing a sharp line between friendship and love" and, in so doing, documented many "marriage-like associations" between men and between women.[14] Scholars who have subsequently studied women's friendships have often replicated Carpenter's strategic decision to conflate friendships with sexual relationships. The single most influential study of female friendship, Carroll Smith-Rosenberg's "The Female World of Love and Ritual" (1975), argued that before psychiatrists popularized the concept of the deviant lesbian, passionate friendship between women was not only accepted among a few female couples but was a norm for many women and an integral aspect of family life. Smith-Rosenberg's prescient identification of the social prominence of female friendship in the United States shaped lesbian studies, but scholars of the Victorian family, while often citing her essay, have not heeded its call to incorporate the study of friendship into the history of family and marriage.

If Smith-Rosenberg's argument has not affected the theorization of family and marriage as she intended it to, the cause lies partly in the way she herself contradicted her primary claim. Even as "The Female World of Love and Ritual" argued that female friendship was "an essential aspect of American society," considered "both socially acceptable and fully compatible with heterosexual marriage," it also segregated intimacy between women in a "female world."[15] Smith-Rosenberg saw female friendships as compensatory, valued because they supplied the emotional warmth missing between wives and husbands in a society premised on separate gender spheres (366, 372, 373). The ideology of separate spheres in fact valorized the domestic intimacy of husband and wife, and we now know that men and women in Victorian England mingled far more than they do in Smith-Rosenberg's characterization of the antebellum United States. Letters and journals attest to genuine affection and intimacy between husbands and wives, alongside conflict and hierarchy, and women had contact with men before and after marriage. The twenty-year-old, unmarried Anne Noel King, for example, spent much of the 1857 London season going out at night with groups of men and women, and married women frequently entertained their husbands' single and married male friends.[16]

Nor was intense friendship confined to a uniquely female world, since men also had deeply romantic friendships with one another before and after marriage.[17]

Another defining move of Smith-Rosenberg's article, though generative at the time, has led to conceptual impasses in theorizing the family, marriage, friendship, and sexuality. By contrasting the twentieth-century opposition between heterosexual normalcy and lesbian deviance to the nineteenth century's failure to sequester friendship from erotic intimacy, Smith-Rosenberg implied that before the advent of sexual orientations, no lines were drawn separating friends, lovers, and family members. To prove the existence of a homogeneous "female world of love and ritual," Smith-Rosenberg indiscriminately cited letters exchanged between sisters, cousins, mothers, daughters, sisters-in-law, married and single women, women of the same age and women of very different ages, lovers, friendly ex-lovers, distraught ex-lovers, and friends with reciprocal and nonreciprocal crushes who never became lovers.[18] As a result, Smith-Rosenberg's concept of romantic friendship between women has proven deeply ambiguous. Its emphasis on a broad "spectrum" of accepted forms of female intimacy suggested that Victorians were more willing to accept female homosexuality than their modern descendants (387). Yet for every scholar who cites "The Female World of Love and Ritual" to explain that Victorian women could have sexual relationships with each other without incurring social stigma, another uses it to prove the sexlessness of the most passionate, enduring, and exclusive love affairs.[19]

Even scholarship that focuses on the central role of queer sexualities in defining Victorian norms adheres to orthodoxies about the family, marriage, and gender relations. After Foucault's *History of Sexuality*, scholars are less prone to characterize the Victorians as sexually repressed, but the image of the Victorian family and marriage as fundamentally heterosexual prevails. The dominant frameworks for relating same-sex bonds to those of family and marriage depend on figures of separateness: the statistical metaphor of deviance, the spatial metaphors of underworld and margins, and the political metaphors of transgression, subversion, and resistance. Whether writing of sexual partnerships or asexual friendships, scholars assume that same-sex intimacy was socially unacceptable and severed from the family and marriage, despite mounting evidence that even lesbian relationships enjoyed an unexpected degree of knowing acceptance. No less an eminence than the archbishop of Canterbury, for example, deferred to his wife Minnie Benson's wish that her female lover move into the home also occupied by their many children.[20] As lenses for viewing the past, the heterosexual paradigm of the family, the deviance paradigm of homosexuality, and the continuum theory of lesbianism have all become cloudy, preventing us from seeing the diverse forms family and marriage took during the very period that witnessed their consolidation as vectors of power and social coherence. Certainly female marriage and erotic infatuation had continuities with female friendship, but the time has come to attend to their significant discontinuities, for only by understanding the differences among conjugality, infatuation, and friendship can we give each of those social relationships its due. In order to distinguish them, we will turn to the lifewriting that provides an atlas of Victorian England's multiple female relations.

VICTORIAN WOMEN'S LIFEWRITING AND RELATIONSHIPS BETWEEN WOMEN

The letters, biographies, memoirs, and diaries that recorded Victorian women's lives are essential sources for differentiating friendship, erotic obsession, and sexual partnership between women. The distinctions are subtle, for Victorians routinely used startlingly romantic language to describe how women felt about female friends and acquaintances. In her youth, Anne Thackeray (later Ritchie) recorded in an 1854 journal entry how she "fell in love with Miss Geraldine Mildmay" at one party and Lady Georgina Fullerton "won [her] heart" at another.[21] In reminiscences written for her daughter in 1881, Augusta Becher (1830–1888) recalled a deep childhood love for a cousin a few years older than she was: "From my earliest recollections I adored her, following her and content to sit at her feet like a dog."[22] At the other extreme of the life cycle, the seventy-one-year-old Ann Gilbert (1782–1866), who cowrote the poem now known as "Twinkle, Twinkle, Little Star," appreciatively described "the latter years of . . . friendship" with her friend Mrs. Mackintosh as "the gathering of the last ripe figs, here and there, one on the topmost bough!" Gilbert used similar imagery in an 1861 poem she sent to another woman celebrating the endurance of a friendship begun in childhood: "As rose leaves in a china Jar / Breathe still of blooming seasons past, / E'en so, old women as they are / Still doth the young affection last."[23] Gilbert's metaphors, drawn from the language of flowers and the repertoire of romantic poetry, asserted that friendship between women was as vital and fertile as the biological reproduction and female sexuality to which figures of fruitfulness commonly alluded.[24]

Friendship was so pervasive in Victorian women's lifewriting because middle-class Victorians treated friendship and family life as complementary. Close relationships between women that began when both were single often survived marriage and maternity. In the *Memoir of Mary Lundie Duncan* (1842) that Duncan's mother wrote two years after her daughter's early death at age twenty-five, the maternal biographer included many letters Duncan (1814–1840) wrote to friends, including one penned six weeks after the birth of her first child: "My beloved friend, do not think that I have been so long silent because all my love is centered in my new and most interesting charge. It is not so. My heart turns to you as it was ever wont to do, with deep and fond affection, and my love for my sweet babe makes me feel even more the value of your friendship."[25] Men respected women's friendships as a component of family life for wives and mothers. Charlotte Hanbury's 1905 *Life* of her missionary sister Caroline Head included a letter that the Reverend Charles Fox wrote to Head in 1877, soon after the birth of her first child: "I want desperately to see you and that prodigy of a boy, and that perfection of a husband, and that well-tried and well-beloved sister-friend of yours, Emma Waithman."[26] Although Head and Waithman never combined households, their regular correspondence, extended visits, and frequent travels were sufficient for Fox to assign Waithman a socially legible status as an informal family member, a "sister-friend" listed immediately after Head's son and husband.

In *A Room of One's Own*, Virginia Woolf lamented that a woman born in the 1840s would not be able to report what she was "doing on the fifth of April 1868, or the second of November 1875," for "[n]othing remains of it all. All has vanished. No biography or history has a word to say about it."[27] Yet as an avid reader of Victorian lifewriting, Woolf had every reason to be aware that in the very British Library where her speaker researches her lecture, hundreds of autobiographies, biographies, memoirs, diaries, and letters provided exhaustive records of what women did on almost every day of the nineteenth century. One cannot fault Woolf excessively for having discounted Victorian women's lifewriting, for even today few consult this corpus and no scholar of Victorian England has used it to explore the history of female friendship.[28] Scholars of autobiography concentrate on a handful of works by exceptional women, and historians of gender and sexuality have drawn primarily on fiction, parliamentary reports, journalism, legal cases, and medical and scientific discourse, which emphasize disruption, disorder, scandal, infractions, and pathology. Lifewriting, by contrast, emphasized ordinariness and typicality, which is precisely what makes it a unique source for scholarship.

The term "lifewriting" refers to the heterogeneous array of published, privately printed, and unpublished diaries, correspondence, biographies, autobiographies, memoirs, reminiscences, and recollections that Victorians and their descendants had a prodigious appetite for reading and writing. Literary critics have noted the relative paucity of autobiographies by women that fulfill the aesthetic criteria of a coherent, self-conscious narrative focused on a strictly demarcated individual self.[29] Women's own words about their lives, however, are abundantly represented in the more capacious genre of lifewriting, defined as any text that narrates or documents a subject's life. The autobiographical requirement of a unified individual life story was irrelevant for Victorian lifewriting, a hybrid genre that freely combined multiple narrators and sources, and incorporated long extracts from a subject's diaries, correspondence, and private papers alongside testimonials from friends and family members.[30] A single text might blend the journal's dailiness and immediacy and a letter's short-term retrospect with the long view of elderly writers reflecting on their lives, or the backward and forward glances of family members who had survived their subjects. For example, Christabel Coleridge was the nominal author of *Charlotte Mary Yonge: Her Life and Letters* (1903), but the text begins by reproducing an unpublished autobiographical essay Yonge wrote in 1877, intercalated with remarks by Coleridge. The sections of the *Life* written by Coleridge, conversely, consist of long extracts from Yonge's letters that take up almost as much space as Coleridge's own words. Coleridge undertook the biography out of personal friendship for Yonge, and its dialogic form mimics the structure of a social relationship conducted through conversation and correspondence.[31] The biographer was less an author than an editor who gathered and commented on a subject's writings without generating an autonomous narrative of her life.

Reticence was paradoxically characteristic of Victorian lifewriting, which was as defined by the drive to conceal life stories as it was indicative of a compulsion to transmit them. This was true of lifewriting by and about men as well as by and about women.[32] The authors of biographies often did not name themselves directly. Instead they subsumed their identities into those of their subjects. Authors who knew their subjects intimately as children, spouses, or parents usually adopted a deliberately impersonal tone, avoiding the first person whenever possible. In her anonymous biography of her daughter Mary Duncan, for example, Mary Lundie completely avoided writing in the first person and was sparing even with third-person references to herself as Duncan's "surviving parent" or "her mother" (243, 297). The materials used in biographies and autobiographies were similarly discreet, and the diaries that formed the basis of much lifewriting revealed little about their authors' lives. Victorian lifewriters who published diary excerpts valued them for their very failure to unveil mysteries, often praising the diarist's "reserve" and hastening to explain that the diaries cited did "not pretend to reveal personal secrets."[33]

Although we now expect diaries to be private outpourings of a self confronting forbidden desires and confiding scandalous secrets, only a handful of authenticated Victorian diaries recorded sexual lives in any detail, and none can be called typical.[34] Unrevealing diaries, on the other hand, were plentiful in an era when keeping a journal was common enough for printers to sell preprinted and preformatted diaries and locked diaries were unusual. Preformatted diaries adopted features of almanacs and account books, and journals synchronized personal life with the external rhythms of the clock, the calendar, and the household, not the unpredictable pulses of the heart.[35] Diaries were rarely meant for the diarist's eyes alone, which explains why biographers had no compunction about publishing large portions of their subjects' journals with no prefatory justifications. Girls and women read their diaries aloud to sisters or friends, and locked diaries were so uncommon that Ethel Smyth, born in 1858, still remembered sixty years later how her elders had disapproved when she started keeping a secret diary as a child.[36]

Some diarists even explicitly wrote for others, sharing their journals with readers in the present and addressing them to private and public audiences in the future. By the 1840s, published diaries had created a popular consciousness, and self-consciousness, about the diary form. In 1856, at age fourteen, Louisa Knightley (1842–1913), later a conservative feminist philanthropist, began to keep journals "written with a view to publication" and modeled on works such as Fanny Burney's diaries, published in 1842.[37] When the working-class Edwin Waugh began to keep a diary in 1847, his first step was to paste into it newspaper clippings about how to keep a journal. One young girl included diary extracts in letters to her cousin in the 1840s.[38] Princess Victoria was instructed in how to keep a daily journal by her beloved governess, Lehzen, and until Victoria became Queen, her mother inspected her diaries daily.[39] Diarists often wrote for prospective readers and selves, addressing journal entries to their children, writing annual summaries that assessed the previous year's entries, or rereading and annotating a life's worth of diaries in old age.[40] Journals were a tool for monitoring spiritual progress on a daily basis and over the course of a lifetime. Diarists periodically reread their journals so that by comparing past acts with present outcomes they could improve themselves in the future. *A Beloved Mother: Life of Hannah S. Allen. By Her Daughter* (1884) excerpted a journal Allen (1813–1880) started in 1836 and then reread in 1876, when she dedicated it to her daughters: "To my dear girls, that they may see the way in which the Lord has led me."[41] Far from being a repository of the most secret self, the diary was seen as a didactic legacy, one of the links in a family history's chain.

Victorian women's diaries combined impersonality with lack of incident. Although Marian Bradley (1831–1910) wrote, "My diary is entirely a record of my inner life—the outer life is not varied. Quiet and pleasant but nothing worth recording occurs," she in fact devoted hundreds of pages to recording an outer life that she accurately characterized as regular and predictable.[42] Indeed, the stability and relentless routine that diaries labored to convey goes far to explain why Victorians were so eager to read the poetry that lyrically expressed spontaneous emotion and the novels that injected eventfulness and suspense into everyday life. Diaries and novels had common origins in spiritual autobiography, and diaries played a dramatic role in Victorian fiction, but although diaries shared quotidian subjects and diurnal rhythms with novels, they were rarely novelistic. Most diarists produced chronicles that testified to a woman's success in developing the discipline necessary to ensure that each day was much like the rest, and even travel diaries were filled not with impressions but descriptions similar to those found in guidebooks. When something unusually tumultuous took place, it often interrupted a woman's daily writing and went unrecorded.[43] There are few differences in this regard between manuscript and published diaries; both are similarly bland, rarely revealing anything that could not have been made public. Those whose papers recorded heady events were among the most likely to destroy them in an era when people regularly burnt correspondence and personal documents.

Keeping a diary was a religious discipline for many Victorians, who recorded their daily work and spiritual lives as part of a mission to develop methodical habits. M.R.D. Foot characterizes William Gladstone's diary as "a mild penitential exercise: a daily occasion for self-criticism."[44] Marian Bradley, an Anglican minister's wife who began to keep a diary in 1854, frequently censured herself for procrastination, impatience, and extravagance, measuring her spiritual life by a rigid moral standard that militated against any hint of worldliness, spontaneity, or selfishness. Like the narrator of a didactic novel, Bradley assessed herself in relation to Christian values and filled her diary with ethical generalizations: "We live but to work, and work while we live, up to the very gates of the other world. How important a work is mine. To be a cheerful, loving Xtian wife, a forebearing and fond wise thoughtful mother—striving ever against self-indulgence and irritability."[45] Using a journal to assess one's virtue and faith was not a religious practice confined to Protestants. Philanthropist Louisa Montefiore (1821–1910), later Lady de Rothschild, was an observant Jew who also kept a diary as a form of "strict self-examination," in the hope that carefully documenting how she managed her time and money and regulated her mind and affections would prevent her from being vain, frivolous, and fanciful.[46]

The motives for publishing lifewriting in the Victorian period were nonetheless often explicitly denominational, and many authors described their works as "Christian biography."[47] The anonymous compiler of the *Letters of Mary Mathison* (1875) justified the privately printed book in a biographical notice: "Those who had the privilege of knowing her will treasure the record of her thoughts . . . and if any . . . should be comforted or helped forward one small step on the heavenward way by any word or thought of hers, they will not have been written in vain, and she 'being dead yet speaketh.'"[48] By allowing the dead to speak, publication of journals and letters typified biographers' fervent belief in resurrection, while the record of an exemplary faith could instruct and convert readers to a similar love of God. Albert Head hoped that his wife Caroline's testimony about Christ, "the Saviour and Friend she loved so dearly . . . might stimulate others to seek for the grace of God" (xiii). So strong was the religious impulse that even those opposed to organized religion adopted its narrative of transformation through faith and good works, with writers telling the life stories of nurses, suffragists, or socialists in order to convert readers to secular causes.

Where Christian biographies emphasized narratives of spiritual evolution that provided readers with models to imitate, other forms of lifewriting appealed to the glamour of the unattainable. Aristocratic memoirs focused on their authors' membership in exclusive social circles and participation in important political events, neither of which could be emulated by the general public. Lifewriting by elite women did not hold up a mirror to the reader but instead offered a visitor's pass for a personal guided tour of privileged lives. In the first half of the twentieth century, when Victorian women's lifewriting surged into print, lifewriting became valued as a form of time travel. Editors and authors no longer argued that works provided spiritual exempla or vicarious entry into an exclusive social circle but instead justified them as having a historical purpose. Victorian lifewriting provided a "picture of a dead world" and a record of a time "fast slipping out of our reach."[49] Its very lack of incident and typicality increased its value for nostalgic readers who were beginning to see the Victorian era as a bygone age of equipoise. With its emphasis on everyday life and interchangeable, representative subjects, Victorian lifewriting fed an appetite for vernacular social history among general readers who anticipated the scholarly interest in the lives of ordinary people by several decades.

In the 1930s a new form of lifewriting, the modernist memoir, began to emphasize inimitable personal details, subjective internal processes, and self-reflexive accounts of the development of perception and expression.[50] Psychoanalytic theory popularized introspection and encouraged individuals to develop elaborate individual mythologies. Works like Eleanor Acland's *Good-Bye for the Present* (1935) abandoned family trees and exemplary religious lives for idiosyncratic, "disconnected glimpses of childish things."[51] Where Victorian lifewriting usually began with familiar topographies and extensive genealogies, modernist memoirs opened with the author's first memory and strove to represent her emerging consciousness. The new style retained some elements from the previous era, but the Victorian lifewriter's inclination to portray individuals as ideal types gave way to deliberately fragmented accounts whose inability to tell a contained, linear story testified to the irreducible singularity of the biographical subject.

FEMALE FRIENDSHIP AS GENDER NORM

Contemporary readers might find themselves almost suspicious of how little there is in Victorian lifewriting to shock or surprise; can their lives really have been this dull? Deficient in arresting details and blandly uniform, Victorian lifewriting does not foster any illusions that it accurately records the historical past. But lifewriting was not pure fiction, and its very adherence to rules and commitment to typical daily life makes it a far more valuable source than conduct literature, medical writings, or police records for understanding how conventions shaped lived behavior. Consider the example of transvestism. Cross-dressing could lead to scandal and arrests, but lifewriting attests that many youths who adopted the clothes of the other sex were treated as amusing pranksters. In her 1857 autobiography Elizabeth Davis recalled "enjoying" herself "extremely" when she dressed as a man to accompany a fellow housemaid to a party and noted that her employers simply "laughed" when they caught her. In the 1840s a young woman living in London wrote to a cousin in the country about putting on a play with other girls for their fathers and mothers: "I have two parts, the good Fairy and the Lord Chamberlain because he sings a song, and he wears a turban and baggy trousers and I wear a beard and moustache." Other accounts described boys dressing as girls and sallying forth in public to the amusement of all in the know.[52]

Victorian lifewriting exposes other gaps between myth and reality. Conduct books confined women to the private sphere, but in fact, many informally participated in politics. Amanda Vickery has pointed out the dearth of research on women's consumption of newspapers, an increasingly political medium after 1750; lifewriting shows that many ordinary middle-class women who complied with gender norms actively read newspapers and discussed political events with their fathers and husbands.[53] Katharine Harris's journal documents how a middle-class teenage girl tracked the revolutions and cholera epidemics of 1848 as carefully as she followed changes in fashion and the dramas of her social circle.[54] Women's diaries and correspondence also modify our image of Victorian feminism as a powerful but marginal movement; though suffrage was a divisive issue, an otherwise silent majority supported female higher education, with many writers asserting that "women have brains, and given equal opportunities, can do as good work as men."[55] Mary, Lady Monkswell (1849–1930) never formally participated in politics except as the wife of a man who held several government positions, but in 1890 she recorded her pride that a woman had attained the highest score on the Cambridge Mathematical Tripos: "Every woman feels 2 inches taller for this success of Miss Fawcett."[56]

Female friendship emerges in Victorian lifewriting as a fundamental component of middle-class femininity and women's life stories. Because the letters women exchanged with male suitors were often deemed too private or compromising for publication, and because wives had few occasions to write to husbands whom they lived with, letters between female friends and kin were the most common and copious source for documenting women's lives.[57] Anna Bower's correspondence with three women who had been her friends since school days made up the bulk of a 1903 edition of her diaries and letters.[58] The *Memoir of Mrs. Mary Lundie Duncan* (1842) drew heavily on the communication between Mary Duncan and a lifelong friend. The many letters included in the published version of Mary Gladstone Drew's diaries and correspondence were addressed to her cousin and friend Lavinia.[59] The editor of Lady Louise Knightley's journals identified the central figure of the early volumes as Louise's cousin and "inseparable companion" Edith, with whom Louise exchanged daily letters when they were separated between 1856 and 1864 (12).

The emphasis on female friendship in Victorian women's lifewriting mirrored the ways in which didactic literature defined it as an expression of women's essential femininity. In *The Women of England* and *The Daughters of England*, Sarah Ellis articulated the tenets of a domestic ideology based on strict divisions between men and women. She counseled women to accept their inferiority to men and to cultivate moral virtues such as selflessness and empathy as counterweights to the male virtues of competitiveness and self-determination. Ellis praised female friendship for several reasons. It trained women not to compete with men by requiring them not to compete with one another; it fostered feminine vulnerability by developing bonds based on a shared "capability of receiving pain"; and it reinforced married love by cultivating the sexual differences that fostered men's desire for women (*Women*, 75, 224). In *The Daughters of England*, Ellis explicitly argued that friendship trained women to be good wives by teaching them particularly feminine ways of loving: "In the circle of her private friends . . . [woman] learns to comprehend the deep mystery of that electric chain of feeling which ever vibrates through the heart of woman, and which man, with all his philosophy, can never understand" (337). Ellis argued that female friendship produced marriageable women by intensifying the opposition between the sexes, but she then undid gender differences by positing similarities between friendship and marriage. The emotions fostered by friendship were also those required for marriage, leading Ellis to call marriage a species of friendship, and friendship "the basis of all true love" (*Daughters*, 388).

Far from compromising friendship, family and marriage provided models for sustaining it; female friends exchanged the same tokens as spouses and emulated female elders who also prized their friendships with women. Marriage rarely ended friendships and many women organized part of their lives around their friends. Louise Creighton (1850–1936), married to an Anglican vicar and eventually the mother of six children, wrote letters to her mother in the 1870s that often mentioned extended visits from her childhood friend Bunnie and other married and unmarried female friends.[60] Just before she acceded to the throne, Princess Victoria wrote of her governess Lehzen as "my 'best and truest friend' I have had for nearly 17 years and I trust I shall have for 30 or 40 and *many* more." On the day Victoria married Albert, Lehzen gave the queen a ring, and their pledges of an enduring bond held true, with Lehzen ensconced at court long after the queen's wedding.[61] Like any monarch, Queen Victoria practiced a politics of display, but what she performed most vigorously was her adherence to domestic middle-class ideals.[62] It is therefore not surprising to find her commitment to lifelong friendship echoed in the aspirations of Annie Hill, a middle-class girl who in 1877 wrote to her friend Anna Richmond, "I do not see why we should not keep up writing to one another all our lives like Aunt Maria and her great friend have done."[63] The friendships that created bonds between individual women also forged a sense of connection between generations.

Friendship and marriage could be overlapping and mutually reinforcing. While engaged to her husband-to-be, Mary Duncan sent him poems and the gift of a hair brooch, and at the same time wrote a poem for her best friend, whom she addressed as "loved one" and "dear one" (163, 179–80, 147). Just as Duncan experienced no conflict in loving her fiancé and her friend, other women expressed affection for friends by hoping they would happily marry. Writing in 1865 of the friend who came "to bless my life," twenty-three-year-old Louisa Knightley fantasized about her eventual wedding with a sense of pleasure rather than incipient loss: "I have grown to love Edie very dearly—the Sleeping Beauty, whom life and the world are slowly awakening. May the enchanted Prince soon come and touch the chord that will rouse her from the dreams of childhood and make of her the perfect woman!" (105–6).

In a long passage from *The Women of England* on women's duties, what begins as a discussion of friendship between women blurs almost imperceptibly into a peroration on marriage between women and men. By the last sentence of this passage, it is clear that Ellis's subject has shifted from female friendship to male-female marriage, but where does the shift begin?

Have [women] not their young friendships, for those sunny hours when the heart expands itself in the genial atmosphere of mutual love, and shrinks not from revealing its very weaknesses and errors; so that a faithful hand has but to touch its tender chords, and conscience is awakened, and then instruction may be poured in, and medicine may be administered, and the messenger of peace, with healing on his wings, may be invited to come in, and make that heart his home? Have they not known the secrets of some faithful bosom laid bare before them in a deeper and yet more confiding attachment, when, however insignificant they might be to the world in general, they held an influence almost unbounded over one human being, and could pour in, for the bane or the blessing of that bosom, according to the fountain from whence their own was supplied? Have they not bound themselves by a sacred and enduring bond, to be to one fellow-traveller along the path of life, a companion on his journey. (47–48)

Ellis's overuse of pronouns, personifications, and body parts to represent people makes it difficult to assign gendered subjects to her sentences. The reference to a faithful hand awakening conscience accords with Ellis's understanding of female friendship's moral benefits, and the "messenger of peace" who enters the opened heart is only figuratively male and could refer to the female friend or the husband. The invocation of "an influence almost unbounded over one human being" invokes an intensity and exclusivity that Ellis associates with marriage and cautions against in friendship, but the gender neutrality of the phrase "human being" makes the phrase applicable to both relationships. Only the final sentence refers unambiguously to the husband, and even then, the emotional solace he receives originates in the "fountain" of female friendship that taught his wife to love. Ellis's use of pronouns similarly underscores the interdependence of friendship and marriage. Her final sentence oddly joins the "one fellow-traveller," who represents the husband, with a plural pronoun, the "they" who have bound themselves to be his companion, and who represent women trained to wifehood by the "mutual love" of friendship. Ellis's suggestive formulation embodies marriage's dependence on prior bonds between women to the point of suggesting that a man marries both his wife and the friends whom she has incorporated into her simultaneously individual and multiple person.

Lifewriting confirms the links conduct literature made between female friendship and conventional femininity, for only women invested in portraying themselves as atypical failed to write of their friendships. Women who succeeded in masculine arenas and advertised their exceptional achievements in published autobiographies often accentuated their distance from standard femininity by downplaying the role that female friends played in their lives. Battle painter Elizabeth Butler (1846–1933), pedagogue and professional author Elizabeth Sewell (1815–1906), and radical activist Annie Besant (1847–1933) all omitted the rhapsodic descriptions of friendship that characterized lifewriting by women eager to demonstrate how well they had fulfilled the dictates of their gender.[64] Outright disdain for female friendship was rare. One of the few extant examples of a woman mocking female friendship is an exception that proves the rule. A sophisticated transplant raised in Paris by parents from the Anglo-Irish gentry who returned to England in 1868, Alice Miles was eager to distinguish herself from her earnest English relatives. In a diary that remained unpublished until the late twentieth century, she wrote that women were obligated to marry for money, not love. Her contempt for British domestic sentiment led her to dismiss the earnest devotion between female friends she encountered in England as hypocrisy or stupidity. She believed instead in "the natural aversion women always seem to entertain towards each other and the still more decided preference they habitually evince towards mankind!" Nevertheless, Miles enjoyed forming a friendships with a young woman "perfectly acquainted" with every "naughty story . . . making the tour of London," whom she praised as "a regular little rose bud . . . looking perfectly bewitching." Even the cynical Miles, who believed that affection between woman was merely a "sign . . . that a man is at the bottom of the emotion," could not resist the pleasure she took in a woman pretty and wicked enough to be a potential rival.[65]

Successful women who represented themselves as proper ladies defined their lives in terms of their friendships with women as well as their devotion to family and church. Anglican novelist Charlotte Yonge (1823–1901) described her life as structured by three great friendships, beginning in childhood with a favorite cousin, "My dear, dear Anne, whom I loved always with all my heart!" (66). Yonge's account of her youthful love for Anne provides an unusual instance of a girlhood friendship being checked by adults:

> [T]he great love of all our lives was getting to be conscious. Anne and I were always together. We wanted to walk about with our arms round each other's waists, but our mothers held this to be silly, and we were told we could be just as fond of one another without "pawing." I still think this was hard, and that tenderness would have done no harm. But I do remember a long walk with the nurses and the little ones round Kitley Point. . . .We gathered [blue-bells] in the ecstasy of childhood among flowers, exchanged our finest clustering stems of blue, and felt our hearts go out to one another. At least I did, so entirely that the Kitley slope—yes, and a white blue-bell—still brings to me that dear Anne and that old love. (83)

The passage depicts mothers attempting to limit how girls express their affection, but not the fondness itself. Yonge's gentle rebuke of the mothers' censure is ratified by her adult status as a novelist whose works were eminently respectable and ladylike. The very act of recollecting Anne and the landscape of their love in the present evades the maternal effort to subdue it in the past. Never an overt rebel, Yonge neutralizes maternal disapproval and strictures by calling the mothers "hard," thus subtly impugning not only their judgment but also their femininity, which suffers in comparison with the "love" between the two girls, hyperfeminine in its "tenderness."

Friends and "Friends"

To understand what friendship between women was, we must first understand what it was not. Before turning to the ways in which female friendship illustrated the play of the Victorian gender system, we must develop grounds for distinguishing it from other relationships between women. This is a detour, for the subject of this chapter is female friendship; erotic desire and marriage between women are the focus of subsequent sections. But friendship, erotic infatuation, and female marriage have so often been conflated, and women's relationships so commonly understood as essentially ambiguous, that the detour is a necessary one. The language of Victorian friendship was so ardent, the public face of female marriage so amicable, the comparisons between female friendship and marriage between men and women so constant, that it is no simple task to distinguish female friends from female lovers or female couples. The question "did they have sex?" is the first one on people's lips today when confronted with a claim that women in the past were lovers—and it is almost always unanswerable. If firsthand testimony about sex is the standard for defining a relationship as sexual, then most Victorians never had sex. Scholars have yet to determine whether Thomas Carlyle was impotent; when, if ever, John Stuart Mill and Harriet Taylor consummated their relationship; or if Arthur Munby and Hannah Cullwick, whose diaries recorded their experiments with fetishes, cross-dressing, and bootlicking, also had genital intercourse.[66] Just as one can read hundreds of Victorian letters, diaries, and memoirs without finding a single mention of menstruation or excretion, one rarely finds even oblique references to sex between husband and wife. Men and women were equally reticent about sexual activity inside and outside of marriage.[67] In a journal that described her courtship and wedding in detail, Lady Knightley dispatched the first weeks of wedded life in two lines: "Rainald and I entered on our new life in our own home. May God bless it to us" (173). Elizabeth Butler, whose autobiography included "a little sketch of [her] rather romantic meeting" with the man who became her husband, was similarly and typically laconic about a transition defined by sexual intercourse: "June 11 of that year, 1877, was my wedding day."[68]

The lack of reliable evidence of sexual activity becomes less problematic, however, if we realize that sex matters because of the social relationships it creates and concentrate on those relationships. In Victorian England, sex was assumed to be part of marriage, but could also drop out of marriage without destroying a bond never defined by sex alone. The diaries and correspondence of Anne Lister and Charlotte Cushman provide solid evidence that nineteenth-century women had genital contact and orgasms with other women, but even more importantly, they demonstrate that sex created different kinds of connections. The fleeting encounters Lister had with women she met abroad were very different from the illicit but sustained affair Cushman had with a much younger woman who became her daughter-in-law. Those types of affairs were in turn worlds apart from the relationships with women that Lister and Cushman called marriages, a term that did not simply mean the relationships were sexual but also connoted shared households, mingled property, and assumptions about exclusivity and durability. We can best understand what kinds of relationships women had with each other not by hunting for evidence of sex, which even if we find it will not explain much, but rather by anchoring women's own statements about their relationships in a larger context. The context I provide here is the complex linguistic field of lifewriting, which brings into focus two types of relationships often confused with friendship, indeed often called friendship, but significantly different from it: 1) unrequited passion and obsessive infatuation; and 2) life partnerships, which some Victorians described as marriages between women.

The most famous and best-documented example of a Victorian woman's avowed but unreciprocated passion for another woman is Edith Simcox's lifelong love for George Eliot, which has made her a staple figure in histories of lesbianism.[69] Simcox (1844–1901) was a trade-union organizer and professional writer who regularly contributed book reviews to the periodical press and published fiction and nonfiction, including a study of women's property ownership in ancient societies, discussed in chapter 5. From 1876 to 1900, Simcox kept a journal in a locked book that surfaced in 1930. Simcox gave her life story a title, *The Autobiography of a Shirtmaker*, that foregrounded her successful work as a labor activist, but its actual content focused on what Simcox called "the love-passion of her life," her longing for George Eliot as an unattainable, idealized beloved whom she called "my goddess" or, even more reverently,

"Her."[70] Simcox knowingly embraced a love that could not be returned, though she was aware of reciprocated, consummated sexual love between women. Her diary alludes to a "lovers' quarrel" among three women she knew (61) and mentions her own rejection of a woman who "professed a feeling for me different from what she had ever had for any one, it might make her happiness if I could return it" (159).

Tellingly, though twentieth-century scholars often refer to Simcox euphemistically as Eliot's devoted "friend," Simcox rarely used the term, and modeled herself instead on a courtly lover made all the more devoted by the one-sidedness of her passion. Simcox defined her diary as an "acta diurna amoris," a daily act of love, and aspired to keep it with a constancy that would mirror her total absorption in Eliot (3). After bringing Eliot two valentines in February 1878, Simcox wrote: "Yesterday I went to see her, and have been in a calm glow of happiness since:—for no special reason, only that to have been near her happens to have that effect on me. . . . I did nothing but make reckless love to her . . . I had told her of my ambition to be allowed to lie silently at her feet as she pursued her occupations" (25). George Lewes, the companion whom Eliot's friends referred to as her husband, was present at most of these scenes, and he and Eliot tolerated and even enjoyed Simcox's attentions, which they consciously construed as loverlike. During a conversation about Elizabeth Barrett Browning's love poems, *Sonnets from the Portugese*, Eliot told Simcox "she wished my letters could be printed in the same veiled way— 'the Newest Heloise,'" thus situating Simcox's missives to her in the tradition of amatory literature (39). In private, Simcox indulged fantasies of a more sensual connection, reflecting on a persistent "love that made the longing and molded the caress," and recalling how "[i]n thinking of her, kisses used to form themselves instinctively on my lips—I seldom failed to kiss her a good night in thought" (136).

In trying to define her love for Eliot, Simcox significantly refused to be content with one paradigm; instead, she accumulated analogies, comparing her love for Eliot to both "[m]arried love and passionate friendship" (60). Like a medieval ascetic, Simcox eroticized her lack of sexual fulfillment, arguing that her love was even more powerful than friendship or marriage because, in resigning herself to living "widowed of perfect joy," she had felt "sharp flames consuming what was left . . . of selfish lust" (60).[71] In an unsent 1880 letter to Eliot, Simcox again found herself unable to select only one category to explain her love: "Do you see darling that I can only love you three lawful ways, idolatrously as Frater the Virgin Mary, in romance wise as Petrarch, Laura, or with a child's fondness for the mother" (120). By implication, Simcox also suggested that there would be an unlawful way to love Eliot—as an adulterer who would usurp the uxurious role already occupied by Lewes. She concluded by explaining that her relationship with Eliot was too unequal to be a friendship (120). In the absence of the sociological and scientific shorthand provided by sexology or a codified subculture, and in the absence of a genuinely shared life that could be represented by a common history or joint possessions, women like Simcox represented their unrequited sexual desire for other women by extravagantly combining incompatible terms such as mother, lover, sister, friend, wife, and idol.

Other women deployed similar rhetorical techniques of intensification and accumulation to express sexual loves that were not equally felt and did not lead to long-term partnerships. At age twenty, Sophia Jex-Blake (1840–1912), one of England's first female doctors and an activist who helped open medical education to women, met philanthropist Octavia Hill (1838–1912). In a biography of Jex-Blake written in 1918 that still adhered to Victorian rhetorical conventions, Margaret Todd called her subject's relationship with Hill a "friendship" but qualified it as one that made "the deepest impression . . . of any in the whole of her life."[72] Jex-Blake considered the degree of love she felt for women to be unusual, writing around 1858, "I believe I love women too much ever to love a man" (78). During a brief relationship that Hill soon broke off, the two women may have been sexually involved, but even so their feelings were never evenly matched. During the period when the women were closest, Hill reduced their bond to mere chumminess by calling herself and Jex-Blake "great companions" (85). By contrast, Jex-Blake was in awe of Hill and described her as both child and mother, roles often eroticized for Victorians, writing in her diary of "My dear loving strong child . . . I do love and reverence her" (85). Even after the relationship ended, Jex-Blake thought of Hill as her lifelong spouse, referring twenty years later to the "fanciful faithfulness" she maintained for her first love, to whom she left "the whole of her little property" in repeated wills (94). Like Simcox, Jex-Blake used intensified language to underscore the uniqueness of her emotions. When she described inviting Hill on a vacation that included a visit to Llangollen, a site made famous by the female couple who had lived there together, Jex-Blake wrote of her "heart beating like a hammer" (85) and then described Hill's response: "She sunk her head on my lap silently, raised it in tears, then such a kiss!" (86). Female friends often exchanged kisses, but Jex-Blake's account took the kiss out of the realm of friendship into one of heightened sensation.

Although it was common for female friends to love each other and write gushingly about it, Simcox and Jex-Blake also wrote of feeling uncommon, different from the general run of women. Simcox identified closely with men and Jex-Blake felt unable to love men as most women did; both were extraordinarily autonomous, professionally successful, and self-conscious about the significance of their love for women. Other women also had intense erotic relationships that went beyond friendship, but were less self-conscious about those relationships, which they rarely saw as needing special explanation, and which usually lasted years or months rather than a lifetime. An example of outright insouciance about a deeply felt erotic fascination between women is found in the journals of Margaret Leicester Warren, written in the 1870s and published for private circulation in 1924. Little is known about Warren, who was born in 1847 and led the life of a typical upper-middle-class lady, attending church, studying drawing and music, and marrying a man in 1875. Her diary attests to a fondness for triangulated relationships that included an adolescent crush on her newlywed sister and her sister's husband, and a brief, tumultuous engagement to a male cousin whose mother was the dramatic center of Warren's intense emotions. In 1872, when Warren was twenty-five, she began to write incessantly about a distant cousin named Edith Leycester in entries that reveled in the experience of succumbing to another woman's glamour: "Edith looked very beautiful and as usual I fell in love with her. . . . Tonight Edith took me into her room. . . . She is like an enchanted princess. There is some charm or spell that has been thrown over her."[73] Numerous similar entries recorded an infatuation that combined daily familiarity with reverent mystification of a sophisticated and self-dramatizing woman.

Warren's fascination with Edith lasted several years. Unlike Simcox and Jex-Blake, Warren never self-consciously reflected that her feelings for Edith differed from conventional friendship, but like them, Warren ascribed an intensity, exclusivity, and volatility to her feelings for Edith absent from most accounts of female friendship. Indeed, Warren rarely referred to Edith as a friend when she wrote of her desire to see Edith every day and recorded their many exchanges of confidences, poetry, and gifts. Warren fetishized and idealized Edith, was fixated on her presence and absence, and used superlatives to describe the feelings she inspired. Within months of meeting Edith, most of Warren's entries consisted of detailed reenactments of their daily visits and the emotions generated by each parting and reunion: "Edith was charming tonight and I was happier with her than I have ever been. She looked beautiful" (287). Warren created an erotic aura around Edith through the very act of writing about her, through a liberal use of adverbs and adjectives, and by infusing her friend's most ordinary actions with dramatic implications. Describing how Edith invited her to visit her country home, for example, Warren wrote, "Edith came in and threw herself down on the chair and said quietly and gently 'come to Toft!'" (291). Although Warren got along well with Edith's rarely present husband, Rafe, she relished being alone with her and described the awkward, jealous scenes that took place whenever she had to share Edith with other women (362, 369).

Warren found ways to dwell on the details of Edith's beauty through references to fashion and contemporary art. Like many diarists, Warren had an almost novelistic capacity to observe and characterize people in terms of prevailing aesthetic forms. She described Edith with flowers in her hair, looking like a pre-Raphaelite painting, and recorded her desire to make images of Edith: "I sd. like to paint her. . . . It wd. make a good 'golden witch' a beautiful Enchantress" (290–91). A ride with Edith inspired Warren to pen another impassioned tableau: "All the way there in the brougham I looked at Edith's beautiful profile, the lamp light shining on it, and the wind blowing her hair about—her face also, all lit up with enthusiasm and tenderness as she leant forward to Rafe and told him a long story . . . I . . . only thought how grand *she* was" (369–70). Shared confidences about Warren's broken engagement to their male cousin became another medium for cultivating the women's special intimacy. By assuring Warren that she did not side with the jilted fiancé, Edith declared an autonomous interest in her: "'I wanted you to come here because—because I like you.' She was sitting at her easel and never looking at me as she spoke for I was standing behind her, but when she said 'because I like you,' she looked backwards up at me with such an honest, soft, beautiful expression that any distrust I had still left of her trueness melted up into a cinder" (290).

Just as Warren heightened her relationship with Edith by writing about it so effusively and at such length, the two women elevated it by coyly discussing what their interactions and feelings meant. Before one of her many departures from London, Edith asked Warren: "'[A]re you *sorry* I am going? . . . How curious—why are you sorry?' Then I told her a little of all she had done for me . . . how much life and pleasure and interest she had put into my life, and she said nothing but she just put out her hand and laid it on my hand and that from her means a great deal more than 100 things from anyone else" (293). Edith's gesture drew on the repertory of friendship, but in the private theater of her journal, Warren transformed the touch of a hand into a uniquely meaningful clasp. This is not to say the relationship was one-sided. If Warren's diary reports the two women's interactions with any degree of accuracy, it is clear that both enjoyed creating an atmosphere of pent-up longing. Edith fed Warren's infatuation with provocative questions and a skill for setting scenes: "She asked what things I cared for now? And I said with truth, for nothing—except seeing her" (303). Three days later, just before another of Edith's departures, Warren paid a call:

When tea was over, the dusk had begun and I . . . sat . . . at the open window. . . . By and bye Edith came and sat near me. . . . The room inside was nearly dark, but outside it was brilliant May moonlight. . . . Edith sat there ready to go, looking very pale and very sad with the light on her face. . . . We did not talk much. She asked me to go to the party tonight and to think of her at 11. . . . She said goodbye and she kissed me, for the first time. (303–4)

Warren is exquisitely sensitive to every element that connotes eroticism: a darkened room, physical proximity, complicit silence, a romantic demand that the beloved remain present in her lover's mind even when absent, a kiss whose uniqueness—"for the first time"—suggests a beginning. Any one of these actions would have been unremarkable between female friends, but comparison with other women's diaries shows how distinctive it was for Warren to list so many gestures within one entry, without defining and therefore restricting their meaning. Warren's attitude also distinguishes her emotions from those articulated by women who took their love for women in a more conjugal or sexual direction. Her journals combine exhaustive attention to the beloved with a pervasive indifference to interrogating what that fascination might mean. Never classified as friendship or love, Warren's feelings for Edith had the advantages and limits of remaining in the realm of suggestion, where they could expand infinitely without ever being realized or checked.

Women who consummated a mutual love and consolidated it by forming a conjugal household were less likely to leave records of their most impassioned moods and deeds than those whose love went unrequited or undefined. Indeed, women in what were sometimes called "female marriages" (a term I discuss further in chapter 5) used lifewriting to claim the privilege of privacy accorded to opposite-sex spouses. Like the lifewritings of women married to men, those of women in female marriages assumed intimacy and interdependence rather than displaying it, and folded their sexual bond into a social one. They described shared households and networks of acquaintances who recognized and thus legitimated the women's coupledom, liberally using words such as "always," "never," and "every" to convey an iterated, daily familiarity more typical of spouses than friends.[74] Martha Vicinus's *Intimate Friends* cites many nineteenth-century women who described their relationships with other women as marriages, and Magnus Hirschfeld's magisterial, international study of *The Homosexuality of Men and Women* (1914) noted that same-sex couples often created "marriage-like associations characterized by the exclusivity and long duration of the relationships, the living together and the common household, the sharing of every interest, and often the existence of legitimate community property."[75] Sexual relationships of all stripes were most acceptable when their sexual nature was least visible as such but was instead manifested in terms of marital acts such as cohabitation, fidelity, financial solidarity, and adherence to middle-class norms of respectability.

Because friendship between women was so clearly defined and prized, one way to acknowledge a female couple's existence while respecting their privacy was to call women who were in effect married to each other "friends." Given that "friends" was used to describe women who were lovers and women who were not, how can we tell when "friends" means more than just friends? Frank Hird's 1904 biography of renowned painter Rosa Bonheur, whose monumental 1853 canvas *The Horse Fair* endeared her to the British public, is a good place to begin to answer this question. Bonheur was French, but Hird was an Englishman writing about her for English readers. The biographer was well placed to understand that terms designating social relationships could have more than one meaning, since he himself was the adopted son of his older male lover.[76] Hird referred to Bonheur's lover of several decades, Nathalie Micas, as her "devoted friend and companion," but he supplemented that term with detailed accounts of Bonheur's feelings for Micas throughout her life and after her death, which he called a deep "blow" to Bonheur.[77] The care of the "friend's" body in the crises of illness and death and in daily life was one sign of a conjugal relationship between women euphemistically called friends. Without ever even hinting that Bonheur and Micas had sex, Hird showed that they had higher levels of involvement and intimacy than even the closest of female friends, who rarely lived together for long periods of time and almost never pooled their wealth or arranged to be interred together. Theodore Stanton, the editor of Bonheur's reminiscences, also made clear that her tie to Micas was in effect a marital one.[78] He cited painter Joseph Verdier's description of Bonheur painting "while Nathalie Micas was taking a bath in a room opening into the studio" (94), and noted that the two women merged finances (103), wrote wills making each the other's primary heir, and arranged to be buried in the same plot (81).

Because female friendship was recognized as an autonomous social relationship with its own duties and privileges, Hird was not simply trivializing or veiling Bonheur's relationship with Micas when he called them friends. At a time when marriage was increasingly conceived as an affective relationship as well as a legal and economic one, husbands and wives also expressed love by calling one another companions. The friendship of a spouse, however, was usually deemed superlative, and when Bonheur used the term to describe Micas, she similarly vested it with the exclusivity that Sarah Ellis identified as "calculated only for the intercourse of married life" (*Daughters*, 336, 337). Micas was "my dearest and best friend," or simply "my Nathalie" in letters Bonheur sent to family, friends, and fellow artists. She assigned Micas multiple roles, describing her as friend and guardian angel and comparing her to a mother and wife (*Reminiscences*, 43, 188). Their social circle followed suit, with friends often referring to them as a "couple" (*Reminiscences*, 8, 81). Bonheur's memoirs cited many sources that referred to the women's "long companionship" and "deep affection," their reciprocal care of each other, and Nathalie's jealousy of Bonheur's other relationships (*Reminiscences*, 99, 101, 109, 102). The editor of those reminiscences fleshed out what he meant by the women's "peculiar friendship" by citing letters in which Bonheur referred to Micas's mother as her mother-in-law, and by devoting an entire chapter to Micas's family history, a treatment usually reserved for a biographical subject's spouse (*Reminiscences*, 122, 110). Although Bonheur insisted "My private life is nobody's concern," she also published the many letters of condolence she received after Micas's death in her memoirs.

There are many instances of published writing acknowledging marital relationships between women by calling them friendships. Victorian women in female couples were not automatically subject to the exposure and scandal visited on opposite-sex couples who stepped outside the bounds of respectable sexual behavior. Instead, many female couples enjoyed both the right to privacy associated with marriage and the public privileges accorded to female friendship. The *Halifax Guardian* obituary of Anne Lister in 1840 recognized her longstanding spousal relationship with Anne Walker by calling her Lister's "friend and companion," a gratuitously compound phrase.[79] Emily Faithfull, whom we will encounter again in chapter 6, was a feminist with a long history of female lovers. An 1894 article entitled "An Afternoon Tea with Miss Emily Faithfull" described her home in Manchester, decorated by "Miss Charlotte Robinson," whom Faithfull readily disclosed "shares house with me."[80] Faithfull left all her property to Robinson in a will that called her "my beloved friend" whose "countless services" and "affectionate tenderness and care . . . made the last few years of my life the happiest I ever spent."[81] To call one woman another's superlative friend was not to disavow their marital relationship but to proclaim it in the language of the day.

The rhetoric of female marriage was best exemplified in lifewriting by and about Frances Power Cobbe (1822–1904). A professional writer and political activist, Cobbe championed feminism, protested vivisection, and lived for decades with Mary Lloyd, a sculptor, whom one acquaintance wrote of as Cobbe's "special woman friend."[82] The social network that embraced the two women included Fanny Kemble, John Stuart Mill, Henry Maine, Charles Darwin, and William Gladstone, many of whom recognized that Cobbe and Lloyd formed a conjugal unit who lived and traveled together and were to be jointly saluted in correspondence and invited as a pair to social gatherings. Renowned actress Kemble, who published several autobiographical works during her lifetime, openly discussed Cobbe and Lloyd as a couple. In an 1877 letter to Harriet St. Leger, published in 1890, Kemble mused: "I think Mary Lloyd really suffers from London; nevertheless not half so much as Fanny would from living out of it. They talk of going away, but . . . I think they are likely to be here for some time yet." Kemble rented a house formerly occupied by Lloyd and Cobbe, and whether writing of how Cobbe had to cancel engagements when Lloyd got lumbago, mentioning that "Fanny Cobbe and Mary Lloyd are coming to lunch with me on Monday," or casually referring to "them," "they," and "their" when Cobbe was her primary subject, she took it for granted that the women were a conjugal unit.[83] Kemble's vision of the relationship corresponded to Cobbe's, who recalled "falling fast asleep while [Fanny Kemble] was reading Shakespeare to Mary Lloyd and me in our drawing-room" and whose own autobiography was peppered with references to "us," "our house," and "our neighbors."[84]

In her own lifewriting, Cobbe combined the rhetorics of friendship and of marriage in ways typical of women in committed sexual relationships with other women. When Lloyd died, Cobbe sent Bonheur a photograph of herself with Lloyd and their dog; Bonheur, who had recently lost Nathalie Micas, responded with a photo of herself with Micas and *their* dog. Like pet names, pets were often a way for women to represent a marital bond. Cobbe multiplied models for her partnership with Lloyd, comparing Lloyd's "soul-satisfying affection" to maternal love and more pragmatically describing Lloyd as "a friend who shared all expense of housekeeping with me."[85] Superlatives abound in Cobbe's descriptions of Lloyd as "my beloved friend" and "my own life-friend," and she made the spousal implications of the second phrase explicit in letters to a married female friend that called Lloyd a "truant husband" when Lloyd was traveling, as well as "my old woman" and "my *wife*."[86] Although Esther Newton influentially argued that only the masculine partner makes the lesbian couple visible, the ease with which Cobbe shifted between describing Lloyd as a wife and a husband complicates the very notion of the "mannish lesbian."[87] Cobbe was indeed mannish: she identified with the masculine world of politics, wore her hair short, and adopted streamlined fashions perceived as male. Yet her proto-butch style was compatible with thinking of Lloyd as both a cozy wife and a rakish husband.

Paralepsis, in which one talks about something by stating that one is not going to discuss it, was another aspect of the rhetoric of female marriage. Cobbe drew attention to her relationship with Lloyd yet kept it private by making telling declarations of information held in reserve. In an article published in *Contemporary Review* in 1900, Cobbe called Lloyd her "life friend," and her autobiography invoked the marital privilege of privacy to explain why she wrote sparingly about Lloyd: "Of a friendship like this . . . I shall not be expected to say more."[88] The 1904 edition of her *Life*, published after both Lloyd and Cobbe were dead, included an introduction that cited Cobbe's account of asking Lloyd's permission to write an autobiography, along with Lloyd's request for "reticence."[89] To communicate that she had consulted Lloyd was a clear announcement of the connection between the two women's lives, for women who were only friends rarely made such requests or demanded that their relationship be kept private. As with Bonheur, paraleptic declarations of discretion were a way to advertise a marital relationship between women that Cobbe never attempted to conceal. In the first edition of her autobiography, published in 1894 while Lloyd still lived, Cobbe ended her story on a note of conjugal triumph, explaining that a recent legacy had made it possible for the couple to live in the family home they had previously been forced to rent out: "I have rejoiced that the comfort and repose of our beautiful and beloved home is secured to my friend and myself." Cobbe bid her readers goodbye noting that they left her "in this dear old house, and with my beloved friend for companion."[90]

Even though Cobbe announced she would not discuss Lloyd at length in her autobiography, she assigned her pride of place in her text. A photograph of "our house" was the frontispiece of a book whose narrative arc situated Cobbe's first meeting with Lloyd as an epoch-making and life-defining event: "[F]rom that time, now more than thirty years ago, she and I have lived together."[91] Cobbe used pronouns to embody her marital bond with Lloyd, peppering her text with references to "we," "our garden," "our home," "our dear little house," and "our pretty little house."[92] Specific anecdotes depicted a life shared with Lloyd at all hours over many years; Cobbe reported, for example, how "one morning before Breakfast [Miss Lloyd] found, and in an incredibly short time, bought the dear little house in South Kensington which became our home with few interruptions for a quarter of a century."[93] Before breakfast, after dinner, during life, after death, Cobbe repeatedly showed how she and Lloyd regularly traversed boundaries that the closest friends rarely crossed. Although her published autobiography opted for the language of friendship over the marital terms she used in letters to close friends, it also openly reported "my friend's" dying words and announced Cobbe's plans to be "laid beside" Lloyd after her own death.[94]

Cobbe's use of terms common to friendship and marriage to represent her love for Lloyd peaked in a poem Cobbe wrote in 1873 that was published only in the second edition of her autobiography, which appeared in 1904, after both women had died. The poem opens with an apostrophe to the "Friend of my life!" and each of its eight quatrains ends with the refrain, "I want you—Mary." In succeeding stanzas, Cobbe evokes nature, domestic scenes, body and spirit, life and death, to build up a picture of her love for Lloyd: "In joy and grief, in good and ill, / Friend of my heart, I need you still; / My Playmate, Friend, Companion, Love / To dwell with here, to clasp above, / I want you—Mary."[95] Cobbe's multiplication of terms and invocation of many registers of intimacy show what she did not directly tell, her spousal bond with the "friend" whose very name, repeated more often than any other word in the poem, was a homonym for "marry."

Women like Bonheur and Cobbe described "friendships" that were de facto marriages by assembling elements of friendship, kinship, marriage, and romance. Their lifewritings demonstrate that terms we might have imagined were fixed for middle-class Victorians, such as "friend" or "wife," were deployed flexibly and could have contradictory meanings. As a result, we can distinguish female friends from female lovers only by situating those words in the fullest possible context. The meaning of an individual statement must be established in relation to a biographical archive, and when that archive is sparse, we may be unable to determine what a given term or exchange meant. In cases where we know that letters and journals were burned or suppressed, the absence of evidence can suggest the existence of an illicit relationship, but it was so common to destroy personal papers that nothing definitive can be concluded from that fact alone. Sexual relationships between women that conformed to a marital model were not considered so illicit that open discussion of a relationship guarantees that it was not sexual. Conversely, just as it is reasonable to determine that sometimes women who called each other "friends" had sexual relationships with each other, in many cases it is equally reasonable to conclude that women were simply friends, despite writing of and to each other in the language of love. Declarations of love are as insufficient to prove a sexual relationship between Victorian women as lack of evidence of sex is to disprove it. But in iterated, cumulative, hyperbolic references to passion, exclusivity, idealization, complicity, private language, and mutual dependence, we can locate a tipping point that separated Victorian women's ardent friendships from the sexual relationships they also formed with one another.

The Repertory of Friendship

Having established friendship's intimate links to proper womanhood, and having demarcated the unrequited passions, obsessive infatuations, and conjugal relationships often conflated with friendship, we can now turn to female friendship itself. What repertory of gestures, emotions, and actions defined friendship? How did women mark their friendships and how did friendships evolve? How did friendship interact with kinship and marital bonds, religious belief, and the Victorian gender system?

One of the most striking differences between Victorian and twentieth-century friendship is how often Victorian friends used "love" interchangeably with weaker expressions, such as "fond of" or "like," and how often women used the language of physical attraction to describe their feelings for women whom a larger context shows were friends, not lovers. In 1864, when Lady Knightley's beloved cousin Edith died, the twenty-three-year-old offset her grief with a romantic quotation: "And yet through all I feel sure / 'Tis better to have loved and lost / Than never to have loved at all'" (71). A year later, Knightley rhapsodized that a new woman, also named Edith, "has come to bless my life. . . . I have grown to love Edie very dearly" (105–6). In 1927, the Dean of Windsor wrote of the "warm tender love" the Duchess of Kent had felt for his aunt, Augusta Stanley, whose "passionate response" led to a "mutual love [that] spelt happiness in both lives."[96] The author of *The Life and Friendships of Catherine Marsh* (1917) wrote of Marsh's 1836 meeting with her friend Caroline Maitland as love at first sight: "[F]rom the first meeting the two girls were mutually attracted" (23). That attraction led to a lifelong correspondence, but the very existence of so many letters shows that the women rarely saw each other in person. Ann Gilbert, a paragon of domesticity, wrote of reaching "blood-heat-fever-heat on the thermometer of friendship" with a neighbor girl (77), but nothing in her lengthy autobiography suggests that the relationship went beyond the "amitié" that Anna Jameson distinguished from "amour" in an 1836 letter to Ottilie von Goethe.[97]

Lifewriting provides many instances of a woman recording her attraction to other women or boasting of being "intimate" with other women in youth and adulthood; Ann Gilbert recalled how as a girl, her sister became "by instantaneous attraction" another girl's "bosom friend" (24, 78). In an 1881 memoir published in 1930, fifty-one-year-old Augusta Becher recalled a youthful meeting with a young woman who "proved just charming—took me captive quite at once" and went to dinner wearing "lilies of the valley I had gathered for her in her hair" (37–38). Ethel Smyth's autobiography discussed her own sexual affairs with women in coded terms but openly described how her mother and the children's author Juliana Ewing "were attracted to each other at once and eventually became great friends" (68, 111). Others wrote of loving (rather than liking) women; in 1837, Emily Shore (1819–1839) wrote of her friend Matilda Warren, "I love her more and more. . . . It is difficult to stop my pen when once I begin to write of her." The two women argued fine points of religious doctrine but concluded "that, after all, we agreed in loving each other very dearly."[98] Addressing her friend Catherine Marsh in 1862, twenty years after they first met, a married woman wrote, "My Katie, you were mine in 1842, and you have been twenty times more mine every year since," reveling in friendship as the proud possession of a beloved intimate (40).

Such expressions of love between friends, as we have seen, were perceived as fulfilling the social function of feminization that led Sarah Ellis to promote friendship alongside motherhood and marriage as one of the duties of women. In *The Bonds of Womanhood*, historian Nancy Cott influentially argues that in the United States, domestic ideology promoted friendship between women as one way of confining women to a female world and to female roles, even as female friendship also laid the foundations for a feminist movement that sought to open the male worlds of education and professional work to women.[99] But even women who were not active feminist reformers enjoyed the ways that friendships allowed them to go beyond the limits assigned to their gender without being perceived as mannish or unladylike. Friendship was both a technology of gender and an enactment of the play in the gender system. As friends, for example, women were able to exercise a prerogative otherwise associated with men: taking an active stance towards the object of their affections. In an 1880s memoir about the 1830s, Georgiana Sitwell, later Swinton (1823–1900), recalled a governess who "was romantic, worshipped the curate, and formed a passionate attachment to our newly imported French governess."[100] Sitwell remembered the governess as uniformly "romantic" in her stance toward men and women, but different in her demeanor toward her male and female objects of affection: deferential and implicitly secretive in her "worship" for the curate, expressive and dynamic in the "passion" she "formed"—that is, chose and shaped—for her fellow governess. Caroline Wigley, later Clive (1801–1873), reflected in an 1838 diary entry about her friendship with novelist Catherine Gore: "When I was so many years younger I used to fall into the most violent friendships and the one I felt for her was nearly the strongest of my passions. Of course she did not return it to an ugly, half-taught, unintelligible girl like me, and I remember crying for half a night because she went out of London without bidding me farewell."[101] By contrast, Wigley was far more reticent about any frustration she felt in her love for Archer Clive, which went unreciprocated for several years. Counseled to be passive in relation to men, women were allowed to act with initiative and spontaneity toward female friends, and friendship enabled women to exercise powers of choice and expression that they could not display in relation to parents or prospective husbands.

Bonds with parents and siblings were given, not chosen, and friendship was for many girls their first experience of an affinity elected rather than assigned. For women who grew up in families with over ten children, friendship was also a girl's first experience of a dyad rather than a swarm. While women had the power to turn down marriage offers and had subtle ways of attracting men they wanted as spouses, they were not allowed to choose a mate too overtly; only in *Punch* lampoons did women propose to men, and it was considered equally improper for women openly to initiate courtship. It was perfectly acceptable, however, for a woman to make the first move toward friendship with another woman, or to solidify amity by writing to a female acquaintance, calling on her, or giving her a gift. Aristocratic women had exchanged gifts, miniatures, and poems for centuries, and in the Victorian era the practice became widespread among middle-class women of all ages. One of adolescent Emily Shore's several intimates, Elizabeth, gave her a "chain made of her beautiful rich brown hair" before leaving England, which Shore considered a token of her friend's affection and looked forward to displaying as a sign of social distinction: "I have generally worn a pretty little chain of *bought* hair, and when people have asked me 'whose hair is that?' I have been mortified at being obliged to answer 'Nobody's.' *Now*, when asked the same question, I shall be able to say it is the hair of my best and dearest friend" (269). Mature women painted portraits of friends and composed poems about them that they then bestowed as gifts, creating a friendship economy based on artifacts whose praise of a friend's beauty, loyalty, and achievements also implicitly lauded their maker for having chosen so wisely.

Female friendship allowed middle-class women to enjoy another privilege that scholars have assumed only men could indulge—the opportunity to display affection and experience pleasurable physical contact outside marriage without any loss of respectability. Women who were friends, not lovers, wrote openly of exchanging kisses and caresses in documents that their spouses and relatives read without comment. Women regularly kissed each other on the lips, a gesture that could be a routine social greeting or provide intense enjoyment. Emily Shore, whose Bedfordshire Anglican family was so proper they did not allow her to read Byron, described in a diary later published by her sisters the "heartfelt pleasure" she obtained from a visit to her friend Miss Warren's room: "She was sitting up in bed, looking so sweet and lovely that I could not take my eyes off her. . . . She made me sit on her bed, and kissed me many times, and was kinder to me than ever [and] held my hand clasped in hers" (203). Writing in 1862 to her friend Mrs. Mary Austin, Jane Carlyle recalled their parting after a recent visit: "Oh, my little woman, how glad I was to recognise your face through the glass of the carriage window, all dimmed with human breath! And how frightened I was the train would move, while you were clambering up like a school-boy to kiss me!"[102] Frances Power Cobbe wrote in her autobiography of how the married Mary Somerville, a good friend but never a lover, "kissed me tenderly [and] gave me her photograph"; Cobbe in turn felt "such tender affection" for Somerville "that sitting beside her on the sofa . . . I could hardly keep myself from caressing her."[103] Cobbe never wrote of caressing

Mary Lloyd, for respectability required lovers and spouses to avoid public signs of a shared sexual life. Friends, by contrast, could openly exchange material tokens of their affection and exhibit themselves giving and receiving the caresses and kisses of friendship.

Female amity gave married and unmarried women the opportunity to play the social field with impunity, since a woman could show devoted love, lighthearted affection, fleeting attraction, and ardent physical appreciation for multiple female friends without incurring rebuke. The editor of Emily Shore's journals noted that when Shore wrote of loving Matilda Warren her diary was also "filled most especially with her passionate love" for a woman named Mary (207). Thomas Carlyle wrote indulgently about Geraldine Jewsbury's affection for his wife Jane as well as about "a very pretty . . . specimen of the London maiden of the middle classes" who "felt quite captivated with my Jane."[104] Marion Bradley, wife and mother, wrote of her deep bond with Emily Tennyson and in an 1865 diary entry observed more casually that her new governess was "a gentle, lively, wise, cultivated little creature. . . . I love her and hope always to be very thoughtful for her and good to her."[105] Equal latitude was afforded to unmarried women. The biography of Agnes Jones (1832–1868), written by her sister and published in 1871, narrated her life in terms of two arcs: achievements as a nurse and love for various women. In adolescence, her sister's "ardent affectionate nature was drawn out in warmest love" for a teacher, followed by an "attachment" to a fellow missionary that "ripened into a warm and lasting friendship" as well as a close connection with another "devoted friend" (15, 21).

In an era that saw no contest between what we now call heterosexual and homosexual desire, neither men nor women saw anything disruptive about amorous badinage between women, and therefore no effort was made to contain and denigrate female homoeroticism as an immature stage to be overcome. Only in the late 1930s, after fear of female inverts had become widespread, did women's lifewritings start to describe female friendship as a developmental phase to be effaced by marriage.[106] Since then, erotic playfulness between women has either been overinterpreted as having the same seriousness as sexual acts or underinterpreted and trivialized as a phase significant only as training for heterosexual courtship. Victorian lifewriting demonstrates, however, that expressions of playful attraction and love were strongest precisely between women who never became lovers, and far from being practice for marriage, were as common after it as before. Jane Carlyle wrote to her unmarried friend Susan Hunter in 1835, "My dear Susan Hunter—What an infidel you are to dream of my ever forgetting your existence or your kindness! Woman though I be, and though Mr. John Jeffrey once said of me . . . that I was 'distinguished as a flirt,' in my time, I can tell you few people are as steady in their attachments. That I was attracted to you, a person of your quick observation could hardly fail to observe. . . . I liked you, and have continued to like you to this hour."[107] Six years after flirting with Hunter by coyly protesting that she was no coquette, Carlyle wrote to her friend, now Mrs. Stirling, of the persistence of their mutual affection: "I rejoice to see that marriage has not spoiled you. . . . I find in your letter . . . proof of . . . admirable good sense. . . . You love me the same as ever."[108] Carlyle's letter raised no Victorian eyebrows; it was published in an edition of her correspondence compiled by her husband and his biographer James Froude.

Victorian society harshly condemned adultery, castigated female heterosexual agency as unladylike, and considered it improper for women to compete with men intellectually, professionally, or physically. But a woman could enjoy, without guilt, the pleasures of toying with another woman's affections or vying with other women for precedence as a friend. In maturity as in youth, women delighted in attracting and securing female friends whom they often singled out for being beautiful and socially in demand. In a letter to her brother in 1817, the unmarried Catherine Hutton of Birmingham (1756–1846) boasted, "I have been a great favourite with a most elegant and clever woman." To a married female friend who often gave her fashion advice she wrote of acquiring yet another "new" friend: "[S]he is beautiful, unaffected, and to me most friendly."[109] Female rivalry over men was discouraged because it implied that women fought for and won their husbands, but women were allowed the agency of competing for one another's favor. Lady Monkswell crowed about having "supplanted" one woman as the "great friend" of Mrs. Edith Bland, and the relative who edited her published letters and diaries included many other instances in which she bragged of similar successes (12). Such relish in contending with women over women was possible without any loss of ascribed femininity, even as it took women well beyond the parameters of womanhood as defined relative to men.

Just as women boasted of making conquests of female friends, they also openly appreciated each other's physical charms. Women commented compulsively in their journals and letters on the appearance of every new woman they met, even when they did not know the woman personally. In an 1874 journal entry penned a few months after her marriage, the twenty-five-year-old Lady Monkswell mentioned a "very nice dinner" attended by "[b]eautiful Mrs. Julian Goldsmid with whom I am in love . . . a fair Italian about 26, with lovely blue eyes, a sweet smile and a sweet voice" (11). After Lady Goldsmid's death in 1892, Monkswell recalled a relish she had felt almost in spite of herself: "She was not the least the sort of woman that I like, but she was kind and nice to us and so very attractive that I feel almost an affection for her" (207). As confirmation that she liked Goldsmid for her looks alone, Monkswell provided an elaborate inventory of Goldsmid's bodily charms, praising her skin, eyes, hair, and teeth, "[d]arling, clever little hands, lovely arms and wrists . . . well shaped legs and feet" (208). Monkswell's tastes were catholic and exuberant. In 1877, after meeting a "most beautiful girl . . . a Miss Graham of Netherby . . . magnificent dark red-brown hair, dark drooping blue eyes, the most beautiful full, red, finely cut lips (and in the words of Rossetti, 'I saw her smile')," Lady Monkswell exhorted, "Let us have a few more girls of this style" (25).

Lady Monkswell was typical in her willingness to write about the pleasure she took in other women's beauty. After marriage, Caroline Clive began to keep a diary jointly with her husband, in which she wrote of an 1845 meeting with poet Caroline Norton in lengthy detail only excerpted here: "[P]erfect beauty, eyes with long eye-lashes on both lids, the lower touching her cheek, a mouth that opens in a way like ideal mouths . . . lovely skin and shape, a flowing, glowing silk gown and cashmere shawl edged with gold" (223). In 1858 Lucy Lyttleton, later Lady Cavendish (1841–1925), described meeting a Mrs. Preston: "*The* most fascinating beauty I have ever seen: shady deep eyes, all expression and grace; and such a lovely classical mouth; figure and manners most winning and refined."[110] Margaret Leicester Warren wrote in 1859, when she was about twelve, of an afternoon spent talking "to the little Lasselses particularly to Amy a very nice and pretty girl of 14"; describing women she met in London three years later, she wrote of Lady Adelaide, "quite beautiful" and Miss Grant, "also very pretty, very light indeed with pale yellow hair and like the women in 'Once a Week'" (vol. 1, 12, 71). Emily Shore wrote of an "exquisitely, perfectly beautiful" woman she saw while traveling with her family in Hastings who impressed her so much she devoted over a page to anatomizing the unknown's features, expression, and dress (144–45). In her *Records of Girlhood* (1879), Fanny Kemble recalled two sisters with "beautiful figures as well as faces" who wore dresses "low on the shoulders and bosom" and wrote of one, "I remember wishing it were consistent with her comfort and the general decorum of modern manners that Isabella Forrester's gown could only slip entirely off her exquisite bust."[111]

A culture of female fandom that spurred girls to worship ballet dancers and opera singers trained them from a very young age to enjoy women's physical attributes even outside the context of personal acquaintance.[112] The special affection girls developed for their favorite female stars is evident in Queen Victoria's girlhood diaries from the 1820s and 1830s, excerpted and published in 1912 under the editorial guidance of Viscount Esher, a married man who had lifelong erotic friendships with men and boys.[113] Perhaps because of his own susceptibility to cross-generational, same-sex attraction, Esher included alongside Victoria's later appreciation of her consort Albert's beauty her warm adolescent responses to the many female performers she saw in ballets and operas and whose costumes she recreated in her extensive doll collection. In 1833, at age fourteen, she wrote of Marie Taglioni, who "danced and acted QUITE BEAUTIFULLY!! She looked *very* pretty. Her dress was very pretty." Two years later, Victoria began an entry praising opera singer Giulia Grisi's "face and neck . . . such a beautiful soft shape. She has such beautiful dark eyes with fine long eyelashes, a fine nose, and a very sweet mouth," and then dilated on Grisi's hair, dress, and manner.[114] In youth as in maturity, Victoria was always eager to adopt middle-class mores, and her interest in the physiques of female performers was as typical of mid-Victorian, middle-class femininity as her later devotion to the roles of mother and wife. In turn, the queen herself became an object of other women's attentive gazes. When Henrietta Halliwell-Phillipps, the wife of a Shakespeare scholar, heard Jenny Lind perform in 1847, she expatiated in what was usually a terse diary on the queen's appearance at the opera: "She was dressed in blue satin with tiara necklace, earrings & bracelets of splendid brilliants & all the front of her dress covered with diamonds. She looked very well & pleased."[115]

Women took note of other women's attractions not only as models to emulate but as pleasurable objects to consume. Women who felt physically attracted to other women were not seen as less feminine because of the attention they lavished on other women's bodies, but more so. Luxuriating in women's charms and viewing women as physical objects are activities some now think of as the prerogative of men. Lesbian enjoyment of women's bodies is considered an appropriation of masculine desire, while heterosexual women are often imagined as inspecting one another in a spirit of hostile rivalry, unable to enjoy feminine beauty unless narcissistically admiring their own. Victorians, however, saw both men and women as inclined to appreciate women's looks, a phenomenon that chapter 3 explores in relation to fashion and consumer culture. Constance Flower, later Lady Battersea (1843–1931), recalled seeing the Empress of Austria at a dinner and finding her "the most graceful, attractive vision that eyes could desire to rest upon." When her neighbor Lord Dudley observed that the Empress and his wife were "the two most beautiful women in the world," Battersea placidly agreed: "And I thought he was right."[116] Adrienne Rich has influentially argued that "compulsory heterosexuality" works by stifling all kinds of bonds between women, from the homosocial to the homosexual, but Victorian society's investment in heterosexuality went hand-in-hand with what we could call compulsory homosociability and homoeroticism for women. The imperative to please men required women to scrutinize other women's dress and appearance in order to improve their own, and at the same time promoted a specifically feminine appetite for attractive friends and lovely strangers.

Conduct literature praised female friendships for developing in women the loyalty, selflessness, empathy, and self-effacement that they were required to exercise in relation to men. Women's lifewriting shows an acceptance of that idealized and ideological version of female friendship; few women left records of conflict or rivalry with friends, though some acknowledged engaging in jealous competition with relative strangers over prized acquaintances and intimates. At the same time, friendship provided a realm where women exercised an authority, agency, willfulness, and caprice for which they would have been censured in the universe of male-female relations. Female friendship provided women with a sanctioned realm of erotic choice, agency, and indulgence, in contrast to the sharp restrictions that middle-class gender codes placed on female flirtation with men. A woman who wrote of spending time alone with a man in his bedroom or giving him a lock of hair without being engaged to him would have transgressed the rules governing heterosexual gender, but to write of doing so with another woman was to describe an accepted means of forming social bonds and acquiring social status in the realm of homosocial gender. The celebration of women's friendships shows that femininity was defined not only in relation to masculinity but also through bonds between women that did not simply tether them to the gender system but also afforded them a degree of play within it.

"Purified and Made One in Jesus"

For every woman whose letters and journals emphasized her frank enjoyment in looking pretty women up and down, there was another who recorded her delight in spiritual communion with a female friend. Evangelical Victorians in particular valued how female friendship reconciled the sacred and the profane. Victorian society was famously riven by contradictory commitments to the material and the spiritual, and scholars have amply shown how men struggled to reconcile physical lust and spiritual love in their sexual lives.[117] Women also struggled to merge the real and the ideal—through marriage, motherhood, and female friendship. Caroline Head's biographer described her as "deeply attached" to several teachers in adolescence, including one "who was greatly used in strengthening her spiritual life, and of whom she wrote in enthusiastic terms to her aunt: 'Dear Miss O. gets more lovely every term, I am *so* fond of her!' Later in life they sought each other's help and sympathy, and the affection never declined." The biographer identifies Head's love for her teacher as a spiritual force providing "help and sympathy," but in the youthful letter the author cites, Head links her fondness to physical admiration for the "lovely" Miss O. (23). In turn, a friend of Head's recalled how the physical and spiritual illumination of first seeing Head's "bright, glowing face" created a bond both romantic and religious as "our hearts were drawn together in union with Christ" (266).

Emily Shore rhapsodized in an 1838 journal entry about how her friend Mary combined actual and angelic beauty: "Oh, Mary! You are still to me something like a fairy dream, too beautiful to be real—a being so pure, so perfect, so lovely, even here so angelically fascinating, that I can hardly believe heaven can add a charm to her; and yet I can actually feel and know that she loves me amongst those she loves most dearly" (268). In an 1834 letter, Mary Lundie Duncan described longing to find "a *friend* to whom I could unfold all my heart. . . . There is *one* here, and when circumstances permit us to meet, a sweet savour is shed around more than one succeeding day.—I have many christian friends, but it requires an attraction of heart, which may be better felt than described, to fill exactly the place Miss ——— does. Now, do not think me a romantic girl, for my love to her is founded on love to God" (129). Aware as she wrote that her affection for her new friend was beginning to sound too similar to worldly "romantic" pleasures, Duncan hastened to assert its basis in religious feeling.

Women wrote of love for God and love for female friends with equal erotic fervor and experienced both as intense sensations that were equally physical and spiritual. Mary Lundie Duncan thanked her best friend for letters that "have not infrequently come when I was in want of quickening and stirring up, and have helped [me] to draw more near to my Saviour, for a time at least" (98). In Victorian lifewriting, passionate references to hearts on fire and burning with love are a sure sign that a woman is about to discuss Jesus. Conversely, women who described joint prayer as a way to develop intimacy borrowed from narratives of seduction to describe religious encounters with new acquaintances. In a letter to her sister, published by her husband in an 1878 memorial volume of correspondence, thirty-six-year-old bible-class teacher Rebekah Taylor wrote of a passionate triangle she formed with another woman and Jesus: "Miss D—— called this morning, and I think we had a nice time together. We beat about the bush a long while, and at last got on to what touched our hearts—the blessed, precious Lord Jesus. . . . To hear it said, when anyone is pouring out a little of the rapture of his soul as he gazes on His beauty, 'He wants cooling a little,' is like an iceberg to me. However, I found a ready response with her. . . ."[118] Taylor's account, like a tale of amorous conquest, begins with an oblique approach, followed by passionate disclosures, rapturous union, and joy in having found a partner who shares her ardor. A letter of recollection appended to the biography of Agnes

Jones similarly described a friendship consolidated through shared religious practice: "I shall never forget my first meeting with her. I made a short call. . . . [H]er quiet, ladylike, self-possessed manner particularly struck me. This call was followed by one or two more, but we did not get below the surface (probably from reserve on both sides) until about the fourth call I made, my darling friend threw herself on the ground at my side, and begged that I would pray for and with her, for she felt 'in great need.' We almost always met twice every week" (386–87). After a gradual disclosure of shared religious feelings through words and gestures, a regular liaison is cemented in which prayer becomes a vehicle for creating a deep bond.

The eroticism of such accounts was all the stronger for being unconscious, unself-conscious, and inseparable from genuine religious feeling. People who thought of God as a friend easily linked friends to God. Between 1800 and 1860, Anglicans and nonconformist Dissenters alike were powerfully influenced by the Evangelical emphasis on religious affect, on emotions experienced as visceral sensations. Where Catholics venerated church authorities, English Protestants valorized a subjective, experiential, personal relationship to Jesus and sought to be near Christ, trust Christ, and be like Christ.[119] After the 1830s, as the Evangelical stress on sin and punishment began to wane, it became common for women to think of Christ as Caroline Head did, as "the Saviour and Friend" whom they "loved so dearly" and with whom they strove to realize "that blessed *personal* relationship 'He is *mine* and I am *his*'" (xiii, 20). Histories of Evangelicalism have focused on its investment in strict gender roles, its male promoters and adherents, and female susceptibility to charismatic male divines, but it clearly also offered women a way to dignify friendship as a factor contributing to spiritual rebirth.

Friends helped each other to receive the grace of faithful, limitless love for their deity, and the love of friends was itself a type of grace. For Caroline Head, a personal relationship with Christ had its earthly equivalent in friendship. Her "best-beloved friend, Emma Waithman" assisted in Head's own spiritual awakening, and both women defined their resulting friendship in religious terms, with Waithman expressing faith in their "bond of union" and Head convinced that the two "shared every spiritual blessing" (19–20, 264). For those who labored to feel what Marion Bradley called "personal feelings of love" for Christ, friendship was a means to personify that love. In her journal Bradley wrote that she felt love of Christ most strongly when spending her "usual Sunday afternoons with [her] dearest" Emily Tennyson and when feeling inspired by her friend's "devoted personal love to Xt." Their religious bond strengthened their friendship, and Bradley wrote of telling Tennyson that she could talk to her "as I never can quite talk with anyone else—she said she felt it also—that we understand each other heart and soul."[120]

Friendship became itself a form of religious training by helping women cultivate self-examination and worldly detachment. The philosophical discourse of male friendship had always emphasized the friend as a truthtelling critic; women similarly saw friends as agents of spiritual growth. Louise Knightley, for example, recorded a dying friend's warning against "'an old fault,'" a sense of superiority to others (63). Friendship also helped women realize the Evangelical desire to detach from the body and the world in order to emulate and approach a God they could not see directly. When conceptualized as a bond that connected souls and thrived even in the face of minimal physical contact, friendship offered women a model of how to love from afar. For Mary Lundie Duncan, the friend shared with God the ability to love without physical presence: "I must love you at a distance, and rejoice to know that . . . I am not forgotten. It is a sweet thought, and if not forgotten by *you*, how much less by Him who has graven my name on the palms of his hands" (235). Loving the faraway friend echoed the human love of a Christ simultaneously distant in his divinity yet proximate in his humanity, and prayer thus became a medium of friendship as well as worship. As a form of religious communication that addressed an invisible deity, prayer lent itself to maintaining connections with friends who were similarly abstracted by physical separation. Duncan maintained contact with a close friend she never saw after leaving school by rising early to compose regular letters to her (97), and by arranging simultaneous prayer sessions that linked the two women when they were apart: "Dearest! May I think that every Friday night you pray specially for me? This is what I mean to do for you, and I think we should both derive much comfort from it" (205).

Friendship helped women to cultivate key tenets of Evangelical Christianity, such as indifference to material gain, acceptance of death, and belief in an afterlife. Victorian Christians often feared that love for a parent, child, or spouse risked becoming a form of idolatry. Hannah Allen wrote in 1838 of her upcoming marriage, "I am fearful at times, lest I should allow my affections to cleave too closely, to the hindrance of my spiritual growth. Oh! that I may make no idol in my heart . . . may we both be ready and willing to yield up our all to thee" (64). Love for kin could become mired in the body, a problem for a belief system that valued the spirit over the flesh. In its attachment to life, love for a husband or child militated against the resolute acceptance of death dictated by faith in heaven. Such love also risked making human beings equal in importance to God, a sacrilege for those who believed in a divine supremacy. Because friendship involved close connection without the primal bodily contact or all-consuming commitment that existed between spouses or parents and children, it was the ideal social relation through which to cultivate belief in resurrection and reunion after death. Deep love for friends who were physically distant helped women like philanthropist Mary Mathison, the wife of a Trinity College fellow, "not to love this world too much" and to practice welcoming death as the gateway to resurrection (103). As Mary Duncan wrote to her best friend, "To love in Christ is the happiest earthly feeling, and I trust it is thus we love each other. It seems a preparation for another state of being, where, indeed, God will be all in all; and, though we are widely separated here, may we not worship together *there*?" (99). On the eve of her friend Margaret Taylor's 1852 emigration to New Zealand, Maria Richmond similarly promised that "once in every 24 hours I shall think of you and all our love, and dwell on the thought of our meeting again and possessing each other when earthly troubles are over."[121]

FRIENDSHIP, KINSHIP, MARRIAGE

By conceiving friendship as facilitating union with Christ and as itself a type of union in Christ, Evangelical Victorians paved the way for understanding friendship as analogous to the most fundamental forms of kinship regulated by religious and civil law. Friends were clearly distinct from spouses and family members in many ways: less physically intimate, more prone to be idealized as perfect than idolized despite their imperfections. Women drew clear distinctions between the love felt for a friend and for a spouse and often articulated their belief that marriage demanded unique feelings of love that went beyond even the warmest friendly devotion. Margaret Warren, for example, experienced great distress when she became engaged to a man for whom she felt only a "kindly affectionate feeling" that she identified as "not . . . the love that a woman should give to her future husband" but "only the love of pity and of friendship" (48).

Marriage thus involved a singular and exclusive form of love, but it was also understood to include and even aspire to the love proper to friendship. Deeply religious women wrote of marriage and friendship as analogous relationships, both based on shared faith and both understood as ultimately a bond with God. Mary Duncan saw her marriage and friendships alike as aspects of her spiritual training. She referred to and addressed her husband-to-be as "friend" (147, 188). She ascribed her happiness after becoming engaged to "joy in being united to one who would serve God with me" (202), just as she defined the "bond" uniting her to her closest female friend as "our fellowship with heaven" (98). Writing to a friend about her engagement to Albert Head, Caroline Hanbury exulted, "We are so perfectly one 'in the Lord'. . . . [W]henever we are together it is always we *three* together, Jesus, Albert and I" (91). For those who took seriously the doctrine "We are all one in Christ," the concrete differences between spouses and friends became less significant.

Less religious spouses similarly aspired to be the best and truest of friends. Sarah Ellis defined marriage in terms of friendship when she wrote in *The Daughters of England* that "friendship is the basis of all true love" because true love and friendship had the "same . . . ultimate aim . . . the moral and spiritual good of its object" (388). In the early 1820s, Richard Low Beck confided to his married cousin and friend Sophy, "I have no other idea of matrimony than its being when well entered into the most exalted friendship this earth affords."[122] The courtship letters exchanged between John Torr and Maria Jackson in the late 1830s articulate married love as a form of friendship, but one more steady than what Torr called "*mere* friendship." Like the women in female marriages who accumulated metaphors for their relationships (supreme friend, sister, mother, wife, lover), Jackson told Torr in 1840, "You are friend, brother, lover, all in one." Convinced that "a perfect degree of friendship can exist only in marriage," Jackson believed that the best marriages were those between people who had been friends before falling in love. She celebrated her luck at contracting a "marriage of affection . . . where friendship was almost perfect before—marriage only placing it on a securer footing and giving opportunities for its exercise."[123] Lady Monkswell inaugurated her diary in 1873 by noting that "On this auspicious day I became engaged to be married to my old friend of 3 years standing—Mr. Collier" (1).

To call a husband a friend was a form of marital decorum that made a relationship based on sex respectable in a society that forbade its open discussion, but it was more than a formula for downplaying the sexual nature of marriage. Because friendship was so effusive, a wife who named her husband her friend was also expressing the warmth of her love for him. Scholars have often characterized middle-class Victorian marriages as distant, and many no doubt were. Revisionist accounts of domestic happiness have drawn primarily on the sentimental outpourings of husbands, but many women wrote openly about their affections for men after becoming engaged to them. Henrietta Halliwell-Phillipps, who defied her father to marry James Halliwell, rarely expressed emotion overtly in her diary, but each year she noted her husband's birthday and the anniversaries of their first meeting and wedding day.[124] In her first journal entry after her 1841 marriage to Lord John Russell, Fanny Elliot Russell (1815–1898) wrote of wanting to become "more and more the companion and friend of him whose heart is mine as truly as mine is his"; two years later she wrote her mother that the "constant sympathy, encouragement, and approbation of John can make everything easy to me."[125] After her husband's death in 1869, Jane Keppel (1804–1883) recalled him as her "dear companion for nearly four and forty years; the sharer of all my thoughts, my joys, and my sorrows . . . the tender admiring *lover* as well as *husband*."[126] Women who were unhappy with their husbands also wrote about it, openly expressing frustration and anger. In the 1830s, utilitarian writer and translator Sarah Austin wrote to a potential male lover about her disappointment in a chronically depressed mate, while Lady Stanley of Alderley (1807–1895) sent acrimonious letters to her husband throughout the 1840s.[127] But like contented female couples, husbands and wives who were happy basked in the ways that their unions combined ardor, friendship, and marriage.

The ease with which women viewed their husbands as friends carried over into a propensity to describe friends as spouses. Just as she recommended that husbands imitate friends, Sarah Ellis explained that a good friend would emulate a good wife, suppressing caprice, ill temper, and selfishness (*Daughters*, 350, 360–61). Sometimes comparisons between friendship and marriage were jocular wishes that presupposed the impossibility of a friend ever becoming a wife. After thanking Anna Richmond for her "demonstrative proofs of love," Annie Hill wrote in 1877: "I wish indeed that you were a 'nice young man,' even *minus* the black whiskers! How happy would I be if I could find a husband that I could love and trust in so thoroughly as I do you."[128] Writing to a friend in 1852, Maria Richmond inched closer to the fantasy of marrying her when she bemoaned the difficulty of finding a perfect husband: "I sincerely hope, dear Margie, that should you continue single . . . you will, however old you may be, come out and marry *me*, helping to farm my little estate and to lecture my nephews and nieces."[129] Others made more solemn comparisons between friends and spouses. Scottish working-class autobiographer Janet Bathgate compared "the love that bound" her to her friend Jenny Burnet "to that of David of Jonathan" and wrote a poem describing their affection as "the tie that binds."[130] Catherine Marsh wrote of how her fifty-year friendship with Harriet Dalrymple "grew and strengthened till Death did us part" (49), and Ann Gilbert described the first of a series of annual summer trips she took with her friend Mary as a "honeymoon of delight" (427).

Women also compared friends to parents and siblings, though as with marriage they were aware of the differences between the two kinds of relationship. The friend could be a surrogate mother, and many women called their friends sisters. Conversely, writers often portrayed close affection between sisters as the highest form of friendship. As Christina Rossetti put it in her poem *Goblin Market*, "[T]here is no friend like a sister."[131] In a more circumspect vein, Sarah Ellis wrote, "[T]here may be faithful friendships formed in after years; but when a sister is a sister's friend, there can be none so tender, and . . . so true" (*Women*, 230). Ellis did not posit an automatic equivalence between sisters and friends but noted instead that sisters were not always friends, thus assuming a distinction between the two relationships that meant they could approximate one another only under the right conditions.

Often compared to a husband, mother, or sister, the friend was nevertheless also in a category of her own. Friends had some of the force and status of spouses, parents, or children, but without sharing households or sex, as spouses did, and without immersing themselves in the total caretaking provided between parents and children. One reason friendship had such allure for Victorians was its unique position as a form of love perceived as moral, uplifting, and genuine even though—or because—it entailed few of the material entanglements and responsibilities attached to middle-class family life. In its concentration of pure sentiment, friendship became a luxury good that expressed freedom from instrumental relationships. A woman who had a close friend was able to display that she could afford to lavish time and attention on someone who did not directly promote her interests. As such, paradoxically, sentimental friendship became a form of labor, for the middle-class values that discouraged women from waged employment taught them to consider emotional work their business.[132]

Middle-class women were the social stratum most prone to emphasize friendship as a matter of sheer emotion. Upper-class women wrote of love for friends but also vaunted acquaintances to prove membership in elite social networks. A few working-class women wrote about intimate friends in their lifewriting, but most avoided overt displays of affect and mentioned female friendships only briefly, focusing instead on relationships with female employers and coworkers that did not lend themselves to unreserved expressions of feeling.[133] A certain degree of physical distance was as necessary to friendship as emotional closeness, and servants and roommates rarely had that kind of space from one another. Like men of all classes, working women understood friendship in terms of what Ellen Ross has called "survival networks" and were most likely to befriend coworkers, roommates, teachers, and employers; only a handful of women infused the shared struggle for existence with a romantic sense of spiritual and emotional affinity.[134] Working-class women thus wrote of friendships primarily in the context of the search for work and shelter, and their memoirs mostly failed to single friendship out as a category. The few that did linked friendship to work or the reproduction of labor; in her autobiography, straw-plait worker Lucy Luck (1848–1922) thus defined one "true friend" as a woman who provided employment and mentioned an acquaintance who informed her about a job opportunity.[135]

Friendship illustrated the play in the middle-class family system by providing women with a relationship outside the family and marriage that
could be imagined as freely chosen, based purely on affinity and affection.
At the same time, however, female friendships were securely connected to
domestic relationships, not simply by analogy but also through concrete
interactions that knit friends to kin. Ann Gilbert wrote of befriending a
pair of sisters with her own sister (78) and of another friend's daughter
becoming her sister's "friend and correspondent" (99). In a literal expression of friendship as kinship, female friends often named their daughters
after one another and stood as godparents to one another's children. Cornelia Crow Carr named her daughter after her best friend Harriet Hosmer,
who in turn called Carr her "best friend and sister" and referred to herself
as little Harriet's aunt.[136] Marriage, kinship, and friendship literally mingled when the children of friends married. Ann Gilbert's lifelong friendship with Anna Forbes was an "intimacy begun in the glow of young
extravagance," then "strengthened . . . matured [and] rivetted by the enduring connection that linked a daughter of hers with a son of mine"
(83). Hannah Allen's "dearest friend" became her sister-in-law when she
married Hannah's brother-in-law (25), and Caroline Head's son married
the niece of her beloved friend Emma Waithman (247).

Courtship and marriage promoted close ties between women when
wives developed affectionate relationships with their husbands' mothers.[137] While relationships between mothers- and daughters-in-law were
not usually termed friendships, in cases of broken engagements the relatively freestanding amity between a woman and her suitor's mother often
came to the fore. When Margaret Warren rescinded her betrothal to her
cousin Amyas in 1871, she was as distressed about upsetting his mother
as she was about disappointing him. One of her diary's most heartfelt
entries recorded telling Amyas's mother she was ending the engagement
even before she informed Amyas himself: "I rose to go and asked if I
might take her hand. She gave it me and kissed me—and then all my pride
gave way and as I knelt by her sofa with my hands in hers as she has often
held them before—we both cried together. . . . I remember saying 'Oh if
I had but loved Amyas one quarter as much as I love you it would have
been all right' and indeed that was true. Her hand was lying on my
hands—her pretty long white fingers with the old blue rings on them and
I could not help it—I stopped down and kissed them before I went" (72).
Warren's life had been disrupted after her own mother's death and the
prospect of acquiring a new maternal figure had made marriage to Amyas
appealing, but she also desired his mother as a friend, an object of affection who would be both an intimate and an ideal.

Courtship, engagement, and marriage often created new friendships
between women linked by a man. Charlotte Yonge wrote enthusiasti-

cally in 1858 of "the beauty and charms" of her brother's new wife
(199). Richard Low Beck, who confided in his married friend and cousin
Sophy about his courtship of Rachel Lucas, was eager for the two
women to get along, writing to Sophy how he was "much gratified . . .
by hearing Rachel has formed a most favourable opinion of thee" and
expressing his hope that Sophy thought equally well of his bride-to-be.
The fact that he and Rachel named their first daughter after Sophy, and
that Rachel faithfully wore a brooch Sophy gave the couple, suggests
that marriage did indeed help Rachel adopt her husband's female friend
as her own.[138] When poet John Keats got engaged to Fanny Brawne, he
asked her to correspond with his sister, and the two women continued
to exchange affectionate letters after Keats's death. Brawne's projected
marriage to Keats created a link between her and his sister that was
consolidated when Brawne helped introduce Fanny Keats to the man she
eventually married.[139]

The complementary relationships among family, marriage, and friendship operated in multiple directions. Family and marriage were compared
to friendship, coexisted harmoniously with friendship, and spawned
friendships; in turn, friendships promoted courtship and marriage. Lady
Battersea wrote of how Louise and Hannah, two women she knew, "became close friends, and Leo's happy marriage [to Hannah's sister] was to
some extent the result of this friendship."[140] The marriage of Lady Augusta Bruce to Arthur Stanley, later Dean of Westminster, was thoroughly
mediated by a female friend who colluded with Stanley's sister to arrange
the social call at which Stanley could propose: "My Dear Miss Stanley
. . . Wd. it facilitate the first meeting if Dr. Stanley and Augusta came to
lunch with me on the 4th. He wd. call upon me and wd. talk of his travels
during the repast, and I wd. slip out (whispering 'On, Stanley, on!') and
they then really ought to arrange everything in 5 minutes." Arrange things
they did, and Augusta, who before her marriage served as lady-in-waiting
to Queen Victoria, explained, "One great value of Dr. Stanley to me
would be that I might continually be talking to him of my darling [Queen
Victoria], and teaching him to love Her!"[141] From start to finish, marriage
was embedded in the world of female friendship.

By helping each other marry, friends expressed their love for one another in a world that valued female friendship but deemed marriage the
most important tie a woman could forge with another adult. In 1885,
William Gladstone's daughter Mary (1847–1927) was among the last of
her friends to get engaged, and since she herself had experienced loneliness
while still single, she was concerned that her remaining unmarried friends
might feel abandoned.[142] Some women managed such feelings by doing
their best to help their friends make good matches, and as a result even
the most intense female friendships promoted the hegemony of marriage.

Fanny Butler (later Kemble) recorded how she was "sorry to leave Phila-delphia on Mrs.———'s account. I am growing to her," but also noted, "She amuses me much by her intense anxiety that I should be married. . . . my single blessedness seems greatly to annoy her."[143] In addition to orchestrating introductions and proposals, friends abetted courtship by persuading their intimates that marriage was emotionally appealing, and married women propounded the joys of marriage to female friends as ardently as any suitor. Ann Gilbert, then Taylor, wrote to her recently married friend Anna Forbes Laurie about every stage of the Reverend Gilbert's courtship, and informed Laurie immediately after accepting his proposal, recalling that her friend had helped persuade her to say yes: "I am learning with tolerable facility to believe what you told me when you said, 'Oh, this delightful, mutual love'" (191).

. . .

The annals of Victorian women's lifewriting point again and again to female friendship's location at the heart of the hallowed middle-class insti-tutions of marriage and family. Female friendship was a very different social bond from female marriage, though both enjoyed degrees of social acknowledgement and approval. It was also distinct from the unrequited loves and infatuations that were rarely disclosed beyond a very restricted private circle. Friendship allowed women to compete for and charm each other, to develop their intellectual and aesthetic tastes, to augment their worldly ties, and to deepen their spiritual ones. Its pleasures and passions were also closely allied to the love of kin and the delights of marriage, and the next chapter thus turns to novels, another important medium for forming desire, representing kinship, and plotting life stories, in order to reveal how that genre's notorious affection for marriage plots depended on female friendship.

CHAPTER 2

Just Reading: Female Friendship and the Marriage Plot

TOWARD THE END OF GEORGE ELIOT'S *Middlemarch* (1871–1872), a scene takes place that exemplifies the power of Victorian novels to fuse marriage and romance. As Will turns to bid Dorothea farewell, she erupts into speech, expressing the vehement feelings her first marriage had smothered: "'Oh, I cannot bear it—my heart will break,' said Dorothea, starting from her seat, the flood of her young passion bearing down all the obstructions which had kept her silent. . . . In an instant Will was close to her and had his arms round her, but she drew her head back and held his away gently that she might go on speaking."[1] As Dorothea and Will embrace in the timeless present of fiction, they exercise over even the most skeptical contemporary readers a pull almost as strong as the one they exercise on each other. It is scenes like these that continue to epitomize the Victorian novel for readers and critics of Anglophone literature. Undergraduates who flock to courses on the nineteenth-century novel consistently distance themselves from the Victorians precisely in the terms Foucault debunked—they were sexually repressed, we are sexually free. Yet they also identify with Victorian novels, especially their concatenation of romantic fulfillment and marriage: "There is no happiness in love, except at the end of an English novel," the narrator of Anthony Trollope's *Barchester Towers* (1857) informs us, with an archness absent from the firm narrative decree issued by an otherwise timid heroine in Charlotte Brontë's *Shirley* (1849): "When people love, the next step is they marry."[2]

Readers enjoy not just the sexuality but the *hetero*sexuality of Victorian novels, an enjoyment all the easier to swallow because of how rarely Victorian novels mark heterosexuality as such. Critics are more self-conscious about the novel's aesthetic dependence on heterosexuality, but insist on it all the more strongly for their awareness of it as a generic marker. Some equate the novel's formal capacity to generate a sense of closure with its embrace of marriage as a social institution (Boone, DuPlessis). Others define the genre in terms of oedipal quests and conflicts that fuel narrative momentum (Barthes, Brooks). Still others posit heterosexual marriage as a principle of social structure or political participation, arguing that novels equate adultery with the breakdown of social hierarchies (Tanner) or the double bind of duty and desire (M. Cohen). Critics have shown how national romances and industrial novels use heterosexuality as a narrative device for depicting the incorporation of ethnic outsiders or the reconciliation of conflicting classes (Trumpener, Gallagher). The female bildungsroman constructs marriage as the only viable outlet for women's erotic and social energies (Armstrong, N. Miller); the male bildungsroman defines the hero's progress as his search for the proper heterosexual partner (Robbins), which requires the suppression of his homoerotic desires and desirability (D. A. Miller).[3]

Queer theory similarly asserts that the novel equates heterosexuality with the real, making lesbianism vanish almost as quickly as it comes into view (Castle), violently banishing lesbians from the precincts of narrative action (Farwell) or from the novel as a genre (Moore), consigning lesbianism to inconclusive plot lines and secondary, eccentric characters (Roof).[4] Eve Kosofsky Sedgwick has shown how the suppression of men's homoerotic desires surfaces in Victorian novels as a Gothic strain of paranoia among male characters who must renounce homoerotic desires but cannot mourn them.[5] Sedgwick recasts heterosexual marriage as a male homosocial relation, an exchange of women that forges eroticized alliances and rivalries between men, and thus unseats heterosexuality as an original, primary, autonomous form of desire. Like other queer theorists, however, Sedgwick identifies literature as a site of violent conflict between the homosocial and the homoerotic that can represent homosexuality only indirectly.

Whether theorists of the novel focus on norms, power differences, or ideological fictions, they understand the social as exhaustive and encompassing, yet also constituted by what it excludes, represses, or pathologizes. That view leads to symptomatic readings that show how the marginal and the invisible are central to narratives that apparently occlude them. In *The Political Unconscious: Narrative as a Socially Symbolic Act*, Fredric Jameson states that the most "interesting" feature of a text is what it represses.[6] The critic's task is "diagnostic revelation of terms or nodal points implicit in the ideological system which have, however, remained unrealized in the surface of the text" (48). Interpretation "always presupposes, if not a conception of the unconscious itself, then at least some mechanism of mystification or repression in terms of which it would make sense to seek a latent meaning behind a manifest one, or to rewrite the surface categories of a text in the stronger language of a more fundamental interpretive code" (60). Symptomatic reading proposes a surface/depth model of interpretation in which the true meaning of the text must lie in what it does not say, which becomes a clue to what it cannot say. The text's gaps, silences, disruptions, and exclusions become symptoms of the absent cause that gives the text its form. While Jameson has little to say about sexuality and focuses instead on politics, class struggle, and the drive to extract a realm of freedom from that of necessity, his method has been seized upon by critics in sexuality studies who show how texts secure heterosexual hegemony by repressing deviant sexualities that are then legible only as the symptoms signifying their exclusion from the text.

Symptomatic reading is an excellent method for excavating what societies refuse to acknowledge, and the twentieth century did indeed define gay and lesbian existence through repression and the resistance to it. But Victorian society repressed so few forms of female relationship that symptomatic reading is not a productive approach for understanding social bonds between women in Victorian fiction. Critics have assumed not only that novels articulate a relationship between desire and social norms, but also that they make heterosexuality the only acceptable mode of desire; that novelists have always defined heterosexuality as the active suppression or implicit negation of homosexuality; and that friendship is best understood as congruent with sexual bonds rather than distinct from them. In fact, nineteenth-century authors openly represented relationships between women that involved friendship, desire, and marriage. It is only twentieth-century critics who made those bonds unspeakable, either by ignoring what Victorian texts transparently represented, or by projecting contemporary sexual structures onto the past. Critics intent on restoring lesbian desire to Victorian fiction have asserted that the marriage plot puts an end to all same-sex bonds—but Victorian marriage plots depend on maintaining bonds of friendship between women.[7] Since Victorians neither repressed female friendships nor policed them as rigidly as they did heterosexual relations, it makes no more sense to produce symptomatic readings of female friendship in Victorian literature than to argue that marriage is the repressed content of nineteenth-century British realism.

In the place of symptomatic readings, the interpretations I offer in this chapter are what I call "just readings." Just reading attends to what Jameson, in his pursuit of hidden master codes, dismisses as "the inert givens and materials of a particular text" (75). In tracing the representation of female friendship in the Victorian novel, I do not claim to plumb hidden depths but to account more fully for what texts present on their surface but critics have failed to notice. I invoke the word "just" in its many senses. Just reading strives to be adequate to a text conceived as complex and ample rather than as diminished by, or reduced to, what it has had to repress.[8] Just reading accounts for what is in the text without construing presence as absence or affirmation as negation. Finally, just reading recognizes that interpretation is inevitable: even when attending to the givens of a text, we are always only—or just—constructing a reading. To pursue just reading is thus not to make an inevitably disingenuous claim to transparently reproduce a text's unitary meaning. Nor is it to propose that we dismiss symptomatic reading; indeed, the just readings I perform here depend on a symptomatic reading of novel theory, since only by attending to what other critics have been unable to explain can subsequent critics build a more capacious interpretive framework.

Symptomatic readings of sexuality in the Victorian novel have assumed that the genre takes shape in relationship to an opposition between a dominant heterosexuality exemplified by marriage and a marginal, repressed homosexuality at odds with marriage and family life, but that premise has rarely been put to the test. The previous chapter showed that Victorian marriage was not defined strictly in terms of sexual difference but as a social relationship that combined sexual passion, economic interests, and spiritual love. As such, marriage was often considered an extension of female friendship and sometimes construed as the best name for sexual bonds between women as well as between women and men. If the Victorian novel depended on marriage for its generic plot, and if marriage was seen as having so many intimate connections to female friendship, one must then ask how novels organized around marriage represented those friendships. If the Victorian novel worked to reproduce gender norms, and if female friendship was one of the relations that defined normative femininity, how did novels incorporate those female friendships into courtship narratives?

Critics have been unable to answer these questions accurately because they have defined femininity in terms of male desire and heterosexual marriage. Criticism has not neglected female friendship in Victorian novels, but it has cast all relationships between women as troubling disruptions or utopian alternatives to the genre's smooth reproduction of femininity, marriage, and heterosexuality.[9] The insistence that relationships between women must heroically oppose the marriage plot has led scholars to define any novel that ends in marriage as hostile to female friendship, rather than attend to the remarkably overlooked fact that almost every Victorian novel that ends in marriage has first supplied its heroine with an intimate female friend. Victorian novels do indeed depend on the union of a man and a woman for their narrative structure—but that union does not negate bonds between women. An a priori assumption that social bonds between women are genuine only if they oppose heterosexual institutions has left critics with nothing to say about the numerous Victorian novels in which courtship between men and women proceeds in tandem with declarations of female amity.

It is thus not surprising that little has been made of another passionate moment in *Middlemarch*, without which Dorothea and Will would never make their pivotal romantic admission. Before Dorothea confesses her love to Will, she confesses it to herself: "[S]he discovered her passion to herself in the unshrinking utterance of despair" (739). Dorothea's dawning consciousness of the love she bears for Will is suffused with gloom because it surfaces only after she has come upon Will with the married Rosamond Lydgate. After discovering the truth of her own feelings, Dorothea strives to see the scene from Rosamond's point of view, "as bound up with another woman's life" (740). Dorothea's sympathy for her rival is both a bid to transcend paralyzing unhappiness through selflessness, and a convenient condescension that allows her to identify with Rosamond in order to "save" her (742). Dorothea's capacity to reach outside the self resembles the narrator's so closely, however, that it is subject only to the gentlest irony, and when Dorothea visits Rosamond the next day, the narrator ratifies Dorothea's sense of "vivid sympathetic experience" (741) by rapidly switching between each woman's point of view. The juxtaposition of each character's unvoiced thoughts formally expresses Dorothea's sense of a palpable connection to Rosamond, matched by their physical proximity in the scene itself. Dorothea takes off her gloves; Rosamond reads Dorothea's face attentively and sees a gentleness there that disarms her; she cannot "avoid putting her small hand into Dorothea's" nor noticing its "firm softness" (745). Rosamond doubts her own "prepossessions"; Dorothea realizes she "had counted a little too much on her own strength" and not factored in how "dangerously responsive" she feels when she sees Rosamond—"she suddenly found her heart swelling and was unable to speak" (745). As the two women sit on chairs that "happened . . . to be close together" (745), Dorothea talks to Rosamond about Lydgate's troubles. As she does so, the narrator notes, "she had unconsciously laid her hand again on the little hand that she had pressed before," and even after Rosamond has "withdrawn" hers, Dorothea's is "still resting on Rosamond's lap" (747).

The gestures that the narrator recounts in such detail are sensual in their physicality and erotic in their power to disrupt each woman's certainties. Rosamond cries helplessly, shedding unaffected tears in another's presence for the first time in the novel. After the resonant narratorial announcement that "[p]ride was broken down between these two," the differences between the two characters start to erode as well (748). Speaking about Rosamond's adulterous interest in Will, Dorothea confesses the dangers that same love posed in her own marriage in a pair of symmetrical, paratactic clauses that merge her identity with Rosamond's: "[W]e are weak—I am weak," she sputters, then stops "in speechless agitation . . . and . . . pressed her hands helplessly on the hands that lay under them" (749). After the clasping of hands comes a kiss, and a confession:

> Rosamond, taken hold of by an emotion stronger than her own—hurried along in a new movement which gave all things some new, awful, undefined aspect—could find no words, but involuntarily she put her lips to Dorothea's forehead

which was very near her, and then for a minute the two women clasped each other as if they had been in a shipwreck.

"You are thinking what is not true," said Rosamond, in an eager half-whisper, while she was still feeling Dorothea's arms round her—urged by a mysterious necessity to free herself from something that oppressed her as if it were blood-guiltiness. . . . Rosamond had delivered her soul under impulses which she had not known before. (749–50)

Rosamond's ensuing admission that Will loves Dorothea, not herself, results from the uncontrollable affects that overtake her in this passage. The kiss, the clasp, the eager half-whisper, the sense that the women are experiencing something mysterious, new, simultaneously fatal and vital, all lend the scene an erotic charge. That the bond between Rosamond and Dorothea remains in the suggestive realm of the erotic without ever becoming the kind of sexual connection Dorothea has with Will does not scant its importance in a novel so concerned with charting every possible filament of community. The kiss Rosamond bestows on Dorothea is a version of the "earnest sacramental kisses" Janet bestows on Mrs. Pettifer in *Scenes of Clerical Life* (1857)—"such kisses as seal a new and closer bond between the helper and the helped" and reinforce the social fabric.[10]

The physical embrace that transports Rosamond and Dorothea to a higher plane of consciousness, connection, and "serious emotion" is inseparable from the resolution of *Middlemarch*'s marriage plot. Without Rosamond's kiss, embrace, and avowal, Dorothea would never know that Will loves her and would not admit her love to him. The confession scene between Rosamond and Dorothea is linked to the subsequent one between Dorothea and Will by the logical necessity of narrative sequence (without the one, the other would not take place) and by resemblance (both depict an involuntary meeting of minds that culminates in a heartfelt embrace). In the terms of classical narrative theory, the rapprochement between the two women is related to the heterosexual plot both syntagmatically (one event clinches the other) and paradigmatically (the two events share sufficient features to come under the same category). Yet our existing theories of the marriage plot cannot account for this moment. Readings that focus solely on the heterosexual dynamics of marriage plots would simply ignore this crucial scene, while a reading premised on the opposition between lesbian and normative desires would read Dorothea's marriage to Will as a panicked retreat from Rosamond.[11] Both readings would err in their assumption that the two currents of desire and affiliation are opposed rather than coexistent and interdependent. Dorothea and Rosamond come together only because of their shared entanglement with Will, and Dorothea and Will tie the knot only because of the electric, decisive affinity Dorothea experiences with Rosamond.

Weak as it is, the bond between the two women is the only force powerful enough to tie up the marriage plot's loose ends.

The pivotal role that one woman's affectionate impulse toward another plays in concluding *Middlemarch* is exemplary of how Victorian novels make female friendship the catalyst of the marriage plot. Rosamond and Dorothea's connection is social, if not public, and therefore affects their connections to others. Like the donor and helper in Vladimir Propp's analysis of the folktale, the female friend is not a static or dispensable secondary character but one with a crucial role to play in achieving the marriage plot's ends. As Propp notes, even in the fairy tale "a helper at times may perform those functions which are specific for the hero," and in complex novels one finds both the heroine and the female friend taking actions that conclude the marriage plot.[12] The female friend is not simply an auxiliary, brought onstage as matchmaker, then whisked off after fulfilling the secondary function to which she would therefore be reduced. She is a mate, an ally, and a critic, the repository of confidences, a bestower of wisdom, a conspirator, nurse or patient, teacher or pupil, a source of physical contact and pleasure, an object of admiration, a link to the past and bridge to the future. Often as securely in place at a novel's end as at its beginning, female friendship has narrative longevity. Marriage plots unite not only a man and a woman but two social institutions, friendship and marriage, which begin as separate but are finally united in a kind of Moebius strip or feedback loop.

Unlike marriage, however, female friendship is rarely a locus of compelling narrative suspense, for it is seldom subject to courtship's vagaries, conflicts, obstructions, and resolutions. Female friendship is thus best described as what I will call a "narrative matrix," a relationship that generates plot but is not its primary agent, subject, or object. The relative stability of a narrative matrix endows it with power and endurance; it is a contributing cause that maintains its identity and presence even after achieving its end. A narrative matrix is not dispensable, since without it the plot would have no sustenance, and would not take the course it does. Nor is a narrative matrix passive, since it has the generative power and dynamism to launch, direct, and resolve a plot. Marriage plots depend on the constantly altering relationships between a heroine and her suitors and on the more or less stable relationship between the heroine and a female friend. The narrative distinctiveness of friendship lies in its ability to make stability a springboard for the adventures that traditionally constitute our notion of the narratable. Though friendship provokes none of the suspense or distress we typically associate with plot, it sustains the reader's interest and attention: with respect to female friendship, Victorian novels succeed in making the reader actively desire that *nothing will happen*. In this sense, female friendship defies Peter Brooks's equation of plot with the dynamic forward movement of plotting, and circumvents the classic distinction D. A. Miller makes between the necessary instability of the narratable and the quiescent plenitude of the non-narratable.[13]

A cursory look at the Victorian canon may inspire some initial skepticism about the claim that female friendship is a central element in the novel of courtship and marriage. Female friendship has little role to play in *Wuthering Heights* (1847), with its antagonisms among Isabella Linton, Catherine Earnshaw, and Nelly Dean, and seems similarly invisible in *The Mill on the Floss* (1861), with its contrasts and rivalry between Maggie Tulliver and her cousin Lucy. In novels like *Vanity Fair* (1848) and *Barchester Towers*, the most important female characters exist primarily in relationship to men, and those novels' compelling antiheroines, Becky Sharp and Madame Neroni, are notable for their overt distaste for other women. *Vanity Fair* describes Becky Sharp as a monster and attributes her deformation to the fact that she "had never mingled in the society of women" (50), although the narrator shares his character's cynicism about female friendship as a mask for female rivalry.[14] When Madame Neroni plans to "create a sensation" at a Barchester party, her goal is "to have parsons at her feet . . . and to send, if possible, every parson's wife home with a green fit of jealousy" (76–77). The narrator is quite clear, however, that Madame Neroni is not a woman but a predatory "spider" (242) and diabolical "basilisk" (361). The novel locates the quintessence of true womanhood in sisters who are the antithesis of Madame Neroni, because their shared adolescent enthusiasm for a neighborhood minister unites instead of divides them: "Having . . . fixedly resolved [on] . . . the pre-eminence of the exalted Green, the two girls went to sleep in each other's arms, contented with themselves and the world" (174).

Maggie, Catherine, Becky, and Madame Neroni are imposing but anomalous characters, refreshing in their deviations from proper femininity but as atypical in their disengagement from female friendship as they are in their demeanor towards men. Indeed, their narrative fates suggest that a heroine who lacks female friends almost always has an uneasy relationship to marriage. That Catherine Earnshaw and Maggie Tulliver lack female allies no more suggests that female friendship is peripheral to the Victorian novel than their unhappy relationship to the marriage plot proves the genre's hostility to courtship and wedlock. *Vanity Fair* and *Wuthering Heights* belong to a canon informed by twentieth-century definitions of subjectivity and gender identity, a worldview in which desire between sexes tellingly called "opposite" was conceived as a battle between the sexes. Ironically, early feminist revisions of the canon shared a similar bias toward novels about heterosexual conflict, celebrating heroines like Maggie Tulliver who defy gender conventions. *Wuthering*

Heights, almost unintelligible to the British reading public for much of the nineteenth century, entered the canon only after the 1950s, when its pairs of men and women locked in ecstatic identification and bitter antagonism seemed to express a structural truth about gender relations. Viewed in light of the twentieth century's stark oppositions between hetero- and homo-, masculine and feminine, the female friendships integral to so many Victorian marriage plots could only appear as excrescences on the formal unity prized among the New Critics who set the Victorian canon, or as an adjunct to the gender struggles crucial to the feminist scholars who expanded it.[15]

One does not have to go outside the canon, however, to show the importance of female friendship in the Victorian novel. It is present in *Middlemarch*, in *David Copperfield*, and even in some of the examples just cited as instances of its apparent absence. The just reader of *Barchester Towers* will have already recalled that toward the end of that novel Madame Neroni commits an act of "unwonted good nature" (371) by helping to bring about a match between Mr. Arabin and Eleanor Bold. What begins as a "good turn" on behalf of a male favorite succeeds only when Madame Neroni decides "to make a present of him" by meeting with Eleanor (437). The scene in which she bestows a husband on Eleanor emphasizes both women's "softened" hearts and "caressingly" grasped hands (439), anticipating in a less earnest register Dorothea's encounter with Rosamond in *Middlemarch*. Another woman finishes what Madame Neroni began when Miss Thorne's "friendship" (461) gives Eleanor's marriage plot its final, decisive push in a chapter entitled "Miss Thorne Shows Her Talent at Matchmaking." Readers of *The Mill on the Floss* may best remember the structural antagonism between rebellious Maggie Tulliver and docile Lucy Deane, but the text does not support a reading of the two cousins as simple rivals for the love of Stephen Guest. Of Maggie, Lucy says, "There is no girl in the world I love so well," and it is that very affection that makes Lucy, according to the narrator, "quite the sort of wife a man would not be likely to repent of marrying . . . a woman who was loving and thoughtful for other women."[16] Though Maggie resents Lucy and injures her by falling in love with Stephen, the plot is almost as driven to reunite Maggie with her estranged female cousin as it is to return her to the alienated brother with whom she ultimately drowns "in an embrace never to be parted" (655), for its penultimate chapter, "Maggie and Lucy," shows the two women similarly "clasped . . . in a last embrace" (643). Even Becky Sharp redeems herself with a final gesture, both self-serving and generous, that helps conclude the marriage between Amelia and Dobbin.

The Form of the Plot

A theoretical abstract of what I call "the plot of female amity," by which I mean the interdependence of female friendship and the marriage plot, would run as follows. The plot begins by contrasting female friendship to the courtship relationship between a man and a woman. Lovers when first meeting often have false first impressions and only declare their love hesitantly, after overcoming many misunderstandings and obstacles. The bond between female friends, in contrast, is either established before the novel begins or coalesces almost instantaneously, intensifies almost effortlessly, and can be expressed clearly and openly. The relative stability of friendship makes it the motor rather than the subject of plot; it generates enormous energy without itself moving much or melting down. The tendency of female friendship to remain constant over the course of a plot is a sign both of its narrative weakness (not much happens to the friendship) *and* of its narrative strength (because of its stability, friendship makes things happen). In the middle phases of the plot of female amity, one friend expresses love for the other by helping her to realize her marriage plot. This can take the form of mediating a suitor's courtship, giving a husband to the friend or the friend to a husband, or helping to remove an obstacle to the friend's marriage. This phase can also take the form of one friend assuaging the other's wounds and bolstering her subjectivity to make her more marriageable. The plot of female amity does not substitute for the conventional marriage plot, since the friend usually does not seek to replace a husband; when she does, the plot of female amity is displaced by the female marriage plot (see chapter 6). In the plot of female amity, marriage and friendship are inseparable, and the woman who promotes a friend's marriage to a man is a forceful agent of the closure achieved once friendship and marriage have become parallel states and the future husband and wife have attained the harmony that already prevailed between female friends.

The plot of female amity is the Victorian novel's purloined letter, hiding in plain sight in the genre's every permutation. The remainder of this chapter makes that point through sustained readings of a few major works, but to give an idea of the plot's range, let me first rapidly survey a sensation novel, a silver-fork novel, a political roman à clef, and a novel of provincial life. Sensation novels, which characteristically emphasize occult powers and deceptive social ties, make female friendship an equally baroque narrative force. In Wilkie Collins's *Man and Wife* (1870), for instance, the attachment between two female friends, Blanche and Anne, is all that can disentangle a marriage plot mired in complex wills, obscure legal loopholes, and vindictive relatives. One friend's "resolution to reunite herself" with the other ultimately enables each woman to be united with a loving husband. Blanche makes her refusal to "give . . . up" Anne a condition of marriage when she tells her suitor: "There's time to say No, Arnold—if you think I ought to have no room in my heart for anybody but you."[17] Anne marries a man she hates in order to secure the legality of Blanche's marriage to the man she loves: "She kissed her—looked at her—kissed her again—and placed her in her husband's arms" (525). As so often happens in the plot of female amity, marriage makes female friends kin when Anne is freed of her villainous first husband and marries Blanche's uncle, who learns to love Anne through the loyalty she arouses in his niece: "'The woman must have some noble qualities,' he thought, 'who can inspire such devotion as this'" (246).

In Frances Trollope's silver-fork novel *The Widow Barnaby* (1839), which combines sentimental fiction with a portrait of high life, a generic preoccupation with virtue and good taste inflects the plot of female amity: the narrative defines the heroine's innate gentility by showing that she can captivate virtuous, well-born women as well as men.[18] One young woman's "enthusiasm" for Agnes, the heroine—whom she finds so attractive "it is with difficulty that I keep my eyes away from her"—shows her good taste, which in turn reflects Agnes's true worth (117). Agnes's responses to other women similarly display her good judgment and capacity to feel desire. The Victorian marriage plot required heroines to be chaste, yet sufficiently ardent and aware of their desires to marry for love. The plot of female amity circumvents the paralyzing effect that this paradoxical demand might have on the marriage plot by using female friendship as a vehicle for depicting a heroine's erotic excitability while skirting, so to speak, the strictures on female heterosexual assertion. When Agnes first meets the "tall, elegant-looking woman" whom she does not yet know is her male beloved's sister, her "whole attention seemed captivated" (228). Once she identifies the woman as the sister of the man she loves, Agnes goes into a paroxysm, "trembling from head to foot with her eyes timidly fixed on the beautiful countenance of Colonel Hubert's sister. . . . [T]here was timidity certainly in the pleasure with which she listened to the voice and gazed at the features of Colonel Hubert's sister; but still it was pleasure, and very nearly the most lively she had ever experienced" (249–50). Within pages, she and Hubert's sister have exchanged the embraces and kisses that are the novelistic sign a happy marriage will soon help their budding friendship bloom, and Hubert's sister approves her brother's choice, exclaiming, "I too am very much in love with Agnes" (342). Trollope can so graphically represent the erotic delight women take and inspire in each other for the obvious reason that the "lively . . . pleasure" of female homoeroticism poses no phallic threat to virginal virtue. But she can also depict their attraction so floridly because a woman's

susceptibility to another woman defined rather than defied femininity—
because even the most erotic bond between women could sustain opposite-sex desire.

As a final pair, consider George Meredith's *Diana of the Crossways*
(1885) and Harriet Martineau's *Deerbrook* (1839). Although both novels
explore community, vocation, and rumor, nothing could be further from
Martineau's expository, prosaic didacticism than Meredith's elliptical,
quicksilver sophistication. Yet both novels conclude with scenes that demonstrate the inseparability of marriage and female friendship. In Meredith's novel, the eponymous heroine, nicknamed Tony, marries only when
her best friend, Emma, proposes on a suitor's behalf. The novel's last
sentences describe Emma's "exaltation" as she "held her beloved in her
arms under the dusk of the withdrawing redness." That "beloved" is the
female friend who has just returned from her honeymoon, and the novel's
last lines focus on the women's reunion: "They sat embraced, with hands
locked, in the unlighted room, and Tony spoke of the splendid sky. 'You
watched it knowing I was on my way to you?' 'Praying, dear . . . [t]hat I
might live long enough to be a godmother.' There was no reply: there was
an involuntary little twitch of Tony's fingers."[19] The stock scene in which
a wife obliquely confesses to her husband that she is pregnant takes place
here between female friends: the "involuntary little twitch" of Tony's fingers is a telegraphic signal that Emma's wish is already reality, a displaced
sign of the fetus's movement within her, and a response whose involuntary
corporeality underscores that a clearly consummated marriage has not
dimmed the romance between female friends.

Deerbrook also ends at dusk, an erotic threshold that blurs light and
darkness, public visibility and shaded privacy, in which day tremulously
balances night and finality seems momentarily suspended. The plot of
female amity is aptly timed to conclude at evening, for it achieves closure
by evenly distributing narrative attention and the heroine's affections
across friendship and marriage, rather than forcing a choice between
them. *Deerbrook* thus ends not only at twilight, but also "on the eve"
of Margaret Ibbotson's happy, long-deferred marriage to Philip Enderby,
which she chooses to spend with her friend Maria.[20] Margaret and Maria
have both loved Philip, but as the plot of female amity dictates, their
shared love has brought them closer instead of driving them apart. In the
novel's final scene, they sit together in Maria's house until they hear Philip's horse, and Maria gives her friend away by telling her to "go and give
Mr. Enderby the walk in the shrubbery that he galloped home for" (523).
The novel's final sentence displays the conjugal couple in the light of female friendship: "Margaret kept Philip waiting while she lighted her
friend's lamp; and its gleam shone from the window of the summer-house
for long, while, talking of Maria, the lovers paced the shrubbery, and let

the twilight go" (523). The reader infers that Margaret leaves Maria's side, but the narrator does not describe her actual departure; instead, she leaps paratactically from a first clause that places the two women in the same room to a second clause that depicts Margaret walking with Philip. That second clause bends over backwards to give the participial phrase "talking of Maria" priority over the clause's grammatical subject, "the lovers," but what the sentence loses in fluency it gains in meaning, since that reversal embodies how Maria presides over Margaret's union with Philip. The passage's articulation of space and vision makes the moment between friends persist in the lovers' walk, for Margaret and Philip are illuminated by Maria's lamp, which Margaret has lit. The novel's final tableau allegorizes the social links that the plot of female amity forges between marriage and female friendship, which appear as closely connected as adjacent moments, cottage and shrubbery, or a light source and the object it illuminates.

FEMALE AMITY AND THE COMPANIONATE MARRIAGE PLOT

Female friendship assumed a crucial role in novels that revolved around companionate marriage and assumed that parents could no longer legitimately choose husbands for their daughters and that friendship should partially or wholly define the ideal relationship between husband and wife. Historically, such philosophers as Aristotle and Montaigne had associated friendship with equality, similarity, and a reciprocal affection based on reason, in contrast to marriage, perceived as a naturally hierarchical relation based on irrational passions that defied control. Beginning in the late seventeenth century, an increasing tendency to view marriage in egalitarian terms transformed it into something like friendship between husband and wife, making friends agents of marriages rather than mere relief from the trammels of wedlock. The liberal democratic principles subtending the companionate marriage plot defined young women as individuals capable of maturation and development, though often within more restricted limits than those placed on men. The heroine of a companionate marriage plot must know herself in order to choose a husband wisely; once freed from the requirement either to obey or reject parental dictates, she is aided in her quest for self-knowledge by friends who are equals and peers. Dorothea ignores the parental figures who attempt to dictate whom she should marry, but her encounter with Rosamond prompts the self-knowledge that leads her to marry Will. Friendship between women becomes a model for managing social bonds in a capitalist democracy that promotes equality and individualism, cohesion and competition. In a novel about community and its fissures, the relationship between Rosamond and Dorothea provides one of the more hopeful glimpses of two very different people speaking openly about what separates and unites them. Their moment of amity converts the jealousy, rivalry, and secrecy that initially divide them into a sense of connection, and as such also provides a model for how men and women, as well as the rival camps of Middlemarch, can resolve their differences.

Friendship between men is too vast a subject to be given its due here, but a brief discussion of its place in Victorian literature and society can help us to understand what was specific about female friendships. The first point to make, because it is the more surprising one, is that Victorians celebrated friendships between men, especially young men, in terms very similar to those used to laud intimacy between women. Lifewriting, conduct books, photographs, and educational treatises praised sentimental, spiritual, romantic, and physical bonds between men and made no fixed connections between male friendships and the legal category of sodomy or the controversial but common practice of sex between older and younger boys at public schools. Friendship between men was believed to promote enlightenment ideals of self-cultivation, sympathetic communion, and civic association. For men as well as for women, such friendships were shot through with erotic yearnings and domestic intimacies that were openly avowed; men did not hide that they slept in the same bed or made plans to live together.[21] For both sexes, friendship was an opportunity to engage in cross-gender behavior with impunity, within the confines of a same-sex relationship. As we saw in the previous chapter, women and girls could act toward female friends in ways they could not toward men; conversely, boys and men could more easily display susceptibility and sentiment with each other than with women, as Thomas Hughes's *Tom Brown's Schooldays* (1857) demonstrates. Friendship for both sexes thus reinforced gender identity and provided respite from gender constraints.

Male friendships also differed from those between women. Friendship between boys was much more likely to be described as a phase that ended when one of the men married, and it was more often understood in terms of rivalry, hierarchy, and sexual difference. Female friendship enforced an altruistic economy of reciprocity and a model of subjectivity based on cooperation, and its repertoire of bodily gestures emphasized contact between undifferentiated body parts such as hands, eyes, and lips. Male friendship feminized both of the boys involved, but was often described as feminizing one more than the other, resulting in a couple modeled more on the exaggerated gender differences of hierarchical marriage. Even when female friends adopted behavior associated with men, their relationship was still seen as intensifying the femininity of both parties. As a result, female friendship was more often compared to companionate marriage, which asked both husband and wife to develop traits associated with feminine forms of sociability.

At its most minimal, female friendship takes the form of neutralized enmity. Thomas Hardy's *Far from the Madding Crowd* (1874) represents even that scant degree of friendship as powerful enough to reconcile female rivals and anticipate friendship between husband and wife.[22] Like *Middlemarch*, Hardy's novel is a *re*marriage plot, in which the heroine learns how to love a husband as a friend only after surviving a disastrous first marriage. For Bathsheba Everdene, learning to overcome jealousy of her husband's erstwhile lover, Fanny Robin, is a crucial step on the road to a companionate union. Bathsheba learns of Fanny's existence only after her death, when Troy flaunts his preference by ordering Fanny an expensive tombstone and planting her grave with flowers. Though it would be consistent with her character for Bathsheba to despise the woman whose demise has only intensified Troy's love, she behaves with uncharacteristic gentleness towards Fanny's body and memory by tending her corpse and then replanting her grave after a storm destroys the flowers Troy had planted. Bathsheba's initial perception of Fanny as a "rival" (229) gives way to a sympathy for the dead woman that constitutes a sort of posthumous friendship.[23]

In the plot of female amity, love between friends develops the emotional disposition necessary for companionate marriage. Bathsheba's retroactive friendliness toward Fanny germinates the compassion that flowers in her marriage to the aptly named Gabriel Oak, which the narrator assesses as a happy union because it realizes the "good-fellowship—camaraderie—... seldom superadded to love between the sexes" (303). The narrator connects female friendship to companionate marriage through the water imagery that dominates both Bathsheba's care of Fanny's grave and the narrator's last words about her marriage to Gabriel. Troy plants flowers on Fanny's tomb but fails to notice that its position directly beneath a rainspout means that the first rain will destroy his blooms, much as his heedlessness helped cut Fanny down in her prime. It is Bathsheba, aided by Gabriel, who repairs the damage done by the "gurgoyle" that channels rainfall into an attacking force echoing her own prior hostility to Fanny: "The persistent torrent from the gurgoyle's jaws directed all its vengeance into the grave" (242). By replanting the uprooted flowers, wiping the mud from Fanny's gravestone, and diverting the gurgoyle's spout, Bathsheba expresses a newfound "superfluous magnanimity" that replaces her initial impulse to reduce an already dead rival to dust (246). That generosity redounds to Bathsheba's credit at the novel's end when she attains with Gabriel a love as "strong as death—that love which many waters cannot quench, nor the floods drown, beside which the passion usually called by the name is evanescent as steam" (303–4). The amicable deed of protecting Fanny's grave from a destructive torrent metaphorically returns in the form of a marital friendship similarly resistant to water's volatility and violence.

Far from the Madding Crowd miniaturizes the plot of female amity: an elegiac gesture of friendship toward another woman begins to teach Bathsheba how to transmute stormy passion into the companionable affection that characterizes her happy marriage to Gabriel Oak. In *David Copperfield* (1850), female amity delivers a similarly happy ending—but to a hero, not a heroine.[24] Like Hardy's novel, *David Copperfield* contrasts a first marriage contracted out of infatuation to a more mature union: David's first wife, Dora, is an incompetent doll; his second wife, Agnes, an angelic domestic manager. David's second marriage is no more egalitarian than his first, since he perceives Agnes as his spiritual superior even as he assigns her the role of a servant, but it is described as significantly more mutual and reciprocal than his conjugal error with Dora.

David's progress towards companionate marriage, his heterosexual sentimental education, is inseparable from the story of the friendship that forms between his first and second wives. When David first meets Dora, her potential deficiencies are foreshadowed by her injudicious choice of female companion, though David falls "headlong" in love with Dora too quickly to heed the unpleasant warning that her confidential friend is his childhood enemy, Miss Murdstone (362, 364). True to the principle that the marriage plot rarely moves forward without a female friend's assistance, the inimical Miss Murdstone quickly gives way to Miss Mills, a friend of Dora's who encourages David's suit with high-flown speeches (448), machinations that help the lovers correspond (486), and the provision of her house as a meeting ground where David can call on Dora (449). When Dora is sequestered with her unmarried aunts after her father's death, Miss Mills consoles David and sustains his affection for Dora by speaking of her constantly and by letting David read the "sympathetic pages" of her diary (519), which keep David's love alive by recording how Dora remains "[b]eautiful in pallor" (518).

In the standard plot of female amity, friendship between women precedes a happy marriage between a woman and a man. *David Copperfield* follows that formula but also varies it, since friendship between a man and a woman produces the female friendship that then goes to work on marriage. Agnes befriends Dora out of love for David, and then advises David how to court Dora and love her despite her faults (525); as David puts it when he declares his love to Agnes at the novel's end, "[M]y love [for Dora] would have been incomplete, without your sympathy. I had it, and it was perfected" (792). Agnes can sympathize and thus complete David's love for Dora because she decides to love the same woman he does. Contemporary readers used to discounting female friendship as a façade may find it especially difficult to credit Agnes's love for Dora as sincere, for at this point in the novel it is clear that Agnes is herself in love with David. David's vision of the friendship that he imagines will develop between his best friend and his future spouse is easy to interpret as a self-serving misprision: "It was as if I had seen [Agnes] admiringly and tenderly embracing Dora. . . . It was as if I had seen Dora, in all her fascinating artlessness, caressing Agnes, and thanking her. . . . I saw those two together, in a bright perspective, such well-associated friends, each adorning the other so much!" (525). The repetition of the phrase "it was as if I had seen" suggests that David's fantasy of the two women pleasuring each other is a false image that he uses to veil the unpleasant truth of the pain he causes Agnes by marrying Dora.[25]

The friendship between Dora and Agnes is not confined to David's hypothetical imaginings, however; it is also conveyed in reported dialogue and accounts of their interactions as straightforward as any can be in a first-person narrative. The women's friendship characterizes their feminine willingness to place David's needs first, but it also establishes each woman's femininity as a matter of same-sex relations. Agnes's kindness to Dora is one more proof of her womanly virtue, and Dora's receptiveness to Agnes another manifestation of her girlish potential for improvement: "[W]hen [Dora] saw [Agnes] looking at once so cheerful and so earnest, and so thoughtful, and so good, she gave a faint little cry of pleased surprise, and just put her affectionate arms round Agnes's neck, and laid her innocent cheek against her face" (563). The women's friendship is never separate from their shared interest in David, but each also claims the other as her own. Dora declares her friendship to Agnes soon after meeting her: "I am so glad . . . that you like me. . . . I want, more than ever, to be liked, now Julia Mills is gone" (564). David's fragmentary memories of his wedding day recall Dora actually holding Agnes's hand when she makes her wedding vows: "Of our kneeling down together, side by side; of Dora's trembling less and less, but always clasping Agnes by the hand" (582). On the verge of departing on her honeymoon, Dora finds it difficult to leave Agnes, "giving Agnes, above all the others, her last kisses and farewells" (584). After her wedding, Dora conjectures that a longer friendship with Agnes would have made her a better helpmate: "I wish . . . that I could have gone down into the country for a whole year, and lived with Agnes!" (594). Dora's wish stems from a desire for the domestic training that would have made her a fitter wife to David, but it also states a desire she shares with her husband: to have chosen Agnes as her first spouse.

The female friend figures as centrally at the wife's deathbed as in her nuptials, and both sites are governed by an altruistic exchange economy in which women do not compete for men but instead give them to each other. Just as Agnes gives Dora to David and in so doing concedes David to Dora, so does Dora assert property in her husband by willing him to her female friend. David famously realizes that his marriage to Dora was "the first mistaken impulse of an undisciplined heart" and resigns himself to adapting to her, since she will not adapt to him (643), but he is quickly relieved of that burden when Dora is struck by a mortal illness a mere paragraph after he announces his brave resolve. The dying Dora asks to have Agnes at her side with a gravity her character is allowed to assume only on the brink of death: "[I]t's not a whim. It's not a foolish fancy. . . . [G]ive Agnes my dear love, and tell her that I want very, very much to see her; and I have nothing left to wish for" (704). Dora dies on Agnes's "bosom, with a smile" (708) while David lies unconscious in another room. We later learn that Dora had asked to see Agnes in order to bequeath David to her, in a perfect coincidence of female friendship and remarriage. As Agnes explains to David after she marries him, Dora "told me that she left me something . . . that she made a last request to me, and left me a last charge . . . [t]hat only I would occupy this vacant place" (794). The perfect reciprocity of Dora's bequest not only relieves David of guilt but also allows Dora to repay her debt to Agnes; just as Agnes helped give Dora to David, Dora's last act is to return the favor by giving her husband back to her friend. The cyclical economy of female friendship matches the circularity of *David Copperfield* as bildungsroman, for female friendship leads David to a more mature marriage that also reproduces his youthful misstep. For all their differences, David's second wife is identified with his first one, as David declares to Agnes herself: "O, Agnes, even out of thy true eyes, in that same time, the spirit of my child-wife looked upon me, saying it was well; and winning me, through thee, to tenderest recollections of the Blossom that had withered in its bloom!" (792). Just as Dora became more like Agnes, Agnes incorporates Dora, the "child-wife" whose spirit shines out of Agnes's eyes, and whose "Blossom" Agnes reincarnates by giving birth to a girl whom she and David name Dora (803).

Female friendship generates the novel's final marriage between a man and a woman, but given the ways that the male hero is also a female one, that ultimate marriage can itself be read as a female friendship. The narrator begins by questioning whether he is "the hero of my own life" and ends by revealing that his autobiography's hero is a heroine, the redemptive Agnes (11). Even before he is born, David is marked by his great-aunt Betsey Trotwood's implacable wish that he be a girl. When he later goes to live with Betsey Trotwood, she enjoins him to "[b]e as like your sister as you can" (195) and dubs him Trotwood after herself and the niece she wishes his mother had produced for her. David's beloved friend Steerforth similarly renames him Daisy (274). The fertile marriage between Agnes and Betsey/Daisy/David provides his aunt with a "real living Betsey Trotwood" (803) and endows David with a relationship that combines marriage, kinship, and amity: Agnes is his wife, his "soul" (806), and his "sweet sister . . . counsellor and friend" (254). At the novel's end, David has incorporated Dora as much as Agnes has, for he now looks up to Agnes, relies on her, and adores her with the same sentimental abandon with which he saw Dora yield to her. His second marriage overcomes the errors of his first not only because David replaces Dora with a better woman but also because David takes Dora's friendship with Agnes as a model for a more companionable marital relationship. By suggesting that the union of a man and a woman derives from and resembles friendship between women, the novel defines marriage as simultaneously based on sexual difference and on sexual interchangeability—the productive paradox at the heart of companionate marriage.

FEMALE AMITY AND THE FEMINIST MARRIAGE PLOT

Where *David Copperfield* shows how female friendship paves the way for a man to find happiness in a companionate marriage, the feminist bildungsroman deploys amity to help female protagonists acquire the autonomy that makes them equal to their husbands. Elizabeth Barrett Browning's *Aurora Leigh* (1856), a nine-book narrative poem that combines epic, kunstlerroman, poetic treatise, and social novel, emphasizes the dilemma marriage poses to a woman who craves love, but dreads that marriage will hinder her artistic ambitions.[26] Like *David Copperfield*, Barrett Browning's poem is a first-person account of a writer's development, and criticism of *Aurora Leigh* has focused on the tensions between its portrait of the artist as a young woman and its ending, in which Aurora finally accepts her cousin Romney, the man she has resisted loving.[27] Readers often focus on Barrett Browning's decision to inflict blindness on the male suitor, but attending too singlemindedly to how Romney must change to become marriageable obscures the importance the poem assigns to Aurora's relationship with another woman. *Aurora Leigh* is deeply concerned with the "condition of England," and friendship between women from different classes is both the poem's most hopeful vision of social cooperation and the matrix that generates egalitarian marriage. The last four of *Aurora Leigh*'s nine books focus on the friendship between Aurora and Marian Erle, a working-class woman introduced as the prospective bride of Romney Leigh, who has proposed to her in an attempt to enact his social ideals. Just before their wedding, the duplicitous Lady Waldemar, herself in love with Romney, persuades Marian to flee the country with a woman who orchestrates a

rape that results in Marian's pregnancy. Aurora eventually finds Marian
on the streets of Paris, hears her story, and the two women move to Italy
together where they form a household with Marian's son. So central is
Marian to *Aurora Leigh* that the story of her life up until her engagement
to Romney takes up most of books three and four, and the story of her
suffering after she leaves England much of book seven.

In *Aurora Leigh*, as in *David Copperfield*, the woman overlooked by the
man she loves transforms rivalry into friendship by claiming her beloved's
beloved as her own. Such altruistic visions strike contemporary readers as
cover stories, for we find it difficult to believe in social relations that equate
self-interest with self-sacrifice, cooperation, and identification. It is now
easier to lend credence to satirical fictions that claim realism by cynically
exposing self-interest as the basis of all social relations.[28] When Henry
James set out to import French aesthetics into the Anglophone novel, for
example, he distanced himself from what he considered the insufficiently
tragic sentimentality of English literature by taking aim at the plot of female amity. As early as *The Portrait of a Lady* (1880–81), James represented that plot as a fiction of female innocence lacking in realism. Isabel
Archer's maturation thus depends on recognizing that the friendship she
contracts in England with Madame Merle—not herself French, but significantly associated with France by her name—only appears to bestow
the gift of marital happiness but is in fact a pretense of friendship designed
to steal her fortune. Isabel thinks she is in an English novel of courtship
and that her friend is her benefactor, only to learn that she is in a French
novel of adultery and that her friend is her rival. In the very act of transforming the nature and value of female amity, however, James still acknowledges its generic primacy for the English novel, for he cannot reform
the marriage plot without simultaneously rewriting female friendship.

The nineteenth-century idealization of female friendship reinforced
constraints on female aggression, but also indicated a commitment to an
intersubjectivity based on mutual fortification rather than on zero-sum
competitions that leave one contestant depleted. The plausibility of that
reciprocal model of subjectivity in Victorian literature is borne out by
Aurora Leigh's representation of female amity from the perspective of a
female participant. After hearing Marian's story of how she became engaged to Romney, Aurora reports, "I kissed the lips that ended.—'So
indeed / He loves you, Marian'" (112). When Romney qualifies that he
and Marian feel "less mutual love than common love" for "the loveless
many" (116), Aurora again "turned / And kissed poor Marian, out of
discontent" (117). Female friendship enables Aurora to express frustrated
love, and Marian is receptive to Aurora's overtures, not least because she
views her own life story in terms of female friendships, first with Rose
Bell, whom "[s]he loved indeed" as a child (98), and later with a fellow
worker whom she is devotedly nursing when she first meets Romney. The

reciprocal importance of female friendship for both Marian and Aurora surfaces throughout the narrative; the antiheroine and false friend Lady Waldemar remarks on the "liking" Aurora took to Marian (173), and the poem retells the women's first meeting from Marian's point of view when she writes to Romney, "Ere you came / She kissed me mouth to mouth: I felt her soul / Dip through her serious lips in holy fire" (133). Marian and Aurora's kiss of friendship incarnates a spiritual affinity that then becomes a model for the ideal synthesis of physical and spiritual love between men and women, for the "sexual passion" that similarly "devours the flesh / In a sacrament of souls" (142).

As in *Far from the Madding Crowd* and *David Copperfield*, the distinction between friendship and marriage in *Aurora Leigh* constantly fades from view: friends experience the sorts of communion associated with spouses; an aspiring husband must learn to approximate the female friend; and female domesticity is the precondition of traditional closure. Marian and Aurora realize Dora's fantasy of living with Agnes before marrying David, and Romney and Aurora disclose their love only after Aurora has shared a household with Marian and her son. After Aurora glimpses Marian in Paris, she imagines proposing friendship to Marian: "Marian! I find you. Shall I let you go? . . . / Come with me rather where we'll talk and live / And none shall vex us. I've a home for you / And me and no one else" (194–95). After Marian tells Aurora of being raped and giving birth, Aurora proposes to Marian directly:

> "Come with me, sweetest sister. . . .
> From henceforth, thou and thine! ye are my own. . . .
> . . . Come,—and henceforth thou and I
> Being still together will not miss a friend,
> Nor he a father, since two mothers shall
> Make that up to him." (219)

Aurora's proposal is proprietary, with its imperatives and possessive pronouns, but she carefully avoids using marriage as the framework of her ownership claim, turning instead to familial terms that evoke equality: she and Aurora will be sisters, friends, and joint mothers.[29] The use of enjambment in the last four lines, however, belies Aurora's assertion of the two women's self-sufficiency by severing the nouns that describe the newly established female unit from their full verbal predicates. "Thou and I" are left hanging, while the isolated phrase "Being still together" suggests motionlessness as much as continuity. In the penultimate line, the four words "since two mothers shall" are an economical replacement of the four that precede them, "nor he a father," but the final line break, which separates the auxiliary "shall" from the main verb "[m]ake," once again implies suspension, this time in an indefinite future.

As in other plots of remarriage where a first union provides the grounds for a second one, the family Aurora founds with Marian is more a matrix than an independent agent. As the plot unfolds it is clear that Aurora's decision to live with Marian makes her even more fulfilling union with Romney possible. Even before subsequent events in the diegesis confirm this, the exegesis suggests that female autarky is destined to produce a union between a woman and a man, because from the outset, that autarky is subtly limited and serves as an occasion to generate rhetorical equivalences between women and men. Even as Aurora appropriates Marian and her son and envisions the self-sufficiency of their household, she inserts Romney into their union by exclaiming, "Oh, Romney Leigh, I have your debts to pay" (219). That statement rhetorically equates Marian and Romney even as it divides them into creditor and debtor; it also signifies Aurora's equivalence to her male cousin. Aurora's use of apostrophe underscores her need to make the absent male beloved a presence in her new household and constructs Romney and Marian as parallel figures, for just as the figuratively addressed Romney literally cannot answer Aurora, Marian makes no verbal response to her invitation: "She looked me in the face and answered not / . . . / But took the sleeping child and held it out / To meet my kiss" (219). Aurora's metaphor of Romney as debtor imagines Marian as both a lacking victim and the owner of a surplus, while it figures Romney as a delinquent who has failed to keep his promises. By substituting herself for Romney vis-à-vis Marian, Aurora corrects his weaknesses but also substitutes her strength for his; both moves are as pivotal to their subsequent union as his feminization through blindness.

Anxious to avoid reducing the working-class female friend to a mere accessory of the heroine's marriage plot, Barrett Browning takes pains not to assign her the role of female poet's muse.[30] The poem makes Marian a subject by assigning her the power to give Romney away to Aurora in marriage, and the novel's final marriage is the result of an exchange between women that asserts the generative energies of friendship. Like all exchanges, the one between Marian and Aurora consolidates the power of the trading partners and secures the bond between them.[31] Critics who have written about the relationship between Marian and Aurora have focused on their class difference and on how Marian renews Aurora's relationship to desire, but not on the active role Marian takes in bringing about Aurora's union with Romney.[32] When Romney appears in Italy, he tells Aurora that he plans to "claim" Marian as his wife because he considers himself responsible for the ills she has suffered (292). Aurora is mute, but the woman whose words she has so often paraphrased speaks out, asking Romney to "Confirm me now. / You take this Marian, such as wicked men / Have made her, for your honourable wife?" (292–93). Marian's speech transforms the rhetoric of the marriage ceremony by rephrasing the cleric's interrogative, "do you take this woman?" as an utterance that hovers between a question and an order. After arrogating to herself the power to officiate over marriage, Marian almost immediately transfers it to Aurora, whom she addresses as the arbiter of Romney's proposal: "Speak. I'm bound to you, / And I'll be bound by only you, in this" (294). Just as Aurora had ordered Marian to live with her ("Come with me"), Marian now commands Aurora to command her.

The power of friendship produces the state of marriage when, in a series of exchanges, each woman attempts to give a husband to the other. First, Aurora bestows Romney on her friend: "Accept the gift, I say / . . . Here's my hand / To clasp your hand, my Marian, owned as pure!— / As pure,— as I'm a woman and a Leigh!" (294). Aurora underscores her commonality with Romney by invoking their shared surname, by offering Marian her hand even as she asks her to take Romney's in marriage, and by claiming a power similar to a husband's to cleanse Marian of her imputed sin by "own[ing]" her "as pure." Female friendship gives form to wedlock, for any subsequent union between Romney and Marian would only reproduce the bonds, gestures, and acts already performed between the two women. When Marian declines to marry Romney, she confirms that Aurora has also proposed by directing her refusal to her female friend: "[C]atch my hands, / Miss Leigh, and burn into my eyes with yours,— / I swear I do not love him" (296).

Men have no monopoly on initiating marriage in *Aurora Leigh*, for the next plan to marry Romney emerges from a second exchange between women. As Romney stands silent, Marian muses aloud that she wishes she could tell Aurora—and in wishing, does tell her—to take Romney as a husband. Explaining that Romney should "wed a noble wife," Marian elaborates, "If I dared / But strain and touch her in her upper sphere / And say, 'Come down to Romney—pay my debt!' / I should be joyful" (298). Echoing Aurora's earlier assumption of Romney's debt to Marian, Marian asks Aurora to pay another debt, this time her own. Marian thus puts Romney in the position she had formerly been assigned by Aurora: that of a wronged lover whose suffering must be redeemed. The female friends swap their debt when Marian simultaneously owns her obligation to Romney and transfers it to Aurora; "pay my debt" becomes equivalent to "marry Romney." An unpaid debt, like an unreciprocated gift in Marcel Mauss's theory, establishes a social connection and a balance of power between giver and receiver. By asking Aurora to pay what she owes Romney, Marian asks Aurora to replace her, but also consolidates their bond, for Marian will always owe Aurora for having paid her debt, just as Aurora will always owe her union with Romney to Marian. In a scene as common in Victorian literature as it has been unremarked, one woman

gives another away in marriage to a man who becomes permanently indebted to the female friend he must learn to emulate.

THE DOUBLE MARRIAGE PLOT: FRIENDSHIP AS CAUSE AND EFFECT

The texts examined so far are unusual because the female friend is absent
from the finale she helps generate. Unlike Fanny Robin and Dora Copperfield, Marian Erle still lives at the end of *Aurora Leigh*, which concludes
before Romney and Aurora formally wed, but when Romney and Aurora
finally merge in a shared vision of the New Jerusalem, neither articulates
whether their new life will include Marian, who simply disappears in
one short sentence: "She was gone" (299). Because Barrett Browning figures female friendship as two women's exchange of *one* man, the
donor must exit to seal the friend's possession of the gift bestowed on her.
In novels with double marriage plots, however, in which female friends
marry male friends or relatives, female friendship can be represented as
marriage's original cause and one of its surviving effects. In Charlotte
Brontë's *Shirley* (1849), the double wedding that concludes the novel sustains the preexisting bond between brides who begin as friends and end
as sisters-in-law.[33] By marrying brothers, Caroline Helstone and Shirley
Keeldar both become Mrs. Moore; when they relinquish their own names
for those of their husbands, they give linguistic form to the social bond
they have already created with each other.

Like *Aurora Leigh*, Brontë's novel addresses class conflict and feminism, and critics have tended to read the novel's final marriages as
reinstating the hierarchies challenged earlier in the plot.[34] The first nine-
teen chapters of the book focus on the antagonism between workers and
mill owners. The middle third of the book shifts to a feminist plot that
concentrates on female characters who, along with the narrator, protest
the limits placed on women, deflate male superiority, and rewrite misogynist myths as gynocentric allegories. The final chapters emphasize a feminine plot of courtship, marriage, and domesticity. Instead of women's
grievances and workers' rebellions, we have Shirley's romantic submission to her tutor, Louis, and Robert Moore's conversion from a harsh
captain of industry into a tender husband who learns to treat his workers
like family.[35]

Female friendships generate feminist critique and at the same time accommodate feminine norms: the friend becomes an agent who is shielded
from charges of unwomanly boldness because she acts on behalf of another. We see this in the interplay between *Shirley*'s plot and its narratorial commentary. In a passage whose loquacity ironically undercuts her

point, the narrator reminds readers of the constraints on women's sexual initiative: "A lover masculine . . . disappointed can speak and urge explanation; a lover feminine can say nothing: if she did, the result would be shame and anguish, inward remorse for self-treachery" (128). Yet the novel proves that although "a lover feminine" can say nothing on her own behalf, her female friend can say a great deal, since Shirley sets Robert's eventual engagement to Caroline in motion by rejecting him as a suitor. Her refusal complicates any simple opposition between male initiative and female passivity, for she reprimands Robert not only for his arrogant presumption that she loved him before he loved her, but also for his confidence that she would be "a traitor to all my sisters," an unwomanly being who "acted as no woman can act, without degrading herself and her sex" (500). Shirley's belief that all women who love first are unsexed defines femininity as reactive to masculinity, but it also defines womanliness in relation to other women by asserting that a woman must be like others of "her sex." Similarity to other women is not simply the condition of being essentially identical to them, but rather a willed solidarity that stems from Shirley's active decision not to be a "traitor" to her "sisters," her resolution not to engage in actions that would separate her from other women.

In the plot of female amity, female friendship absorbs, neutralizes, and transmutes female rivalry. Shirley rejects Robert not only out of loyalty to all women but also out of fidelity to one woman, her friend Caroline Helstone, who suffers from unreciprocated love for Robert. Conduct literature discouraged women from vying over men in order to secure the difference between female passivity and male competitiveness, but Brontë folds female rivalry into female friendship in order to establish women's equality with men. To depict women competing for a man would be to define femininity as a lack that a man must supply and that a woman overcomes only at the expense of another, who then becomes a loser twice over: deprived of the prestige a man confers, defeated by another woman. *Aurora Leigh* resolves this problem by making a man into a gift that one friend bestows on another; *Shirley* resolves it by focusing on rivalry as a false problem in a bountiful economy that provides a man for each woman who desires one. Shirley quickly acts to dispel Caroline's concerns about her as a possible rival when she protests that she would like to "call out" Robert: "He keeps intruding between you and me: without him we should be good friends; but that six feet of puppyhood makes a perpetually recurring eclipse of our friendship. . . . If we were left but unmolested, I have that regard for you that I could bear you in my presence for ever" (264). The economy of female amity devalues even the most traditionally appealing attributes of manhood when Shirley demotes Robert Moore's imposing physique to "six feet of puppyhood." It rates female friendship higher than sexual love when Shirley's eclipse metaphor equates "friendship" with the sun. Robert interests Shirley only as a model and medium for attracting Caroline, as bait to draw Caroline into conversation through the "irresistible . . . temptation" of talking about him (275). "We will talk of Moore, then, and we will watch him," Shirley proposes to Caroline at a party, and as Caroline looks for Moore in the crowd, "she looked . . . into Miss Keeldar's eyes" (309). One friend's willingness to promote the other's desire for a man means that for a woman to look at her male beloved is also to look with, and into, another woman's eyes.

One of the hallmarks of the plot of female amity is its insistence on a reciprocity that makes friendship and courtship mutually reinforcing. Just as the male beloved becomes a pretext for binding two friends more closely, friendship becomes a mechanism for uniting a friend with her male beloved—a union that can be realized only when it, too, comes to be governed by the principle of reciprocity. Only because Shirley rejects Robert is he available to marry Caroline, and only because of Shirley's effect on Caroline can Robert and Caroline make an equalizing declaration of friendship before they become engaged (558, 561). As Caroline explains to Robert, she learned to view him in a less worshipful light after Shirley revealed that he had been willing to marry for money but without love, and she regained hope that he might love her only after Shirley intimated to her that she was not Caroline's rival. Shirley makes these communications indirectly, and the narrator is unusually indirect in her depiction of the scene in which Shirley drops her telling hints. While most scenes between Caroline and Shirley are narrated in linear order, with the dialogue between them reported fully and directly, we learn of the night when the two women "occupied the same room and bed," "did not sleep much," and "talked the whole night through" in a flashback, where Caroline discreetly paraphrases for Robert the earlier conversation she had with Shirley (559). That analeptic narrative structure embodies the imbrication of female friendship and the marriage plot: a prior intimacy between female friends leads them to share information that then produces admissions of love between a man and a woman. The reader learns of that earlier, crucial confidence only after it becomes a matter of discussion between lovers who can share secrets because female friends have already done so. Female confidences take precedence at the level of the linear story, but courtship between a man and a woman is the precondition for representing those confidences in the narrative discourse. The reversal of precedence in the order of the story and the order of the discourse cancels any priority friendship might have over marriage or marriage over friendship. This episode creates yet another similarity between friendship and marriage by shrouding both in privacy: just as we never directly see the friends in bed together, we do not witness the wedding night that Shirley's nocturnal conversation with Caroline precipitates.

Contemporary literary criticism has set female development in opposition to marriage, arguing that while the hero of a bildungsroman realizes his ambitions when he chooses a spouse, the heroine relinquishes hers when she consents to wed. The plot of female amity complicates that schema by showing that in many Victorian narratives, female friendship is a vector of both marriage and feminism; it bolsters the female self and thus ensures that a heroine's marriage follows from her strength, not her weakness. Female friendship can inspire a timid woman to emulate a more independent and ambitious one; after Caroline befriends Shirley, who shares her Romantic sensibility and intellectual interests, she plans voyages, challenges men, pursues outdoor exercise, and undertakes philanthropic work with other single women. The novel's frequent identification of Shirley with masculinity (213, 331) underscores how her friendship with Caroline prefigures and models the novel's later marriages; in becoming independent and lively around her "gentlemanlike" female friend, Caroline learns to be less abject in relation to her future husband. Where romance between men and women depends on obstacles and miscommunications and inflicts pain and illness, female friendship enables women to express emotion through energetic speech and robust gestures. Shirley declares to Caroline, "[Y]ou and I will suit. . . . Kiss me—and good-bye" (226), and places "her hand into Caroline's with an impulsively affectionate movement. . . . '[Y]ou had better make much of me. . . . I began to flatter myself we were thoroughly friends; that you liked Shirley almost as well as Shirley likes you: and she does not stint her regard'" (245–46). Even when mired in erroneous jealousy of Shirley, Caroline makes a declaration that discounts Virginia Woolf's claims about female friendship's absence in literature before the twentieth century: "Shirley, I like you" (265). Echoing the narrator of *Far from the Madding Crowd*, who identifies true love between a man and a woman as a friendship stronger than passion, Caroline openly tells Shirley that the "affection" she feels for her is one "that no passion can ultimately outrival, with which even love itself cannot do more than compete in force and truth" (265).

Shirley's double marriage plot is matched by a double friendship plot. In a narrative that insists that equivalence and reciprocity structure the relationship between friendship and marriage, the one character to challenge the primacy of Caroline's love for Shirley is not a male suitor but another woman, Shirley's governess, Mrs. Pryor. After focusing on the growing friendship between Caroline and Shirley, which culminates in chapter 19 when they run to witness the attack on Moore's mill, the novel's mobile narrator shifts her focus to Caroline's budding relationship with Mrs. Pryor, who is "as well-disposed to cultivate Caroline's acquaintance as Shirley" (226). Even before the older and younger women know each other well, they share a sensitivity to each other's bodies. When Mrs. Pryor first visits Caroline, the younger woman notices that the elder one is flushed and "gently sought to relieve her by opening her shawl and removing her bonnet. Attentions of this sort, Mrs. Pryor would not have accepted from every one. . . . [T]o Miss Helstone's little light hand, however, she yielded tractably" (227). Mrs. Pryor returns Caroline's tenderness when she observes that Caroline has grown wan: "[S]he . . . swept Caroline's curls from her cheek as she took a seat near her [and] caressed the oval outline" (244).

In the plot of female amity, nursing reinvigorates both patient and caretaker. Mrs. Pryor's love for Caroline reaches its summit in chapter 24, when she helps Caroline through a dangerous illness and the two women "coalesce . . . in wondrous union," with the "patient . . . as willing to be cherished as the nurse was bent on cherishing" (401). In that chapter, more than halfway through the novel, the narrator also reveals what she has carefully kept secret until this late stage of her story: in a scene bathed in the romance of the "moonlight" (409), Mrs. Pryor confesses that she is Caroline's mother. Critics often ignore Brontë's dramatic decision to conceal that familial connection for much of the text. That narrative feint is striking, however, both because *Shirley* depends so little on the Gothic secrets and unreliable narration of *Jane Eyre* and *Villette*, and because it forces the reader to construe an earlier scene between Caroline and Mrs. Pryor as a marriage proposal. In chapter 21, entitled simply "Mrs. Pryor," the two women walk in a "wooded ravine," the kind of landscape that Ellen Moers identified as a metaphor for female sexuality and that here becomes an emblem of the fertile union of female bodies in the absence of men: "This was no trodden way: the freshness of the woodflowers attested that foot of man seldom pressed them: the abounding wild-roses looked as if they budded, bloomed, and faded under the watch of solitude, as in a sultan's harem" (360).[36] The references to flowers invoke female reproductive sexuality, but the analogy between a harem and solitude and the allusion to the rarely present "foot of man" underscore that in this fruitful bower, men are superfluous.

The plot of female amity uses narrative sequence and narrative resemblance to depict female friendship and heterosexual marriage as logically related, structurally similar, and mutually reinforcing. *Shirley* comes close to replacing the plot of female amity with the plot of female marriage, for the walk Mrs. Pryor takes with Caroline culminates in one of Victorian fiction's most vivid scenes of courtship between women. After Caroline confides in Mrs. Pryor that she would like to go far away and work as a governess, Mrs. Pryor warns her of the difficulties of that life and proposes instead that she and Caroline pledge to unite their lives together.

Mrs. Pryor presents her suggestion as both a departure from marriage and a version of it. She begins hesitantly, commenting that "the young . . . frequently—anticipate—look forward to—to marriage as . . . the goal of their hopes" (365), and then gains assurance, declaring "romances . . . pernicious," marriage "never wholly happy," and "Let all the single be satisfied with their freedom" (366). In the place of a husband, Mrs. Pryor offers herself:

> "I possess a small independence, arising partly from my own savings, and partly from a legacy. . . . [W]henever I leave Fieldhead, I shall take a house of my own . . . [T]o you, my dear, I need not say I am attached; with you I am happier than I have ever been with any living thing. . . . Your society I should esteem a very dear privilege—an inestimable privilege, a comfort, a blessing. You shall come to me then. Caroline, do you refuse me? I hope you can love me?" (368)

Even as Mrs. Pryor presents her proposal as an alternative to marriage, she formulates it according to the rhetorical rules of a Victorian proposal: she begins with an account of the financial resources that justify her right to speak at all, continues with an assertion of her high regard for the woman she offers to support, and concludes with an anxious inquiry about whether her love will be reciprocated and her overture accepted. Caroline responds by kissing her and telling her, "I love you dearly" (369). The appearance of this proposal scene *before* Mrs. Pryor reveals her maternity shows that although it was unusual for the plot of female amity to shift into a female marriage plot—the narrator comments on the "peculiarity" of Mrs. Pryor's interest in Caroline—Victorian novelists found it thinkable that friendship between two women could culminate in an informal marriage (229). Brontë presents female marriage as antagonistic to courtship between men and women; unlike the female friend, the female suitor criticizes male-female marriage and replaces it with monogamous marriage between women. Even before proposing that Caroline live with her, Mrs. Pryor diverts Caroline from her frustrated love for Robert by offering a "new channel" for Caroline's thoughts and by paying Caroline attentions as "vigilant, assiduous, untiring" as Robert's are fitful. As Robert himself puts it after he has finally proposed to Caroline, "She was faithful when I was false" (595).

The ability of a mother to adopt the guise of a female suitor hints at the maternal erotics I explore in chapters 3 and 4, but *Shirley* ultimately absorbs the plot of female marriage into the plot of female amity, for once Mrs. Pryor admits that she is Caroline's mother, she assumes a friend's symbiotic relationship to the male-female marriage plot. Mrs. Pryor literally keeps Caroline alive for Robert by restoring the health Caroline loses when she despairs of ever receiving Robert's love. Gaining a mother makes Caroline stronger and hence more marriageable; when Robert asks

Caroline to explain why she has started to "look brightly; move buoy-antly; speak musically," she explains, "For one thing, I am happy in mamma: I love her so much, and she loves me" (557). The symbiosis between marriage and friendship works in both directions, for marriage to a man also sustains the intimacy between daughter and mother. Caro-line's male and female loves become interchangeable; when Caroline gazes at Venus, "the Star of Love," and feels a hand "circle . . . her, and rest . . . quietly on her waist," she assumes it is her mother's, but discovers instead that it is Robert's. Maternal friendship is both a contributing cause of marriage and one of its effects. When Caroline tells Robert, "I cannot break her heart, even for your sake," he assures her that her mother has already accepted his invitation to live with them after they wed (595).

Unamiable *Villette*: Lucy Snowe's Passion

The interdependence of marriage and female friendship in Victorian fic-tion suggests that a challenge to one would seriously perturb the other. No female friendship without marriage in the Victorian novel—and by the same token, no marriage without female friendship. Although it is famously difficult to find a Victorian novel whose female protagonist sur-vives her failure to marry, Charlotte Brontë's *Villette* (1853), which de-flects a definite marital conclusion for its heroine, is an exception.[37] Critics often interpret *Villette* as an account of repressed desire, but remarkably few have suggested that the desires its heroine denies include lesbian ones.[38] This is, after all, a novel in which the first-person narrator, Lucy Snowe, has passionate responses to several other female characters, takes immense pleasure in partially dressing as a man and flirting with a woman during the course of a school play, and is haunted by a nun— a figure for lesbian sex since Diderot—who ends up in Lucy's bed and whom Lucy discovers is a hoax only after she hurls herself on her in a stunningly physical attack (569). A contemporary resistance to imagining desire be-tween women may explain this gap in the criticism, not least because *Villette* is so open about Lucy's attraction to many of the women she encounters. The novel's failure to end in marriage has less to do, however, with the heroine's desire for women than with her idiosyncratic rejection of female friendship.

Lucy's queerness is distinctly Victorian: it inheres in an anomalous dis-taste for other women's amity, not in a transgressive preference for wom-en's love. That refusal of female friendship never varies, though the women offering it run the gamut from flirtatious coquettes to virtuous paragons, and the contact they offer ranges from fleeting to intense. When a woman on board the ship Lucy takes to Villette comes "tripping up" to offer "the accommodation" of a stool, Lucy tersely rebuffs her overture: "I declined it" (113). She turns down each of the fellow teachers at Madame Beck's school who make her "overtures of special intimacy" (194). The trio of feminine types represented by coquettish Ginevra Fanshawe, exemplary Paulina Home, and commanding Madame Beck provide Lucy with opportunities to spurn female friendship in all forms. The most persistent, and persistently rejected, is Ginevra Fanshawe, who "would . . . have made of me a sort of friend and confidant" (148). Always sensitive to women's "fine forms" (286), whether in a chambermaid's "trim . . . waist" (106), the figures of her fellow theatergoers, or her young female students, Lucy appreciates the "fascinatingly pretty" (207) Ginevra's "fair, fragile style of beauty," but scorns her "teazing peevishness" and "unsparing selfishness" (118). On occasion, Lucy succumbs to Ginevra's physical charms—"Notwithstanding these foibles . . . how pretty she was!" (149)—but more often she is "crusty" with Ginevra in spite of her good looks.

Lucy's dislike of Ginevra is as ambivalent as her attraction to her; for example, Lucy admits that she always chooses to give her morning bread to Ginevra, a softer incarnation of crustiness that she claims to be unable to explain: "I don't know why I chose to give my bread rather to Ginevra than to another; nor why . . . I always contrived that she should be my convive" (312–13). Nor can Lucy's constant rejection of Ginevra be separated from her relish in recounting the scenes between them: Ginevra brings Lucy her hose to repair, Lucy refuses to mend them (149); Ginevra comes to Lucy's "chamber to show herself in all her splendour. . . . [S]he was going to bestow on me a kiss, but I said 'Steady!' . . . and so put her off at arm's length, to undergo cooler inspection" (152). That chilly rejection allows Lucy to indulge in an "inspection" all the more thorough for being "cooler." Though Lucy may spurn Ginevra every time she comes "[t]hrowing herself without ceremony on my bed" (352), she knows that the girl "liked me no worse for it" (118). Just as there is no having Ginevra, there is no getting rid of her, either, since the more Lucy pushes her away, the more Ginevra seeks her out.

Lucy's demeanor toward Ginevra is contradictory, but the openness with which she expresses attraction to her suggests that Lucy's scorn is not the negation of an erotic desire she is barred from articulating. When Dr. John refers to Ginevra as Lucy's friend, Lucy internally scoffs: "Friend, forsooth!" (262). The narrator is clear about why Lucy is drawn to Ginevra: she finds her pleasant to look at and enjoys her unquenchable need to solicit Lucy's attention (394). At the same time, Lucy frames Ginevra's desire for her in terms of a heterosexual rivalry that is the antithesis of the female friendship Victorians idealized. Much of Lucy's irritation with Ginevra stems from the younger woman's wish that Lucy admire, envy, and cater to her in ways that underscore Lucy's inferiority as a female social actor. Lucy imagines that Dr. John sees her as the "humiliated, cast-off, and now pining confidante of the distinguished Miss Fanshawe" (263), and Ginevra dismisses Lucy as a "dear grandmother" (574), even demanding that Lucy join her in front of a mirror and acknowledge that there is no possible parity between them: "I would not be you for a kingdom" (215). At other points, Ginevra demands that Lucy take a man's role and be her foil: she calls Lucy "Timon" (312) and "dear old Tim" (573), and asks to take Lucy's arm as they walk, but "when she took my arm, she always leaned upon me with her whole weight; and, as I was not a gentleman, or her lover, I did not like it" (393).

Victorians defined female friendship as absence of rivalry, but Ginevra positions Lucy as even less than a rival, a predetermined loser in any competition between them. Lucy thus feels "suffocate[d]" by Ginevra's hyperfemininity, her "girlish, giddy, wild nonsense" (576). One reason Lucy refuses other women's friendship is that their presence undoes her sense of femininity instead of bolstering it. Standing before Madame Beck's beautiful pupils, she comments, "In beholding this diaphanous and snowy mass, I well remember feeling myself to be a mere shadowy spot on a field of light" (200). Gazing at other women does not produce identification but radical erasure—the "snowy mass" makes Snowe invisible, the field of light makes Luce/y a shadow. Lucy makes friendly overtures to Ginevra or entertains romantic thoughts about her only on the rare occasions when she can imagine them both within the circuit of male-female desire. Thus the one time Lucy does not shed Ginevra's arm, she wants to "make her useful by interposing her" between herself and M. Paul as part of a complicated flirtation with her male colleague (470). Similarly, Lucy's only beneficent fantasy of Ginevra makes her "a sort of heroine" in a romantic "illusion" (231) that stems from Lucy's vision of the "electric chord of sympathy" that she believes exists, not between Ginevra and herself, but between Ginevra and the "faithful hero" whom Lucy also loves (230).

In the plot of female amity, women who love the same man refuse to compete for him and thus smooth the way for marriage by affirming the femininity that Victorians equated with altruism and reciprocity. Since women's desire for men in *Villette* always involves rivalry, female friendship cannot generate marriage. The famous scene in which Lucy plays a man's part in a school play, dressed half as a man and half as a woman, illustrates how Lucy's desire for Ginevra is inseparable from erotic contests. The play stages a rivalry between a fop and a "sincere lover" dubbed the *Ours*, or "bear" in French (210). Ginevra shows a "marked fondness, and pointed partiality" for Lucy in her role as fop in order to show Dr.

John, who is in the audience, that she prefers the dandy de Hamal to him (210). Lucy throws herself into her performance not in order to woo Ginevra directly but to make a point to Dr. John, whom she detects is both the target of Ginevra's act and its most sedulous observer:

> [I]t presently became evident that she was acting *at* someone; and I followed her eye, her smile, her gesture. . . . There was language in Dr. John's look . . . it animated me: I drew out of it a history; I put my idea into the part I performed; I threw it into my wooing of Ginevra. In the "Ours," or sincere lover, I saw Dr. John . . . I . . . rivalled and out-rivalled him. I knew myself but a fop, but where *he* was outcast *I* could please. . . . [M]y longing was to eclipse the "Ours." (210)

Unlike the heroines of the plot of female amity who claim friendship explicitly and then bestow men as gifts on one another, Lucy and Ginevra create a bond of mutuality—"ours"—by playing against the male *Ours*. At the same time, they "eclipse" the "ours" they share by competing for him. Lucy woos Ginevra to punish Dr. John for having effaced her by preferring Ginevra; her goal is to show him that his love for Ginevra the flirt is like Ginevra's love for the fop. The erotic heat associated with negative, aggressive affects like jealousy, humiliation, and punishment circulates freely between Ginevra and Lucy, but the warmth generated between them dissipates into what each sees as a more primary contest over men.

So resistant is *Villette* to female friendship that even "delicate, intelligent, and sincere" Paulina Home does not lend herself to the idealization, spiritual affinity, and feminine reinforcement that defined female amity (461). Paulina's "refinement, delicacy, and perfect personal cultivation" make her a "singular contrast" to her cousin Ginevra (346). Yet though Lucy finds Paulina's "attractions . . . very real and engaging" (359), she is as reluctant to befriend her as she is to become intimate with Ginevra. Lucy declares her appreciation of Paulina and notes how rare it is: "I liked her. It is not a declaration I have often made concerning my acquaintance, in the course of this book" (461). Yet even liking a good woman who reciprocates her affection (463) creates a sense of deficiency in Lucy that risks turning friendship into rivalry. She thus refuses Mr. Home's offer to become Polly's paid "companion" because she declines to be a "bright lady's shadow" (382), and rebuffs John's wish that she give him the "delight" of seeing Polly discuss him with Lucy, complaining that he "wanted always to give me a role not mine" (403–4). Polly's good qualities are exactly what cause John to transfer his affections from Ginevra to her, but as John's worthy beloved, the virtuous Polly is as much Lucy's rival as the capricious Ginevra was.

In novels governed by the economy of female amity, intimate confidences and caresses are the currency of friendship between women equally guaranteed of securing husbands if they want them, but in *Villette*'s universe of scarcity, Paulina's amiability becomes a galling reminder of her unwitting victory over Lucy. In *Middlemarch*, the plot of female amity is expressed as a sequence: one woman strokes another's hand and experiences a communion that inspires a confession that produces marriage. *Villette*'s treatment of the same gesture exemplifies the novel's rejection of the plot of female amity: when one woman takes another's hand, she severs the traffic between female friendship and marriage. Paulina touches Lucy only in order to express her love of John; as she asks Lucy's opinion of him, she "held my hand between hers, and at each favourable word gave it a little caressing stroke" (462). Lucy herself disappears in relation to Paulina just as she disappears in a sentence whose syntax effaces Lucy as the subject who produces "each favourable word." With nothing to gain from friendship with Paulina, Lucy refuses to mediate her courtship and spurns an invitation to share the couple's love: "It was best to answer her strongly at once, and to silence for ever the tender, passionate confidences which left her lips, sweet honey, and sometimes dropped in my ear—molten lead" (520). In her final novel, Brontë refuses the self-sustaining economy of female amity, which turns men into objects whom female friends bestow on each other, and replaces it with a vision of the marriage market as a corrosive force that turns friendly gestures into blistering attacks.

Nothing may seem more natural to us than female rivalry over men, but nothing seemed more odd to Victorian readers, who found Lucy Snowe unaccountably "morbid" and unduly sarcastic, especially in her "bitterness" towards other women. "There is something peculiarly unamiable," wrote one reviewer in 1853, "in the severity and rigour of the judgments which [Lucy] passes upon the young girls of the school in which she is placed as governess." The novel's vision of relations among women ran so contrary to the reviewer's expectations that he hastened to attribute it to the peculiar character of the observer rather than accept her "painful . . . picture" of girlhood as "a true representative of the reality."[39] The gender trouble that has led critics such as Joseph Allen Boone to align *Villette* with modernist literature left its Victorian audience nonplussed, not least because Lucy so morosely departs from the Victorian definition of womanliness as a relish for femininity.[40] Prone to perceive women as gall and wormwood, Lucy mistrusts her attraction to femininity in its most comforting manifestations—sweetness and prettiness. Even when she encounters those feminine qualities in a man, Ginevra's suitor Alfred de Hamal, Lucy is unsparing in her contempt, dismissively contrasting him to Dr. John, whose features are "not delicate, not slight like those of a woman" (219), and dismissing de Hamal as a "little dandy . . . his lineaments were small, and so were his hands and feet; and he was pretty and smooth, and as trim as a doll" (216). Lucy does not link de Hamal's effeminacy to any sexual proclivity for men; she is as contemptuous of his interest in Ginevra and in a painting of Cleopatra as she is of his "womanish feet and hands" (281). Rather, the effeminate man allows Lucy to give full rein to her ambivalence about femininity in women.

Lucy's contempt for de Hamal is inseparable from her desire for the sweetness and prettiness he exemplifies, since she craves charming things and tasty morsels as consistently as she fears that her appetite for them will be denied.[41] Cordials, honey, and sweet wine are the narrator's favorite metaphors for emotional and material blessings (452, 311, 324), and she is surprisingly detailed in her descriptions of the literal food she eats at school or on visits (130, 138). Lucy values M. Paul as a bestower of sweets who perceives that she is a "[p]etite gourmande" (444) and keeps her "bonbonnière . . . well supplied with chocolate comfits" (511). When M. Paul gives Lucy a house, she delights in a salon that exhibits the very preciousness she rejects in de Hamal, noting that the room was "very tiny, but I thought, very pretty," with "ornaments in biscuit china" (584). Asked if she likes de Hamal, Lucy replies cuttingly, "As I like sweets, and jams, and comfits" (217), but she belies her own sarcasm in her genuine appetite for those very treats. Observing de Hamal at the picture gallery, she internally derides him: "What a very finished, highly-polished little pate it was!" (281). Yet the very word Lucy uses to mock his head, "pate," has already appeared, modified only by accent marks, to describe what Lucy most longs for when, "excessively hungry" on the day of the school play, she recalls seeing "a basket full of small pâtés à la crème, than which nothing in the whole range of cookery seemed to me better" (205). Lucy can acknowledge her "relish for these dainties" (205) because her appetite for them can be satisfied, but her conviction that she is unamiable makes her loath to desire sweetness in feminine form, whether as the cloying Ginevra, the delicate Paulina, or the doll-like de Hamal.

Lucy is consistently stymied in the female friendships she constructs as obstacles rather than conduits to marriage. Yet she does experience a *passion* for femininity, as for everything else she desires: her feelings for women and men alike take shape as suffering, pain, and privation. To a vision clouded by anachronism, Lucy's passion for femininity is as indistinguishable from the love between female friends as pâté from pate. For Brontë's readers, however, such passion was as different from female friendship as French from English. Victorians valued female friendship as a compound of the qualities they prized and therefore imposed on women: self-effacement, self-sacrifice, reciprocity, altruism, responsiveness, self-control, sweetness, prettiness, and vulnerability, and the Victorian novel made female friendship a matrix for marriages that in turn reinforced friendship. Dorothea Brooke, Aurora Leigh, Caroline Helstone, and Agnes Wickfield marry their true loves only after each gives her all to another woman and receives all that other woman has to give. Victorian literature was relentless in its drive to unite men and women in marriage, and equally determined to base those marriages on anterior bonds between women; not for nothing does Mrs. Pryor, the woman whose offer of life companionship rouses Caroline Helstone into marriageability, have a name that is a homonym for "prior." In Victorian fiction, it is only the woman with no bosom friend who risks becoming, like Lucy Snowe, one whom no man will ever clasp to his heart in marriage, a friendless woman who remains perpetually outside the bosom of the family.

PART TWO

Mobile Objects: Female Desire

CHAPTER THREE

Dressing Up and Dressing Down
The Feminine Plaything

I went with Emily to the skating on asphalt at Princes in Hans place. I never saw a prettier sight—some 200 young women all in more or less graceful motion and dressed in all manner of print dresses with most astonishing and picturesque hats. The beauty of the girls was something to make one scream with delight. The older I grow the more slave I am to beauty.

. . .

[A]lthough I suffered cruelly from the violence of my new mistress, it was from no want of affection towards me, but simply from a desire to imitate her mother, by whose occasional fits of fury the little girl was so wonderfully impressed that, after having undergone any unmerited punishment, she always acted the scene over again upon my unlucky self.

. . .

I know one very expensive school for young ladies in Kensington, where for certain offences, whatever their age, the young ladies are birched as follows. . . . On entering she is told by a matron to lie across a narrow ottoman which occupies the middle of the room. . . . The matron then buckles a strap, which, passing across the culprit's waist, fastens her to the ottoman. She then, without a word, removes the loose dress from below her waist, selects a rod from a stand of rods, and slowly administers on Miss ———'s bare person the prescribed number of strokes, counting each as she gives it.

These passages were not written by pornographers, prurient men about town, or denizens of a secret sexual underworld. The first is an 1874 diary entry by Mary Collier (later Lady Monkswell), a married twenty-five-year old woman whose son edited and published her journals in the 1940s. The second is taken from a children's book by Julia Pardoe entitled *Lady Arabella; or the Adventures of a Doll* (1856), in which the eponymous doll, who narrates her own tale, bemoans the ill treatment she receives from her "mistress," a girl named Jane. The third excerpts an 1870 letter from "A Rejoicer in the Restoration of the Rod," which appeared in the *Englishwoman's Domestic Magazine*, a fashion journal for middle-class matrons that for several years published correspondence about the propriety of adult women using corporal punishment to discipline girls.[1] Taken together, these representative passages illuminate the everyday homoeroticism of a Victorian ladies' world in which women's magazines and girls' literature sound remarkably like the pornography that proliferated alongside them.

Fashion, dolls, pornography, mothers and daughters: to link them is on first sight both provocative and predictable. On the one hand, their grouping suggests an outrageous loss of border control, a shocking traffic between the feminine and the masculine, the adult and the juvenile, the licit and the illicit, the respectable and the obscene, and the aesthetic and the scatological. On the other hand, to claim a resemblance among dolls, pornography, and fashion has been a critical commonplace since feminists first argued that all three turn women into narcissistic, passive objects to be looked at by men. That an active pleasure in looking *at women* could be a requisite element of heterosexual femininity has been a logical impossibility for a theory that declares active spectatorship and desire to be masculine and limits women to passive identification with the feminine image or active identification with the male gaze.[2] Scholars have thus argued that Victorian fashion plates constructed woman as "an object to be looked at rather than an actor or a self," and "located femininity as object in a sexual dynamic where the gaze was assumed to be male."[3] The fact that fashion plates assumed a female gaze becomes irrelevant, since the framework asserts that images create the gender of their spectators.

The passages with which I opened this chapter, however, demonstrate that Victorian women as well as men enjoyed objectifying women and entertained active, aggressive impulses towards femininity. Victorian commodity culture incited an erotic appetite for femininity in women, framed spectacular images of women for a female gaze, and prompted women's fantasies about dominating a woman or submitting to one. Victorian society accepted female homoeroticism as a component of respectable womanhood and encouraged women and girls to desire, scrutinize, and handle simulacra of alluring femininity. Rather than engage in elaborate juggling acts that translate female spectators, authors, and image makers into masculine ones, this chapter confronts the fact that Victorians organized heterosexual femininity around women objectifying women and develops a theory for that historical evidence. It may at first seem contradictory to say that heterosexual women eroticized women—wouldn't that make them lesbians? To the contrary, Victorians did not oppose female heterosexuality to lesbianism, and thus considered a woman's erotic interest in other women compatible with her roles as wife and mother. A reputable wife had to take an erotic interest in images of fashionable ladies; an engaged mother had to relish dressing and disciplining her daughters; and a proper girl had to worship at the altar of femininity by idolizing, caressing, or tormenting her female doll.

Many scholars have depicted desire between women as subversive and intensely policed, but I am not suggesting that women had to turn to objects or children as outlets for desires that would have been censured if directed at real adult women. As we saw in chapter 1, women who sexually desired other women were able to live with other women in relationships recognized as marriages, and female friends explicitly appreciated one another's physical charms. Fashion was a way for women to enjoy femininity as a freestanding object of visual pleasure. In the passage that opened this chapter, for example, Mary Collier's eye for fashion is also an eye for the ladies. She glides from careful attention to "print dresses" and "picturesque hats" to an unabashed, almost ecstatic relish for the "200 young women" wearing them. Her pleasure is avowedly visual—"I never saw a prettier sight." She eroticizes the aesthetic as something to which one submits when she declares herself a "a slave . . . to beauty." Her rapture is also commonplace and collective, the sight that thrills her "something to make *one* scream with delight" (emphasis added). Lady Monkswell exemplifies the latitude accorded to female homoeroticism in an era when lesbianism was neither avowed as a sexual identity nor stigmatized as a deviant sexuality. Today, a woman so susceptible to another woman's attractions would be obligated to qualify her screams of delight by explaining whether she was or was not a lesbian. Though contemporary representations of mainstream femininity constantly invoke lesbianism, they also consistently disavow it.[4] Nothing could be further from the world of Lady Monkswell, which never delineated a clear lesbian social type and thus accepted female friendship, female marriage, and female homoeroticism as components of conventional femininity. Precisely because Victorians saw lesbian sex almost nowhere, they could embrace erotic desire between women almost everywhere. Female homoeroticism did not subvert dominant codes of femininity, because female homoeroticism was one of those codes.

Homoeroticism is thus neither a synonym nor euphemism for lesbianism or sex between women; nor does it refer simply to mental representations of sex. "Erotic" and "sexual" are not used here as interchangeable terms. The erotic and the sexual can and do intersect, but only the sexual refers to acts that involve genital arousal. Sexual desires are wishes to perform or fantasies about engaging in such acts. These restrictive, literal definitions of the sexual enable a corresponding latitude in defining the erotic in a way that does justice to the complexity and ingenuity of desire.

Because the erotic has no necessary connection to sex acts, to describe a dynamic or relationship as erotic requires no evidence of sex. In *Sade/Fourier/Loyola*, Roland Barthes defines the erotic as an affective valence defined by intensity, obsessiveness, theatricality, and pleasure. Barthes locates the erotic not in sexual acts but in practices of classifying, ritualization, and image-making and in emotional states such as "humiliation, jubilation, fear, [and] effusion."[5] Erotic relationships involve intensified affect and sensual pleasure, dynamics of looking and displaying, domination and submission, restraint and eruption, idolization and humiliation. Those erotic dynamics can exist between two people or between a person and an object, image, or text. To say that a woman had an erotic relationship with a woman or an image of a woman does not mean that she wanted to have sex with that woman or masturbated to that image. Erotic dynamics can lead to sexual excitement or activity, but even when they do not, they remain qualitatively different from the more neutral responses people have to the majority of people and things in their environment. A fashion plate is not overtly sexual, but it is designed to evoke erotic feelings in ways that a sewing pattern is not. In some cases, eroticism is in the eye of the beholder: books, cars, or pets are neutral objects for many but erotic objects for those who love them. In other cases, an object's eroticism has mass appeal. Voluminous sales of dolls and fashion plates in the Victorian era, for instance, prove that women responded eagerly to their presentation of femininity as a voluptuous, pliable spectacle.

This chapter argues that the female homoerotics of fashion and doll play had a counterpart in clandestine pornographic literature, which used obscene words and descriptions of sexual acts to arouse readers. To posit close connections between homoerotics and sexual discourse might seem to contradict the distinction between the erotic and the sexual, but my point is not that pornography was the naked sexual truth of fashion and dolls, nor that fashion plates and dolls were symptoms of repressed sexual desires. Pornography is not the sexual underbelly of culture; rather, pornography and mainstream culture share an erotic repertoire. Even at its most graphic, pornography prompts sexual acts and sensations because it represents and inspires the erotic affects of fascination, excitement, transgression, absorption, disgust, and shame.[6] Fashion, dolls, and pornography all emphasized the display and concealment of the body; each offered rule-bound systems for creating distinction, and each was structured by extremes of idealization and degradation, adoration and aggression, submission and dominance. Each dramatized self-discipline and the internalization of prohibitions, or displayed their inversion as humiliation, excess, and the violation of rules. And all three thrived on the tension between limitless desire and finite satisfaction in modern consumer culture, which promotes reveries and attaches desire to specific objects as sources of pleasure.[7] In his classic study of luxury and capitalism, Werner Sombart defined fashion as a sensual pleasure independent of procreation and reproduction, but nevertheless "essentially the same" as erotic pleasure.[8] The eroticism of commodities like fashion plates and dolls reverberated in Victorian pornography because all three were designed to appeal to the imagination and to the senses by marshaling the tactile and visual pleasures of texture, sensation, form, and color.

Conventional wisdom assumes that fashion and dolls embody what women want to be and what men want to have, that women identify with simulacra of femininity and men desire them. Since the distinction between identification and desire was invented precisely to separate in theory the homosexuality and heterosexuality that so often converged in practice, it is not surprising that identification has been used to explain away the homoeroticism inhabiting heterosexuality. Yet just as homo- and heterosexual desires and fantasies coexist within one subject, identification and desire merge within one viewer.[9] Identification is not identity; it depends on viewers' lack of identity with the image, on a distance and difference from the glamorous things that generate desire.[10] In longing to become like the images and dolls they admired, studied, and handled, Victorian women and girls necessarily experienced those icons as palpably separate from themselves. Dolls and fashion plates were impossibly distant but also sensually satisfying, tantalizingly unattainable objects of fascination but also miniature images within easy control.

To theorize the erotic as a set of dynamics rather than as a function of fixed gender relations or literal sexual acts is to assume that women can and do feel the same forms of desire as men. Like men, women direct their desires at both masculine and feminine objects. Victorian women who organized their sexual lives around men had erotic lives that also included girls and women. Binary gender does not determine desire, although gender is susceptible to eroticization and can become a source of excitement as a spectacle or boundary.[11] Erotic fantasies have no fixed relationship to gender roles, to sex acts, or to social power relationships. To show that women had sadistic fantasies about girls or that girls enjoyed punishing dolls is neither to diagnose female misogyny nor to valorize female agency and lesbian desire. At a given historical moment, gender can become a differential principle for distributing erotic agency or legitimacy. In restrictive heterosexual regimes, only men are allowed to be agents of desire, and then only if women are their objects. In the Victorian era, however, women as well as men could permissibly eroticize femininity. Victorian consumer culture thus presents a "female world of love and ritual" very different from the reciprocal, nurturing, pastoral sphere Carroll Smith-Rosenberg evoked when she coined the phrase. In spectacular contrast to the idealized universe of female friendships and

female marriages explored in Part One, fashion magazines and doll literature portrayed rituals replete with the voyeurism, objectification, and
domination that have been mistakenly declared the sole property of heterosexual men.

FASHION AND FANTASIES OF WOMEN

In his notes on fashion for *The Arcades Project*, Walter Benjamin comments, "To be *contemporaine de tout le monde*—that is the keenest and
most secret satisfaction that fashion can offer a woman."[12] In one economical sentence, Benjamin evokes the sexual, psychological, social, and
historical theories of fashion. By equating fashion with female "satisfaction," Benjamin captures the debate between those who view fashion as
a technology of women's subordination and those who see it as a venue
for women's pleasure, invention, and power.[13] To refer to the "most secret
satisfaction" fashion offers not women but "*a* woman" evokes fashion's
psychological appeal to an interiorized individual who defines herself in
terms of solitude, depth, and concealment, and clothes as intimate objects
that activate desire and promote reveries of beauty, leisure, and power.
Where psychology emphasizes the individual, sociology studies the group,
and Benjamin links the two when he predicates the fashionable woman's
"most secret satisfaction" on being contemporary with "*tout le monde*,"
literally with "everyone," but also with the social realm of worldliness
connoted by "*le monde*." For sociologists, fashion is a distinctly modern
phenomenon that constitutes group identity through imitation and simultaneously promotes an individualist ethos dedicated to relentless innovation.[14] Fashion is a weapon in the battle for distinction when rank is no
longer fixed by birth and sumptuary laws.[15] For women who do not vie
directly in the economic marketplace, fashion becomes a way to demonstrate facility with the rules of propriety that rationalize bodies in space
and time.[16]

The fashion that makes its female follower everyone's "contemporary"
confers historicity by marking the passage of time. Clothing styles identify
eras, and thus fashion becomes an index of history.[17] At any given moment, fashion imposes homogeneity, but over time it mandates constant
change. That variability represents both the relentless innovation imposed
by global capitalism's drive for profits and the triumph of individual fancy
over nature, tradition, and fixed authority.[18] Since what is novel one day
becomes passé the next, to conform to the movements of fashion is to
embody history's dialectic of old and new, maturity and youth, tradition
and novelty, the eternal and the transitory. Barthes observed that even
more than it expresses sex and gender, fashion signifies age.[19] Fashion

confers membership in a generation and thus becomes a transaction between generations. Fashion can cause generational conflict when adolescents adopt fashions that alienate their elders, or, as in Victorian society, it can be shared between mothers and daughters. Victorian mothers consulted fashion magazines to dress themselves and their daughters in the latest modes. To help them marry men, mothers willingly draped daughters in clothes that exposed or accentuated breasts, waists, and hips. But the gaze solicited by women's fashionable dress belonged most often to women, for Victorian manliness directed men to admire women's bodies while deriding the fashions that clothed them.[20]

Dense as it is, Benjamin's aphorism about fashion is thus incomplete, for in probing fashion's depths, he overlooked its surface: the most overt pleasure Victorian fashion offered women was looking at other women and being looked at by them. The elaborate color plates that circulated in Victorian fashion magazines and epitomized Victorian femininity depict women who solicit and return other women's fascinated, admiring, and probing gazes, who lock eyes, walk arm-in-arm, and stand so close to each other that their hands and dresses overlap (fig. 1). Fashion plates were one of the most popular forms of imagery targeted at women, and by the end of the nineteenth century over a million women had been exposed to them in France alone.[21] Though similar to other types of images that depicted dress in detail (clothing-trade plates, costume prints, caricature), the term "fashion plate" is reserved for images that promoted fashion by depicting women wearing the most current clothing styles.[22] Before the 1770s, European royal courts set and disseminated fashions by exporting life-size dolls garbed in actual clothes. Portraiture, historical surveys of national costume, and women's amateur art paved the way for iconography to replace the clothes themselves. By the 1770s, French and British magazines supplying fashion news included hand-colored fashion plates. By the mid-nineteenth century, fashion plates were displayed in shop windows, sold as freestanding images, and appeared regularly in the women's periodical press, often accompanied by patterns that enabled women to see and sew the latest dresses.[23] During those decades, industrial innovations in fabric manufacture and the popularization of home sewing machines fostered an appetite for new clothes among the middle and upper classes and increased the pace of fashion.

Fashion depends on quick dissemination in time and extensive distribution in space; a fashion is one only if many people simultaneously learn of it, adopt it, then renounce it. Like newspapers, fashion periodicals provided previews and updates of quickly passing events and were thus a crucial factor in the rise of fashion.[24] Fashion flourished in a modern press organized around immediacy, vividness, novelty, and conformity, and women's journals provided wide distribution for the fashion images that

SUPPLEMENT — The Queen, THE LADY'S NEWSPAPER AND COURT CHRONICLE — 3 November 1866

LATEST PARIS FASHIONS

Presented to the subscribers to the Queen The Lady's Newspaper and court chronicle

Paris, Boulevart des Italiens. 1

Figure 1. E. Préval, plate from supplement to *The Queen*, 1866.

shaped collective taste. After the 1840s, increased train travel and the abolition of paper taxes expanded the market for all journals, including those reporting on dress trends. As Margaret Beetham has shown, the elite fashion publications of the 1830s were supplanted in the 1840s and 1850s by domestic magazines directed at a middle-class female readership and focused on daily household management as secular female morality.[25] After the 1840s, the most successful women's magazines both represented the latest fashions and taught women household skills, thus mediating between aristocratic and bourgeois codes by reconciling display with regulation and restraint. As Beetham explains, women's magazines were commodities that "gave entry into a world of commodities."[26] Their seriality promoted the endlessly displaced desire that fueled consumer society, and their regularity incorporated the domestic woman into the temporal cycles of a rationalized, industrial world.

Many of the fashion images in women's periodicals were produced by female artists. The *Englishwoman's Domestic Magazine*, which published fashion plates in each issue, advertised among its readers for women who could produce wood engravings, needlework patterns, and fashion blocks.[27] The majority of fashion plates, however, were signed by well-known artists and engravers, most of them French, for British fashion *was* French fashion. French publishers produced international co-editions of their fashion gazettes, and the major British fashion magazines had Paris offices and employed French artists to illustrate Parisian trends.[28] The most important and prolific producers of fashion plates in both the French and British press were Jules David and the women of the Colin family, better known by their married names: Héloïse Leloir (1820–1874), Laure Noël (1827–1892), Anaïs Toudouze (1822–1899), and her daughter Isabelle. The Colin sisters were trained and skilled artists immersed in the world of illustration and design. Their father was an artist, they married painters, engravers, and architects, and their own artistic work extended beyond fashion plates. Leloir, for example, also painted portraits, illustrated books, and taught art to girls.[29] In addition to producing numerous plates for French design houses and French fashion magazines, the Colin sisters published work in British fashion journals, including *La Belle Assemblée* (an English publication with a French name), *The Queen*, and the *Englishwoman's Domestic Magazine*.

Produced by women, for women, fashion plates solicited a female gaze for images that put women, their bodies, and the objects that adorned them on display. Fashion imagery objectified women as sexually attractive figures designed to be looked at; women in fashion plates wear clothes that accentuate eroticized body parts, especially breasts and waists. Like other erotic imagery of the day, fashion plates often portray women in couples, and though the two women in any given plate wear different

THE VENUS OF MILO; OR, GIRLS OF TWO DIFFERENT PERIODS.

Chorus. "Look at her Big Foot! Oh, What a Waist!—and what a Ridiculous Little Head!—and no Chignon! She's no Lady! Oh, what a Fright!"

Figure 2. "The Venus of Milo; or, Girls of Two Different Periods," *Punch Almanack for 1870.*

clothes, their facial features are often almost identical. Those interchangeable faces concentrate the viewer's attention on their vividly differentiated bodies, which take up a disproportionate amount of space and are depicted in far greater detail than their countenances.[30] Features are minute and lightly sketched, while hats and dresses are highly colored; individual visages flatten and fade while clothed bodies project volume through saturated color and illusionistic shading.

The objectification of female figures in fashion plates paradoxically enhanced the subjectivity of the women who apprehended them. Women as well as men experience mastery when viewing human figures depicted solely as objects to be looked at. Women of fashion had the power to inspect, admire, and evaluate one another, as we see in an 1870 cartoon from *Punch* (fig. 2), which depicts women criticizing the Venus de Milo's fashion sense. The cartoon ridicules women's lack of true taste, but shows them using fashion as a standard for making aesthetic judgments, wielding the social powers of denigration and exclusion, and scrutinizing a partially nude female figure. In fashion plates, women's power is evident in artists' preference for brunettes, whom Victorians typed as bold, passionate, and decisive.[31] Scholars have characterized women in fashion imagery as passive and imprisoned, but plates depict them in the acts of writing, shopping, strolling, attending exhibitions, horse races, and the theater, playing badminton, rowing boats, traveling on trains without men, riding horses, and hunting with guns (fig. 3). Images of fashionable women, like those of well-dressed men, are not so much passive as impassive. The fashionable figure, arrested in the midst of leisure activities, embodies the unhurried pace and relaxed stance of a luxurious life.[32]

Fashion plates were images of women designed for female viewers, and that homoerotic structure of looking is intensified by the content and structure of the images themselves. Fashion plates almost never depicted women singly or coupled with men, but most often portrayed two women whose relationship is uncontained and undefined. An 1879 plate shows a woman on horseback staring intently at another woman whose back is to us and appears to return the rider's gaze; a male figure in the background appears to look toward and reflect the viewer, who watches the two women as they inspect one another (fig. 4).[33] The park setting and the physical distance between the two women code them as passing strangers, intensifying the erotic valence of their mutual scrutiny. The composition suggests that the two women are about to move toward one another even as the horse appears to move out of the picture frame; the frontal orientation and precarious seat of the woman riding sidesaddle suggest that she could easily slip off her horse to approach the standing woman, whose dog appears similarly inclined to move into the picture plane toward the woman on horseback. Fashion, often associated with a sexually charged inconstancy, becomes a respectable version of promiscuity for women, a form of female cruising, in which strangers who inspect each other in passing can establish an immediate intimacy because they participate in a common public culture whose medium is clothing.[34] That collective intimacy extended to the fashion magazine itself, consumed by thousands of female readers separately, but simultaneously.

A woman who looked at a Victorian fashion plate did not simply find her mirror image, for in that plate she saw not one woman but two. Fashion plates reflected her gaze itself, for in most, one woman stares at another who does not directly return her look. The woman who looked at fashion plates thus saw an image of a woman who, like herself, was able to gaze unobserved at a desirable vision of fashionable femininity. Fashion plates further thematized the female viewpoint that constituted them by placing various kinds of optical apparatus in women's hands, usually instruments that bring what is far near, an action that reflects the plate's work of bringing distant fashions and higher status closer to the female viewer. In an 1845 plate, one woman looks through a telescope just past another who nevertheless poses for the woman who holds the telescope

Figure 3. Isabelle Toudouze, plate from *Le Follet*, 1875.

Figure 4. Jules David, plate from the *Société des journaux de mode réunis*, 1879.

and for the woman who views the plate (fig. 5). In an 1891 plate, the optical instrument becomes a fashion accessory with the power to duplicate the gaze one woman directs at another (fig. 6). The woman on the right looks not at the woman next to her, but at her lorgnette—and the lorgnette looks back. Held by a female hand, angled at a fashionable woman, and floating against an empty background, that lorgnette figures the fashion plate's mobile feminine gaze.[35]

Figure 5. Plate from *Le Petit courrier des dames*, 1845.

Figure 6. Plate from *Le Journal des demoiselles*, 1891.

Figure 7. Anaïs Toudouze, plate from *Le Follet*, 1857.

At the center of an 1857 plate by Anaïs Toudouze, one woman hands another binoculars held at an angle that creates a literal line of sight between their waists (fig. 7). The raised hand, inclined torso, and slight smile of the figure on the right suggest that she is offering the glasses in a gesture that repeats the fashion plate's invitation to women who like to look. The plate shows four women, three snugly enclosed within the velvety curves of the opera box that forms the image's lower frame. The frame suggests pleasurable excess, not containment: the line that runs past the lower left-hand edge opens the box out beyond the frame; the seated woman's opulent nosegay rests outside the box and repeats its vulval imagery; and the woman on the left is literally outside the box as she stands behind it but keeps her hands near the seated woman's back. The central placement of the binoculars draws attention to the backside of the woman positioned directly behind them. Her back to us, she reproduces the viewer's physical position in front of the image, even as her image in the mirror gazes off to the side, avoiding a visual confrontation that might discomfit the beholder.

Fashion plates linked visual pleasure to tactile enjoyment, making the desire to become fashionable as inseparable from an erotics of looking and touching as the plates make looking and touching inseparable from each other. Along with the female gaze they solicit and represent, fashion plates evoke a female world saturated by a tactile sensuality represented through carefully rendered drapery and studied contrasts between the soft, curved folds of clothing and the hard angularity of objects. Often accompanied by sewing patterns, the plates touched on the technical manipulations necessary to put fashion into practice: selecting, handling, and sewing fabrics, and measuring, fitting, and dressing bodies. Women touch in many plates; in some their figures are contiguous and overlapping, in others they touch the same object, and in others they touch each other directly as they clasp each other's hands or wrap an arm around a waist or shoulder (fig. 8).[36] Their proximity to the front of the picture plane intensifies the illusion that the viewer could reach out and grasp them, representing touch as the promise of an exchange, the transfer of modish beauty as an actual handing over of body parts or fashionable objects. That exchange never quite takes place, for the viewer cannot grasp the image, and the figures themselves are never shown completing their transactions. Instead, they are captured in the midst of them, limned by the very imminence that defines consumer culture. Fashion plates relegate the viewer's desires to a realm of fantasy, in the sense of something imagined but not yet realized, a powerful promise of transformation and satisfaction that is never definitively fulfilled or thwarted.[37]

Although fashion plates link look and touch, the two are often asymmetrical. In paradigmatic fashion plates, one woman looks at and even touches another who either turns completely away from the woman looking at her or looks in her direction but not directly into her eyes (fig. 9). In many fashion plates in which women touch but do not meet eyes, tracing the direction of the apparently vacant gaze shows that the figure who seems to stare into space is looking not at nothing, but at another wom-

Figure 8. Plate from *Revue de la mode*, 1885.

Figure 9. Plate from *Le Journal des demoiselles*, 1888.

an's breasts, hips, or genital area. Anaïs Toudouze's 1848 plate of two women and a girl at the races (fig. 10) aligns the seated woman's gaze with the standing woman's breasts and also draws the viewer's attention to those breasts by making them the point at which lines drawn from the waving banner and the upraised hand of the girl would meet. What ini-

Figure 10. Anaïs Toudouze, plate from *Le Journal des jeunes filles*, 1848.

tially appears to be an abstracted stare looks purposeful and disingenuous when we see where it is directed. Its surreptitious eroticism is heightened by Toudouze's representation of the seated woman's hands: with one she grazes her shawl, while with the other she presses the standing girl's fingers into her lap, precisely where the absence of buttons on her skirt suggests a gap or opening.

The convention of posing one woman to look at another who does not return her gaze creates an erotic atmosphere redolent of voyeurism. Like the beholder who looks at the fashion plate, the woman who looks at another in the plate does so all the more freely because she is unobserved. An aura of autoerotic reverie envelops many of the figures in fashion plates, inviting their beholders to indulge in similar meditations. Modern fashion has always been associated with fantasy, with whimsical invention and erotic fabrication; in fashion plates, the blank faces of the figures make them appear to be fantasizing, enjoying vision without consequence and looking liberated from acting.[38] In some fashion plates, those blank looks allow obscene touches to appear as the polite gestures of everyday intimacy. In an 1881 plate, the ruffle on the wrist of the woman in the center blends imperceptibly into the lace at her bosom, so that the woman on the left who politely grasps her companion's wrist also appears to graze her breast (fig. 11). An 1888 plate shows a seated woman, one hand buried deep in a small bag that rests on her thigh just below and alongside her crotch, the other hand resting on a table but also tangled in the fur trim of the dress of the woman standing in the center (fig. 12). Since the standing woman looks down, away from her visitor, the woman who touches her does so unobserved. While furtively handling her social peer's dress, the seated woman gazes at the well-dressed servant who, eyes slightly averted, hands her tea and also has a hand buried in her pocket. The servant's decorum creates a masturbatory allusion that links the maid and her mistress's guest.

Other plates play with the dynamic of grasping and unattainability inherent in the fashion image by translating fashion's processes of observation and imitation into visual plays on reaching for the clothed female body. An 1854 plate takes up a motif popular in nineteenth-century pornography, the game of blindman's buff, played here by three women with a statue of Diana behind them (fig.13).[39] A blindfolded woman touches a woman who looks at her, while a third woman peeks at them both from behind the statue. As is frequently the case in fashion images, the woman who looks is shown with a hand at crotch level, where she gathers up her skirt so that, barely touching the blindfolded woman's skirt, we see a minuscule foot whose scale and form make it resemble a displaced clitoris. The outspread arms of the blindfolded figure and the central placement

Figure 11. Plate from *The Queen*, 1881.

of the scarf that covers her eyes and cascades down her neck accentuate
that she is offered up to the viewer as well as to the two female figures
flanking her. The composition comments on the delights of fashion plates
themselves, which provide the pleasure of looking at an image of a woman
who cannot look back and represent the appeal of physical contact without resistance or confrontation.

Figure 12. Plate from *Le Journal des demoiselles*, 1888.

Fashion plates frequently depicted girls whose elaborate clothing and poised stances reflected their incorporation of maternal taste and discipline. Victorian culture represented girls as epistemological paradoxes, so innocent that they could be intensively eroticized without raising comment.[40] But unlike images and stories that eroticized girls for a mixed audience of men and women, fashion imagery displayed girls in erotic dynamics with adult women for the delectation of a female audience. In

Figure 13. A. de Taverne, plate from *Le Petit courrier des dames, 1854.*

The History of Sexuality, Foucault argued that the intensification of family ties in the nineteenth century also sexualized them, and fashion plates show that in the process all cross-generational ties were eroticized, including those between adult women and girls. In many plates, the girl becomes an accessory or toy like a fan, lorgnette, purse, pet, or doll. Indeed, children's literature and pattern books explicitly called girls their mothers' "live dolls."[41] Many images position a girl between two women; in some cases both women touch her, in others one appears to offer her to the other. Some plates arrange girls as worshipful supplicants at the altar of an adult woman's beauty, gazing at a woman from her shorter height or from a kneeling position (fig. 14). Others depict a girl who attempts to attract adult women's attention by clasping a dress, arm, or hand, or by twisting her body to face them (fig. 15). Designed to be objects of an appreciative female gaze inside and outside the image, girls in fashion plates also embody a desire to look at and touch a woman, a desire figured as both self-abasing and self-important. Fashion plates make evident the girl's desire to be seen as well as to see; they activate a female pleasure in looking at women that triggers an equally strong desire to be looked at by them.

Victorian fashion iconography disproves the still influential claims that men look and women are looked at, that only male viewers enjoy corporeal spectacles of femininity, that voyeuristic scopophilia is split from exhibitionistic fetishism, and that the beholder must choose between desire or identification. Fashion plates were popular because women who wanted to turn themselves into spectacles of femininity took pleasure in looking at images that reduced women to lovely bodies filling out beautiful clothing. Far from creating a utopian reciprocity that bypassed objectification and voyeurism, fashion plates trained Victorian women to assume the appearance of middle-class femininity by indulging their pleasure in looking at female bodies, their longing to touch them, and their desire to control them.

DISCIPLINE AND PUNISHMENT IN THE FASHION MAGAZINE

The fantasy of a woman exhibiting and disciplining another woman's body attained its most spectacular form not in the visual images but in the printed pages of England's leading fashion magazine. In 1868, almost every fashion plate in the *Englishwoman's Domestic Magazine* included a girl alongside two adult women, and that same year a debate raged in letters to the editor about whether parents, especially mothers, should use corporal punishment to discipline children, particularly girls past puberty. The fashion plate's image of the quietly contained, fashionable girl who

Figure 14. Plate from *Le Journal des demoiselles*, 1887.

Figure 15. Plate from *Le Journal des demoiselles*, 1882.

worships her female elders became a story of unruly daughters and stern mothers. The fashion image's obsession with dressing and covering the body became the reader's drive to expose it; the proud mien of the plate's figures mutated into narratives of humiliation and shame. Only one element remained constant from image to text: the world in which both rituals were staged was dominated by female actors and objects.

"I put out my hands, which she fastened together with a cord by the wrists. Then making me lie down across the foot of the bed, face downwards, she very quietly and deliberately, putting her left hand around my waist, gave me a shower of smart slaps with her open right hand. . . . [R]aising the birch, I could hear it whiz in the air, and oh, how terrible it felt as it came down, and as its repeated strokes came swish, swish, swish on me!"[42] This description of a girl being birched by a woman first appeared in an 1870 supplement to the *Englishwoman's Domestic Magazine* that extended a debate about corporal punishment raging in the journal since 1867. Editor Samuel Beeton justified publishing the monthly supplements, each consisting of eight large, double-columned pages of small type, by citing the overwhelming volume of letters received on a topic "which, of late years," had "aroused . . . intense, not to say passionate interest."[43] Beeton priced the supplement at two shillings and made it available by post, thus guaranteeing its accessibility to middle-class readers. Like the *Englishwoman's Domestic Magazine*, a respectable family publication that advertised in the pages of *Cobbin's Illustrated Family Bible*, the supplement presumed an audience of housewives who would be drawn to its advertisements for *Beeton's Book of Home Pets* and *The Mother's Thorough Resource Book*.[44]

The *Englishwoman's Domestic Magazine*, as its title announced, was aimed at the middle-class women whose homes defined the nation. By the 1860s, the thirty-two-page monthly cost sixpence and reached roughly 50,000 readers per issue.[45] With two color fashion plates in each issue, a republican editor who supported women's employment and suffrage, and articles on "The Englishwoman in London," "Great Men and Their Mothers," and "Can We Live on £300 a Year?" the journal combined fashion, feminism, and thrift.[46] Fashion magazines had always had heterogeneous content—astronomer Mary Somerville first encountered algebra while reading "an illustrated Magazine of Fashion"—and the *Englishwoman's Domestic Magazine* prided itself on being learned and political as well as practical and stylish.[47] The magazine had both women and men on its staff, and Isabella Beeton codirected it with her husband until her death in 1865, soon after she completed a best-selling opus on household management.

The publication of correspondence revealing women's preoccupation with corporal punishment and its overlap with pornography might surprise us today, but only because we erroneously assume that Victorians imagined women and girls to be asexual unless responding to male initiative. Victorians themselves did not set such limits on female desire, and many found the letters on corporal punishment published in the eminently respectable *Englishwoman's Domestic Magazine* provocative, with their use of onomatopoeia, teasing delay, first-person testimony, and punning humor, all typical of Victorian pornography. A letter from "A Happy Mother," published in 1869, explained that the author put cream on her children before whipping them, so that punishing them produced whipped cream: "I scream—ice cream."[48] Some readers denounced the correspondence as indelicate and indecent, warning that it might arouse male readers, and accusing women who flogged children of improper motives.[49] In the 1870 supplement, a "mother" worried about how a gentlemen might respond to finding an otherwise "useful" publication marred by "immodest" descriptions of punishments by "ladies."[50] One letter fulminated against "people who take pleasure in giving . . . exact details of the degrading way in which they punish their children." A correspondent signing "A Mother Loved By Her Children" condemned "the indelicacy in which every disgusting detail is dwelt on" by a woman who described a punishment she had received from another woman. "A Lady" protested "the offence to decency and propriety in publishing vulgar details" about "the removal of clothes and 'bare persons.'"[51] Readers who protested the indecency of the letters recognized that reading about punishment could provoke sexual sensations in both men and women.

The voluminous correspondence began as a short query in 1867: "A Young Mother would like a few hints—the result of experience—on the early education and discipline of children." The first two published responses opposed whipping, arguing that mothers who resorted to physical punishment would lose the self-control needed to discipline children properly.[52] Though Beeton himself opposed corporal punishment, he published many letters in favor of it. The debate quickly became more specific: whether it was proper for adult women to punish girls, especially those past puberty, by whipping them on the "bare person." Whether writing for or against corporal punishment, correspondents provided detailed accounts of inflicting, receiving, and witnessing ritual chastisements in which older women restrained, undressed, and whipped younger ones. Letters described mothers, aunts, teachers, and female servants forcing girls and young women to remove their drawers, tying girls to pieces of furniture, pinning back their arms, placing them in handcuffs, or requiring them to count the number of strokes administered. Some letters were written from the point of view of mothers and guardians who had to impose discipline, others from the perspective of those reminiscing about having been disciplined. Many women provided testimonials that began with recollections of having "screamed, and shrieked, and implored" to no avail and ended by celebrating the moral benefits of chastisement.[53]

Fashion plates obsessed with dressing the female body metamorphosed into miniature narratives intent on undressing it. Repeated references to punishing girls "the old-fashioned way," on bare, exposed buttocks, cast a new light on the fashion plate's tendency to view women and girls from behind.[54] Letters even debated exactly how girls should be undressed. In a letter framed as a memory of being whipped by an uncle and thus converted to the benefits of corporal punishment, a woman urged that the "child must actually take off *for herself* such garments as are in the way, and must be whipped till she submits without fighting."[55] Correspondents to the women's magazine pedantically explained that exposing the girl's "bare person" was "the very soul of the chastisement" because it activated "the important agency of shame" and increased the pain inflicted.[56]

Corporal punishment is where pornography, usually considered a masculine affair, intersects with fashion magazines targeted at women. Both types of publications were mass-produced commodities that created an aura of luxury, and both depended on the relative democratization inherent in an economy organized around consumption and leisure.[57] Pornographic publications and monthly women's journals had similar formats: both combined short stories, poems, historical essays, serial fiction, current events, and letters to the editor; both featured detachable color prints that could be sold separately; and both released special Christmas issues.[58] Their common interest in corporal punishment led to even more concrete links between pornography and fashion magazines. John Camden Hotten, the publisher of many pornographic works, advertised a pseudoscientific study of *Flagellation and the Flagellants* in the supplement to the *Englishwomen's Domestic Magazine*.[59] Other pornographic publications actually reprinted verbatim material first published in fashion magazines.[60] In his exhaustive bibliography of pornography, Henry Spencer Ashbee mentioned the "remarkable and lengthened correspondence" about flagellation in "domestic periodicals" alongside his discussion of flagellation in "bawdy book[s]" such as *Venus School-Mistress* and *Boarding-School Bumbrusher; or, the Distresses of Laura*.[61]

The *Englishwoman's Domestic Magazine* was more available to women readers than pornography, but Victorian pornography was not the exclusively male province it is often assumed to be.[62] Like the fashion press, pornographic literature expanded during the middle decades of the nineteenth century; between 1834 and 1880, the Vice Society confiscated 385,000 prints and photographs, 80,000 books and pamphlets, and 28,000 sheets of obscene songs and circulars.[63] Who wrote and read pornography remains a mystery: publishers falsified dates and places of publication; authors wrote under pseudonyms; and individuals left few public traces of their purchases and reading experiences.[64] The scant evidence we have suggests that pornography was a predominantly but not entirely male domain. Newspapers reported women publishing and selling obscene books and texts; one woman has been documented as the author of a French pornographic novel that circulated in England; and women of all classes frequented the Holywell Street area where obscene books and prints were sold and often visible in shop windows.[65] After publisher and bookseller George Cannon died in 1854, his wife ran the business for ten more years; in 1830 a police officer testified that Cannon hired women who "went about to . . . boarding schools . . . for the purpose of selling" obscene books, "and if they could not sell them to the young ladies, they threw them over the garden walls, so that they might get them."[66] Women did not have to purchase pornography directly to read it, however, since they might easily find any sexually explicit books that male family members brought home.

Women did not need to turn to pornography to encounter sexually arousing descriptions of older women disciplining younger girls; they could read material in the pages of a ladies' home journal that would be reprinted as pornography. The correspondence about corporal punishment blurred distinctions not only between pornography and the women's press but between male and female readers. Some worried that the magazine had become so obscene that it needed to be hidden from both; Olivia Brook wrote in 1870 that she now put the magazine "out of reach of any casual observer, and where especially no gentlemen can read it."[67] Some of the letters Beeton published were written by real mothers, others suggest men impersonating women, some seem to describe actual events, others have the hallmarks of fantasy, but all appeared in a magazine directed at women interested in fashion, gardening, and housekeeping.[68] The letters appeared in a "Conversazione" section that interspersed accounts of corporal punishment with requests for advice about etiquette, courtship, cosmetics, stain removal, and medical problems. The quotidian details of women's everyday domestic lives existed alongside with letters that described the "real struggle for mastery" between older and younger women.[69]

The popularity of corporal punishment as a topic in both the *Englishwoman's Domestic Magazine* and pornography attests to the convergence of women's and men's erotic fantasies about discipline. Although twentieth-century scholars have represented the Victorian interest in flagellation as a quintessentially male obsession, beating fantasies were not the property of any one gender, social group, or psychological type. In Victorian England, a birching scene could surface in the journal of an unremarkable upper-class girl who spent her days studying, practicing the

piano, and taking walks. In 1850, thirteen-year-old Anne King wrote a
short play in her journal about a schoolmistress who catechizes a boy
about his German; as he stutters, she "holds up" and "shakes" a cane
that she then uses to punish him:

SCH.: You naughty boy I declare
Take care that the tense is perfect next time. . . .
(She takes the cane and punishes the pupil who laughs heartily in spite of his
terror and who at last escapes).
Oh! That naughty Tommy, will he always be so idle? He *shall* make his imper-
fect tense perfect before he comes to me again.[70]

Like many pornographers, King used dramatic form to create a sense of
immediacy and to encourage the implied reader to picture her characters'
bodies on display.[71] And like many pornographers, King associated discipline with the pun, which simultaneously follows and breaks linguistic
rules. That combination of submission and defiance is echoed in the pun's
content, which plays on the two meanings of "imperfect"—lack of mastery, and a grammatical tense to be mastered.

Anne King's miniature drama of punishment shows that flagellation
scenarios represented, interpellated, and excited women as well as men,
and that the power differences inherent in scenes of discipline and punishment were erotically charged in any gender configuration. Her scenario
focused on a female teacher birching a boy, but ritualized accounts of
older women whipping adult men or girls were also common. In *The
Other Victorians*, Steven Marcus influentially argued that all pornographic accounts of whipping, even those that represent women birching
or being birched, were nothing but displaced versions of repressed fantasies about father-son sex.[72] That interpretation assumes that erotic desire
between women was irrelevant to Victorian society, and that sex between
men or family members was impossible to represent directly. In fact, the
only impulse Victorian pornography repressed was repression itself. Victorian pornographers represented same-sex acts of all kinds and freely
indulged their obsession with incest, including sex between fathers and
sons. A typical book-length narrative depicted a protagonist of either sex
progressing from sex with servants, neighbors, friends, and distant relatives, to sex with brothers and sisters, then with mother and father. The
male character who pens *Letters from a Friend in Paris* praises "the fine
parental prick" and describes a man who "had under his eyes while sod-
omising his wife the beautiful form of his loved daughter writhing in all
the lust of her mamma's exciting titillations," while in *The New Ladies'
Tickler*, a niece "admire[s] the softness and beauty of the charms" her
aunt exposes in the process of birching her.[73] The psychoanalytic schema
assumes that desires forbidden by internalized prohibitions can find only
oblique expression, but the carnivalesque world of Victorian pornogra-

phy acknowledged prohibitions by defying them and turning them into a source of sexual pleasure.

Victorian pornography helps to explain how the family could simultaneously be organized around sexual difference and be a site of homoerotic desire, for in it the family is a hotbed of sex, but same-sex acts do not imply fixed sexual identities. Representations of sex between men and sex between women were never confined to specialized publications. Sex between women was regularly featured in pornographic texts and in images that depicted two or more women engaging in tribadism, oral sex, anal sex, digital penetration, mutual masturbation, and sex with dildos.[74] Flagellation literature described women achieving orgasm from punishing girls and penetrating girls with fingers and dildos while birching them.[75] But the notion of an exclusively homosexual orientation—or an exclusively heterosexual one—had yet to emerge. *The Sins of the Cities of the Plain* (1881), often cited as one of the first texts to express gay sexual identity, made its protagonist's "early development of . . . Pederastic Ideas" compatible with diverse sexual combinations. The male narrator has sex with a female cousin and with another woman while her brother spies on them; the sister and brother then have sex while the narrator penetrates the brother.[76] In the second volume, the famous male cross-dresser Ernest Boulton appears and recalls seducing a beautiful female milliner while passing as a woman; after engaging the milliner in conversation about fashion, Boulton goes home with her and performs oral sex on her in his female guise.

The convergence of pornography and women's magazines on the topic of flagellation points to their common origins in nineteenth-century liberal democracy, which promoted the free circulation of ideas among individuals who could demonstrate self-control and tasteful judgment. Pornography had affinities with Enlightenment and utilitarian ideals regarding the empirical investigation of nature and quests for knowledge, increased well-being, and merit-based rewards.[77] Fashion was a feminized version of liberal democracy, for it depended on a woman's ability to train her taste and accommodate her individual style to fluctuating group rules. By following fashion codes, women learned to fit their bodies into a social mold; by improvising on those codes, as fashion itself demanded, women developed the kind of restricted autonomy associated with liberal subjectivity. As Mary Haweis explained in *The Art of Beauty* (1878), clothing was a form of individual aesthetic expression and therefore had to follow "the fundamental principle of art . . . that *people may do as they like*."[78] The liberty underlying the art of dress also upheld of liberalism's ideal of personal freedom as a source of originality and political renewal.

The correspondence columns of fashion magazines allowed women to participate in the public discourse central to liberal politics. Corporal punishment was a matter of genuine disagreement for the readers of the *Englishwoman's Domestic Magazine*, split between those who abhorred it and those who thought it instilled obedience to traditional parental authority.[79] Editor Samuel Beeton highlighted the fashion magazine's engagement with liberalism by titling the correspondence column a "Conversazione," an allusion to the traditions of Italian civic humanism. He defended the publication of controversial letters by calling them a "debate" and reminded readers of the intrinsic merits of airing majority and minority opinions when he urged them to be "wise enough to hear both sides, and determine for themselves what is best to do under their own particular set of circumstances. . . . [F]reedom has been given to all to express their opinions, for without such liberty nothing can be thoroughly sifted, and we have no desire to repress the candid thoughts of writers because they may differ from ourselves or from the majority."[80] The discourse of liberalism helped Samuel Beeton to justify publishing letters whose very popularity branded them as the obscene limit of public discussion.

The overlap between pornography and fashion magazines underscores the eroticism of the Victorian interest in punishment, but what remains to be understood is how both kinds of media connected punishment to fashion. In pornographic texts as well as in the *Englishwoman's Domestic Magazine*, birching was often a question of style. Punishment itself was subject to sudden changes in mode. A letter to the *Englishwoman's Domestic Magazine* from "An English Mamma" described exposing the girl's bare buttocks as "the old-fashioned style."[81] Discipline could become an excuse to shop for and show off costumes and accessories. Letter-writers asked for the addresses of stores selling birch rods and suggested other instruments more suited to ladies.[82] "A Lover of Obedience" wrote, "I object to the rod as unfeminine, so up to ten or twelve years old, I whip all my children . . . with a slipper."[83] Correspondents argued about whether girls should wear special costumes for punishment; one letter used French, the language of fashion and sex, to refer to the "toilette des condanées," while another recommended forcing children to wear the clothes of the opposite sex as a form of punishment.[84]

Pornographic texts echoed the terminology of fashion magazines in lavish descriptions of costumes designed especially for birching. The narrator of *The Merry Order of St. Bridget* spends almost as much time describing clothing as she does recounting flagellation scenes. Each woman holds a rod purchased in Paris and "tied up with ribbons which corresponded with the colours of her dress."[85] The servant who narrates the adventures of "the order of the rod" in letters to a female friend notes that she works for a "Queen of Fashion," and that upon initiation into the group, she receives "a chemise of fine lawn, trimmed with Valenciennes lace and insertion; a soft white flannel petticoat worked round the bottom with silk," and a bodice and slippers that she describes in similar detail, using the language of fashion-plate captions.[86] Dress matters all the more in texts where it is removed. In *The Romance of Chastisement*, a lady about to punish a girl whom she calls "that fine young lady from the Fashions [sic] Book" comments that it is "a pity to disarrange so elegant a costume," then substitutes the outfit for the girl by nicknaming her "the Sprigged Muslin."[87]

Fashion magazines and pornography both represented corporal punishment as a matter of forming social networks. Modish clothing created class bonds through emulation, pornography represented women banding together to enjoy their taste for birching theatricals, and correspondence in fashion magazines gathered readers into a community, formed by print. One writer even suggested that "advocates of chastisement would do well to communicate with each other" directly.[88] Just as readers reproduced the clothes in fashion plates, correspondents described imitating what they had read in letters about corporal punishment. "EMMA" wrote that "though not an advocate of corporal punishment, on the 1st of last month I was so much struck . . . by the description by A SCHOOL-MISTRESS of a most ceremonious method of inflicting punishment that I determined to follow exactly the same method and try it the same morning."[89] The pornographic *Merry Order of St. Bridget* similarly emphasized that corporal punishment was a social activity that resulted in competitive emulation. The women form a club, "a regular whipping society," which demands that whipping be a collective affair; after learning that one woman retires every day to birch her husband, a club member declares, "[W]e won't have any private practice here."[90]

Fashion expresses rank, and letters published in the *Englishwoman's Domestic Magazine* set forth corporal punishment as yet another ritual display of distinction. Those who opposed corporal punishment labeled it unfeminine, degraded, and vulgar, while those who upheld it warned that it had to be carried out in a stately manner, reminding readers that it was practiced on "[b]oys of the very highest birth" and in "high-class ladies' boarding-schools."[91] Pornographic representations of birching similarly associated it with prestige.[92] The rules of the *Merry Order of St. Bridget* require each member to devise a special outfit that becomes a sign of her refinement, and fashion and whipping converge as ways to acquire status through imitation. The servant who narrates explains that since joining the whipping club and acquiring her own whipping costume, "I am as ardent a votary of whipping now as any of the ladies I have served."[93] Becoming as well-dressed and as devoted to whipping as "the ladies" allows the narrator to place her service to them in the past tense, suggesting that sharing her employers' taste for corporal punishment has raised her to their level.

Though often accused of promoting excess, fashion demonstrated its adherents' discipline by displaying their ability to contain their bodies and desires within the parameters set by rigid dress codes. The *Englishwoman's Domestic Magazine* correspondence described corporal punishment as requiring and instilling similar qualities of "duty," "obedience," and "discipline" in both punisher and punished.[94] Sometimes the restraint was literal; one writer recommended handcuffing disobedient girls.[95] Other letters understood restraint and self-control in terms of comportment. A letter from a mother who signed herself "Pro-Rod" testified that whipping her daughters had produced "very good, well-behaved girls"; those who wrote against whipping emphasized that it was incompatible with the self-control required of mothers as disciplinarians.[96] In fashion, restrictive clothing symbolized the self-control and leisure of the lady of rank; in corporal punishment, the self-contained adult who punished an unruly and humiliated child signified the adult's superior status. One writer speculated about whether one should lay an adolescent to be punished "across the knee" in order to treat her "just like a child"; another that a girl must "make all her own arrangements for her punishment" and thus lose her "sense of power."[97]

Just as corporal punishment undid the clothes so carefully arranged in the fashion plate, it transformed the plate's authoritative glamour into the power to inflict humiliation: "There must be a certain amount of uncovering, and I think the party administering the chastisement should herself unfasten and lower the girls' drawers after she is placed over the knee. This adds to the feeling of shame produced, and convinces the child that there is an authority which it would be well for her not to set at nought."[98] Another writer described punishment as a loss of self: "[T]he proceeding so surprised and humiliated my proud self that I could hardly believe in my own identity."[99] The dissolution of the self in shame was also understood, however, to lead to tonic reform of the castigated subject. Both fashion plates and corporal punishment promised to create a better, more appealing self through identifications with powerful, idealized figures. As we have seen, the admiration that fashion plates provoked in the viewer were reflected in images of girls who gazed adoringly at aloof women; letters about corporal punishment described the awed attachment that those punished felt for their adult disciplinarians. A male correspondent explained how punishment could bolster both parties: after being flogged at fifteen by the head governess at his school, the author "felt ever afterwards . . . a sort of sentimental devotion towards this noble and stately-looking young lady."[100]

Like the fashion magazine, pornography represented corporal punishment as a matter of abjection and idealization, capable of creating generational hierarchies even among adult women. In *The Romance of Chastisement*, a magnificently dressed schoolmistress punishes her French teacher, who then "flung herself at her Majesty's feet, kissed her hand, pressed it to her breast, and . . . implored her pardon with tears, calling her Mistress—like a little child."[101] "Fear and shame . . . the strongest passions" of those punished, translated easily into veneration. In *Romance*, one female cousin recalls in a letter to another, "I . . . never lost my terror of the rod, yet doted on the hand that wielded it, as if it were a lover's, and in the very agony of discipline would seek to gratify my tormentress by the freest display of my naked person."[102] Those words are spoken by a woman who remembers a childhood whipping she received from a well-dressed woman who became the "object" of her "adoration," and whose gaze mirrors both her own image and the older woman's desire: "I saw my nakedness with her eyes, and exalted in the lascivious joy that whipping me afforded her."[103] In an "Exhibition of Female Flagellants," a woman testifies that she "could never see a woman of elegance, with a hand and arm she liked, without wishing and seeking the pleasure [of a whipping] from her," while another "idolize[s] Lady Caroline's hand and arm" and cannot "bear to see it hold the rod without the ornaments of pearls, bracelets, a wedding and diamond rings."[104] Pornography equated the effects of punishment with those of fashionable dress; both reduce other women to abject admiration and self-abasement.

Pornography and women's magazines alike linked fashion to scenes of female punishment, but pornographic descriptions of birching had one obvious difference from those published in the *Englishwoman's Domestic Magazine*: they were more explicit and enthusiastic about the sexually arousing effects of birching, being birched, or writing and reading about corporal punishment. Correspondents who supported corporal punishment never admitted to feeling sexual pleasure in administering or receiving it, while opponents alluded euphemistically to the "indecent" pleasures of birching only to condemn them. Victorian pornographers, by contrast, wrote openly of the satisfaction whipping gave women and men. *The Birchen Bouquet*, one of the pornographic compendia that reprinted letters from the *Englishwoman's Domestic Magazine*, remarked, "That a number of ladies take a secret pleasure in whipping children with a birch rod, particularly grown up boys and girls, is too well credited to need comment."[105] A story in the pornographic periodical *The Boudoir* described one woman birching another, then rushing "on her victim with all the energy of an excited tribade, turning the girl over on her back and burying her face between Miss Bessie's thighs, as she licked and sucked up every drop of spendings from her victim's quivering q-m, to the great delight of Miss Polly, who sat down and frigged herself in sympathy at the voluptuous sight."[106]

Pornography satirized fashion-magazine correspondence for confining the sexual pleasures of whipping to the tacit realm of innuendo. A rhyming exchange between a spinster and a matron, entitled "The Charm: A Dialogue for the 'Englishwoman's Conversazione,'" claimed that the only implausible element of the correspondence in the *Englishwoman's Domestic Magazine* was its disavowal of the joys of birching. After hearing the spinster recount how she birched her niece, the matron responds: "How nice to hear of an authentic whipping. / Those stories in the Ladies' Magazines / Are scarcely credible, that is to say, / They *may* be true, but brought behind the scenes, / The sense of being there they don't convey," because they conceal that "it's *pleasant* while you're whipping." Mothers and other female guardians wrote letters about copying the punishments detailed in the *Englishwoman's Domestic Magazine*, but none did so with the brio of the matron in "A Charm," who responds to the spinster's description by declaring, "I'll go at once and give it to the Girls!"[107] Where the fashion magazine created a gap between longing and fulfillment, pornography promised to close it by making language interchangeable with action: to hear about a whipping is to execute one; to read about sexual pleasure is to experience it.[108]

Pornography attributed women's pleasure in whipping girls to the joy of asserting power and privilege, including the prerogative of sexual knowledge and pleasure. *Indecent Whipping*, a publication hovering between pornography and the fashion magazine, included a letter from a "schoolmistress" who discovers that her female pupils "indulged" in "conversation of the filthiest type . . . and the most disgusting practices." She then forces the girls to "undress . . . to their shoes and chemises" to be birched.[109] Girls are punished for voluntarily displaying bodies that older women can expose or conceal at will. In *The Birchen Bouquet*, a girl who whips another and views her "nakedness" is then punished by an adult women and forced to give her "a sight of those parts which you are so fond of exposing."[110] In another tale, female teachers show "evident excitement" as they "make the tips of the rod twine round" a student's thighs, belly, and buttocks to "take the bad thoughts out of her."[111] Prohibition and indulgence merge in the act of punishment, but are separated along generational lines. The sexual excitement forbidden to girls can be openly exhibited by women, for whom the act of driving out the girls' "bad thoughts" arouses their own. Pornography flaunted what fashion-magazine correspondents acknowledged only as an outrage: the erotic thrill that Victorians of both sexes felt at the prospect of a female authority bending a girl to her will.

Live Dolls

Where fashion magazines offered images of women with girls who could be dressed, caressed, and abused like dolls, children's literature tendered stories of imperious girls punishing, desiring, adoring, and displaying dolls that resembled fashionable adult women. In Victorian children's literature, dolls are to girls what, in the fashion press, girls were to women: beautifully dressed objects to admire or humiliate, simulacra of femininity that inspire fantasies of omnipotence and subjection. Today we are most familiar with Victorian depictions of girls as utterly innocent angels threatened by demonic, hypersexual men, as Little Nell is by Quilp in Charles Dickens's *The Old Curiosity Shop*. But as we have seen, Victorians did not confine objectification, domination, and idealization of women to men. The stories they told about girls and their dolls show that Victorians imagined girls as well as adult women enmeshed in idealizing and aggressive homoerotic fantasies.

Take two examples, one of idealization, one of aggression. The first is from the early-twentieth-century memoirs of Anna Klumpke, as told to Lilian Whiting, whom we will encounter again in chapter 6. Anna Klumpke (1856–1942) was born in the United States to a mother who encouraged her daughter's artistic ambitions. Whiting singled out one childhood incident as prefiguring the subsequent course of Klumpke's life: her intense response to Rosa Bonheur's painting *The Horse Fair*, and subsequent acquisition of a Rosa Bonheur doll dressed in the men's clothes Bonheur wore in a famous portrait:

> As a nursery treasure it was a great success. . . . Her enthusiasm was deeply stirred, and her mother continued to excite her childish fancy. Taking Anna on her lap, she taught her these lines from Longfellow . . . Lives of great men all remind us / We can make our lives sublime, / And, departing, leave behind us / Footprints on the sands of time.[112]

As an adult, Klumpke became both a painter in her own right and Bonheur's second spouse. Past and present, replica and original, miniature and life-size coalesced when childhood dream became adult romance. Looking back on her life for Whiting, Klumpke recalled her identification with the ideal represented by the Bonheur doll and Longfellow's "great men," along with the "enthusiasm" stirred by the doll and the "fancy" excited by her mother. The doll prefigures the adult Klumpke's marital and maternal bond with the much older Bonheur, who in turn raffishly courted her young lover by telling her, "If I love you it is because at times you remind me so much of my mother."[113] Mother, doll, and female lover merge as ideal objects of perfectly realized desire.

In Klumpke's idyllic tale, a female doll dressed in men's clothes comes to life to be loved for life, but many Victorian children's books were equally interested in the other side of doll play, in which girls exercised absolute dominion over dolls who resembled ladies of fashion. Fantasies of girls punishing dolls and being punished by them appeared regularly in fiction for young readers, such as Clara Bradford's *Ethel's Adventures in the Doll Country* (1880). The story begins after Ethel's doll runs away because Ethel has punished her. The narrative that follows is governed by the dream logic of texts like *Alice in Wonderland*; events abruptly start and stop and inanimate objects come to life. Ethel follows her plaything to doll country, which is populated by hundreds of birch rods, who speak, "leer" (50), and rub their hands in anticipation of beating Ethel for having mistreated her doll (fig. 16).[114] The rods, we learn, "punish all incivility" to the inhabitants of doll country, "'And we enjoy doing it,' said the voice of the Rod. 'Oh, don't we just, ah ha!'" (35). When Ethel tells the Rod she is tired of him, he rejoins, "'But I am not tired of you: you are such a charming child that I should like to have the pleasure of'—'Whipping me, I suppose?' asked Ethel. 'Quite so, my dear! What wonderful penetration you have!'" (40–41). The Rod pops up everywhere: he swings himself over Ethel's head (50), "wriggle[s] about as though whipping someone," (78), announces "*my* business is to bring up little girls properly," and reminds Ethel, "Little girls should always be submissive to their superiors" (76). When the Fairy who rules doll country cautions Ethel that if she speaks, she will be punished, the Rod comments, "'Shan't I like it?' and . . . smacked his lips" (80).

The little girl also puts herself in the Rod's place: "Ethel could hear him saying to himself—'What fun it will be! Won't she scream?'" (112). Ethel can so easily envisage the pleasures of a birch rod because she takes a similar delight in meting out punishment to her doll. Resentful of her poor reception in doll country, she mutters, "I shall just whip those disagreeable dolls tomorrow . . . for coming here—showing off their forlorn condition—to excite pity, I suppose" (83). When the damaged doll testifies against the girl who harmed her, we learn the history of Ethel's relationship to her plaything; the doll recalls how, after an initial period of receiving clothes, furniture, attention, and love, Ethel rejected her for a showier new "lady" doll: "'[T]he more the merrier,' said my fickle little mistress" (172, 152). Faced with the doll's piteous testimony about the punishments she subsequently received, Ethel remains unrepentant: "[T]he doll was mine, and I could do as I liked—besides, she deserved it" (175). Like birching narratives, doll stories created polarized states of abjection and idolization, and here the doll worships the lovely girl who abused her: "[I]n my eyes she looked altogether beautiful," she testifies (126), and recalls that even when she ran away, she pictured Ethel's "curls shaking

Figure 16. From Clara Bradford, *Ethel's Adventures in Doll Country*, 1880.

about her shoulders. They were such pretty curls, and fell softly on your face when she was dressing you!" (178). Though the doll airs her grievances, she maintains her submissive attitude towards her mistress: "[L]et me beg of your majesty to be lenient with dear little Ethel, for after all, *I love her still*!" (180).

Ethel's Adventures in the Doll Country is one of many doll tales that depict the little girl as a fickle lover, imperious mistress, and beloved idol, and dramatize the girl-doll relationship as one involving visual fascination, sensual contact, domination, and submission. The ease with which both Ethel and her doll shift between the opposite poles of those erotic dynamics is also typical of doll tales: Ethel is threatened by the whip as she threatens her doll; the formerly admired doll is debased and acquires a potential for vengeance. *Ethel* stands out from the dozens of other doll tales published between 1826 and 1890 in only two ways: it is the only tale to personify an instrument of punishment, and one of the few to abjure a moral conclusion. Ethel never shows remorse for tyrannizing her doll; when the Rod chides Ethel that she would not like to receive the treatment she metes out to her dolls, Ethel haughtily replies that she is not a doll, and mocks the Rod's reminder to "[d]o unto others as you would be done by" (84). Like women in fashion magazines and pornography who asserted their right to do as they liked with their young female charges, Ethel claims the right to inflict suffering on a doll to whom she attributes sentience, precisely because the doll's imagined pain yields the girl pleasure.

The affinities between fashion media and doll tales, evinced by their shared attraction to scenarios of idealization and aggression, are not surprising, given the many links between fashion and dolls in modern Europe. Before economic and technological developments made it easy to disseminate fashion plates, Europeans exchanged life-size mannequins dressed in new clothing styles, called "fashion dolls."[115] Like fashion, doll manufacture expanded in the nineteenth century. In addition to cheap and plain dolls made of rag, wood, and leather, many stores began to sell more expensive wax and porcelain dolls, often with elaborate wardrobes. Seraphina, the narrator of *The Doll and Her Friends* (1852), epitomizes the doll as luxury item, "six inches high, with jointed limbs and an enamel face, a slim waist and upright figure, an amiable smile, an intelligent eye, and hair dressed in the first style of fashion."[116] France led the production of fashionably dressed dolls, although Germany and England were also prominent doll producers, and an English company invented paper dolls.[117] As in the fashion industry, many leading dollmakers were men, but women did much of the artisanal labor, and several directed dollmaking firms and published doll magazines.[118]

Print and visual culture continued to link dolls and fashion long after plates replaced dolls as a means of disseminating new clothing styles. Fashion magazines reported on dolls, carried doll advertisements, and offered patterns for doll clothes.[119] Dolls appeared in fashion plates on the laps of mothers or held aloft by girls whose hands disappear under the dolls' long skirts (fig. 17). Dolls and fashion became so identified with each other that in the 1860s several magazines were devoted to doll clothes and used the pictorial conventions of fashion plates to depict dolls garbed in lavish outfits and captured mid-action (fig. 18). Over the

Figure 17. Jules David, plate from *Englishwoman's Domestic Magazine* (detail), 1867.

course of the nineteenth century, as children's literacy rates rose, as sales of books and toys increased, and as technological improvements made illustrated books more popular, dolls and their fashions became a favorite topic in printed matter aimed at girls.[120] Although some doll tales cautioned against the perils of vanity, others forthrightly advertised dolls

Figure 18. Plate from *La Poupée modèle*, 1866.

as an effective way to train girls to appreciate clothes.[121] The cover of *Dolly's Outfit* (1872) explains that "[t]he girl who takes a pride in dressing her doll well is thereby learning to dress herself in a suitable and tasteful manner."[122]

Like the images of women in fashion plates, dolls exemplified ideals of genteel female appearance. Doll literature provided exhaustive inventories of clothing, and books like *The Well-Bred Doll* (1853) equated the doll's beauty with her wardrobe.[123] Dolls who narrated their own tales in the first person based their literary authority on their ability to embody and evaluate fashion. The doll who recounts *Victoria-Bess, or the Ups and Downs of a Doll's Life* (1879) boasts that her wax face and limbs were "modelled to perfection after the most approved forms of feminine beauty" (10); the narrator of *Dolly's Story Book* (1889) sagely notes that "dolls think a good deal of dress."[124] Although dolls who narrated their own stories often drew attention to the gap between their perceptive and expressive powers, Victoria-Bess is at no loss for words when she skillfully assesses that her new owner's mother has a "slender figure exactly like those we see in fashion-plates" (49). Possessed of the attributes that defined the figures in fashion plates, literary dolls embodied the standards applied to girls and women.

Dolls and fashion plates both created mimetic illusions that combined realism and fantasy; both depicted vividly colored, self-contained figures who represented luxury, elegance, and leisure, and both were designed to inspire a passion for femininity in girls. Depending on how they were dressed, Victorian dolls could represent adult women or girls, but regardless often had the same voluptuous hourglass contours as women in fashion plates (fig. 19).[125] Dolls representing mature girls or adult women dominated the market throughout the nineteenth century, and baby dolls sold in large numbers only after 1914.[126] Victorian girls who fancied dolls were in a similar position to adult women who gazed longingly at fashion plates: both yearned to possess an idealized image of mature female beauty. Girls worshipped their playthings the way mothers doted on prettily dressed daughters and on the adult figures in fashion imagery.

Just as fashion plates invited women to possess the feminine attractions portrayed within them, dolls invited girls to consummate their desire for femininity by possessing an object that represented it. On the cover of a book produced by a major doll company, a young girl holds her mother with one hand and with the other gestures toward dolls in a shop window who, according to the book's title, return her interest with the importunate salutation, "Purchase me, young lady" (fig. 20). In *La Poupée de Mademoiselle Lili*, a little girl goes to a toy store to "buy herself a little girl," and in *More Dolls* (1879), the less imperious Milly encounters the gift of a doll with wonder at her new ownership: "Is this Beauty really for me?"[127] Doll tales personify commodities in terms of their desire to be sold. As one doll narrator puts it, "My long-cherished wishes were fulfilled, and I was bought" (23). The moment of purchase in turn realizes the girl's desire to possess the doll completely, which culminates in her demand that the doll come to life: "Oh, my pretty dolly . . . how I wish you were alive. . . . I want to have you alive all for my own," says the girl at the center of Annabella Browne's *Live Dolls* (1874).[128]

For many Victorian feminists, the doll was a metaphor for women's status as inferior playthings. Some memoirs and novels described girls rebelling against the constraints placed on them by ignoring, attacking, or heroically rescuing their dolls.[129] Today many decry both fashion and dolls for objectifying women and encouraging them to internalize misogynist limits on female autonomy.[130] While toys are often described as liberating children's imaginations and emotions, dolls are considered deadening influences that teach girls to be dependent, passive, and constrained. The most notorious twentieth-century theory of dolls interprets them as symbols of what girls lack and therefore long for—penises and infants— a theory that only became popular when baby dolls began to dominate the market after 1914.[131] Yet dolls do not predetermine submission; they appealed to girls who later questioned the strictures placed on women or wielded considerable power as adults. Feminist Lucretia Mott recalled that a doll was her "childhood treasure"; author Ann Gilbert wrote that

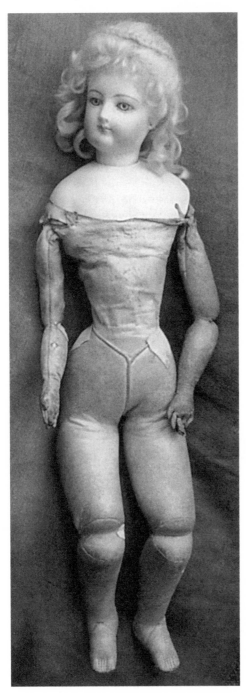

Figure 19. Photograph of nineteenth-century doll.

Figure 20. Cover of *Purchase Me Young Lady,* nineteenth-century advertising booklet published by Maison Jumeau.

"the natural avidity with which a little girl . . . seizes, caresses, loves a doll, seems to indicate the suitableness of the amusement"; and until she was fourteen, Princess Victoria kept a stable of over a hundred dolls whom she dressed as court ladies and ballet stars.[132]

Victorian dolls embodied the play of the system: dolls were volatile entities that could appear to be both object and subject, young girl and mature woman, inert and uncannily lifelike. Roland Barthes notes that fashion discourse, with its emotional, domestic, infantilizing and seductive rhetoric, encourages women to think of clothing as a doll, "sometimes loving, sometimes loved," able to signify both mother and child (*The Fashion System*, 241). In Victorian doll tales, girlish love for dolls combines maternal tenderness and maternal aggression; a daughter's infatuation and passionate dependence; the sensual intimacy and companionship of sibling and marital love; and greedy lust for a beautiful object that can be purchased, then abandoned at will. In their role as objects, dolls did not transmit their passive state to the girls who played with them; indeed, to endow dolls with the power to foist passivity on girls paradoxically assumes that dolls are supernaturally active and women and girls already so passive they could hardly be made more so. As the literary example of Ethel shows, when dolls were portrayed as helpless, their vulnerability did not mirror the girl's weakness but instead magnified her mastery and cruelty. Even texts that praised doll play for increasing a girl's empathy, responsibility, and selflessness did so to defend it against an equally recognized capacity to stimulate a girl's vanity, capriciousness, and greed.

Dolls were literary subjects as well as material objects. Though nineteenth-century doll tales cannot tell us what girls actually did with dolls, they do convey adult fantasies about how girls played with their toys, and tell us what authors thought children and parents wanted to read.[133] Like the world of fashion, the literary doll universe was a feminine one; doll stories focused on girls and female dolls, were written primarily by women, and were often explicitly addressed and dedicated to girls. Children's literature in the nineteenth century oscillated between instruction and amusement, reason and imagination, and juvenile fiction treated dolls as lifelike objects that could both impart lessons and rouse a girl's pleasure and fantasy.[134] Mrs. Robert O'Reilly, the author of *Doll World; or Play and Earnest: A Study from Real Life* (1872), characterized "Doll world" as one of "mimic joys and sorrows . . . caricatures of those that burden older lives, yet perhaps not altogether unfaithful copies of them."[135]

Dolls were an apt subject for children's literature because, like fiction itself, they were amusements justified by their ability to teach sympathy. Tales approvingly portrayed girls projecting feelings onto inanimate dolls and argued that doll play extended the girl's moral capacity to imagine the feelings and thoughts of infants, animals, and the poor. Doll tales praised girls for considering toys human; the preface to *Memoirs of a Doll* (1854) calls dolls "the pivot of humanity" because the way girls treat them determines how, once grown, they will care for their children (vi). Mrs. Gatti's *Florence and Her Doll* (1865) made a girl's future dependent on her ability to sympathize with the inanimate doll: "The little girl who is careful and tender even of a doll, that cannot feel, deserves to be trusted with the care of a living creature."[136] Fantastic tales that showed dolls coming to life conveyed the didactic message that even inanimate objects deserved a girl's kindness. Just as novels paradoxically taught readers to sympathize with fictional characters who did not really exist, doll tales showed that girls could and should imagine the feelings of entities who were only apparently mute and immobile.

Doll tales taught lessons besides sympathy. Many showed the influence of Evangelical notions of domestic, Christian femininity, which emphasized obedience, good works, preparation for the afterlife, and a strong sense of sin and punishment. Readers learned that the contemptuous and vain would be humbled and chastened. As the narrator of *Rosamond: Dolly's New Picture Book* (1870) puts it when describing a proud doll who is consigned to a corner of the garret after being burned: "It is a hard lot—but after all, has she not deserved it? Therefore, dear Dollies, let Rosamund's story be a warning to you, and be always modest and obedient, and then you will be sure to thrive."[137] Virtuous dolls teach girls to become industrious, prudent, neat, gentle towards the weak, generous to the poor, and loyal instead of fickle. Some tales suggested that girls should be as silent, dependent, and acquiescent as dolls, while others showed that dolls improved a girl's intellect by serving as pupils to whom the girl could repeat her lessons or providing an occasion to learn about the industrial processes that produced toys.[138] Doll fiction gave lessons in philanthropy by showing how the plaything who was a source of pleasure could also become a token of sacrifice; in many tales, a girl decides to give up her prized possession to a poorer girl who lacks her comforts. Doll tales were sociology for girls: stories that charted a doll's decline as she migrated from a wealthy household to a poor one offered readers a panoramic survey of the nation's many classes.[139]

Many doll tales took the form of first-person memoirs that milked the pathos of beings who can perceive and communicate as narrators but remain mute and motionless within their fictional universe. In continental modernist writing, the doll's combination of figural realism and inanimate mechanism was often seen as uncanny, but in English doll tales, it was more often the occasion for sentiment.[140] As the doll who narrates *The Doll and Her Friends* puts it, "[N]ot having the gift of speech, I could only listen submissively" (35). Another doll narrator notes, "Silent people think the most"; observing festivities in which she cannot participate, she explains, "[A]s I could not speak I thought quietly over all I had heard and seen."[141] Doll narrators come alive in the act of narration, but in the fictional world they inhabit, they can only react. The doll who narrates *Memoirs of a Doll* wittily expresses the strain this puts on character and narration when she comments on her own reported speech: "Ah! said I, inwardly (indeed I cannot discourse in any other way)"(9). Doll memoirs expose the gap between narration and authorship that realist fiction encourages readers to forget, for their narrators often remind readers that they cannot physically write the tale they tell; in *The Doll and Her Friends*, Lady Seraphina explains that she dictates her memoirs to an enamored pen (91). In first-person memoirs, dolls become pure interiority; as characters they never act but are only transacted, but as narrators they become the center of consciousness through which all action filters.

Victorian doll tales taught girls about fashion, altruism, and the finer points of fictional narration, but they can teach us about the Victorian eroticization of childhood. Historians see the nineteenth century as the culmination of a long process that defined childhood as a unique, inevitably lost period of innocence, human spontaneity, closeness to nature, and immersion in a maternal, feminine world.[142] To that essentially Romantic conception of childhood, Victorians added an Evangelical notion of original sin, which emphasized strict discipline and an insistence on breaking the child's will. The influence of Romantic ideals of childhood on Evangelical anxieties about the Fall made children focal points of narratives about suffering and redemption.[143] Some Victorians saw childhood as a distinct stage marked by asexuality, others saw the child as prone to vice, in need of careful monitoring, and possessed of a disobedient will to be broken by adult authorities. Whether innocent or guilty, children were eroticized. Their alleged lack of sexual knowledge created a vacuum to be filled by adult desires, and their innate guilt made them signs of the sinful desires that required regulation.[144]

Like the fashion discourse they often echoed, doll tales demonstrate how women eroticized girlhood and saw girls as bearers of homoerotic desires. Scholars have paid ample attention to the erotic dynamics of Victorian father-daughter relationships and Victorian men's sexual preoccupations with girls, but the desires of adult women for children of either sex have remained a virtually taboo topic.[145] Only Carol Mavor, writing about photographs a Victorian woman took of her adolescent daughters, has explored how mothers experienced daughters as dolls, "objects dressed to entice and to invite play," who enabled adult women to express their desire for "young feminine bodies."[146] Doll fiction, written almost entirely by women, eroticized girls and women's familial relationships from a dizzying variety of positions. Relative to dolls, girls become erotic subjects who assume the roles of ardent mother, sister, daughter, or suitor. Like the subject of the next chapter, Miss Havisham in *Great Expectations*, girls in children's books sequester themselves with a doll who represents both a daughter and a mother.[147] In *Live Dolls*, the proud owner of a new doll finds a summerhouse that she claims for the mother-daughter dyad she forms with her plaything: "This is my house where I shall live with my little girl" (5). In "The Doll's Ball" (1864), a girl compares one doll, "the loveliest creature she had ever seen," to her older sister, then dreams that she sees another pretty doll who resembles her "mamma," a "lovely lady who put out her hand and asked her to a ball."[148] In *My Dolly*, a girl bestows ardent kisses on both her mother and her doll, who embodies what the girl imagines her mother wants from her and what she wants from her mother: "I don't like a Dolly that talks too much. And I do like one that never tires of listening. . . . [E]ven mamma is sometimes too busy to hear me. But my Dolly listens and listens to all my stories, and never thinks them too long" (21, 22, 26, 87). Conversely, dolls who tell their own tales express the erotic contentment of a girl in the arms of an adored mother. The narrator of *Memoirs of a London Doll* remarks that her first "new mamma, the little Lady Flora, was very pretty," and her story ends when she is "placed in the soft little arms of my present dear mamma" (40, 125).

Dolls enabled writers to mobilize the traffic between both sides of the generational divide and between opposing poles of erotic dynamics. The pseudo-philosophical preface to *Memoirs of a Doll* asks, "What is there more innocent, more true, more loveable, than the delicious little personage [the doll] who preceded us in the arms of our mother, and who, long before our grandsons, will sit on the knees of our daughters?" (v). Both innocent and delicious, a token of the mother's presexual childhood and a harbinger of the daughter's sexual future, the doll could embody the erotic extremes of idealization and humiliation, rapture and indifference, tenderness and cruelty. As *Memoirs of a Doll* explained, dolls exist to be "whipped with . . . choler, or embraced with . . . ardour" by girls who punish, forgive, long for, admire, envy, exhibit, dress, undress, and caress their feminine playthings (vi). Children's fiction portrays boys as the doll's "natural enemies," but boys are not alone in their attacks on dolls, for heroines also frequently mutilate and deface their manikins.[149] In *Jimmy: Scenes from the Life of a Black Doll* (1888), the eponymous narrator catalogues his young "mistress's" cruelty by describing how she whips him daily.[150] In some tales, the doll's fragmented body signifies the power of middle-class girls to inflict social misery on the poor and enslaved. Others invert that extreme aggression by portraying the magical reparations performed by a beneficent young woman who heals a doll ravaged by neglect or abuse.

In children's fiction, girls who subject dolls to violence usually reenact the discipline of mothers and other female caretakers. In *Memoirs of a Doll*, a girl "whip[s]" her doll, telling her, "I am always being plagued and scolded about my lessons and so I shall plague and scold you too" (32, 38). In *My Dolly*, two girls imitate their mothers' conversation as they chat about cod liver oil and how to handle disobedient dolls (132). *Live Dolls* begins with a girl named Mabel declaring "*I want a live doll to do just what I like with*" (6). No sooner has the doll come to life than Mabel slaps and scolds her. Although the manifest moral of the tale is to teach girls to appreciate the efforts of those who are "older, wiser, and better" at caring for the helpless, it also exposes the pleasures of unfettered maternal power (123). When scolding her live doll, Mabel feels "the grand delight of 'making herself minded'. . . . Mabel enjoyed the idea that now it was her turn to rule, and that Rosabella must obey her" (20). Just as pornographic texts linger over bullying matrons who extract abject apologies and promises from the girls they punish, *Live Dolls* shows Mabel forcing Rosabella to say that she is "sorry and will never do it again" (30). In *Doll World*, two older girls demonstrate that to play with a doll is to punish her, as they plan to "[t]each her lessons . . . and whip her and put her in the corner. Now, Miss Doll, hold up your head and put your hands behind your back!" (224).

Where some tales emphasize how girls who play with dolls mimic their mothers, others accentuate how the doll mirrors the girl's subordination to maternal omnipotence. In *The Doll and Her Friends*, a doll who is the "duplicate" (36) of her young owner receives duplicate lessons in bodily comportment: "[S]he cured me of poking my head forward, of standing on one leg, of leaning against the furniture while I was speaking, of putting my elbows on the table" (38–39). In *Doll World*, a girl corrects her doll, then commiserates with her surrogate: "You need not look so miserable; I can feel for you. I have gone through it all. They were always *at me*" (209). In other cases, the boundless power mothers wield over girls, and girls exercise over dolls, becomes the doll's own. In *Memoirs of a Doll*, a misbehaving girl imagines that her doll is a "spy on all my actions" (34), and in *Sybil's Dutch Dolls* (1887), a girl dreams that her dolls come to life and warn her, "*We* shall play with *you*, and *you* will have to mind what *we* tell you."[151]

The fantasy of a girl wielding absolute power over a female figure also emerged in comparisons between the girl's selection of a doll and the purchase of a female slave for a harem. Tales describe dolls in stores waiting "to be chosen and sold" to girls whom doll narrators call their "mistresses," and girls in doll tales fantasize about owning and mastering a female object.[152] Lady Seraphina, in *Doll and Her Friends*, declares, "I belong to a race the sole end of whose existence is to give pleasure to others" of "the female sex. . . . We are a race of mere dependents; some might even call us slaves . . . forced to submit to every caprice of our possessors" (1–2). The comparison makes the doll a symbol of feminine subordination, but with a difference: when dolls become slaves, girls become masters who go to market to select and purchase a beautiful companion. Lady Seraphina explains, "Personal beauty" is "the badge of all our tribe," and hopes that as a result she will be able to inspire "strong attachment" or "love" in a prospective female buyer (3). Like women in Victorian society, dolls are valued for their looks, but in doll world, the purpose of feminine beauty is to appeal to girls.

In addition to representing the girl's slave, the doll could also represent a girl's wife or husband, a role that in doll world merged with visions of love between mother and daughter. In her 1935 memoir Eleanor Acland recalled her possessive love for her childhood doll: "Lady Fair was Milly's very own. . . . The devotion that Milly felt for her was a jealous passion. . . . Milly adored the very name she had invented for her beloved."[153] Girls in children's books take uxurious pride in their dolls' beauty and virtue. In *Dolly and I* (1883), an allusion to a biblical passage compares the doll to the proverbial good wife: "Dearer far than rubies / My lovely Doll I prize. / And she loves me, my Dolly! / Oh! no one will deny; / We dearly love each other!— / Dolly and I."[154] *Memoirs of a Doll* notes that as the girl's first love object, the doll represents the future child and the future husband. The author warns men considering marriage to investigate a prospective wife's former relationship to her doll, because "the doll . . . was himself in the past" (vi).

The homoerotic love between a girl and her doll merged with heterosexual narratives of romantic courtship and marriage. Doll tales describe a process that begins with love at first sight, leads to a honeymoon period spent in bed, and culminates with social reintegration through the paying of calls to exhibit the new love object. The longing and fascination for an unattainable object so dear to courtly literature also mark the beginning of doll narratives describing how a girl and doll fall instantly in love despite the obstacles that separate them. In *More Dolls*, a doll recounts the story of a mermaid who, smitten with a little girl, lures her into the water. Before allowing her to return to land, the mermaid asks that they spend one special night together: "[T]onight you will sleep with me in my coral cave. . . . Presently Ella and Tiny lay down on a bed of sea-moss, and Tiny wound her wee arms about Ella's neck, and put her lips close to Ella's ear and sang to her so gently, so gently, that Ella soon fell sound asleep" (65–66). The mutual, sensual fascination between the mermaid and the girl mirrors and combines that between girl and doll, mother and daughter, and mutually entranced lovers.

The girl's visual pleasure in the doll's spectacle of femininity becomes itself a sight to behold, for both the narrating doll and the tale's implied reader. In many tales, a plate-glass window and the doll's high price are the only barriers separating lover from beloved. The poor girl who enters a toy shop in Jessie Armstrong's *Celestine and Sallie; Or, Two Dolls and Two Homes* (1890) is immediately seduced by a wax doll who resembles a fashionable adult lady: "[A] cry, a peculiar cry of childhood, broke from little Mary's lips; a cry of mingled delight and longing. . . . [T]he beauty which had caused this stir in Mary's heart was no less a person than her highness the Princess Celestine." From this point forward, the narrator tells us, "Mary had eyes only for the lovely Celestine herself. 'O, father!' she cried, 'look at the beauty there! O, I must have her!'"[155] The eponymous heroine of *Minnie's Dolls* receives a new doll and looks "with rapture at her treasure" (62). In *Rosamond*, another girl viewing her doll for the first time "remained speechless for a while, as if spell-bound by the magic of Rosamond's appearance" (n.p.).

The crystallization of love at first sight leads to the transports of the first night together. In her autobiography, Charlotte Yonge recalled how after receiving "the largest and best doll I ever had," she "lay in bed with my hand over my treasure."[156] In *Rosabella*, a doll recounts being given to a girl who "crept into bed and took me in her arms, keeping me cuddled up quite close. My eyes shut up whenever I am laid on my back, and so they did now" (19). The description of the doll's mechanical attributes make the girl's passion for her slightly ridiculous, but they also highlight the doll's erotic pliability as a love object. Where Victorian novels elide the first night of marriage, doll tales amplify the scene of a girl who takes her new doll "in her arms," and makes her a "bedfellow" to talk to "at night, when we were in bed," while also conveying the feelings of a doll experiencing the "great happiness of passing the whole night in the arms of my first mamma."[157] Doll tales graft the ecstasy of mother-infant bonding onto romantic passion, making the pleasures of the doll with her "mamma" indistinguishable from the delights of newlyweds. In *Rosamond*, the girl who receives a new doll spends their entire first night together "dressing and undressing her" (n.p.), while the poverty-stricken girl who obtains the damaged Victoria-Bess calls the doll "my queen— my beauty" (152), promises to "always care for 'er" (155), and celebrates the prospect of constant companionship with "a dear little dolly to cuddle, and to talk to nights" (156).

The social codes of the married couple also govern the phases that succeed the honeymoon period. In *Memoirs of a Doll*, a father interprets his daughter's acquisition of a new doll as marriage when he writes on the doll's behalf to one of her former owners that "having now become the doll of another, I cannot with propriety reciprocate the solicitude which you are pleased to entertain for me, nor can I . . . address you in similar terms of affection" (60–61). During the early phases of their union, the girl's love for her doll is limitless, as Lady Seraphina attests in *The Doll and Her Friends*: "My young mistress devoted every spare moment to the enjoyment of my company, and set no limits to her caresses and compliments" (24). The girl fusses over the doll like a wife over a husband, but she also plays husband to Lady Seraphina's wifely plaything, as the doll narrator observes: "[T]he object of my existence was plain enough, namely, to give innocent recreation to my young mistress" (29). Initially, doll and girl are inseparable, and the girl takes her doll everywhere so that she can "exhibit" her when paying calls.[158] Like a proud new spouse or parent, the girl has trouble separating from her new love, and the doll who narrates *Rosabella* describes how her mistress "bent down and kissed the tips of my shoes" before leaving her for the day.[159]

As in novels that describe the effects of the boredom and restlessness that set in after the initial glow of marriage fades, doll tales recount the jealousy and infidelity that arise when fickle girls abandon their erstwhile loves. A mother wryly notes the transience of her daughter's passion for a "waxen beauty" when she comments that a doll about to be discarded "was such a great favourite at one time. Why, I was almost jealous of Sophronia myself." [160] Dolls watch the girls who once adored them like faithful husbands turn into libertine rakes when they receive new playthings. The doll in *Ethel's Adventures* recalls how her "fickle little mistress" held a "rival in her faithless arms" (152, 158). In *Victoria-Bess*, a father remarks aloud on his daughter's "fickleness" and wonders "how long *this* favourite will last" (51), and the new beloved realizes that one day she might have "a rival in my mistress's affections" (52).

Like a mythical figure, the doll simultaneously embodied opposed states: adult and child, husband and wife, slave and mistress, adoring and adored, punisher and punished, subject and object. Doll fiction presented dolls as having the human qualities of perception, sensation, and emotion, but they also depicted them as commodities that merely simulated human form. As a commodity, the doll gave girls a purchase on their desire for femininity. When girls bestowed dolls as gifts, they demonstrated their worth in a feminine economy that measured women in terms of selflessness. When a girl relinquished the doll she treasured to another girl who desired her, the doll became a medium for transferring enjoyment and creating social bonds through credit and debt. In travelogues that used dolls of different nations to explain national customs, the English doll became a counter in the imperial marketplace. In one tale, an Algerian girl instantaneously prefers an English girl and her doll: "'I love you,' said the Algerine child, 'and I like your doll best.'"[161] Like the English culture that Victorians dreamed would stay intact no matter where they traveled, the doll was currency in female transactions the world over, a sign of the love and envy, hierarchy and identification, abjection and adoration incessantly circulating between women.

• • •

Fashion, dolls, and pornography have always been considered erotic, but only as reflections of masculine desires for femininity. As we have seen throughout this chapter, they also conveyed women's desire for femininity. Ironically, female homoeroticism can be discerned most clearly if we define gender as secondary to eroticism rather than primary to it. Eroticism consists of dynamics that do not depend on gender or genitalia, instead relying on domination and helplessness, adoration and abjection, faithfulness and promiscuity, possession and rejection, and visual and tactile pleasure. Most theories of sexuality insist on equating those dynamics with heterosexual or masculine desire and with gendered structures such as castration anxiety, penis envy, and the Oedipus complex. Most theories of sexuality also define desire between women as the refusal or absence of the drives that putatively define heterosexuality or masculine desire. This has been considered to be supremely true of the Victorians, to whom we often attribute a refusal to recognize female sexual desire.

Just as chapters 1 and 2 demonstrated that Victorians did not see social bonds between women as distinct from or antithetical to familial and marital ones, this chapter has shown that women's status as sexual objects for men did not preclude their erotic interest in and for other women. Like the father-daughter relationship, the mother-daughter bond became a template for desire that could prefigure marital ties and overlap with the everyday homoeroticism of commodity culture. Because Victorians did not oppose heterosexuality and female homoeroticism, they did not see desire between women as imitative or secondary; because Victorians did not define lesbianism as an autonomous identity, they were not concerned that female homoeroticism might lead women to disclaim sexual relationships with men. Fashion magazines, pornography, and doll literature were all products of a world in which women and girls were as thrilled and enthralled by femininity as men and boys were. Desire for women was the crucible in which femininity was formed. As we will see in the following chapter, that desire could also become the model for a boy's erotic fascination with a girl who serves as an older woman's live doll.

CHAPTER 4

The Female Accessory in *Great Expectations*

GREAT EXPECTATIONS (1860–61) HAS ALWAYS been read as a tale of guilt, shame, and obsessive, thwarted desire.[1] The concept that dominates the criticism is repression: of time, growth, experience, empire, and origins.[2] Interpreters have attributed almost every imaginable form of desire to the male protagonist—Oedipal, masochistic, sadistic, autoerotic, and male homoerotic—in order to argue that the novel's cyclical plot corresponds to a narrative of arrested male development.[3] Yet the form of desire that most distinguishes the novel and that impresses itself most strongly on Pip—desire between women—is oddly absent from critical readings, perhaps because its importance to the narrative is so obvious it has been consistently overlooked.

At the figurative and literal center of *Great Expectations* is Pip's encounter with the couple formed by Miss Havisham and her adopted daughter, Estella, who live "associated and secluded" together in the grand estate Miss Havisham inherits from her father.[4] In chapter 29, at the midpoint of the novel's middle volume, the adult Pip travels from London to visit Miss Havisham, who reunites him with a newly mature and even more captivating Estella. This scene, like many in the novel, finds Pip "trembling in spirit" before Estella and "worshipping the very hem of her dress" (233), while Estella is composed and "inaccessibl[e]" (236). As always, Miss Havisham matches Pip in the "ravenous intensity" (237) with which she absorbs Estella's beauty, and the narrator repeatedly draws the reader's attention to Miss Havisham's possessive pleasure in the younger woman. In the one chapter, Miss Havisham directs a "greedy look" at Estella (232), plays with her hair (233), kisses a hand to her (237), and places jewels in Estella's "hair, and about her bosom and arms" (240). Pip gazes at Estella, but the play of looks in this triangle is considerably more complex. Miss Havisham has trained Pip to desire Estella, requires him to witness *her* passion for Estella, and takes pleasure in observing his awareness that he is excluded from the female dyad. The younger woman takes Pip in only to express contempt for him, while the elder scrutinizes him in order to relish his pain.

This scene is even more noteworthy because its detailed unfolding belies that it has already been narrated several times before. Here is Pip's first visit to Satis House: "Miss Havisham beckoned [Estella] to come close, and took up a jewel from the table, and tried its effect upon her fair young bosom and against her pretty brown hair. 'Your own, one day, my dear. . . . Let me see you play cards with this boy'" (58–59). Pip's second visit replays the same scene, slightly but crucially modified: "Miss Havisham watched us all the time, directed my attention to Estella's beauty, and made me notice it the more by trying her jewels on Estella's breast and hair" (88). In the first instance, Pip is relatively external to the female dyad: he watches Miss Havisham adorn Estella's "fair young bosom" and listens to her refer to him categorically and in the third person as "this boy," even as she announces her plan to watch him. In the second scene, Pip is included with Estella as an object of Miss Havisham's gaze—she "watched us"—but only insofar as she greedily enjoys seeing the girl she adores reject the boy who admires her. In the second scene, Miss Havisham teaches Pip to identify with her desire by training him to attend to the sights she enjoys most—Estella, and his own discomfiture.

The vision that Pip cannot tear his eyes from structures his subjectivity around ongoing attempts to occupy Estella's or Miss Havisham's place in what is for him a foundational scene of desire between women. Although critics have isolated one female character from the other in order to focus on how Pip relates to each, Estella and Miss Havisham appear together in almost every scene, and as a result, both Pip and the reader experience them as a dyad.[5] Throughout the novel, Pip attempts to merge with a female couple that simultaneously solicits and excludes him by identifying with both of its members. In the case of Miss Havisham, Pip identifies primarily with her desire: her desire for Estella, and her desire that he desire Estella. Just as Miss Havisham calls her wish to see a boy play a "sick fanc[y]" (58), Pip describes his desire for Estella as one of his "fancies" (128) and follows Miss Havisham's order to reproduce her own fascination with the girl and her consuming passion for the fiancé who betrayed her. She tells him, "I bred her and educated her, to be loved . . . . Love her . . . giving up your whole heart and soul to the smiter—as I did!" (237). Pip follows suit by putting Miss Havisham's words into his mouth: "Far into the night, Miss Havisham's words 'Love her, love her, love her!' sounded in my ears. I adapted them for my own repetition, and said to my pillow, 'I love her, I love her, I love her!' hundreds of times" (241). This moment encapsulates the mimetic structure of desire that shapes the entire novel, in which the older woman's hungry admiration for Estella produces Pip's equally consuming love.

Pip's desire to have Estella is inseparable from his desire to be Miss Havisham, but it is also intimately related to a wish to occupy Estella's place as a fashionable doll, set off by jewels and lovely clothes, attracting the admiration of a wealthy woman of leisure. As Miss Havisham's erotic object, Estella models what Pip wants and wants to be. The narrative cannot separate Pip's desire for Estella from his ambition to become her, and the narrator poignantly expresses his love for Estella as his incorporation of her. Pip figures his self as a receptive channel that takes Estella in and merges with her: "it was impossible for me to separate her . . . from the innermost life of my life" (233); as he later tells her, "You are part of my existence, part of myself" (360). Even Pip's speech becomes the feminine body he wishes to have when the narrator describes how the words he spoke to Estella "welled up within me, like blood from an inward wound, and gushed out" (360). In seeing Estella as part of himself, and in figuring his innermost being as a bleeding, gushing orifice, Pip imagines transforming himself into a female body part so that he can inhabit the female dyad. In a variation on René Girard's schema of mimetic desire, Pip emulates both the desiring subject, Miss Havisham, and her desired object, Estella, copying both and competing with both.[6] Because the homoerotic female dyad is Pip's model of desire and his standard of social value, he wants both to win the prized object from Miss Havisham (more fundamentally his rival than even Bentley Drummle), and to win Miss Havisham's attentions away from Estella.

None of the extant theoretical models for triangles consisting of two women and a man explains the threesome at the center of Dickens's male bildungsroman. *Great Expectations* has some interesting analogies to the lesbian pulp fiction of the 1950s, whose stock plot revolved around a possessive and embittered woman who hates men and seduces a beautiful and less experienced woman. In lesbian pulps, a hypervirile man wrests the younger woman away from the older one, who jealously resists his attempts to seduce her lover. In *Great Expectations*, by contrast, Miss Havisham actively invites Pip to love Estella, Pip seeks to ingratiate himself with both women, and his love for Estella never definitively triumphs. The situation of a man watching two women has typically been interpreted as a fantasy of total access, of the male gaze capturing the female couple so that the male organ can intervene between them.[7] In Dickens's novel, however, a boy repeatedly witnesses the spectacle of his irrevocable exclusion from the female dyad. Perhaps more appropriate would be the Proustian model: as a youth, a male, first-person narrator has a formative encounter with lesbianism that ends with the women he spies on blocking his access to the scene, and thus begins an obsession with women who desire women.[8] But even here the analogy is only partial, for Proust's interest in the secret, concealed world of "inverts," whom he views as a distinct sexual species, differs notably from Dickens's unselfconscious exhibition of Miss Havisham's overt relish for Estella.

The eroticism of Estella's relationship with Miss Havisham merits closer attention than critics have accorded it, but cannot be understood using twentieth-century frameworks as out of joint with the historical moment of *Great Expectations* as the spectral Miss Havisham is herself out of joint with time. Indeed, Victorian reviewers who denounced Miss Havisham as implausible, eccentric, and "bordering on the monstrous and loathsome" attributed her pathology only to her monomaniacal refusal to recognize the passage of time. Her relationship with Estella did not seem remarkable to readers who believed that passionate devotion between women was essential to the formation of ideal womanhood.[9] Rather than deform the mother-daughter bond out of all recognition, Miss Havisham's relationship with Estella simply intensified the normal dynamics of the Victorian mother-daughter relationship represented in fashion magazines and doll stories: the maternal determination to make a daughter an irresistible marriage prospect, or the appeal of turning a young girl into a pretty poppet to be adorned and adored. The fetishism, objectification, scopophilia, exhibitionism, and sadism that we saw at work in mainstream Victorian representations of mothers with their daughters and girls with their dolls are reproduced in more concentrated form in *Great Expectations*, which draws a man into a female world of love and ritual organized around women's aggressive objectification of femininity.

Rather than read the novel as failing to adhere to a heterosexual norm or exposing that norm's fissures, I propose that *Great Expectations* shows how a man's desire for a woman is shaped by his identification with the desire between women woven into the fabric of the family, everyday life, and consumer culture—the very stuff of the Victorian novel. Dickens was himself well acquainted with the worlds of fashion and dolls. A known dandy when it came to his own clothing, Dickens was attentive enough to female dress that a character from his novel *Barnaby Rudge* (1841) inspired the "Dolly Varden" look of the 1870s. An eccentric dollmaker is one of the more memorable characters in *Our Mutual Friend* (1864–1865), and as the father of several daughters, Dickens would have been familiar with dolls as material objects and as subjects of children's literature. He certainly knew of the children's book *The Enchanted Doll* (1846), which author Mark Lemon dedicated to two of Dickens's daughters.[10] Estella's icy demeanor and her eventual humbling at the hands of a violent husband recall cautionary doll tales in which a cold, vain doll falls from grace. Miss Havisham echoes the neglected, withered playthings that litter doll tales, such as the inmate of a toy shop in *Dolly Dear* (1883), "a bride arrayed in all her glory" who has "been waiting so long for her expected husband, that her white satin dress was beginning to show a yellow tinge."[11] Dolls were literally at the origin of *Great Expectations*, for Dickens based Miss Havisham on a newspaper article about a woman who lived in a house filled with hundreds of toy soldiers that in the novel become one treasured female doll.[12]

Though *Great Expectations* originated with a metamorphosis of the masculine into the feminine, the novel itself focuses on a man's effort to place himself in a female world. Unlike fashion plates and doll stories, which assumed a female audience, *Great Expectations* tells the story of a woman and her coveted, fashionable doll from the point of view of a boy who desires the doll but can never possess her. The boy who cannot have the doll can, however, aspire to be her. Having learned to envy Estella's status as Miss Havisham's beloved plaything, Pip concludes, as we will see, that he must doll himself up to be loved. He consents to be toyed with and fashions himself into a splendidly clothed doll so that by patterning himself on Estella, he will become as desirable to her as she is to Miss Havisham. Pip grafts a longing for social mobility onto his sense that he must become a feminine object in order to obtain the woman he desires; the result is a novelistic universe premised on what I call gender mobility, in which women become men and men become women. Ultimately, however, *Great Expectations* shifts the terms of womanhood from the hierarchical, fetishistic world of fashion and dolls to a more sentimental universe, a move that wins Pip the friendship of each member of the female dyad but denies his initial desire to become one with them by becoming one of them.

Because Dickens is often described as anticipating psychoanalysis, while Freud is often seen as theorizing Victorian family practices, it is worth clarifying at the outset how different Dickens's Victorian doll story is from Freud's modern one. Freud wrote about dolls in his essay on "Femininity," which took castration and masculinity as absolute reference points for the formation of gender and sexuality in both sexes. In Freud's narrative, girls and boys share a primary attachment to the mother, but only girls relinquish it. Girls turn away from the mother out of anger at the prohibitions she places on their sexuality and disdain for her lack of the penis that Freud considered equally desirable to girls and boys.[13] In Freud's narrative, the girl transfers the power she invests in the penis to her doll, which compensates for what she lacks by representing a baby and a phallus. In Dickens's narrative, a woman requires a doll as a weapon against men because she feels wounded by them, but despite the text's attentiveness to female injury at men's hands, it also depicts the doll as an effective instrument of feminine power. It is Estella's feminine "completeness and superiority" that make Pip feel inferior to her (234).

The certainty and rapidity with which Pip adopts Estella's degrading view of him as a contemptible working-class boy with "coarse hands" and "thick boots" (59) matches the velocity of Freud's account of the little girl who first sees a penis, but reverses its gender hierarchy, for the narrator equates femininity with social superiority. Pip explains to Joe, "there had been a beautiful young lady at Miss Havisham's, who was dreadfully proud, and . . . she had said I was common, and . . . I knew I was common, and . . . I wished I was not common" (69). Compare Freud on the little girl's first sight of a penis: "She makes her judgement and her decision in a flash. She has seen it and knows that she is without it and wants to have it."[14] Freud asserts that girls measure their bodies against a standard defined by the penis and console themselves for their deficiencies with baby dolls that represent the organ they lack. Dickens depicts a boy who measures himself against a beautiful girl and finds his masculine body both deficient and excessive by comparison. Estella's doll-like femininity represents a gold standard of gentility that makes masculinity as undesirable as manual labor. Unlike the Oedipal triangle, which associates being with femininity and having with masculinity, the boy's encounter with the female dyad defines both being and having as feminine positions.

Freud and Dickens are as divergent in their account of the mother-daughter relationship as in their interpretations of what the doll symbolizes about the relative value of masculinity and femininity. Freud focuses on the separation of mother and daughter as the girl transfers her affections to her father—or to a doll that, for Freud, symbolizes the girl's missing, envied, desired penis. Dickens emphasizes the enduring power of the self-contained bond between the hyperfeminine doll-daughter and the mother who lavishes on her the passion she withholds from men. Estella has no paternal rival for her mother's affections; the wedding cake moulders, but Miss Havisham's appetite for her daughter never flags. The monomania that memorializes Miss Havisham's injury by a man guarantees that she will dwell almost indefinitely on the attractions of the weapon that avenges it. Nor does Miss Havisham, certain that Estella always acts as an extension of her own desires, show any jealousy of Bentley Drummle, the man Estella marries. Estella in turn asserts that she embraces Miss Havisham and her wishes; when she complains that Estella is "proud" and "hard" to her, Estella reminds her, "I have never been unfaithful to you or your schooling" (301). The erotic resonance of "unfaithful" confirms the sense that Miss Havisham's lessons have created a bond between women as loaded and direct as that between husband and wife or pupil and student. If, as Catherine Robson has argued, Victorian men believed that "perfect childhood" was "exemplified by a little girl" who enjoyed undisrupted seclusion with the mother, then the ideal mother-son relationship was conceived as a mother-daughter one, for boys had reason to believe that girlishness secured a mother's love.[15] In the Freudian model of mother-son love, the son imagines the mother to be like him and responds traumatically when he discovers she lacks a phallus. *Great Expectations* casts the boy as devastated when he discovers his difference from girls, convinced he must make himself over as feminine in order to obtain a woman's love.

Women and the relations between them have a formative influence on how the hero of *Great Expectations* experiences his body and his desires. The social and psychic bonds between women are usually understood as accessories to the desire between men and women, but accessories are not always subordinate and secondary. In law, an accessory bears responsibility for an act even if absent from its commission, and in fashion, accessories pull together an ensemble. Estella is Miss Havisham's accessory, and as such is essential to her character. Accessory has the same root as access—the right to approach, enter, or make use of. While Miss Havisham may seem to be a mere accessory to the love story between Estella and Pip, she is the gatekeeper who controls Pip's way to his lady love. Pip's determining encounters with the female dyad at the center of *Great Expectations* teach him that to gain access to a woman he must embrace the path of femininity and transform himself into a female accessory.

THE FEMALE DYAD AND THE ORIGINS OF DESIRE

In the world of Victorian fiction, notorious for revolving around dead, absent, and idealized mothers, the women of Satis House represent an unusually sustained portrayal of a mother-daughter relationship.[16] Clad in a decaying gown whose "fillings and trimmings . . . look . . . like earthy paper," possessed of a body like those "buried in ancient times, which fall to powder in the moment of being distinctly seen," Miss Havisham initially seems more mummy than Mummy (59). Her living death, however, makes her all the more vivid a presence, and characters interpret her adoptive maternity as both deficient and absolute. When Pip asks "what relation" Estella is to Miss Havisham, Herbert first utters only a curt negation: "None. . . . Only adopted" (175). Yet that minimal maternity implies a total identification, for Estella is nothing but her adoptive mother's creation, as Herbert also points out when he announces, "There has always been an Estella, since I have heard of a Miss Havisham" (181), his use of the indefinite article suggesting that each woman is the other's chief object.

The female dyad is organized around men, for the daughter is trained to avenge her mother's disappointment at a man's hands by executing the maternal command: "Break their hearts my pride and hope" (93). At the same time, Miss Havisham's adoptive maternity makes the female dyad relatively autonomous from men. As an unmarried woman and the sole heir of a wealthy father, Miss Havisham rules her household according to her whims alone. Without submitting to a husband, who under English law would be the sole bearer of parental rights, she acquires a daughter to whom she transmits her name: "'Estella's name. Is it Havisham, or—?' I had nothing to add. 'Or what?' said [Jaggers]. 'Is it Havisham?' 'It is Havisham'" (239). The repetition of Miss Havisham's name in this brief dialogue, and the suggestiveness of Pip's realization that he has "nothing to add" to it, underscores the female dyad's self-sufficiency. Indeed, Pip perceives the two women as inseparable, a joint entity modeled as much on a married couple as on mother and daughter. Pip sees "Miss Havisham and Estella" together in the landscape (107, 108) and "combine[s]" them with the "prospect" on which he gazes (125). When he broods over how his household differs from the upper-class Satis House, he compares how Joe and Mrs. Joe take meals to Miss Havisham and Estella, who "never sat in a kitchen," thus equating the two women with a husband and wife (71). The unit the two women form is less a mother-daughter unit, which has separation as its horizon, than a conjugal one joined until death. Even when Estella marries, the man she chooses resembles the adoptive mother who already treated her daughter as a spouse. His nickname, "the Spider," suggests his affinity with Miss Havisham's spider-filled rooms, and his courtship technique of "doggedly watching Estella" (305) recalls the equally persistent looks Miss Havisham directs at her adopted daughter.

Like the woman beholding a fashion plate, the mother disciplining a daughter, and the girl playing with her doll, Miss Havisham creates a desirable image of femininity that she can visually possess and indulges her lust for power by animating a feminine object whose every act she commands. Estella calls both herself and Pip "mere puppets" subjected to Miss Havisham's wishes (264), and late in the novel she tells Miss Havisham, ending on a note of erotic invitation: "I am what you have made me. Take all the praise, take all the blame, take all the success, take all the failure; in short, take me" (300). Critics often dismiss Estella's relationship with Miss Havisham as inorganic and inert by describing the younger woman as the elder's "instrument," "appendage," "ornamental object," "thing to be bartered in the marriage market," "trained to be desired and to be the object of appetite," "valuable as property to be owned and used."[17] In condemning Miss Havisham for depriving Estella of the autonomy and vitality proper to sexual subjects, however, critics miss the sexiness of their own formulations—the erotic appeal of having or being an instrument, object, or appendage, and the piquancy of attributing the desire for a female object to a woman.

Having acquired a girl of her own without submitting to a father or husband, Miss Havisham turns that girl into a phallus, in Judith Butler's revisionist reading of the term as a "purposefully instrumentalized body-like thing" that can be decoupled from the male body to become "transferable or plastic property."[18] Another way to put this is that Miss Havisham turns Estella into a dildo, a surrogate appendage "mould[ed] into the form that her wild resentment, spurned affection, and wounded pride, found vengeance in" (394). The analogy is not as historically scandalous as it may seem, since dildos appeared often in English pornographic literature.[19] Like a dildo, Estella is endowed with the power of the woman who wields her but has no sensation of her own. "Sen[t] . . . out to attract and torment and do mischief . . . set to wreak Miss Havisham's revenge on men," Estella is both attached to and detachable from Miss Havisham, who directs Estella's actions and uses her as an instrument to give men the shaft (298). Like the "crutch-headed" stick into which Miss Havisham presses her body, Estella is a powerful extension of Miss Havisham's witchlike forces (83).

Put differently, Estella is Miss Havisham's fashion plate and doll, trained to toy with men. Like a doll, Estella cannot feel, but like a doll, her inanimate state makes her susceptible to multiple personifications. Miss Havisham exhibits her as the embodiment of invulnerable female beauty, while Pip infuses her with the sensitivity she avowedly lacks. The doll is both weapon and love object, for Miss Havisham's enjoyment of Estella is inseparable from her keen awareness of Estella's power to inflict pain, not only on others but also on Miss Havisham herself. Miss Havisham never exempts herself from her mission to make Estella irresistible, and the love she lavishes on Estella resembles her self-sacrificial affection for her faithless former lover: "Did I never give her a burning love, inseparable from jealousy at all times, and from sharp pain!" (300). Miss Havisham describes Estella's effect on her as one that mingles comfort and suffering when she recalls how she took Estella "into this wretched breast when it was first bleeding from its stabs and . . . and lavished years of tenderness upon her" (300). The visceral imagery positions Estella as at once weapon, wound, and balm: it opposes Estella to the stabbing knife, imagining the girl entering Miss Havisham's breast to staunch its wound, but also likens Estella to a knife that can inflict "sharp pain." Even Miss Havisham's mode of utterance mingles pain and pleasure as she "moan[s]" of Estella's cruelty, producing sounds associated equally with suffering and sexual excitement (301). Estella's resemblance to an object—hard, cold, insensate—creates a contrast between her "cold, cold heart" and Miss Havisham's "wild heat" (300) that only accentuates the intensity of the older woman's desire.

To the "malignant enjoyment" of the pain Estella inflicts on her and on others, Miss Havisham adds a sheer pleasure in possessing Estella, figured as her oral and visual consumption of the younger woman (114). Always attuned to every nuance of the female dyad's interactions, Pip observes Miss Havisham "fixing" her eyes on Estella (236), consuming her many moods with "miserly relish," and embracing her with "lavish fondness" (93). Miss Havisham hides from others to eat literal food, but she flaunts her uncontrolled ingestion of Estella: "[T]here was something positively dreadful in the energy of her looks and embraces. She hung upon Estella's beauty, hung upon her words, hung upon her gestures, and sat mumbling her own trembling fingers while she looked at her, as though she were devouring the beautiful creature she had reared" (298). Just as Miss Havisham's fingers become mouths when they "mumbl[e]," her eyes become orifices when they ingest Estella with a "greedy look" (232). Her hungry gaze even feeds on the looks others direct at her daughter: "Miss Havisham would often ask me in a whisper . . . 'Does she grow prettier and prettier, Pip?' And when I said yes . . . [she] would seem to enjoy it greedily" (93).

In a reading of hands as figures of sexuality in *Great Expectations*, William Cohen asserts that "there is little of interest to say about Estella's hands" and implies that the same holds true for Miss Havisham's by giving no account of them at all.[20] But Cohen's analysis unwittingly provides yet another confirmation of the novel's preoccupation with desire between women, for *Great Expectations* cannot leave either woman's hands alone. When Estella wants to offer proof of her loyalty to Miss Havisham, she uses her hand: "'When have you found me giving admission here,' she touched her bosom with her hand, 'to anything that you have excluded?'" (301). The autoerotic gesture that accompanies Estella's speech—"she touched her bosom with her hand"—displays the female hand as a conduit of one woman's devotion to another, figured here as a declaration of negative penetration, implying that Estella contains only what she has let Miss Havisham place inside her. Miss Havisham's hands are also always in play and often endowed with sexual power—swelling and throbbing, manipulating sticks and striking bosoms, dressing Estella up or wildly gesturing when she dresses Estella down in outbursts that resemble lovers' quarrels. When Pip witnesses the older woman say goodbye to the younger, he draws attention, over several sentences, to the "clenched hand" that Miss Havisham kisses to Estella "with a ravenous intensity" (237). Miss Havisham is all hands when she tells Pip to love Estella: "She drew an arm round my neck. . . . 'Love her, love her, love her! How does she use you?'" To the "passionate eagerness" of her voice Miss Havisham adds the tumescent power of her grasp: "I could feel the muscles of her thin arm round my neck, swell with the vehemence that possessed her" (237). Witnessing Pip's desire for Estella compounds Miss Havisham's delight in her, and she expresses her pleasure with a physical directness notable in a figure who otherwise aspires to wraithlike disembodiment.

Gender Mobility I: Masculinity as Castoff

Pip is present, as both character and narrator, every time Miss Havisham displays her erotic investment in Estella. Indeed, the two women stage many of those scenes for Pip's benefit—or to his detriment. To understand the novel we must therefore analyze how the female dyad that dominates *Great Expectations* structures Pip's erotic wishes and social ambitions. Blind to the pivotal role played by desire between women in the novel, most critics treat Pip's desire for Estella as too natural to merit analysis, the straightforward desire of one man for one woman. Others have assessed Pip's passivity and frustrated desire as aberrations of proper masculinity, which they define as dominion over women and identification with men.[21] But the narrative suggests that male desire for women requires men to identify with women's desire for each other, for Satis House teaches Pip that what most satisfies a woman is to have or to be another woman's doll.[22]

Fashion and dolls symbolize wealth and leisure as well as alluring femininity, and *Great Expectations* is of course as much about thwarted social mobility as it is about frustrated desire.[23] Pip's identification with the female dyad is motivated by his desire to enter their privileged class as well as by his wish to join a beautiful girl's inner circle. To become a gentleman in *Great Expectations* is both to acquire a lady through marriage and to incorporate her fashionable appearance and detachment from manual labor. The novel presents gentility as originally feminine, for Pip first encounters elite leisure and display in the exclusively female world of Satis House. Leisure makes ladies and gentlemen alike into pampered, adored dolls, while labor masculinizes even the novel's female characters. Pip consistently perceives working women (his sister, Biddy, Molly) as dirty, coarse, or violent—precisely the qualities he associates with the criminal Magwitch and seeks to expunge in himself. The lesson Pip learns about desire's origins in the female dyad is inseparable from one that equates masculinity with degradation and work, and he leaves his first visit to Miss Havisham and Estella convinced that he "was a common labouring-boy; that my hands were coarse, that my boots were thick . . . and generally that I was in a low-lived bad way" (64).

Because Pip believes that to rise in class he must distance himself from his debased boyhood, his narrative of social mobility is also a story of gender mobility, a dual process that involves casting off masculinity and adopting fashionable femininity. Pip contends with Estella and Miss Havisham's contempt for his sex by embracing it. His distaste for masculinity is itself a form of gender mobility, for it enables him to identify with the female dyad's aversion to men and in so doing, to evade the status they assign him.

Great Expectations begins by pronouncing the death of a masculinity that apparently cannot die, since the rest of the novel relentlessly repeats its inaugural belittling of manhood. The novel opens with a gravestone that announces the death of Pip's mother and of his father, whose name, Philip Pirrip, is truncated twice over in Pip's. The "five little stone lozenges" that stand for Pip's "five little brothers" add to the portrait of masculinity as foreclosure when the narrator dryly comments that his male siblings "gave up trying to get a living, exceedingly early in that universal struggle" (3). When Jaggers asks Estella about Pip, she belittles masculinity with the shortness of her response: "'Whom have we here?' . . . 'A boy,' said Estella" (81). Jaggers follows with a pronouncement that consigns all boys to the lowest ranks: "I have a pretty large experience of boys, and you're a bad set of fellows" (81).

Pip's need to annihilate his masculinity stems both from his conviction that desire exists only between women and from his mimicry of the prestigious Estella, who looks on boys with "supreme aversion" (60). When Estella teaches Pip that jacks "ought to be called knaves" (61) and obeys Miss Havisham's command to "beggar" Pip at a card game (59), she dramatizes the novel's constellation of masculinity, working-class origins, and criminal violence, embodied in the equation of "Jacks" with scoundrels.[24] Pip readily adopts Estella's belief that he will become genteel only if he abandons his equally "coarse and common" gender and class (105). His desire to be a gentleman is also a desire not to be a boy, for to be a boy in *Great Expectations* is to be deficient relative to girls, gentlefolk, and adults.

But to become a man of any sort only increases the masculinity that Miss Havisham and Estella hold in such low regard. On his second visit to Satis House, Pip describes his reaction to the "ghastly" Miss Havisham by stating, "I shrank under her touch" (83), a figure of speech that becomes literal when Miss Havisham rejects Pip for growing too tall (96) and Pip attempts to diminish the male bulk she finds objectionable. Pip associates advances in manhood with loss of status. His apprenticeship, for example, coincides with his being mistaken for a criminal and receiving an image of disabled masculinity, a "woodcut of a malevolent young man fitted up with a perfect sausage-shop of fetters" (103). At a dinner to celebrate his orders, he feels like "an excrescence" (103), and is flooded by a "melancholy" (103) sense of superfluity that recalls his earlier dejection after first encountering and incorporating Estella's disdain for his hands as "vulgar appendages" (61). The novel represents Pip's masculinity not as vigor and supremacy but as bondage and monstrosity.

Pip dislikes masculinity in others as well as in himself. He loves Joe, and persistently associates him with femininity. He calls Pumblechook "that detested seedsman," a phrase that also expresses Pip's loathing for his own masculinity, for he is himself a seed, or pip, that he hopes will not mature into a man. He rejects Magwitch's manliness along with his criminal past when Magwitch's return topples Pip's dreams of class elevation and undoes his ambition to leave masculinity behind. Magwitch's relentless address of Pip as "dear boy" (315), his insistence that he is "father" to Pip's "son" (315), and his appearance as "a muscular man, strong on his legs . . . browned and hardened by exposure to weather" (310), all undo Pip's assiduous efforts to mute his own maleness. By immediately insisting on "the abhorrence in which I held the man, the dread I had of him, the repugnance with which I shrank from him," Pip retreats into his identification with a female dyad that disdains overt shows of masculinity (315).

Pip's encounters with Trabb's boy offer a spectacular example of how his attempts to exorcise humble beginnings are inseparable from a desire to excise masculinity. Like Pip at Satis House, Trabb's boy is first referred to simply as "the boy" (148). The tailor's contemptuous treatment of his employee reenacts Pip's previous humiliation at Satis House even as it distances Pip from the boy he once was. When Trabb's boy follows Pip through town as he shows off his new clothes, uncannily appearing out of nowhere to mock Pip's snobbery, the irrepressible boy whom Pip cannot shake also embodies the masculinity he cannot unload. As Pip walks through the streets pretending to see no one, he imitates the haughty Estella, but Trabb's boy leaps out incessantly to expose Pip's pretensions, recalling Pip to his gender as well as to his class origins: "[H]e was a boy whom no man could hurt; an invulnerable and dodging serpent who, when chased into a corner, flew out again between his captor's legs, scornfully yelping" (243). For Pip, Trabb's boy impersonates a bestial, uncontrollable priapism inseparable from low social status. The boy who flies out between his captor's legs can only be "a boy who excited Loathing in every respectable mind" (243), and Pip associates him with a serpent, as he later associates Magwitch with a snake. If masculinity in *Great Expectations* is a wound, then those who remind Pip of his masculinity are wounding. When Trabb's boy surfaces once again, late in the novel, he reappears as an injurious reminder of failed gender mobility. Now inflated into "Trabb's overgrown young man" (425), this embodiment of resurgent masculinity accompanies Startop and Herbert to rescue Pip from Orlick's attack. As he helps Pip's "violently swollen and inflamed . . . throbbing arm" (425) into a sling, Trabb's boy is yet another narrative demonstration that a man's enlarged appendage is equivalent to his weakness, pain, and violation.

GENDER MOBILITY II: PIP AS DOLL AND FASHION PLATE

Dickens based Miss Havisham on a woman who lived in a house with hundreds of male dolls, but when developing his fictional character, he changed the eccentric woman's cohabitant to a single, perfect female doll. Pip similarly jettisons undesirable masculinity for a femininity that represents both desire and desirability. Pip's first view of Estella instantly conveys to him that her superiority is inseparable from her sex: "She seemed much older than I, of course, being a girl, and beautiful and self-possessed; and she was as scornful of me as if she had been one-and-twenty, and a queen" (55). Because Pip measures the distance between himself and Estella in units of femininity, even his fantasies of marrying her revolve around closing the distance between them by transferring her femininity and social status to him. When Pip asks himself "whether Miss Havisham intended me for Estella," both senses of the word "intended" resonate in a query that wonders whether Miss Havisham means him to marry Estella *and* whether she takes him for her (145).

Great Expectations rarely describes Estella's beauty directly but instead materializes her charms in terms of accessories easily transferred from one body to another, such as the "beautiful jewels" that represent Miss Havisham's investment in Estella as a lapidary object of desire.[25] Like jewelry, Estella is hard, brilliant, and coveted, and Pip identifies Estella as gemlike, her beauty full of "glitter and colour" (240).[26] Elsewhere in *Great Expectations*, jewelry is cited as a prime example of "portable property," and its mobility makes it a ready means for Pip to transform himself into an object desirable to women—that is, to transform himself into a bejeweled doll (199). The boy who watched Miss Havisham drape Estella in jewels becomes a man who cannot keep his hands off jewelry and always has it to spare on hand. Pip's first debts are "not unwholly unconnected . . . with jewellery," (271), and he acquires so much of it that when he needs money, he converts "some easily spared articles of jewellery into cash" (377). "Jeweller's account, I think," Joe says of Pip's creditors, as though the uncertainty of Pip's property in his jewelry made even his dispossession of it dubious (456). But the very tenuousness of Pip's claim to his jewels exhibits how his new self mimics Estella, for just as Estella borrows her jewels from Miss Havisham, Pip never owns his outright.

Pip's adult reunion with Magwitch shows that in adopting Estella's look, Pip has also assumed her indebtedness to an imperious benefactor. Like Miss Havisham, Magwitch puts his adopted child's jewels on display: "'Look'ee here!' he went on, taking my watch out of my pocket, and turning towards him a ring on my finger, while I recoiled from his touch as if he had been a snake, 'a gold 'un and a beauty: *that's* a gentleman's, I hope! A diamond all set around with rubies; *that's* a gentleman's, I hope!'" (316). Magwitch refers, of course, to his wish to find that his wealth has transformed Pip into the English gentleman that the transported convict cannot be himself. But the doubts about class and gender inscribed in Magwitch's repeated optative—"that's a gentleman's, I hope!"—are not simply rhetorical, for while a watch was a male accoutrement, a ring could be worn by a man or a woman. Magwitch's desire that Pip be a gentleman conflicts with the wishes of the narrator who reports it, because although Pip enjoys displaying his gentility, he hates to be reminded that he is a man. When Pip compares Magwitch to a snake and recoils from him, he associates Magwitch's lowly criminal status with a serpent's phallic masculinity and refuses both.

It is no accident that Pip makes his most determined efforts to realize gender mobility through jewelry, hair, footwear, and clothing, for those are the very elements that visually define the novel's female dyad and associate it with the carefully rendered features of dolls and fashion plates. Estella is repeatedly associated with beautiful dress. Miss Havisham's tattered dress may seem to place her at the antipodes of the impeccably composed figures in fashion plates, but she is nonetheless, like any fashionable lady, defined by her appearance. The decayed splendor of her outlandish costume makes her a parodic fashion plate, an assemblage of negative fetishes that simultaneously symbolize and compensate for her losses.

Visual objects produce ways of seeing, and Pip, defined by the regard in which he holds Miss Havisham and Estella, has an eye formed by fashion. Once he becomes a gentleman, dress becomes Pip's business, and he maintains that occupation even after the spectacular demise of his expectations, for the chastened adult who narrates the novel continues to exercise a telling eye for appearances and costume. Far from being the gratuitous detail Barthes associated with the reality effect, clothes in *Great Expectations* reveal a sartorial imagination that sees the world in terms of clothing and whose most fleeting glance registers even the most ephemeral characters' dress. The reader knows that Miss Havisham fetishizes shoes, "rich materials—satins, and lace, and silks" only because Pip pays such close attention to her outfit (56). His obsession with clothes is so total that rather than see clothing as a language, he construes letters as clothing. He assumes, for example, that the "large old English D" Biddy gives him to copy is "a design for a buckle" (72), and conflates text and textile when he hallucinates Miss Havisham hanging by the neck, "the faded trimmings of [her] dress . . . like earthy paper" (63).

Pip repeatedly uses clothing to express or effect a transformation. After a miserable visit to Miss Havisham, he finds himself turning to fashion as an antidote, "loitering down the High-Street, looking in disconsolately at the shop windows" (114). Clothes may never adequately console Pip, but no distress can deflect his attention from dress. After being severely burned in his attempt to save Miss Havisham, Pip takes time to observe how his injury has affected his outfit: "I could only wear my coat like a cloak, loose over my shoulders and fastened at the neck" (399). As an expert in the use of clothes to conceal shameful origins, Pip finds it impossible to countenance Magwitch's taste in disguise: "[E]verything in him that was most desirable to repress, started through that thin layer of pretence" (334). Pip's objection to Magwitch's costumes is less a protest against dissembling disguises, however, than an assertion of superior taste. He frames his disapproval of Magwitch's costume as a moral critique of artifice, but his participation in Magwitch's fabrications is what alerts him to their failure: "The more I dressed him and the better I dressed him, the more he looked like the slouching fugitive on the marshes" (333). Rather than abandon the project of clothing Magwitch, Pip overrules the convict's outdated and overstated fashion sense with his own by convincing him not to wear shorts and to wear "his grizzled hair cut short" (334). Even when Pip breaks with his irresolute past self, he retains his zeal for clothes, expressing his newfound vigor by going on a shopping spree. Determined to help Magwitch leave England unscathed, Pip devises a plan that once again involves assembling an outfit: "I . . . went from shop to shop, making such purchases as were necessary to the change in his appearance" (331). Pip's assertiveness may be new, but he remains to the end the fashion victim he has been since his first encounter with Miss Havisham and Estella, loyal to consumer society's credo that when the going gets tough, the tough go shopping.

In his efforts to become a doll to rival and attract Estella and Miss Havisham, Pip must find his own equivalents for the flowing hair, dangling shoes, fine frocks, and brilliant jewels upon which he has learned to train his gaze. During the Regency period in which the novel is set, fashion and display were the province of men as well as women, and an interest in flashy clothing would not automatically indicate a desire to become feminine.[27] *Great Expectations* was written, however, in 1860, during the heyday of polarized male and female fashions, when plain severity prevailed for men and colorful, elaborate clothing was the rule for women.[28] The novel itself takes pains to associate Pip's attention to clothing with Miss Havisham's. When Pip first sees Miss Havisham's room, he picks out as "prominent . . . a draped table with a gilded looking-glass" that he qualifies as "a fine *lady's* dressing table" (56; emphasis added). Pip spends most of the novel seeking a place at that table by acquiring for himself the "bright jewels . . . dresses . . . watch and chain . . . handkerchief, and gloves, and . . . flowers" he first singles out as Miss Havisham's property (56). Pip later buys many of the same objects—jewels, watch, a dressing gown with a "flowered pattern" (217)—and reproduces

Miss Havisham's aesthetic of excess and eccentricity by developing "lavish habits" that lead him to "to be always decorating the chambers in some quite unnecessary and inappropriate way or other" (216) with "incongruous upholstery work" (269). The narrator's boot fetish replicates Miss Havisham's shoe fetish, noted in his first encounter with her, when he observes that she wears one shoe on her foot and keeps the other "on the table near her hand" (56). Just as Miss Havisham's shoes are never quite where they should be, boots crop up in the most surprising places once Pip transforms the "thick . . . common boots" of his youth into luxurious signs of his social ascent (59, 61). He hires a servant he calls the Avenger, "a boy in boots—top boots—in bondage and slavery to whom I might have been said to pass my days," just as he is in thrall to a boyhood spent getting the boot from Estella (216). Pip sees and even hears boots everywhere: Joe's best boots are too big for him (214); Pip wakes to hear Wemmick cleaning his boots (207); he finds Jaggers "in his dressing-room surrounded by his stock of boots" (214); and a servant named none other than "Boots" gratuitously appears at the Blue Boar (228).

Great Expectations has been interpreted as a stalled bildungsroman about a male protagonist who never fully matures, but understood as the story of a man's desire to insert himself into a female dyad, Pip's tale is marginally more successful. In between attracting their contempt and atonement, Pip makes a spectacle of himself in Estella's and Miss Havisham's eyes by becoming a fashion plate. In *The Fashion System*, Roland Barthes asserts that fashion avoids pathos and renounces temporality in favor of situations and decor, but clothes in *Great Expectations* have a plot.[29] They exemplify the novel's themes of social pretense, stolen identity, and the grip of the past, and they have a dynamic role to play as the means to realize the desire to have and to be the female accessory that women desire. Pip's first act on learning of his great expectations is to have himself measured for a new suit, and he alerts the tailor that he wants "a *fashionable* suit of clothes" (148, emphasis added). Even after additional and immediate visits to "the hatter's, and the bootmaker's, and the hosier's" (149), his fashion career is only beginning, for when he arrives in London, he receives "the cards of certain tradesman with whom I was to deal with all kinds of clothes" (168). To be endowed with a fashionable wardrobe is to become—like Estella for Miss Havisham—the object of a hungry gaze, for each shopkeeper who learns of Pip's fortune "ceased to have his attention diverted through the window by the High–street, and concentrated his mind upon me" (149). Even sensible Biddy wants to see Pip's new outfit: "You will show yourself to us; won't you?" (142).

To be a female fashion accessory demands that Pip have feminine fashion accessories, such as the "little hand-portmanteau" (156) that he fingers as obsessively as Miss Havisham nervously taps her stick, "repeatedly unlocking and unstrapping my small portmanteau and locking and strapping it up again" (156). The narrator has to emphasize the littleness of the "small" portmanteau because the word usually referred to a large leather suitcase with two hinged compartments. The portmanteau's hinged design allows Pip to pivot from one compartment to another in a mechanical equivalent of his social shifts from debased masculinity to elite femininity. It becomes a container for Pip's femininity, and when he stores it on a coach journey, he tellingly remarks that "My little portmanteau was in the boot under my feet," placing the portmanteau in a boot that is the antithesis of his boyhood boots (227). The boots Pip wore on his feet kept him under, but the boot under his feet signifies his ability to travel in style, with a pampered ease that is no longer the monopoly of Estella and Miss Havisham. Packed into Pip's portmanteau are the clothes he hopes will place him on the same footing as Estella and make him her equal in social class and feminine finery. Indeed, Herbert identifies the portmanteau with Pip's desire for Estella when he tells Pip, "You brought your adoration and your portmanteau here, together" (244–45). The portmanteau is a figure of infinite containment and endless envelopment, a holder for the clothes that enclose Pip that can itself be placed in another container. Like Pip's adoration for Estella, the portmanteau materializes his desire to combine incorporation of a feminine other with envelopment by her.

The Sentimental Education of the Female Dyad

Great Expectations equates Pip's desire to have Estella with his desire to be her, a longing he expresses by cloaking himself in the fashionable accessories that he hopes will attract the female dyad's gaze. Pip's urge to metamorphose from a laboring boy with "black face and hands" (106) into a fashionable gentleman who wins the woman in white's beautiful doll is inseparable from a wish to see himself reflected in the gilded looking glass of Miss Havisham, whose gaze confers social and erotic value. Pip's new wardrobe briefly gives him access to a position previously occupied only by Estella when he displays his new clothes to Miss Havisham and becomes the object of her admiring gaze and her relatives' envious looks (154–55). Pip comes closest, however, to realizing his desire to be the object of the female dyad's gaze in a charged scene in the third volume, when he confronts both women with his love for Estella and his knowledge that Miss Havisham let him mistake her for his benefactor. The scene begins with a typical configuration of the female dyad excluding the male spectator and climaxes when Pip finally succeeds in attracting each woman's gaze to himself alone. At the outset, Pip describes Miss Havisham "looking on" at Estella, who knits at her feet and only glances at Pip. The narrator begins his tableau in the continuous past tense ("was looking," "pausing," "motioning"), which conveys the unchanging rhythm of Satis House. Once Pip makes the women look at him, the narrator shifts to the simple past, dramatizing the importance of an event happening for the first time in the novel: "They both raised their eyes as I went in, and both saw an alteration in me. I derived that, from the look they interchanged" (354). That moment does not eliminate female homoeroticism as the template of desire, since Pip knows what the women see in him only from the look they exchange with each other. It does, however, mark the dissolution of the female dyad, for it is the last glimpse the novel provides of Estella and Miss Havisham together. That structural decision suggests that once Pip attracts Miss Havisham's gaze away from Estella and onto himself, he displaces her as its object. In Pip's final view of the two women together, each has finally taken her eyes off the other and fixed them on him: "Estella looked at me merely with incredulous wonder . . . Miss Havisham . . . seemed all resolved into a ghastly stare of pity and remorse" (360). When Pip next visits Miss Havisham, she is alone, and he is the sole focus of her visual attention: "her eyes rested on me" (391).

The coincidence of Miss Havisham's attention to Pip's emotional outburst with her sudden capacity to feel "pity" and "remorse" casts a new light on the impasse Pip reaches in his drama of desire and identification. The obstacle he confronts is not his sex but rather his wish to combine two incompatible forms of social relationship prevalent between women: on the one hand, the altruism and reciprocity embodied in the ideal of female friendship, and on the other, the sadistic objectification inherent in the female homoeroticism of consumer culture. Pip's aspirations to femininity are not in and of themselves barriers to his happiness, but his attempt to combine two incompatible modes of femininity is doomed to fail. Were he willing to embrace the altruism, reciprocity, and egalitarianism of the plot of female amity (see chapter 2), he would marry his social equal and spiritual superior, Biddy, just as David Copperfield marries Agnes—or, in a counterfactual fictional universe, he would receive Estella as a gift from Miss Havisham just as David's dying first wife arranges for him to marry her friend. But the plot of female amity in *Great Expectations* confronts an insuperable obstacle in the compelling eroticism of a commodity culture invested in hierarchy, aggression, and submission—in one woman worshipping at the foot of another, a mother disciplining her daughter, or a girl dominating her doll.

As many critics have observed, Pip fully embraces not only the accoutrements of fashion culture and doll fiction but also their dynamics of pain, pleasure, and objectification. Where Estella has the good looks and high price of an expensive and unattainable doll, Pip has the sentimental value vested in literary dolls who accept abuse and neglect as their lot and come to life only to articulate the pain they submit to at their mistress's hands (see chapter 3). Like many narrators of first-person doll tales, Pip is aware that he is only a plaything for Estella, who taunts and slaps Pip and takes "pleasure, from giving me pain" (128).[30] Like many a doll, Pip suffers "torture" at Estella's hands (296) and a "sense of dependence and even of degradation" (298) in her presence. Victorian doll tales criticize insensitive children who treat dolls as objects, contrasting their deficient humanity to the more benevolent feelings of dolls who appear inanimate but whose narration reveals them to be sentient subjects. *Great Expectations* similarly contrasts Miss Havisham's inhumane treatment of Pip as "a model with a mechanical heart" to the narrator's reminders that he feels "pain" (319).

The punishment scenarios that dominated Victorian fashion discourse, pornography, and doll literature surface in *Great Expectations* as recurring scenes of chastisement and humiliation.[31] Victorians thought of Dickens as an opponent of corporal punishment, and a letter on the topic to the editor of the *Englishwoman's Domestic Magazine* denounced women who advocated birching as worthy of marriage only to "one of the Murdstone or Squeers species."[32] Yet the ease with which that correspondent associated sadistic mothers with not one but two Dickensian villains also illustrates Dickens's lifelong preoccupation with physical discipline. The birching woman appears in *Great Expectations* as Mr. Wopsle's great-aunt, who occasionally makes "an indiscriminate totter at [her students] with a birch-rod" (71), and as Mrs. Joe, who more effectually wields the Tickler, "a wax-ended piece of cane, worn smooth by collision with my tickled frame" (9). The obscenely named Tickler—a pornographic text published in 1866 was entitled *The New Ladies' Tickler*—merges the punishment of the cane with the pleasure of tickling, and evokes Miss Havisham, who uses Estella to tease and cut Pip.[33] Estella herself occupies the top rung in the novel's ranks of punishing women, and Pip finds himself in thrall to her icy demeanor—"hard and haughty and capricious to the last degree"—which reflects the stance of the lady of fashion so prized in flagellation narratives (174–75). Estella embodies the restrained contempt and arbitrary exercise of power that correspondents in Victorian fashion magazines deemed far more "ceremonious" than the determined display of "irritation" that both fashion magazines and *Great Expectations* associated with angry women like Pip's working-class sister.[34]

Great Expectations ends on a notoriously indeterminate note, but to the extent that the final volume provides a sense of closure, it does so by shifting Pip's desire to join the female dyad from the discipline and punishment of fashion to a terrain where Pip can easily outclass Estella: sentiment. Estella feels nothing for Pip, not because his dress fails to impress, but because she can feel nothing at all; as she herself explains to Pip, "I have a heart. . . . But I have no softness there, no—sympathy—sentiment—nonsense!" (235). Pip, on the other hand, has sentiment in abundance, and his relationship to Estella highlights that, in this one regard, he possesses what she lacks. As Herbert puts it when he seeks to persuade Pip to "detach" himself from Estella, Pip's love for an unfeeling woman is all the more dangerous because it is "rooted in the breast of a boy whom nature and circumstances made so romantic" (247). Estella's bosom, which attracts Miss Havisham's jewels, is a mere surface relative to the emotional profundity of Pip's breast, and the novel achieves tentative closure by changing the definition of femininity from a matter of fetishistic surfaces to an ideal of emotional depth.

Having achieved only partial success as a fashion plate, Pip introduces a new standard of femininity that allows him to supplant Estella. In his role as the consummate Dickensian daughter to Magwitch, Pip replaces Magwitch's biological daughter, Estella.[35] Magwitch explicitly views Pip as a substitute for his daughter, telling Herbert that Pip recalls to him "the little girl so tragically lost" (402). Like a good daughter, Pip holds Magwitch's hand throughout his trial (451) and receives his last kiss as the dying man lets Pip's hand sink "upon his breast" (455). The use of the word "breast," with its feminine connotations, underscores how the sentimental dyad formed by Pip and Magwitch replaces the antisentimental couple formed by Estella and Miss Havisham, characterized by a very different play of hands on bosoms.

The novel's structure reinforces this replacement, since once Magwitch reappears, the narrative depicts Estella and Miss Havisham together only one final time, in the fifth chapter of the third volume. In that chapter, as we have seen, Pip finally enters the women's world, taking Miss Havisham's seat by the dressing-table and attracting both women's gazes. He does not claim their attention with fancy dress, for this is one of the few instances when Pip visits Satis House without mentioning his clothing or portmanteau. Instead, Pip induces Miss Havisham "to look steadily" at him (355) and possesses her "gradually concentrating attention" (357) by speaking the language of sentiment in a "passionate" declaration of love for Estella. Where Pip's costume never fully succeeded in transforming him into Miss Havisham's object, his outburst of feeling shifts the work of gender mobility from him to her. His emotional display translates Miss Havisham's femininity from its habitually spectacular register into the sentimental one she had rejected, and allows him to assume and redefine Estella's role as Miss Havisham's reflection. As she puts it, "Until I saw in you a looking-glass that showed me what I had once felt myself,

I did not know what I had done" (394). Earlier Miss Havisham sat before a literal mirror and made Estella a material reflection of invulnerability, but here Pip becomes the figurative mirror of her past and present sorrow. Once a fetishist and voyeur whose handiwork was the unfeeling Estella, Miss Havisham suddenly becomes a contrite woman whose hand no longer fondles crutch or daughter, but instead rests penitently on her newly revived "heart" (360).

In making Miss Havisham over in the image of sentimental femininity, *Great Expectations* finds Pip a role within the doll narrative, though not as the fashion doll whose part he coveted. Instead, Dickens appropriates didactic doll narratives that conclude on a repentant note, with speeches by girls who regret mistreating their dolls or by doll narrators who realize the worthlessness of merely physical beauty. The humbled doll who narrates *Victoria-Bess* (1879) echoes Miss Havisham's and Estella's last speeches when she explains, "Affliction's stern but kind discipline had purified me of so many of my faults, my overbearing pride for one thing."[36] Miss Havisham's last outburst is similarly one of "earnest womanly compassion" (395). Where she once hung over Estella to gloat, she now trembles over Pip to weep. The hands that placed jewels in Estella's hair are now "tremulous" (391) and outstretched in a plea for forgiveness: "she . . . pressed that hand of mine which was nearest to her grasp, and hung her head over it and wept" (394). Miss Havisham's conversion to sentimental womanliness finally incorporates Pip into the female dyad, for he becomes the sentimental subject of Miss Havisham's effusions as Estella had been their fetish object. When Miss Havisham asks his forgiveness, she drops "on her knees at my feet; with her folded hands raised to me in the manner in which, when her poor heart was young and fresh and whole, they must have often been raised to heaven from her mother's side" (393). Kneeling at Pip's feet as she once sat at her mother's, her once restless hands folded in prayer, Miss Havisham now plays worshipful daughter to Pip's divine mother.

Just as the desire to punish cannot be expunged from even the most moralistic doll narratives, which chastise girls for having punished their dolls, Pip's sentimental mother-daughter relationship with Miss Havisham cannot fully displace the sadism and fetishism of the original dyad she formed with Estella. Miss Havisham's self-abasement before Pip glorifies him and humbles her, much as she had once humiliated him, and the narrative itself aggressively eliminates Miss Havisham when, almost immediately after she kneels at Pip's feet, her dress catches fire and she dies of burns before the chapter ends. The sentimental warmth that melts Miss Havisham's iciness becomes a flame that incinerates her. Doll narratives preach that aggression can only play its role when veiled as impersonal justice, and any glee Pip might feel over Miss Havisham's suffering is confined to the way that his effort to rescue her from death resembles an attempt on her life: in his effort to put out the flames that engulf her, he throws her down and they "struggl[e] like desperate enemies" (397).

That conflagration allows Pip finally to triumph over Miss Havisham sartorially, for he puts out the fire that reduces her signature outfit to dust by covering her in his "double-caped great-coat . . . and . . . another thick coat" (397). With "every vestige of her dress . . . burnt" (398), Miss Havisham reverses positions with Pip. Now it is she who lacks adequate clothing and Pip who has layers to spare, she who is coated in another gender's trappings when Pip wraps her in garments rendered useful by the masculine thickness and superfluity he had been taught to consider undesirable. Yet Pip still lacks Miss Havisham's acknowledgment that he has succeeded as a female accessory, and the implausible rapidity with which Miss Havisham's demise follows her conversion to sentimentality suggests that her character is no longer interesting once she has relinquished the cruelty that was inseparable from her compulsive attention to dress. Wrapped in a white sheet, her dying speech repetitive and "blank," Miss Havisham vanishes along with the clothes that were the key to her value in Pip's tale (399).

Great Expectations ends by drawing the previously impervious Estella into a sentimental dyad with Pip. The novel's famous final phrase, "I saw the shadow of no parting from her," has always been read as an ambiguous comment on Pip's marriage to Estella, a deliberately stilted phrase with several possible interpretations. It can mean that Pip has no fear they will part, or that he sees Estella's gloom-inducing "no" departing from her. On the other hand, the novel's final sentence could be Pip's commentary on Estella's statement that they will "continue friends apart" (479). The narrator's final words might then mean that Pip has yet to renounce his delusions about Estella (he sees them together although she does not), or that he understands that his vision of them not parting is illusory, a mere shadow rather than a reality.

The conclusion's eloquent obscurity suggests that marriage between a man and a woman has never been the narrator's goal; as we have seen, the union Pip desired with Estella was always more that of one fashionable woman with another. A marital ending thus remains shrouded in ambiguity even when Estella unambiguously reenacts Miss Havisham's reduction to repentant sentiment. Like Miss Havisham, Estella asks for Pip's forgiveness now that she has "been bent and broken" by suffering (478). Somewhat diminished in beauty, her eyes "saddened," "softened," and filled with "tears," Estella is no longer supremely cruel or indifferent but instead embraces Pip's allegiance to feeling and sympathy (477). Admitting that suffering "has taught me to understand what your heart used to be" (478), Estella extends her "once insensible hand" in a "friendly touch" (477) that signifies her acceptance of the sentimental standard that will always award Pip precedence in any competition between them.

The adoption of sentimental reciprocity as a new basis for the bond between Estella and Pip only adds to the melancholy of the novel's conclusion:

> "Be as considerate and good to me as you were, and tell me we are friends."
>
> "We are friends," said I, rising and bending over her, as she rose from the bench.
>
> "And will continue friends apart," said Estella. (478–79)

Estella and Pip rise together "as" one, and in "rising and bending over her," Pip balances a gesture of mastery with one of subservience. Their exchange enacts the symmetry to which friendship aspires, as they trade the word "friend" back and forth without the contradictions and qualifications that characterized their former exchanges. When Pip asserts, "We are friends," he echoes Estella, whose final utterance mirrors his repetition of hers and extends his present claim into the future. As a fragment that begins with a conjunction, the phrase "And will continue friends apart" embodies Estella's continuity with Pip, and though her words threaten separation, they also allude to friendship's independence from physical embodiment. The narrator's next words, "I took her hand in mine," appear to contradict Estella's and suggest that he is not yet ready to relinquish the play of hands he had so envied in her relationship with Miss Havisham. Yet that unadorned clasp of hands, free of rings, gloves, and watches, in the one scene between Pip and Estella to make no mention of what either one wears, only adds to the conclusion's pathos. By the end of the novel, Pip has allied himself with both members of the primal female dyad—through sentiment rather than fashion. But to deprive Miss Havisham and Estella of their trappings in the primal scene is also to acknowledge his failure to assume them himself. Whether Pip's heartfelt grasp of Estella's hand means that Pip and Estella marry or separate, remain friends together or apart, their ultimately neutral embrace cannot be disentangled from the ruin of his greatest expectation, that he will join the female dyad by commanding their recognition of his successful transformation into a fashionable female accessory.

PART THREE

Plastic Institutions: Female Marriage

CHAPTER 5

The Genealogy of Marriage

DOES MARRIAGE HAVE A HISTORY? And if so, is it only the history of alliances between men and women? Social historians have answered the first question with a resounding yes, and in the past several decades have traced marriage's evolving relationship to the state, civil society, and private life, to friends and kin, to consent, contract, and pleasure. But most have also taken for granted that until very recently, marriage has been defined as the union of male and female.[1] In 2004, when legalization of same-sex marriage in Massachusetts sparked awareness that many same-sex couples were eager to wed, those on all sides of the ensuing debate viewed gay marriage as a sudden development with relatively shallow historical roots. Opponents charged that same-sex marriage lacked a past and would be the end of history, calling it a threat to "the most fundamental institution of civilization."[2] Supporters saw it as a new phenomenon made possible only by the very recent intersection of a gay civil rights movement and the modernization of heterosexual marriage. As Stephanie Coontz put it in a defense of same-sex unions, "Gays and lesbians simply looked at the revolution heterosexuals had wrought and noticed that with its new norms, marriage could work for them, too."[3]

Changes in heterosexual marriage have made lesbian and gay unions possible, but the influence has not been unilateral. For over a century, same-sex unions have also affected innovations in heterosexual marriage. To be sure, until very recently legal marriage has only been available to opposite-sex couples, most people have long taken it for granted that marriage takes place between men and women, and for decades, lesbian and gay activists have focused more on criticizing marriage than on demanding the right to it (as many continue to do). But the meaning of marriage is not exhausted by its legal definition, and socially accepted forms of marriage that exist outside the law have long informed legal changes to the institution. Far from having to wait for heterosexuals to make marriage more flexible, same-sex couples helped create that flexibility by using marriage as a model for their relationships and by actively working to change the laws governing unions between men and women.

Same-sex unions have been part of the history of marriage since at least the nineteenth century. As we saw in chapter 1, the female relations of Victorian England included women who lived together, owned property together, made vows of fidelity to one another, and were described as spouses by themselves and by others in their social networks. Women in female marriages created relationships that, like legal marriage, did the work assigned to sexuality in the nineteenth century: the management of shared households, the transmission of property, the expression of emotional and religious affect, and the development and care of the self.[4] Through individual, customized legal agreements, women in female couples obtained some of the rights that the state automatically conferred on married couples. Their legal status as unmarried women allowed them to have a socially recognized spouse and to keep the economic autonomy that legally married wives relinquished under the doctrine of coverture. Women in female marriages were thus in the vanguard of the movement to modernize marriage, for their relationships anticipated the increasing equality of husbands and wives gradually written into law over the course of the nineteenth and twentieth centuries. More concretely, several women in female marriages played a small but pivotal role in advocating for civil divorce, the property and custody rights of wives, and expanded opportunities for unmarried women. Although female marriages were the exception, not the rule, women in them were able to play a significant role in the history of marriage because they belonged to social networks that included legislators, journalists, activists, and anthropologists. They were, to use Michael Lucey's terms, agents "who both *work within* and *do work on* . . . social forms."[5] The pressures exerted by forms of kinship outside the law but inside the social were a crucial factor in making marriage a plastic institution.

Just as the "homosexual" is a recent invention, so too is the opposition between marriage and homosexuality. Nor is the history of same-sex unions congruent with the emergence of lesbian and gay identity, for same-sex unions existed long before sexology invented the "invert." Only once medical writers and social thinkers in the 1880s began to equate inversion with the infantile, the primitive, and the undoing of a civilization premised on monogamous, heterosexual marriage did homosexuality come to seem antithetical to marriage. Since then, many have perpetuated the association between homosexuality and primitivism by warning that gay marriage will lead to an undifferentiated presocial state in which anything goes. As United States senator Rick Santorum notoriously put it in 2002, if the right to privacy were extended to gay sex, then "you have the right to bigamy, you have the right to polygamy, you have the right to incest, you have the right to adultery. You have the right to anything."[6] In that view, gay sex is so external to the social order that it has the power to reverse the course of civilization by catapulting culture into a state of nature.

In the service of a diametrically opposed political vision, Gayle Rubin made a similar argument in her pathbreaking 1995 essay, "The Traffic in Women," when she famously observed that a critique of anthropological and psychoanalytical theories of culture relegate homosexuality to a precultural realm: "[T]he incest taboo presupposes a prior, less articulate taboo on homosexuality. A prohibition against *some* heterosexual unions assumes a taboo against *non*heterosexual unions." Prefiguring a point that Judith Butler developed in *Gender Trouble* and subsequent writings, Rubin showed that anthropological theories of kinship that posit the incest taboo and male exchange of women as necessary for the emergence of culture also exclude homosexuality from civilization, and thus establish an implicit equivalence between them.[7] Psychoanalysis and structural anthropology, by emphasizing that the incest taboo and the taboo on homosexuality make social and psychic coherence possible, raise the specter that to legitimate homosexuality would dissolve the very structure of kinship.

Homosexuality does indeed haunt Claude Lévi-Strauss's *The Elementary Structures of Kinship* (1949), one of Rubin's key texts, but interestingly, Lévi-Strauss does not associate homosexuality with incest or with the precultural. One can see the case for Rubin's argument that Lévi-Strauss's concept of the incest taboo assumes a prior taboo on homosexuality, for Lévi-Strauss's theory is not overtly hospitable to the possibility of formalized same-sex relationships and there is little in it to salvage for progressive sexual politics today. "[T]he rules of kinship and marriage," Lévi-Strauss wrote, "are not made necessary by the social state. They are the social state itself."[8] The rule of marriage is the prohibition on incest, which regulates the relation between the sexes as a dictate that men must exchange women (23). It would thus follow that sexual relationships that do not involve male exchange of women could not be part of the social state. Lévi-Strauss accordingly dismissed theories of kinship that depended on what he called "feminism"—by which he meant any explanation that assigned agency and autonomy to women. In this sense, 1940s structuralist anthropology proved less willing to recognize the possibility of female autonomy than its Victorian avatars, with their accounts of early matriarchy and polyandry. Victorian anthropologists, however, also argued that primitive societies lacked incest taboos. By asserting that the incest taboo was universal, Lévi-Strauss conferred structure and sociality on primitive society—and simultaneously aligned "the social state" with marriage, defined as male authority over women, and with culture, posited as a set of rules that require men to exchange women.

Surprisingly, however, Lévi-Strauss was also willing to recognize the sociality of homosexuality. He noted that homosexuality and fraternal polyandry can both be "solutions" to the scarcity of wives (38).[9] Responding to Brenda Seligman's argument that blood-brotherhood "disputes that the woman is the sole or predominant instrument of alliance," Lévi-Strauss conceded, "It is far from our mind to claim that the exchange or gift of women is the only way to establish an alliance in primitive societies" (483). He even claimed that before Seligman did so, he himself had already shown that among some groups, the cross-cousin and potential brother-in-law "is the one with whom, as an adolescent, one indulges in homosexual activities" (484). That is, he glossed, brothers-in-law are the same "whether they play the role of the opposite sex in the erotic games of childhood, or whether their masculine alliance as adults is confirmed by each providing the other with what he does not have—a wife—through their simultaneous renunciation of what they both do have—a sister" (484).

Lévi-Strauss recognized homosexuality only to the extent that he could subsume it within heterosexuality, but in the process he characterized homosexuality as cultural, as a form of alliance within the social, not banished from it. The universality of the incest taboo means not that homosexuality is equally taboo, but rather that even homosexuality is ultimately governed by the prohibition on incest and the imperative to exogamy. Hence the assertion that homosexual relationships are governed by the same rule of exchange as heterosexual ones: "[M]arriage serves as model for that artificial and temporary 'conjugality' between young people of the same sex in some schools and on which Balzac makes the profound remark that it is never superimposed upon blood ties but replaces them" (480). An artificial, temporary, imitative conjugality—Lévi-Strauss barely conceded the existence of homosexuality as such. But precisely because he could barely see it as different from heterosexuality, he did not distinguish between heterosexuality and same-sex alliances, nor did he locate homosexuality in a primordial state of nature before incest was prohibited.

FEMALE MARRIAGE IN THE NINETEENTH CENTURY

Members of respectable Victorian society were also able to perceive women as married to one another, and they rarely confounded female marriages between white, middle-class women with the polygamous or incestuous arrangements they attributed to the peoples they sought to subjugate, using Christian ideals of marriage to justify the imperial mission. The life of Charlotte Cushman (1816–1876), documented in letters and memoirs, shows that even a woman who did have an illicit affair with her daughter-in-law differentiated between that illicit, quasi-incestuous affair and a more marital relationship, conducted in full view of her friends and the public, with a woman she called her wife. Charlotte Cushman was one of the most acclaimed and financially successful American actresses of the nineteenth century, best known for playing Romeo in the 1840s. Born in the United States, she lived outside it for most of her life, first in England and then in Italy, but returned often to play sold-out national tours. As Lisa Merrill has shown in a brilliant biography, Cushman used the language of marriage to conceptualize many of her sexual relationships with women, which after her rise to stardom usually consisted of a primary relationship with a peer and a secondary, clandestine relationship with a much younger woman, often a fan.[10] Cushman described her primary relationships as marriages that created a spousal bond and kinship network. In 1844, she noted in her diary, "Slept with Rose," and the following day wrote "'R.' Saturday, July 6th 'married.'" (9). As in heterosexual marriage, sex made marriage and marriage created kinship: Cushman called Rose's father "Father," as though he were her father-in-law, or as though in marrying Rose she had become her sister (74).

Cushman was involved in two long-term relationships with women: one with Matilda Hays, an author, translator, and feminist activist, and another with the sculptor Emma Stebbins, whom she met in 1857. Stebbins is best known today for her sculpture *Angel of the Waters*, which stands in Central Park's Bethesda Terrace and features prominently in Tony Kushner's *Angels in America*. Until her death in 1876, Cushman cultivated a public persona as a respectable artist and lived openly with Emma Stebbins in an elegant apartment brimming with friends and pets. After Cushman's death, Emma Stebbins wrote a biography of her former spouse that, with the reticence and impersonality typical of the lifewriting discussed in chapter 1, made only one direct statement about their relationship: "It was in the winter of 1856–57 that the compiler of these memoirs first made Miss Cushman's acquaintance, and from that time the current of their two lives ran, with rare exceptions, side by side." But Stebbins attested to her marital connection with Cushman through the very act of writing the biography as a memoir, in her pointed exclusion of Cushman's other lovers from her account, in her detailed description of their shared apartment in Rome, and in a ten-page inventory of their pets, including dogs named Teddy and Bushie.[11]

One of the women's many pets became the subject of a eulogy by Isa Blagden, a writer who lived in Florence and was close to Stebbins and Cushman, for whom she composed "To Dear Old Bushie. From One Who Loved Her," cited in full in Stebbins's biography. It would be naive to think that the Victorians were so naive as to be unaware of the connotations of "Bushie" as a pet name, so to speak, for female genitalia. The use of pronouns rather than proper names in the subtitle "From One Who

Loved Her" invites us to read the poem symbolically, as a lament for a beloved dog and as an anticipation of the death of a beloved woman. That conflation is facilitated by the poem's rhetorical decision to apostrophize the absent dog directly in the second person as an unnamed but personified interlocutor: "Much loving and much loved, dare I, / With my weak, faltering praise, / Record thy pure fidelity, / Thy patient, loving ways; / Thy wistful, eager, gasping sighs, / Our sullen sense to reach; / The solemn meaning of thine eyes, / More clear than uttered speech?" The rest of the poem argues that animals equal humans in love and fidelity, and concludes, "A life-long love lies in thy dust; / Can human grave hold more?"[12] In its emphasis on the true devotion of a passionate love that remains tacit, the poem signals Blagden's genuine affection for Bushie and her appreciation for the "life-long love" between the two women with whom the dog lived.[13]

Cushman herself described her relationship to Stebbins as a marriage when she warned her young lover Emma Crow that she was not a free woman; as she put it, "Do you not know that I am already married and wear the badge upon the third finger of my left hand?" (211). Cushman began a clandestine relationship with the much younger Crow in 1858, soon after she exchanged rings with Emma Stebbins and began living with her. Cushman met Crow while touring the United States; their affair lasted years, spanned continents, and is documented in Cushman's many letters to Crow, which Crow preserved and bequeathed to the Library of Congress, despite her lover's many anxious requests that she burn them. In that correspondence, Cushman frequently tried to naturalize her adulterous betrayal of Emma Stebbins by calling the younger Emma Crow her daughter, niece, and baby, as if to suggest that Crow was not Stebbins's rival but simply an addition to the family. "Never did a mother love her child so dearly. Never did Auntie think so sweetly so yearningly of her Niece. Never did Ladie love her lover so intensely," Cushman wrote.[14]

Cushman took the incestuous fantasy of sex as kinship to its literal limits when she encouraged Crow to marry Cushman's nephew and adopted son, Ned Cushman. Cushman's plan was to have Crow live near her as her daughter-in-law, a situation to which Cushman's wife, Emma Stebbins, could not object. Crow was so in love with Cushman that she agreed to the arrangement, and she and Cushman continued their affair well after Crow's marriage to Ned made Charlotte Cushman young Emma's mother-in-law and aunt to the children Emma had with Ned. After Crow married Ned Cushman, Charlotte continued to address Emma as her lover, but also as a "dear new daughter" who had, in taking the Cushman name, also become in some sense Cushman's wife. Cushman called Emma's marriage with Ned her own "ultimate entire union" with Emma, and her letters to a pregnant Emma convey a sense, as biographer Lisa Merrill puts it, "that she and her 'little lover' were having this baby together." With a grandiosity that came easily to a rich and famous actress, Cushman arrogated to herself the roles of husband, wife, father, mother, aunt, and lover, saluting Emma as "Dearest and Sweetest daughter[,] niece, friend and lover" and referring to herself in other letters as "Big Mamma."[15]

Cushman's matrilineal, incestuous, adulterous, polygamous, homosexual household seems to realize the conservative fantasy of the primitive family in which no distinctions are made, no restrictions imposed, and patriarchal monogamy does not contain the promiscuity that results when women reign unfettered. For that very reason, Cushman provides an excellent point of departure for interrogating the equation of homosexuality with primitive sexual anarchy. Her affair with Emma Crow does not in fact show that those who disregard the taboo on homosexuality will also flout the prohibitions on incest and polygamy. Instead it demonstrates that, like most Victorians, Cushman's desires were shaped by taboos that incited the very desires they prohibited. Vows of monogamy, even when not legally binding, made adultery all the more alluring, and as Foucault shows in the first volume of the *The History of Sexuality*, nothing in the Victorian family was more normative than its obsession with incest. In societies that make "the family . . . the most active site of sexuality . . . incest occupies a central place; it is constantly being solicited and refused; it is an object of obsession and attraction, a dreadful secret and an indispensable pivot. It is manifested as a thing that is strictly forbidden . . . but it is also a thing that is continuously demanded in order for the family to be a hotbed of constant sexual incitement."[16] The mother-daughter axis was as subject to eroticization as any other aspect of family life, and incest fantasies, veiled and overt, were a prominent feature of Victorian culture (see chapters 3 and 4). Cushman's letters to Emma Crow blurred the lines between lover and family member in the same way as Dinah Mulock Craik's 1850 novel *Olive* did when describing a wife's love for her husband: "She loved him at once with the love of mother, sister, friend, and wife."[17] Pornographic novels obsessively depicted incest of every variety and in every possible gender configuration (see chapter 3), and Henry James easily translated his acquaintance with Charlotte Cushman's history into the heterosexual plot of *The Golden Bowl*, in which a father marries his daughter's husband's lover, also named Charlotte.[18]

The normative cast of even Cushman's most hidden desires helps to explain why she was not branded as deviant in her lifetime and why the relationships with women that she did make public were accepted by those surrounding her. Cushman was a recognized and often admired type: a nineteenth-century woman whose financial independence made it relatively easy for her to form a couple with another woman. Cushman

enjoyed playing male roles on stage, and like many middle-class and aristocratic women in female marriages, she adopted masculine dress and
nicknames.[19] But she lived openly with other women as a woman, and
identified with both feminine and masculine roles. Cushman called Emma
Stebbins her better half and described herself as married to her first lover,
Rose, but she did not consistently or exclusively see herself as a husband.
The language of marriage described the quality of her commitment to a
sexual partner rather than a gendered division of roles. In this respect
female marriage appears, on the basis of current historical evidence, to
have been a primarily middle- and upper-class phenomenon. Working-
class women who earned their own money also formed couples with other
women, but it was more common for one member of the couple to live
as a man. Such alliances were therefore not perceived as female marriages.
Although in some technical sense they could be called marriages between
women, in the eyes of the law, the couple's community, and even the couple themselves, they were marriages between a woman and a man. If
caught or exposed as women, some female husbands were legally censured and mocked in ballads and broadsides for seizing male privileges,
but others were not.[20] An 1869 article on "Modern Amazons," for example, wrote approvingly of two women who assumed the roles of "man
and wife" and "lived together in good repute with their neighbours for
eighteen years."[21]

Examples of two women using the language of marriage to describe
their relationships in the relatively private context of journals and letters
abound across the nineteenth century. Eleanor Butler referred to her beloved Sarah Ponsonby in her journals as "my better half."[22] Sculptor Harriet Hosmer, one of Cushman's friends in Rome, called the widowed Englishwoman Lady Louisa Ashburton "my sposa" and referred to herself
as Ashburton's "hubbie," "wedded wife," and daughter. Writing to Ashburton of a marriage between monarchs, Hosmer added, "They will be
as happy in their married life as we are in ours"; in another letter she
promised "when you are here I shall be a model wife (or husband which-
ever you like)."[23] Early in the century, Anne Lister and Anne Walker decided to become "companions for life" in a relationship that would, according to both, "be as good as marriage." Lister sealed her union with
Walker by giving her a ring and arranging to receive communion with
her, along with a legal ceremony in which each woman willed the other
her unentailed property.[24] An 1892 obituary of English-born Annie Hindle in the *Chicago Herald* reported that in 1886 the famous male imper-
sonator was married to her "dresser and faithful companion" Annie
Ryan, "a pretty little brunette of twenty-five" by "a minister of the gospel,
Rev. E.H. Brooks," who "solemnly pronounced Annie Hindle the husband of Annie Ryan." Hindle married in male dress, using a male name,

but the article noted that following the wedding she lived with Ryan while dressed as a woman: "The neighbors respected them. . . .That they could live together openly as man and wife, the husband always in female attire, and yet cause no scandal, is the best proof of the esteem in which those around them held them."[25]

The idea of female marriage was not simply a private metaphor used by women in same-sex relationships; it was also a term used by the legally married to describe relationships that were conducted openly and discussed neutrally in respectable society. Even among middle-class Victorians, marriages were not defined by law alone, and for couples with no legal status, social acceptance provided legitimation and established rules for beginning and ending relationships.[26] Charlotte Cushman assumed that many in her circle were aware of sexual romance between women, since she warned Emma Crow in an 1860 letter that "there are people in this world who could understand our love for each other, therefore it is necessary that we should keep our expression of it to ourselves."[27] The historical context leaves it surprisingly unclear whether Cushman demanded secrecy because Crow was a woman, or because Cushman was afraid of being exposed as adulterous. There are no similar records of Cushman attempting to conceal her relationships with Eliza Cook, Matilda Hays, or Emma Stebbins, which far from being open secrets were explicitly acknowledged by her social circle and in newspapers. Cushman and her lovers displayed their intimacy for all to see. In the 1840s Cook published a fervent poem, "To Charlotte Cushman," which described the two women as "captive in Affection's thrall," and when Hays published her translation of George Sand's *La Petite Fadette* in 1851, she dedicated it to Charlotte Cushman. On a tour of United States theaters in 1849, Cushman traveled with Hays, and a newspaper article praising Cushman as a "woman . . . worthy of homage and esteem" added, "Miss Cushman will be accompanied by her friend, novelist and translator, Matilda M. Hays."[28]

When grasping for a vocabulary to describe relationships between women, Victorians often, as we saw in chapter 1, resorted to a qualified, hyperbolic lexicon of friendship, but they also applied the concept of marriage to female couples. Elizabeth Barrett Browning wrote to her sister Arabel in 1852 about meeting Matilda Hays and Charlotte Cushman: "I understand that she & Miss Hayes [sic] have made vows of celibacy & of eternal attachment to each other—they live together, dress alike . . . it is a female marriage. I happened to say, 'Well, I never heard of such a thing before.' 'Haven't you?' said Mrs Corkrane [sic], . . . 'oh, it is by no means uncommon.' They are on their way to Rome, so I dare say we shall see a good deal of them. Though an actress . . . Miss Cushman has an unimpeachable character."[29] Barrett Browning's informant was the wife of journalist John Frazer Corkran, a correspondent for the *Morning Chronicle*. Browning's reference to vows of celibacy suggests an equation of female marriage with sexual renunciation, but the conjunction of the women's celibacy with their "eternal attachment" to each other redefines celibacy as a mutual vow never to leave one another to marry men, one way of predicating Barrett Browning's next term, "a female marriage." The offhandedness of Barrett Browning's "I happened to say" sits uneasily with the emphatic nature of what she does say—"Well, I have never heard of such a thing"—but suggests her desire to demonstrate that she has already absorbed the lesson in urbanity imparted by her married interlocutor, who remarks, "[I]t is by no means uncommon." Browning's final comment on Cushman's reputation for respectability makes no connection, positive or negative, between her female marriage and her "unimpeachable character." Far from suggesting that she might want to avoid Cushman and Hays, Browning writes that she expects to see a good deal of them—and she did, often bringing along her husband and their young son.

To understand the social position of women in female marriages, it is helpful to distinguish between a subculture and a network. Charlotte Cushman did not belong to a subculture, a type of social group that tends to be organized around a limited number of shared traits and that coheres through its separation from the mainstream. She did, however, belong to a network, a form of social alliance whose strength derives from its relative openness and internal variety and from its links to other networks. Overlapping sets of acquaintances as well as shared identities define networks; the stronger the network, the greater the number and type of groups to which it is linked. Cushman's network thus included women in or interested in relationships with other women and had many links to people who were not in same-sex couples. Her circle overlapped considerably, for example, with the Browning circle, which consisted of highly respected artists who lived in Italy to get distance from their immediate families, access to a warmer climate, and exposure to Italy's historic culture. Charlotte Cushman's integration into multiple networks shows how easily same-sex relationships between women were assimilated to the model of marriage. Indeed, as Merrill notes, Cushman's relationships with Matilda Hays and Emma Stebbins helped incorporate the actress into many networks by giving her an aura of propriety and respectability (190).

Women in female marriages or interested in sexual liaisons with women banded together but also entered social circles organized around legally married couples. Robert and Elizabeth Barrett Browning spent time not only with Cushman and Hays but with several other women whose charged same-sex relationships included giddy flirtations, tempestuous infatuations, short-term love affairs, and long-term partnerships. The Brownings' letters recount numerous dinners, picnics, and excursions with Harriet Hosmer, Isa Blagden, Kate Field, and Frances Power Cobbe, as well as with Cushman and Stebbins. In some cases, the ties were deep: Blagden was one of Robert Browning's chief correspondents, Hosmer made a famous cast of the Brownings' hands, and after his wife's death, Robert gave Field a chain and locket Elizabeth had worn since childhood, adding to it some of his wife's hair.[30] Cushman, Hosmer, and Cobbe were on good social terms with married women such as Jane Carlyle, Mary Somerville, and Margaret Oliphant, and often socialized with their husbands as well. Harriet Hosmer adopted boyish dress and manners and flirted openly with women, but Victorian lifewriting attests that dozens of respectable Englishwomen traveling to Rome were eager to meet her. She knew the Gladstones, Sir William Boxall (director of the National Gallery and portraitist of leading figures of the day), and the Layards (Austen Layard was an archeologist, politician, and ambassador to Madrid in the 1870s; his wife was the daughter of Sir John and Lady Charlotte Guest). Her visitors in the late 1860s included a diplomat's wife, a philanthropic Christian woman, and Anne Thackeray, who traveled to Rome with Lady de Rothschild.[31]

In the 1860s and 1870s, a period when few knew of the sexological idea of inversion and many still associated sodomy with sexual acts absolutely opposed to nature and virtue, the female couple was accepted as a variation on legal marriage, not treated as a separate species. This suggests that Lillian Faderman and Carroll Smith-Rosenberg were absolutely right that Victorians considered love between women to be perfectly normal, whether that love involved intense, sensual friendships that existed alongside marriage to men (Smith-Rosenberg) or lifelong partnerships that replaced marriage to men (Faderman).[32] It also shows how they were wrong. Smith-Rosenberg erred in defining intimacy between women as a supplement to male-female marriage, for women in female marriages did not supplement marriage, they appropriated it. Faderman was wrong to argue that acceptance of female couples depended on the perceived asexuality of their relationships; the use of marriage as a term to describe female couples suggests that people believed sex was involved, for marriage, unlike friendship, was never an asexual term. For Victorians, marriage meant the union of sexual and spiritual impulses, the reconciliation of sexuality with propriety. Marriage was a socially acceptable exhibition of sexual intimacy because it was predicated on fidelity and thus advertised not only the sexuality of spouses but also their acceptance of restraints and limits. For this reason, female marriage was not associated with a savage state of sexual license but instead was readily integrated into even the most restrictive ideas of social order. As we will see, however, female marriage also differed from legal marriage between men and women in significant ways, and those differences made it a model for reformers seeking to modernize legal marriage.

FEMALE MARRIAGE AND VICTORIAN MARRIAGE REFORM

Until 1857, legal marriage in England was defined by its effective indissolubility, since divorce with the right to remarry was prohibitively complicated and expensive. The law of marriage also mandated the formal inequality of husbands and wives, since coverture dictated that they were legally one person, the husband. Serious reform of those laws began when Barbara Leigh Smith submitted a petition to Parliament in 1856, requesting a change to the laws governing married women's property, which belonged entirely to husbands unless protected by the law of equity. Although that petition's immediate success was only partial, it influenced politicians to create a civil divorce law the following year. Eager to collect signatures from women who were not married to men and were therefore considered disinterested supporters of reform, Smith ended up soliciting signatures from several women who at some point in their lives were in female couples, including Isa Blagden, Geraldine Jewsbury, Amelia Edwards, Charlotte Cushman, and Matilda Hays.

That a number of women more interested in relationships with women than in marriage to men signed a petition calling for a Married Women's Property Act suggests an affinity Smith may not have anticipated between same-sex relationships and marriage reform, one that cannot simply be explained in terms of a feminist desire to increase the rights of all women. Hays had always been a feminist, and she remained one well after signing the 1856 petition, but her support for divorce also stemmed from her experience with female marriage. When her relationship with Cushman ended in 1857, Hays returned to her feminist circle in London, where she helped run the *English Woman's Journal* and the Society for Promoting the Employment of Women, and eventually formed another relationship with Theodosia, Dowager Lady Monson.[33] She also supported herself as a translator and writer, and her novel *Adrienne Hope* (1866) included characters based on herself and Lady Monson, Miss Reay and her constant companion, the solicitous, widowed Lady Morton. Miss Reay declares her support for women's rights and notes, "Until quite lately a married woman was only a chattel . . . absolutely belonging to her husband. . . . The new Divorce Court has mended this state of things."[34] In an earlier work, *Helen Stanley: A Tale*, one character makes a didactic speech arguing that divorce is a valid solution to the problem of marital unhappiness and daringly asserting that one could love more than once.[35]

In her political and literary work, Hays developed practical and ethical underpinnings for divorce by working to increase women's economic autonomy and by countering the pervasive accusation that divorce licensed a purely carnal promiscuity.

Hays's feminist vision of laws that would give women legally married to men more freedom incorporated the definition of marriage she had developed in forming and ending her own female marriage. Although women in a female marriage did not have the benefit of a legally recognized union, they already enjoyed two of the privileges that women married to men fought for over the course of the century: independent rights to their income and property, and the freedom to dissolve their relationships and form new ones. They also created unions that did not depend on sexual difference, gender hierarchy, or biological reproduction for their underpinnings, as most Victorian marriages between men and women did in legal theory if not in social fact. Like many who supported new divorce or property rights for wives, Hays asserted that marriage could and should be based on the equality and similarity of spouses. As we will see in the next section, "contract" was the term that summed up the view that legal, opposite-sex marriage should be dissoluble and grant equality and independence to wives—and "contract" was a term that already described most female marriages. Anne Lister and Anne Walker used wills and deeds to formalize their relationship, and Rosa Bonheur drew up detailed wills with her first and second spouses, Nathalie Micas and Anna Klumpke. Like male and female suitors, who combined sexual and romantic passion with economic calculations (think of the negotiations that accompany courtship in Trollope novels), women in female marriages made formal agreements that combined mutual love with financial interests. When Rosa Bonheur asked Anna Klumpke to live with her, she first warmly declared her love, then wrote to Klumpke's mother explaining their decision to "unite [their] existence" and assuring her that Bonheur would "arrange before a lawyer a situation where she [Anna] will be considered as in her own home."[36]

Women like Bonheur and Klumpke modeled their relationships on romantic marriage, defined in terms of love and fidelity, but they also adopted a daringly modern notion of marriage as contract. Radical utopian William Thompson contended in 1825 that marriage was not really a contract because it was an unequal, indissoluble relationship whose terms were determined by the state.[37] By mid-century his critique had been absorbed into liberal and feminist arguments for the reform of legal marriage between men and women, some made by women in female marriages based on contractual principles. Contract marriage was egalitarian relative to legal coverture because it assumed a mutually beneficial exchange in which each side received consideration. Bonheur's will explained that she was leaving all her assets to Klumpke because she had asked her "to stay with me and share my life," and had therefore "decided to compensate her and protect her interests since she, in order to live with me, sacrificed the position she had already made for herself and shared the costs of maintaining and improving my house and estate."[38] Forced by necessity to construct ad hoc legal frameworks for their relationships, nineteenth-century women in female marriages not only were precursors of late-twentieth-century "same-sex domestic partners," but also anticipated forms of marriage between men and women that were only institutionalized decades after their deaths.

Women in female marriages used principles derived from contract to dissolve their unions as well as to formalize them. Indeed, the very act of ending a union depended on the analogy between marriage and contract. As Oliver Wendell Holmes put it in *The Common Law* (1881), the essence of contract was that each party was "free to break his contract if he chooses." The law did not compel people to perform their contracts, only to pay damages if they did not perform them.[39] After Cushman met Emma Stebbins and her relationship with Matilda Hays began to fray in 1857, Hays threatened to sue Cushman for damages on the grounds that she had sacrificed a literary career to follow Cushman to Italy. Cushman did not take pains to keep Hays's demand a perfect secret; Harriet Hosmer knew of it, and Anne Brewster, an early lover and ongoing friend of Cushman's, dilated upon it in her diary. Hays's demand that Cushman pay some type of alimony may have been a subtle form of blackmail, but the threat Hays wielded was not the revelation of a relationship already open enough to be mentioned in newspapers and known to everyone in their social circle. Rather, the potential source of scandal was the revelation that Cushman's infidelity was the cause of their rupture. To quiet reports of her adultery and to acknowledge that she was breaking their agreement to live together, Cushman paid Hays one or two thousand dollars, a substantial amount of money at the time, and a sign that she, like Hays, interpreted their union in terms of a basic principle of contract: that the party breaching an agreement must pay damages.[40]

Female marriages had their share of troubles and were as plagued by infidelity, conflict, and power differences as legal ones, but because the state did not bind female couples for life, their unions exemplified the features that British activists fought to import into marriage between men and women: dissolubility, relative egalitarianism, and greater freedom for both spouses. These were matters of some urgency: the doctrine of coverture dictated that a wife's income and property unprotected by equity belonged absolutely to the husband alone, as did the couple's children. Until 1891 a husband was legally allowed to hold his wife in custody against her will and there was no legal concept of marital rape.

In the 1850s, feminists seeking to end coverture and obtain independent rights for legally married women joined forces with liberal utilitarians interested in rationalizing the law and transferring authority from church to state. Together they proposed the property act that Hays and Cushman supported and helped to pass the controversial 1857 Divorce and Matrimonial Causes Act, which made divorce available to many more people than ever before by shifting jurisdiction from an ecclesiastical court to the nation's first civil divorce court.[41] The new law did not end coverture or hierarchical marriage, and it codified a double standard that made it more difficult for wives to sue for divorce than husbands. Nevertheless, it was widely perceived as undermining husbands' power and prestige. A satiric set of sketches in *Once a Week* portrayed the divorce court as a place where wives tricked and victimized husbands, and the *Englishwoman's Domestic Magazine* noted in 1864 that "the revelations of the Divorce Court show that there are bad husbands as well as good."[42] Statistics give some sense of the law's actual effects: when divorce had to be finalized by parliamentary decree, only 190 were granted between 1801 and 1857, while in the ten years between 1858 and 1868, the new civil court granted 1,279 decrees.[43] The 1857 legislation provided an appealing new option for ending marriage, especially for women: before its passage, only four women had ever obtained a parliamentary divorce decree, but between 1858 and 1868, wives initiated 40 percent of divorce-court petitions and were successful about as often as husbands in dissolving marriages.[44]

The 1857 Act had cultural ramifications that went far beyond its legal ones. As Bessie Rayner Parkes put it in 1866, a "universal discussion of first principles . . . accompanied the passing of the New Divorce Bill."[45] Abstract debates about marriage as an institution were accompanied by a new public appetite for sensational news about marital breakdown. Divorces were granted to hundreds of spouses, but divorce trials were followed by thousands of readers, and journalistic reports of divorce-court proceedings exposed the variability of marriage as a lived institution.[46] The general public discovered through trial reports that violence, adultery, incestuous adultery, bigamy, and even sex between women (an issue in two notorious divorce trials, the 1864 Codrington trial and the 1885 Dilke-Crawford trial) could be part of married life in Britain. A spate of novels about bigamy, adultery, and divorce, mostly published between 1857 and 1865, also fed the appetite for stories about marriages that broke the rules. Calls to censor divorce reports in order to protect privacy and public morality were ineffectual. One advocate of censorship, W.E.H. Lecky, also wrote a popular history of morals that placed European civilization at the acme of human development because of its Christian concept of lifelong monogamy. His call to suppress accounts of divorce trials suggests that he understood how effectively they exposed the difference between what married couples practiced and what the laws of marriage preached.[47]

The 1857 law of divorce also changed the terms of celibacy, producing much journalistic discussion about whether marriage was necessary at all, especially in light of census figures that showed an increasing number of men and women never marrying. Victorian feminists charged that the social compulsion to marry consolidated male domination, since women entered marriages that made them inferiors only because the unmarried state entailed economic dependence and social death. Those who felt that the only suitable fate for a woman was to become a dependent wife made the unmarried "spinster" an object of pity: "A single woman! Is there not something plaintive in the two words standing together? . . . No woman is single from choice."[48] Others described the single state as unnatural: "There is nothing single in nature; celibacy was never contemplated in creation."[49] Feminist John Stuart Mill countered that as a result of such stereotypes, the desire to marry was really a revulsion against the stigma of being unmarried, since a "single woman . . . is felt both by herself and others as a kind of excrescence on the surface of society, having no use or function or office there."[50] For marriage between men and women to be equal, feminists argued, single women had to be able to lead practicable and pleasurable lives. The demand to reform marriage began as a quest to make it more equal and more flexible, then evolved into a demand to make it less obligatory. To change the quality of life for the unmarried would alter marriage itself.

While some drew attention to the difficulties unmarried women faced, others argued that life was already easier for unmarried women than many believed and that marriage was no longer the only desirable female destiny. In the 1860s, unmarried women became visible as activists, philanthropists, and artists whose labor earned them a place in a society made more porous by a general emphasis on reform. The spectacular effectiveness of single women during the Crimean War increased public respect for them. Imperialist rhetoric exhorting England to live up to its values of democracy and equality at home in order better to disseminate them abroad contributed to an increased appreciation of all women's social contributions. Feminist Caroline Cornwallis warned readers in 1857 that "to tie the hands of one half of mankind . . . is a suicidal act, and unworthy of a nation whom an omnipotent will seems to have marked out as the great civilizer of the world."[51] By the 1860s, writing about single women had become enough of a trend for a book reviewer to comment, "If in the multitude of counsellors there is safety, how blest must be the security of single women!" Turning single women into dependents needing guidance from a "multitude of counsellors," the reviewer concluded that marriage was the best state, because "[m]an and woman need to be One." Yet even he granted that women who lacked husbands needed work as an outlet for their talents.[52] Others suggested that single life might be preferable for women, especially in light of the marital miseries publicized by divorce court proceedings. Anne Thackeray noted in her essay "Toilers and Spinsters" (1858) that a single woman "certainly does not envy poor Mrs. C., who has to fly to Sir Cresswell Cresswell [a divorce-court judge] to get rid of a 'life companion' who beats her with his umbrella, spends her money, and knocks her down instead of 'lifting her up.'"[53]

Even passionate advocates of marriage hostile to feminism began to accept that some women would never marry. As an example of this, take the most famous Victorian article about single women, W. R. Greg's "Why Are Women Redundant?" (1862).[54] Greg's article is frequently cited as evidence of the contempt Victorians heaped on unmarried women, because his strong commitment to marriage led him to propose sending "redundant" Englishwomen who could not find husbands to colonies where men outnumbered women. But Greg's article also demonstrates the growing acceptance of single women. Although he pleaded that every woman who could be paired with a man should be, he assumed that because adult women outnumbered adult men, single women were as natural as monogamy. Nature rules that "marriage, the union of one man with one woman, is unmistakably . . . the despotic law of life," but "she not only proclaims the *rule*, she distinctly lays down the precise amount and limits of the *exception*" (279). Greg quantified the natural exception in terms of census figures showing 106 women over twenty years old for every 100 men in the same age group. What Greg considered a startling anomaly was the census finding that 30 percent of women over twenty were unmarried. By contrast, Greg deemed the "redundant six per cent for whom equivalent men do not exist" (282) a normal exception consonant with "a thoroughly natural, sound, and satisfactory state of society" (282) and proportionate to the "precise percentage of women whom Nature designed for single life" (279). So natural was the single woman for Greg that he personified Nature herself as a single woman, busily making designs and laying down "the despotic law of life" with no husband to guide her.

Greg decried the rising number of unmarried women in England, but he also identified a fixed number of women for whom celibacy was required. He defined those women as "natural anomalies" who lacked femininity, loved independence, wanted to serve humanity, or were "almost epicene" in their genius and power: "Such are rightly and naturally single; but they are abnormal and not perfect natures" (280). The abnormal is imperfect, but it is also natural, and Greg thus asserted that unmarried women (but not unmarried men) were inevitable and socially necessary.

Despite his vehement promotion of marriage, he noted dispassionately that some women "deliberately resolve upon celibacy as that which they like for itself" (281). In a footnote Greg even suggested that single life was the happier choice for many women: "In thousands of instances [maiden ladies] are, *after a time*, more happy [than wives and mothers]. In our day, if a lady is possessed of a very moderate competence, and a well-stored and well-regulated mind, she may have infinitely less care and infinitely more enjoyment than if she had drawn any of the numerous blanks which beset the lottery of marriage" (299). Greg's acceptance of single life as natural transformed marriage from a fatal necessity into a lottery, a game of chance whose risks women could rationally choose not to incur.

The changing view of single women indicated the burgeoning of new ideas about marriage. Across the political and rhetorical spectrum, writers in the 1860s testified to the growing awareness that marriage between men and women was not a universal element of social life. In "What Shall We Do with Our Old Maids?" (1862), Frances Power Cobbe used the same statistics as Greg to show that single women were becoming a constitutive and transformative element of England's social landscape.[55] Cobbe and others argued that single women were happier than they had ever been, and that when unmarried women enjoyed the good life, marriage itself would also change. The suggestion that people could survive independent of marriage also undid the notion of marriage as the union of opposite sexes, each requiring the other in order to supplement a lack, and harmonized with a modern understanding of companionate marriage based on similarity and friendship. Feminist John Stuart Mill, one of Cobbe's many personal acquaintances, echoed her sentiments when he wrote in *The Subjection of Women* (1869) that "likeness," not difference, should be the foundation of true unions, and that marriage should be modeled on what "often happens between two friends of the same sex."[56]

If marriage was defined by love and patterned on same-sex friendship, then what happened between two friends of the same sex could also be understood as a marriage. In an 1862 essay, "Celibacy v. Marriage," Frances Power Cobbe wrote that women who did not marry men could still be happy by forming "true and tender friendships"; the celibate woman need not fear "a solitary old age" since she could easily "find a woman ready to share" her life.[57] In later lectures on *The Duties of Women*, Cobbe mused, "I think that every one . . . must have the chance offered to them of forming a true marriage with one of the opposite sex or else a true friendship with one of their own, and that we should look to such marriages and friendships as the supreme joy and glory of mortal life,—unions wherein we may steep our whole hearts."[58] Cobbe subtly shifts her use of conjunctions, from "marriage . . . or . . . friendship" to "marriages *and* friendships" (emphasis added), thus transforming marriage and friendship from mutually exclusive alternatives into inter-changeable bonds for which the sex of the partners makes little difference to the quality of the union.

The triumph of companionate marriage as an ideal not only changed the relationship between husband and wife, but also transformed the status of unmarried people and provided grounds for valorizing same-sex unions. The belief that without love it was better not to marry made those who refused to wed out of expediency spiritually superior beings. Cobbe argued that women would marry for love only if the single state were "so free and happy that [women] shall have not one temptation to change it save the only temptation which *ought* to determine them—namely, love."[59] Her reasoning shrewdly framed her rejection of compul-sory heterosexuality as a desire to improve marriage, and called on de-fenders of virtuous marriage to support the unmarried woman's right to happiness. Implicitly, Cobbe also rallied those who believed in marriage to ratify any union based on affection. In doing so, she may have had in mind a union like her own. As we recall from chapter 1, although Cobbe never legally wed, for over thirty years she lived with a woman she pub-licly called her "beloved friend," sculptor Mary Lloyd.[60]

Cobbe's life is an example of how social networks and informal, extra-legal relationships affected the political and the legal. Because female marriage was not a marginal, secret practice confined to a subculture, but was integrated into farflung, open networks, women like Cobbe could model their relationships on a contractual ideal of marriage and propose that legal marriage remodel itself in the image of their own unions. Cobbe belonged to a network of feminist marriage reformers that included John Stuart Mill, Barbara Leigh Smith, Charlotte Cush-man, and Geraldine Jewsbury, as well as to a wider network of politi-cians, philanthropists, and journalists that comprised Walter Bagehot, Matthew Arnold, Lord Shaftesbury, Cardinal Manning, and Lady Bat-tersea, whose memoirs remarked on Cobbe's short hair and unconven-tional dress but also described her as "one of my most honored friends."[61] Cobbe was even friends with W. R. Greg, her antagonist in the debate about unmarried women.[62] Through her writings and her pro-fessional and personal connections, Cobbe was able to shape legislation and policy. Her article on "Wife-Torture in England" (1878) led to the passage of laws making it easier for poor women to obtain separation orders from husbands convicted of assaulting them.[63] Cobbe achieved all this while living openly with another woman in a relationship that she and others perceived to be modeled on marriage. The important role she played in Victorian debates about celibacy, marriage reform, domestic violence, and women's work is further evidence of the influence female marriage had on the changing forms of marriage between men and women. Although Cobbe herself could not vote and was legally bound to Mary Lloyd only by individual agreements such as wills, her writings in the public sphere and her secure position in a highly ramified social world contributed to legal and political change.

The traffic between female couples and the legal institution of marriage ran in two directions. Because relationships between female couples were understood as marriages, they provided models for more flexible, egalitarian, and voluntary marriages between men and women. Conversely, the drive to change the laws governing marriage between men and women showed that the institution of marriage was already relatively plastic, one that could be molded into a permanently new shape without fracture or rupture. As a result, female couples and their friends found it plausible to use the language of marriage to describe their relationships. English society in the 1850s and 1860s did not perceive female marriages as dangerous or unspeakable, even at a time when most saw sodomy as a sexual act completely at variance with nature or virtue. Female couples were not a separate species but rather a middle-class equivalent of bigamous working-class couples whose alliances were illegal but nonetheless regulated by informal rules, marked by some form of wedding ritual, and recognized by the couple's peers, who knew that at least one member of the couple was legally married to somebody else.[64] Marriages were not defined by the law alone, and for couples with no legal status, social acceptance replaced law as marriage's legitimating sign. Victorians who applied terms like "wife" or "marriage" to female couples accepted them as a variation on legally married couples and conferred respectability on same-sex unions.[65] At the same time, to describe two women as married turned marriage, the supposedly stable ground of the comparison, into a plastic figure flexible enough to embrace the female couple.

The Debate Over Contractual Marriage

The features of contract that created a common ground between female marriage and reformed marriage between men and women were equality and dissolubility. The debates about the 1857 Matrimonial Causes Act hinged on whether or not marriage should be a contract, and if it were a contract, what that should mean. By and large, those who supported greater equality between wives and husbands advocated understanding marriage as a contract. In 1890 feminist Mona Caird summed up decades of feminist argument when she wrote, "As soon as the principle of equality between the sexes is sincerely accepted, there remains no valid reason against the immediate adoption of contract-marriage."[66] An 1857 article opposed to changes in "the greatest, oldest, and most universal of all social institutions, the great institution of marriage," argued that only a "lower conception of marriage" treated "it as a purely civil contract between individuals," that Christianity defined marriage as "a lifelong compact . . . which never can be rightfully dissolved"; and that "the principle of divorce" was "handed over from Paganism" and "barbarism." Arguing that marriage "derives its essential and specific character from restraint: restraint from the choice of more than a single wife; restraint from choosing her among near relatives by blood or affinity; restraint from the carnal use of woman in any relation inferior to marriage; restraint from forming any temporary or any other than a life-long contract," the author equated Christian marriage with civilization because it prohibited certain acts (incest, polygamy, divorce) associated with a state of nature in which men had the freedom to treat women as instruments of their pleasure.[67]

Although those who upheld traditional hierarchical marriage believed that promises to marry required mutual consent, and that Christian marriage made men and women spiritual equals, they also insisted that marriage was defined by the difference between the sexes and was transcendent and irrevocable in ways that contracts were not. As one opponent of reform put it, the "common law of England . . . in entire accordance with the principles of Christianity, made a man's wife and children completely dependent upon him,—placed them, both as to person and property, completely under his control."[68] A judge ruling in an 1869 divorce case made a similar point when he explained, "The law . . . recognizes the husband as the ruler, protector, and guide of his wife; it makes him master of her pecuniary resources; it gives him, within legal limits, the control of her person; it withdraws civil rights and remedies from her, save in his name."[69] To argue for coverture was to take a stand against divorce and its implications of contractual marriage. In an unsigned 1856 article, Margaret Oliphant wrote, in an almost parodically uxurious voice, that the "justice which means an equal division of rights has no place between those two persons whom natural policy as well as Divine institution teach us to consider as one. . . . Marrying is like dying—as distinct, as irrevocable, as complete."[70]

Contract is a crucial term in both British political history and in contemporary feminist theory, and it is worth recalling those contexts when studying Victorian marriage debates. Since the seventeenth century, contract has defined the political relationship between individuals and the state in terms of a balance between freedom and obligation. This political history helps to explain why contract became such an important term in Victorian discussions of marriage and divorce. In a study of natural law, Ernest Bloch argues that philosophers since Epicurus have identified the essence of contract with the fact that it can be terminated.[71] Victoria Kahn points out in her study of seventeenth-century writing that contracts were considered distinct from promises because only contracts could legitimately be broken.[72] Contracts have signified freedom in English political thought most clearly when they have been equated with ongoing consent; even John Milton, who advocated that wives submit to husbands, recognized that to define marriage as a contract rather than a covenant meant granting wives more freedom.[73] But as Kahn also shows, the formative political debates of the seventeenth century often posited contract as the antithesis of a married state based on natural, divinely ordained differences; indeed, the absolute sovereignty of a king over his people was often compared to the unquestioned dominion of a husband over a wife.

In recent years important critiques of liberal notions of contract have emphasized the exclusions and inequalities built into contract theory to such an extent that it now seems difficult to conceive that women once used contract to press claims for freedom.[74] P. S. Atiyah, for example, has argued that because nineteenth-century liberal politics mandated a separation of public and private, contract law could be applied only to the public marketplace, never to private, familial relationships such as marriage.[75] In fact, nineteenth-century judges frequently applied contract law to promises to marry and to agreements between spouses.[76] In one 1886 case, a judge asserted that marriage was indeed a generic contract, whose "validity . . . must be tested and determined in precisely the same manner as that of any other contract."[77]

While some have argued that the liberal public sphere excluded marriage from the contractual realm, others have warned that to include marriage within the purview of contract is to misrepresent women's coercion into sexual subjugation as consensual. For Carole Pateman, the social contract of political participation presumes a sexual contract that defines women as naturally deficient in the rationality, autonomy, or equality a subject must possess to enter a contract freely. Marriage is the one contract women are required to enter, she claims, because it is the contract most reducible to the hierarchical structure defining all contracts.[78] Yet Pateman's argument about contract is contradictory, for she defines contract as freedom when women are excluded from it, and as subjection when they are included in it (135–36). Because Pateman cannot decide if contract is essentially free or unfree, she cannot determine whether marriage should be made more or less contractual (156, 165), nor whether sexual difference is dangerous (167) or desirable (185). Monique Wittig provides a contrasting view of contract theory's relation to gender and sexuality in "On the Social Contract," where she distinguishes between the heterosexual contract and the social contract and argues that women must break the heterosexual contract in order to become part of the general social contract. Since the category of sexual difference is crucial to the heterosexual contract, its disappearance is one necessary component of what Wittig understands as an ongoing process of constantly remaking the social contract.[79]

Readings of canonical political theory alone cannot establish the valence of a term like "contract" in Victorian discourse, but the differences between Pateman and Wittig can shed some light on why Victorian feminists used "contract" as a watchword in their fight for equality between husbands and wives. Nineteenth-century writers associated contract with the marital relationship between men and women; according to the narrator of Wilkie Collins's novel *Man and Wife* (1870), marriage was the ultimate contract, "the most important contract of civilized life."[80] Victorian feminists used the tension between the social and sexual contracts identified by both Pateman and Wittig to draw attention to women's ambiguous position in marriage, which required their free consent to a relationship that was hierarchical and difficult to dissolve. Mary Shanley points out that Victorian feminists "drew heavily on liberal principles of individual liberty and bodily autonomy" in seeking to reform marriage, and many of the male politicians who supported marriage reform did so because they wanted to extend the liberal principles of self-government to private as well as public life.[81] While many feminists accompanied demands for equal rights with equally fervent support for the idea that women were essentially different from men, others acknowledged that to make marriage more egalitarian necessarily involved making good on the premises of liberal universalism by undoing differences between male and female.

When feminists argued that marriage should become more contractual, they understood contract in terms of the *social* contract, as a voluntary agreement between equals that either party could terminate. Feminists argued that marriage was not yet truly contractual, because in marrying under English law, women gave away equality (wives were not equal to husbands), autonomy (wives were absorbed into their husband's legal personality), and freedom (wives could obtain a divorce only under very limited conditions).[82] Dissolubility became the definitive feature of contractual marriage, because it was a legally necessary element of any contract and contained within it the ideas of consent and equality. The ability to exit from contracts was as crucial to their definition as the ability to enter them freely, and those who advocated contractual marriage thus expressed strong support for divorce. In an 1830s essay on marriage laws, John Stuart Mill asserted that women were "ripe for equality" but that it was "absurd to talk of equality while marriage is an indissoluble tie." Mill imagined divorce as the logical corollary of a radically voluntary marital relationship: "[A] woman ought not to be dependent on a man, more than a man on a woman, except so far as their affections make them so, by a voluntary surrender, renewed and renewing at each instant by free and spontaneous choice." Like "the other relations voluntarily contracted by human beings," marriage should "depend for its continuance upon the wishes of the contracting parties."[83] In *The Subjection of Women* (1869), Mill repeated that marriage should be like a business contract, with each " free to cancel the power [of the other] by withdrawing from the connexion.[84] The dissolubility implied by contract came to represent the freedom, consent, and equality that feminists believed should define marriage as an ongoing process.

Opponents and proponents of contractual marriage alike shared the assumption that contractual marriage needed to be understood in terms of a progress narrative of civilization. Some saw liberalized divorce laws that created greater equality between spouses as a step back in time. William Lecky, for example, criticized the Romans for making marriage a "coequal partnership," "merely a civil contract, entered into for the happiness of the contracting parties, its continuance depende[nt] upon mutual consent," an agreement that "[e]ither party might dissolve . . . at will."[85] Lecky unfavorably compared dissoluble contract marriage to Christian marriage, which by imparting an "essentially religious and even mystical character . . . to marriage" also insisted on the "absolute sinfulness of divorce" as a repudiation not only of one's spouse, but of one's faith in God (351–52). Feminists demanding the right to be included in the liberal English polity often reproduced Lecky's belief that certain social customs were incompatible with civilization, even if they disagreed about what those customs were. Caroline Cornwallis called laws depriving married women of rights relics of an earlier "state of semi-barbarism." In an 1846 review of books about the condition of women, Anna Jameson wrote that each proved "that the chief distinction between savage and civilized life, between Heathendom and Christendom, lies in the treatment and condition of women . . . that on her power to exercise her faculties and duties aright, depends . . . the progress of the species."[86]

The writings of John Stuart Mill exemplify what we might call a feminist civilizational framework that made women's equality the key to development and progress.[87] In his earliest writings on divorce, Mill placed contractual marriage in an anthropological narrative: "When women are merely slaves, to give them a permanent hold upon their masters was a first step towards their evolution. That step is now complete: and in the progress of civilization, the time has come when women may aspire to something more than merely to find a protector" ("Early Essays," 83). In *The Subjection of Women*, Mill translated his liberal belief in unfettered individual development into the anthropological idiom of social plasticity. Dismissing attempts to fix women's nature, Mill wrote that it was impossible to generalize about sexual characteristics given "the extreme variableness of those of [human nature's] manifestations which are supposed to be most universal and uniform" (149). But Mill sought to give that variability a linear direction in which change would increase the good of an ever-increasing number of people. As part of that utilitarian liberal framework, he argued that changing women's position in marriage was part of the shift from primitivism to civilization. Over and over again, Mill stated that married women's inequality in the present was a "relic of the past," an instance of "the primitive state of slavery lasting on," a survival that seemed compatible with "modern civilization," but in fact impeded progress toward a society based on consent, freedom, equality, and unconstrained self-development (*Subjection*, 136, 132). In the kind of move Nietzsche later overturned (see chapter 6), Mill argued that modernity begins when superiors make and keep promises to inferiors and thus create a realm of equals who make contracts with one another. To make marriage contractual, in that view, was to differentiate it from the savagery that all sides in the marriage debates identified as anathema.

Victorian Anthropology and the History of Marriage

Victorians disagreed about whether contractual marriage represented civilization or savagery, and about whether civilization had already been achieved or had yet to be attained, but even thinkers as dissimilar as Mill and Lecky agreed that it was possible to demarcate the line between the primitive and the modern and that modernity was the superior state. Nineteenth-century imperial powers divided societies into stages, identifying Christianity and the West with the acme of human development and dismissing other religions and regions as stuck in a primitive past. That mode of thought is often described as anthropological, because many of the nineteenth-century writers who first began to compare cultural and social forms presented their findings as narratives charting the evolution of one set of customs and laws into another. One school of nineteenth-century anthropology sought to make the nascent discipline more scientific by measuring racial differences, while another produced theoretical accounts of language, myth, law, religion, and kinship.[88] Those who elaborated narratives about the origins of culture, society, and the state studied symbolic systems, religious thought, political structures, and economic exchange. Their speculative histories distinguished primitive societies based on myth, force, enslavement, fixed status, and clan rule from modern societies based on reason, equality, promises, consent, the rule of law, and state formations distinct from kinship ties.

As marriage underwent radical changes in the Victorian present, writers began to conjecture about the forms it had taken in the past, and many anthropologists who wrote comparative histories of kinship posed the question with which we began: does marriage have a history? The 1860s saw the publication of major studies of marriage and kinship customs by Henry Sumner Maine, Johann Bachofen, Lewis Morgan, and John McLennan, leading Friedrich Engels to comment in his own study of *The Origin of the Family, Private Property and the State* (1884) that "[b]efore the beginning of the sixties, one cannot speak of a history of the family."[89] The temporal coincidence of divorce reform and family studies is one reason that scholars have suggested a connection between the 1857 Matrimonial Causes Act and early anthropology, but anthropology and marriage law reform were also linked in remarkably concrete ways. Sir James Wilde, later Lord Penzance, was both a divorce-court judge and a member of the Anthropological Society.[90] Many of the writers now called Victorian anthropologists were trained as lawyers, and their interest in cross-cultural studies of marriage and kinship was inspired by their engagement with contemporary legal codes. Henry Maine (1822–1888) began his career as Regius Professor of Civil Law at Cambridge and after 1861 was a legal member of the Viceroy's Council in India. His work in comparative jurisprudence influenced early anthropological and sociological theorists by defining law as a form of social expression and then studying its temporal evolution.[91] Johann Bachofen (1815–1887) was a Swiss jurist and historian of Roman law, and Lewis Morgan (1818–1881) studied and practiced law, as did John McLennan (1827–1881), who described his study of *Primitive Marriage* (1865) as a branch of his work on the "early history of civil society."[92] All of these writers were interested in the connections between laws past and present. Maine viewed legal codes as replete with archaisms that survived even when the social formation to which they corresponded no longer existed and believed that those relics from the past held the keys to its reconstruction. McLennan focused on a primordial past that antedated written law but also contended that one could use the "legal symbols" of the present as clues to the past (12).

In addition to being influenced by the ways in which marriage was changing in contemporary society, anthropologists were also strongly influenced by Darwin's *The Origin of Species* (1859) and its emphasis on variation and evolution.[93] Darwin's *Origin* did not theorize variations in the sexual instinct, and his study of sex, *The Descent of Man*, presented human sexuality as uniformly heterosexual.[94] But *The Origin of Species* did theorize development as flux and defined nature itself in terms of successive variations, positing the reproductive system as a source of individualizing changes rather than as a mechanism for identical replication. For Darwin the identity of any species was ephemeral, since distinct species had shared origins in the past and "not one living species will transmit its unaltered likeness to a distant futurity."[95] Even monstrosities—"a considerable deviation of structure in one part"—were on a continuum with the variations essential for natural selection, and could not "be separated by any clear line of distinction from mere variations" (101, 72). *The Origin of Species* thus provided a way of thinking about change over time in which commonality and difference were intertwined. When Darwin famously wrote that "our classifications will come to be . . . genealogies," he meant that those who studied species over time would have to study both their common origins and their constant transmutations (456). In *Ancient Law* (1861), Maine adopted a Darwinian approach to the history of marriage by arguing that it followed two historical axes of change: one legal, one social, and each moving at a different pace. Contemporary social opinion was "always more or less in advance of the Law," and legal fictions, equity law, and the passage of new legislation were needed to coordinate laws and social practice (23).

Under Darwin's influence, anthropologists saw monogamous marriage as only one of many variations. I began this chapter by citing contemporary associations of homosexuality with fantasies of primitive disorder—incest, promiscuity, polygamy. Victorian anthropologists helped to invent those fantasies of sexual savagery, yet many also affirmed the continuities between early and modern societies, and in so doing, affirmed that there was no fixed, natural form of marriage law.[96] The Darwinian understanding of life as variable led to an understanding of law and social customs as equally adaptable and plastic. Anthropologists writing conjectural histories of marriage often saw intimate links between Christian Europe and the primitive past, thus investing savage customs with the prestige of origins. In *Primitive Marriage*, McLennan wrote that promiscuity was "the most ancient form of kinship" (160) and that forms of marriage considered barbaric in nineteenth-century England, such as polyandry, "must be accepted as a stage in the progress towards marriage proper and the patriarchal system" (225).[97] Bachofen's *Mother Right* corrected historians who rejected the theory that "lower, unregulated sexual relations" preceded marriage, and warned that a "bitter surprise is in store for those who look on marriage as a necessary and primordial state."[98] In *Kamilaroi and Kurnai* (1880), a study of group marriage, Lorimer Fison and Alfred Howitt argued that "some of the more important institutions of civilized states must be sought, in their rudimentary forms, in this very condition of savagery from which they originate." In a chart that used the quintessentially English names John, Jane, Smith, and Brown to diagram Turanian and Ganowanian kinship patterns, the authors even suggested that primitive and civilized marriage systems were interchangeable.[99] Edith Simcox, the professional author and labor organizer encountered in chapter 1 as George Eliot's unrequited lover, proclaimed in an erudite study of *Primitive Civilizations* (1894) that no aspect of "modern family life . . . can be put forward as so pre-eminently and absolutely natural as to be universal."[100] Simcox argued that primitive civilization was not only as natural as modern life, it was in some respects superior. Demonstrating that wives in the past had owned property, possessed rights to their children, and enjoyed legal autonomy, Simcox implied that wives could enjoy the same independence in the present without undermining the social fabric.[101]

If primitive society began with incest, consanguine marriage, promiscuity, communal marriage, infanticide, and polygamy, then one could not universalize the incest taboo, nor argue that indissoluble, monogamous, hierarchical marriage was fundamental to human nature or human society. Because anthropologists acknowledged that multiple forms of marriage could constitute a cultural and social system, those who believed that monogamous, indissoluble marriage represented an advance in civilization over primordial promiscuity were put in the extraordinary position of having to explain what made it more civilized than its antecedents. In so doing, they also had to take a stand in contemporary debates about marriage as contract, and their positions were often discordant. In *Kinship and Marriage in Early Arabia* (1885), W. Robertson Smith wrote that patrilineal monogamy advanced "progress towards civilised ideas of conjugal fidelity" because it placed a woman "specially under the protection of one man," a position that presumed that in civilized marriage, the husband remained stronger than the wife.[102] For others, polygamy was primitive because it depended on men's violent capture of women, and monogamy was civilized because it was more likely to involve the woman's consent. Although Engels famously contended that monogamy, far from being "the reconciliation of man and woman," was "the subjugation of one sex by the other," his contrarian remark set out to overturn the received wisdom that only in monogamous marriage "does woman assume the position of the equal of man."[103] In the *History of European Morals* (1869) Lecky thus wrote, "[T]he whole tendency of civilisation is to diminish the disparity between the different members of the family"; in the shift to monogamy, "the wife from a simple slave becomes the companion and equal of her husband." Only with the end of wife purchase and the establishment of monogamous marriage did the wife "cease to be [the husband's] slave, and become in some degree a contracting party."[104] Lecky thus agreed with Maine's famous formulation of the course of history as a move from status to contract, the "free agreement of individuals" (163).

Just as anthropologists debated whether monogamous marriage meant that spouses became contractual equals, they also divided over whether monogamous marriage was compatible with legal definitions of contract as a dissoluble agreement between individuals who retained the right to terminate their agreement at will. Maine made a strong stand for the individual rights of wives when he charged that Christian marriage laws "deeply injured civilisation" by consolidating "the proprietary disabilities of married females" (152–53) and making it more difficult for wives to obtain divorces. Others believed that contractual marriage undid civilization, because dissolubility militated against the equality created when Christian law made the marriage bond equally permanent for husband and wife, restrained the sexual passions of both sexes, and made it impossible for husbands to repudiate wives at will. In an article on "Marriage and Modern Civilization" (1901), W. S. Lilly called Christian marriage "the Magna Charta of woman in modern civilisation" because it established marriage as the "lifelong union of two equal personalities." Lilly warned "that to degrade indissoluble marriage to a *mere* dissoluble contract . . . will be to throw back modern civilisation to that wallowing in the mire from which she rescued it."[105]

In some cases, a single author divided against himself on the question of whether dissoluble marriage elevated women and advanced civilization. Robertson Smith described a pre-Islamic form of contractual marriage, *mot'a* marriage, as more primitive than forms that assigned unequal status to husbands and wives. In *mot'a* marriage the woman was called "Sadica," or "female friend," an apt term for a contract in which "the wife is not under her husband's authority but meets him on equal terms" (93). Smith defined *mot'a* marriage as "a purely personal contract, founded on consent between a man and a woman, without any intervention on the part of the woman's kin" (84). In *mot'a* marriage, both spouses have divorce rights, the woman stays near her kin, and any children born belong to her (83, 85). The woman's right to dissolve her marriage is linked to "her right to dispose of her person" (91), which she loses in a subsequent form of marriage that Smith translated as "marriage of dominion," in which a husband owns a "subject wife" (93). On the one hand, Smith criticized marriage of dominion for its basis in capture or purchase, opining that Islam "set a permanent seal of subjection on the female sex" by abolishing *mot'a* marriage (121). On the other hand, he himself relegated *mot'a* marriage to a primitive, rudimentary matrilineal stage that predated patrilineal kinship (37).

Kinship includes parenthood as well as marriage, and anthropologists also debated where to place various forms of generational affiliation on the scale of civilization. Those who saw biological reproduction as the aim of marriage made sexual difference a constitutive element of wedlock. Others were willing to entertain the possibility that contract rather than sexual difference should define the relationship between parents and children as well as the relationship between spouses. Maine, for example, was particularly interested in the ancient Roman law of adoption, "which permitted family relations to be created artificially" (125), thus making kinship and citizenship independent of biological reproduction. Adoption law emerged from the confluence of *patria potestas* and the idea that the family was the basis of the state. To absorb new people into the state required that they be thought of as biological kin, but in a society that defined the family solely in terms of paternal authority, being of the same blood became less important than being under the same paternal power (144), and adopted children thus had the same status as biological offspring. Over time, *patria potestas* lost ground, but the legal fiction of adoption—what Maine called "factitious extensions of consanguinity" (127)—remained a way to perpetuate and enlarge the family by means other than marriage and heterosexual reproduction (125). Because the family, adoptive and biological, remained a basis for imagining social bonds, adoption also became a model for making political communities that were not based on shared blood.

Maine viewed adoption as crucial to civilization and suggested that to equate the family with heterosexual reproduction was a relic of primitive culture: "[W]ithout . . . the Fiction of Adoption which permits the family tie to be artificially created, it is difficult to understand how society would ever have escaped from its swaddling clothes, and taken its first steps towards civilisation" (26). Adoption shows that "the composition of the state uniformly assumed to be natural, was nevertheless known to be in great measure artificial. . . . The earliest and most extensively employed of legal fictions was that which permitted family relations to be created artificially, and there is none to which I conceive mankind to be more deeply indebted" (125–26). In her laudatory study of *Primitive Civilization*, Edith Simcox also noted that adoption was prevalent in ancient Babylonia, where women had many civil rights, egalitarian marriage was idealized, and "deeds of adoption [were] executed with formalities closely resembling those of marriage contracts" (377). For Maine and Simcox, the progress of civilization depended on conceptualizing the relationship between parent and child, like that between husband and wife, as a legal form that made kinship into a constructed agreement between individuals. Perhaps not surprisingly, adoption was also associated with same-sex love; in the 1840s, a sophisticated pornographic periodical published an essay on "The Loves of Sappho" that cited examples of Roman patricians who formalized their "personal love" for attractive male youths by adopting them.[106]

SAME-SEX UNIONS AND THE HISTORY OF CIVILIZATION

Tracing how anthropological texts understood the relationship between marriage and contract has returned us to the question of same-sex unions.

Historical hindsight reveals that contract undermined the idea that kinship depended on sexual difference, but did Victorian histories of marriage ever explicitly discuss same-sex unions, and if so, where did they place them in their evaluative scales? We can begin to answer this question by pointing out that several anthropologists who argued that marriage was not essentially defined by sexual difference belonged to social networks that included women in female marriages. Edith Simcox never lived with another woman, but she knew women in female couples and triangles (see chapter 1). Charles Darwin and Henry Sumner Maine both knew Frances Power Cobbe well enough to be aware that she lived with Mary Lloyd. Darwin's father had known the Ladies of Llangollen, another famous female couple, and Darwin himself lived near Cobbe and Lloyd while writing *The Descent of Man*. During that time, Lloyd lent her neighbor Darwin a pony, and he, like others in their circle, treated her as part of a unit, referring to "you and Miss Lloyd" when he wrote to Cobbe.[107] Though scholars today question whether Maine's liberal individualism produced a conservative or progressive view of marriage, Cobbe identified him as a feminist ally whose "interest in the claims of women and . . . strong statements on the subject, made me regard him with much gratitude."[108]

A handful of participants in the Victorian marriage debates explicitly discussed the role that same-sex relationships played in progress narratives of kinship. Some perceived same-sex relationships in exactly the terms Gayle Rubin's reading of anthropological theory would lead us to expect: as a practice antithetical to kinship, permissible only in states of presocial, precultural savagery and primitive promiscuity. Lecky, for example, equated polygamy and pederasty. His natural history of morals anatomized the "virtues . . . appropriate to each successive stage of civilisation" (ix) and warned that "[w]hen the passions of men are altogether unrestrained, community of wives and all eccentric forms of sensuality will be admitted" (103). Lecky linked the proliferation of courtesans in ancient Greece to male involvement with "that lower abyss of unnatural love, which was the deepest and strangest taint of Greek civilisation," named in a footnote as "paiderestia" (294), and identified with the story of Harmodius and Aristogeiton, "united by an impure love" (295). Engels made the inverse point in *The Origin of the Family, Private Property and the State*, which valorized the collectivism of primitive social forms over the individualism of modern ones. Where Lecky saw homosexuality as indicative of society before Christianity, Engels depicted homosexuality as an artifact of the rise of private property and the monogamous family. Noting that historically monogamy had always been "*for the woman only*, but not for the man," Engels criticized ancient Greek marriage for sullying wives and encouraging sodomy among husbands: "[T]his degradation of the women was avenged on the men and degraded them also till they fell into the abominable practice of sodomy and degraded alike their gods and themselves with the myth of Ganymede" (128).[109]

Although Engels shared Lecky's negative view of Athenian pederasty and wrote scathingly about "Urnings" in a letter to Karl Marx, he inadvertently proposed that same-sex marriage was an element of the stage of kinship he found most promising: the era "[b]efore incest was invented," when the family was structured by "the principle of promiscuity—the absence of any restriction imposed by custom on sexual intercourse" (101). Engels described an early kinship structure called the consanguine family, in which "[b]rothers and sisters, male and female cousins of the first, second, and more remote degrees, are all brothers and sisters of one another, and *precisely for that reason* are all husbands and wives of one another" (102). "All husbands and wives of one another"—Engels takes it for granted that only men can be husbands to women, only women wives to men. But precisely for that reason he produces a phrase that literally states that in the primitive family, everyone is *both* husband and wife to everyone else, without regard to sex. When Engels writes "[b]rothers and sisters . . . are all brothers and sisters of one another," he deploys kinship terms that are not limited by the sex of their object: women are sisters of both women and men. That gender inclusiveness extends grammatically to the sentence's final clause, which turns to sexual relationships; syntax transforms semantics, so that "husbands and wives" can be defined like the siblinghood that determines them. Women are the wives of their sisters and brothers, men the husbands of their brothers and sisters.

Engels makes the same grammatical slip when he comments on the punaluan family, in which several sisters are the common wives of common husbands, who unlike those in consanguine marriages are neither each other's brothers nor brothers of the sisters whom they marry. The term "punalua" refers not to different-sex relationships but to same-sex ones: "husbands . . . no longer called themselves brothers, for they were no longer necessarily brothers, but punalua—that is, intimate companion, or partner. Similarly, a line of natural or collateral brothers had a number of women, *not* their sisters, as common wives, and these wives called one another *punalua*" (104). In this "classic form of family structure . . . whose essential feature was the mutually common possession of husbands and wives within a definite family circle," wives are the intimate partners of other wives, husbands the intimate associates of other husbands (104), and marriage establishes relationships between women and between men as well as between men and women.

Where Engels unwittingly suggested that same-sex relationships were a component of primitive group marriage, and thus equated same-sex unions with a form of incest that he valued for its group harmony, Johann Bachofen explicitly described same-sex unions as a feature of civilization and modernity. In *Mother-Right* (1861), Bachofen described sexual relations in primordial nature as reproductive, fecundating, fulfilling the needs of the material world alone, and exclusively heterosexual. Civilization advances only when women and men move away from the primitive state Bachofen calls "hetairism," in which sexuality is violent and concerned only with biological reproduction. In a lengthy discussion of Sappho, unusual in its day for its frankness about her sexual relationships with women, Bachofen calls Sappho "chaste," defining chastity not as sexuality's absence but as its idealizing regulation:

> The love of women for their own sex [in Lesbian poetry] was equivalent to Orphic [male homosexuality]. . . . Sappho's striving to elevate her sex was the source of all her sorrows and joys, and it was Eros who inspired her in this attempt. Her ardent words flowed not from maternal solicitude but from amorous passion, and yet this enthusiasm, which seized upon the sensuous and the transcendent, the physical and the psychic, with equal vigor, had its ultimate and richest source in religion. Love and identity of sex, which had seemed exclusive, were now united."[110]

For Bachofen, lesbianism, like monogamous marriage, is a form of culture because it requires a degree of self-restraint; both convert materialist lust into spiritual love without abandoning sensuality. By interpreting sapphic love as an advanced stage of civilization, Bachofen implicitly argued against any absolute equation of civilization with heterosexual monogamy and reproduction.

• • •

If nineteenth-century Europeans did not uniformly assume that the union of man and woman was the only civilized form of marriage, it was due in part to the antic heterogeneity of public opinion about what form the institution should take. The 1850s and 1860s were defined by arguments, not agreement, over what constituted marriage and family, and same-sex relationships informed those debates. Participants in those debates had varying degrees of familiarity with women in female marriages, and several historians of marriage explicitly and implicitly deemed same-sex relationships compatible with values such as respectability, civilization, and progress. This does not redeem the empirical and ethical flaws of systems that relentlessly discriminated among religions, nations, and eras. But it does alert us to crucial differences between the twentieth-century concept of homosexuality and the nineteenth-century custom of female marriage. The homosexual and the lesbian were defined by secrecy, stigma, and their asocial deviance from married couples, while those in female marriages had a place in a social system as acceptable variations on legal spouses.

For decades, scholars hampered by twentieth-century prejudices obscured the facts of nineteenth-century female marriage, and as a result it has only recently become possible to identify the role that female marriage played in political, social, and intellectual life. Until the 1990s, biographies of Charlotte Cushman, Frances Power Cobbe, Anne Lister, and Emily Faithfull never mentioned their relationships with women unless to protest too much that they were utterly asexual friendships. Subsequent scholarship established the sexual nature of those relationships, but in the process reclaimed them for lesbian history by insisting on their marginality and opposition to marriage. Rosa Bonheur and Charlotte Cushman were, however, international stars beloved by the public, connected to artistic and intellectual luminaries, who lived openly with women they considered spouses. Frances Power Cobbe never feared that her well-known relationship with Mary Lloyd might compromise her status as a champion of women's rights inside and outside marriage. Writers like Henry Sumner Maine and John Stuart Mill advocated definitions of marriage that asserted the benefits of equality and likeness between spouses. Johann Bachofen explicitly linked lesbianism to modern enlightenment.

One of the great lies of present-day narratives of civilization is that in the past, values were fixed, and that until very recently there was an unbroken consensus that marital relationships could exist only between a man and a woman. One hundred and fifty years ago, however, Victorian values were already in flux. Legislators, journalists, and anthropologists debated the legitimacy of divorce and the meaning of marriage. While many warned that civilization was coming to an end, many also believed that dissoluble unions between legally equal spouses were the future of marriage—not least because of the example offered by the female marriages of their day.

CHAPTER 6

Contracting Female Marriage in
Can You Forgive Her?

As one of Victorian literature's most assiduous and complacent manufacturers of marriage plots, Anthony Trollope may seem a startling focus for a chapter about female marriage and the Victorian novel. A self-proclaimed conservative who voiced antifeminist views and sought to please his middle-class readers, Trollope produced the literary equivalent of the status quo. His position in the mainstream of Victorian literature and society makes him an excellent example for testing the previous chapter's argument—that Victorian debates about divorce and marriage indicate a general awareness of the plasticity of marriage. From the 1850s through the 1870s, as legislators, activists, and journalists acknowledged that it was possible to change the legal terms of marriage between men and women, historians of the family similarly recognized that marriage could be the name for a bond between two women or two men. Social recognition also played an important role in expanding the vernacular meaning of marriage, and acquaintances, friends, relatives, and colleagues conferred marital status on female couples who could not marry under the law but whose relationships exhibited marital features such as cohabitation, financial interdependence, physical intimacy, and agreements about fidelity.

Even Anthony Trollope knew women in female marriages, and a novel he began writing in 1863, *Can You Forgive Her?* (1864–1865), suggests that he understood that some women without husbands did not reject marriage altogether but instead chose a variation on it. Trollope wrote realist narratives of courtship, and many of his works deployed the plot of female amity analyzed in chapter 2, in which female friendship generates marriage between women and men. As I have shown throughout this book, however, female friendship and female marriage were distinct social relationships, and Trollope's interest in the plot of female amity would not necessarily promise a corresponding curiosity about unions between women. *Can You Forgive Her?* is unique among Trollope's many novels for its sustained engagement with female marriage, for it depicts courtship between a man and a woman as coterminous with one woman wooing another. Trollope wrote the novel in the wake of 1857 legislation that established England's first civil divorce court and spawned heated public debate about whether marriage could or should be a contract, and Margaret King and Kathy Psomiades have shown that Trollope's novels registered anxieties about women's increasing economic and political agency.[1] The presence of *female* marriage among feminist reformers and in Trollope's text has gone undetected, however, because of the assumption that same-sex relationships and marriage have until quite recently been mutually exclusive.

Can You Forgive Her? exhibits some agitation about female marriage, but not because Trollope equated any and every kind of love between women with subversion of the social and aesthetic orders. Like most middle-class Victorians, Trollope valued intimacy between women as a component of normative femininity and hence as a basis for marriage. Female marriage perturbed Trollope because of its links to a troubling innovation in marriage between men and women—the feminist reform of marriage into a dissoluble and egalitarian contract. In *Can You Forgive Her?*, Trollope represents a woman's choice between two male suitors as a contest between contractual marriage and hierarchical marriage that is simultaneously a struggle between female marriage and female amity. Hierarchical marriage and female amity are the ultimate victors, and the novel invokes the civilizational narratives explored in the previous chapter to portray sexual equality as a form of false progress that unleashes a savagery curable only by a return to a traditional rule of force in which men govern women. To narrate the triumph of hierarchical marriage and female amity, however, Trollope must acknowledge the existence and attractions of contractual and female marriage as viable social forms legible within the realist novel's aesthetic order.

Trollope, Feminism, and Female Marriage

Victorian feminists argued that marriage should be a contract between autonomous equals who could dissolve their agreement by mutual consent, and they obtained a great deal of publicity for their vision of marriages based on similarity between spouses. John Stuart Mill argued that because equality and likeness were the foundations of true unions, marriage should emulate what "often happens between two friends of the same sex."[2] Reformers equated egalitarian marriage with civilization, progress, and modernity and condemned hierarchical marriage as primitive, savage, and barbaric. Upholders of tradition, conversely, argued that contract and divorce would degrade marriage by returning it to its origins in primitive promiscuity. The question of whether same-sex relations represented primitive promiscuity or modern egalitarianism also surfaced, with Johann Bachofen aligning same-sex unions with the advance of modern civilization.

The publicity surrounding the 1857 Matrimonial Causes Act made divorce, adultery, bigamy, and cross-dressing popular literary topics.[3] Despite his reputation as a purveyor of anodyne fiction, Trollope explored those controversial issues in the early 1860s, just before he began *Can You Forgive Her?* George Smith, editor of the *Cornhill Magazine*, refused to publish two stories Trollope submitted in 1860, describing them as unfit for a family journal. "The Banks of the Jordan" described a man attracted to a male travel companion who turns out to be a cross-dressed woman, and "Mrs. General Talboys" portrayed English expatriates in Italy who assert that the marriage tie is "by no means necessarily binding" and divorce no longer "the privilege of the dissolute rich." After Trollope succeeded in placing the stories elsewhere, readers complained about their risqué subject matter.[4]

Trollope incurred nothing but gratitude, however, when he contributed two stories free of charge to feminist Emily Faithfull, whose Victoria Press produced anthologies designed to showcase women's work as compositors and illustrators.[5] Trollope never hid how much he relished receiving payment for his writing, and his decision to donate fiction to an overtly feminist publication complicates the antifeminist stances he often took in his writing and lectures. In content as well as venue, the stories Trollope gave Faithfull suggest his sympathy with women's desires for mobility and independence. "The Journey to Panama" (1861), which appeared in Faithfull's *Victoria Regia*, describes a young woman who decides not to marry after an inheritance leaves her financially independent. "Miss Ophelia Gledd" (1863), Trollope's contribution to Faithfull's second compendium, *A Welcome*, portrays a self-willed woman who does eventually marry, but whom Trollope modeled on his unmarried friend Kate Field.[6]

Trollope's social and professional involvement with Kate Field and Emily Faithfull speaks volumes about his awareness of female marriage and erotic relationships between women. Kate Field has traditionally been the closest thing in Trollope studies to a study in scarlet, the only hint that Trollope was ever less than completely faithful to his wife.[7] But to examine Field only through the lens of Trollope's romantic fantasies about her is to overlook the more lavender shades that tinged her life. Field and Trollope were linked by a social network that united same-sex couples, legally married opposite-sex couples, and unmarried men and women whose sexual interests varied, and they shared connections to many of the women in female marriages discussed in earlier chapters. Field and Trollope first met in Florence in 1860, where Trollope's mother and brother belonged to an Anglo-American expatriate circle that included Walter Savage Landor, the Brownings, and Mary Somerville, as well as women in female marriages and having affairs with women, such as Charlotte Cushman, Emma Stebbins, Isa Blagden, Harriet Hosmer, Frances Power Cobbe, and Mary Lloyd.[8] A favorite of both Brownings, Field had gone to Italy to recover from unrequited love for a married aunt and thus arrived primed to appreciate the same-sex relationships she encountered there. While in Florence, Field flirtatiously referred to her hostess Isa Blagden as "Hubby," exchanged presents with Frances Power Cobbe, and observed Lady Ashburton kneel before her lover, Harriet Hosmer.[9] Having previously met Charlotte Cushman in the United States through her aunt, Field slyly saluted the actress's erotic and quasi-marital relationship with Emma Stebbins by addressing Cushman as "Beloved Romeo" and referring to Stebbins as "Juliet."[10]

Field and Trollope maintained regular contact after meeting in 1860, but their relationship was always strained by Field's allegiance to the female independence she had witnessed in Italy. Trollope was not universally hostile to women who supported themselves and who married other women instead of men and was even on friendly terms with many of them. His correspondence documents cordial interactions with Frances Power Cobbe, Rhoda Broughton, Isa Blagden, Amelia Edwards, and Emily Faithfull.[11] He was aware of the close connections among the women in Cushman's circle; when writing to Field, he sent his love to Blagden, and when writing to Blagden, he forwarded a note from Field.[12] He helped Isa Blagden contact British publishers and sought out the acquaintance of Amelia Edwards, a writer who openly lived with another woman. He contributed to *Victoria Regia* along with Matilda Hays, who had been Charlotte Cushman's partner in the 1850s and then formed a long relationship with Theodosia, Lady Monson.[13] In Field's case, however, Trollope was less tolerant, and his platonic romance with her consisted mostly of berating her for not marrying a man. Even as Trollope helped Field pursue a career as a writer, he badgered her "to go & marry a husband," and in 1862, wrote her that he didn't "at all understand how you are living, where—with whom—or on what terms," registering a confusion that would last for much of their friendship.[14]

Field did eventually settle down—with another woman. Trollope died the year Field met the woman who became her partner, so we cannot know how he would have responded to learning that his friend had finally heeded his advice, after a fashion. We do know that the Victorian middle class defined marriage in terms of shared households, financial support, bequests of wealth and property, the care of the body in life and death, and vows and practices of exclusive commitment and unique spiritual communion. By those criteria, Field clearly had a spouse, for wherever we turn in the record of her later life, we find one woman. The woman to whom Field entrusted her body for burial was the same woman who inherited Field's letters, journals, and possessions, wrote a loving biographical tribute to Field, penned a memoir about her encounters with Field's ghost, and was buried next to Field in Mount Auburn Cemetery: Lilian Whiting.[15]

Whiting was a journalist, poet, and figure of some literary repute in Boston. Like Field and Trollope, Lilian Whiting knew many women in female marriages or involved in extramarital affairs with women, including Rosa Bonheur, Anna Klumpke, Harriet Hosmer, and Emma Crow Cushman.[16] Whiting's biography of Anna Klumpke gave a remarkably explicit account of how Rosa Bonheur proposed that Klumpke become her second spouse. Elsewhere Whiting noted that Bonheur left her estate to Klumpke and called Klumpke's biography of Bonheur "the most intimate" work ever written about the artist.[17] The parallels to Whiting and Field were clear: Field left Whiting all her papers, and Whiting wrote Field's biography. Nor was that biography the only book Field inspired Whiting to write. She dedicated a volume of poems to Kate Field in 1895, and after Field's death in 1896, published a spiritualist memoir about her communications with the spirit of Kate Field—"the central interest of my life" and its "magnetic centre"—in order to prove that "[l]ove is not barred by death."[18] Whiting wrote of "she—who was dearest of all to me" sending messages that Whiting experienced as a "mysterious thrill . . . like contact with an electric current." *After Her Death* openly advertised the identity of the title's "*her*—my beloved friend" by reproducing a portrait of Kate Field as its frontispiece, and reviewers explicitly identified the work as "a graceful and touching tribute . . . to the memory of the late Kate Field."[19]

A few years after Field's death, Whiting wrote a biography based on the papers she had inherited from Field as well as on the numerous "private letter[s]" Field had sent her daily whenever they were apart.[20] *Kate Field* follows nineteenth-century biographical conventions that encouraged authors to stay invisible even when writing about family members and spouses whom they knew intimately.[21] Whiting rarely uses the first person, and she refers to herself only as "the biographer" and "the writer of this book" even when describing direct interactions with Field.[22] Yet she also tells the reader, almost in passing, that "the biographer" and her subject lived together whenever Field was not traveling, that Field wanted to support Whiting financially, and that Whiting asked Field to destroy the personal letters she had sent her.[23] Through frequent, casual references to what Field "always" did or felt, Whiting subtly conveys intimacy with her subject, just as she communicates their erotic relationship by naming her own "memory" as the source of a sensuous rhapsody about Field's beauty.[24]

Although Trollope claimed to find Field's life incomprehensible, their shared acquaintance with women like Cushman, Cobbe, Hosmer, and Emily Faithfull shows that he had a context for understanding Field's choices. When Trollope contributed a story based on Field to Faithfull's anthology in the early months of 1863, he did so as a "friendly lark . . . chiefly for the sake of Emily Faithfull herself."[25] He also showed his commitment to Faithfull at a time when rumors had begun to swirl about her relationship with Helen Codrington. Born the daughter of a country parson in 1835, Faithfull came to London and joined the Langham Place feminist movement in the 1850s. During several of those years, Faithfull lived with Helen Codrington and her husband, and when Admiral Codrington sued his wife for divorce, Faithfull was a crucial witness in a widely reported trial that publicized her overly intimate relationship with a woman accused of adultery.[26] The actual trial did not begin until July 1864, but Admiral Codrington filed divorce papers in November 1863, and when Trollope began *Can You Forgive Her?* several months earlier, in August of that same year, he would have probably heard the rumors that caused a few of Faithfull's feminist friends to sever personal and professional contact as early as 1862.[27]

While some feminists were anxious lest sexual scandal taint their political endeavors, the less vulnerable Trollope continued to socialize with Faithfull, spending time with her in June 1863 and again on February 16, 1864, when Faithfull visited Trollope's home at Waltham Cross.[28] On April 28, 1864, Trollope finished writing *Can You Forgive Her?*. About two months later, he saw Faithfull again, when she lunched with him and his wife in Greenwich on June 15, 1864, only six weeks before giving evidence in the Codrington trial. On both occasions, Faithfull brought along Emilie Wilson, daughter of an MP and Faithfull's intimate since 1862.[29] Two months later, Faithfull was rehearsing her evidence for a trial initiated in November 1863, when Admiral Codrington first filed the divorce papers attesting that his adulterous wife, Helen, had shared a bed with Emily Faithfull for years. In November 1863, Anthony Trollope was at work on the chapter that lies at the literal and figurative center of *Can You Forgive Her?*, "Among the Fells." That chapter provides a key to the link Trollope made between Emily Faithfull and Kate Field, for in it, a character named Kate Vavasor—who like her namesake Kate Field never marries a man—proposes marriage to her cousin Alice.[30]

FEMALE MARRIAGE AND CONTRACTUAL MARRIAGE IN *CAN YOU FORGIVE HER?*

Trollope's novels seem to leave little room for female marriage, crowded as they are with the multiple male suitors who exemplify his trademark variation on the marriage plot. Rather than focus on the obstacles to courtship between one man and one woman, a typical Trollope novel charts the dilemmas of a heroine who must choose between two or more suitors and arrive at a decision final in both senses: timed to coincide with the novel's end and pronounced with the permanence of a marriage vow. The central heroine of *Can You Forgive Her?* must also choose between two suitors, but the novel undoes the certainties of the marriage plot by beginning where most Trollope novels end, with her engagement to be married.

The narrator emphasizes that his starting point inverts conventional novel form when he concludes his first chapter with a dramatic declaration about his heroine, Alice Vavasor: "And now for my fact. At the time of which I am writing she was already engaged to be married."[31] Readers are left wondering where Alice could possibly go from there, and though the book was popular and profitable, reviewers were predictably impatient with a plot that recounts how Alice repeatedly breaks and remakes engagements with two different men. "[F]or so thick a book," commented Henry James, "there is certainly very little story."[32] The suitor to whom she is engaged at the novel's start and whom she ultimately marries is the upright John Grey; the suitor to whom she gets engaged after breaking with John is her shifty cousin, George Vavasor. Each man has a female counterpart who advocates on his behalf: Alice's cousin Glencora favors John, while George's courtship of Alice is almost entirely conducted by his sister Kate Vavasor, who is also Alice's closest friend.

Margaret King has argued that *Can You Forgive Her?* chastises its heroine for her aspirations to be something other than a man's wife, but Alice does not simply resist marriage per se. Rather, she rejects one kind of marriage in order to embrace another; she turns from John, an indomitable superior who insists on the permanence of marriage promises, to George, who allows Alice to define marriage as dissoluble, egalitarian, and contractual. Alice's engagement to George can take place only because she dissolves her promise to marry John, and the narrator and various characters construe Alice's decision to end that engagement as equivalent to making the marriage bond itself impermanent. Promises to marry did not customarily have the same weight as marriage vows, but in Trollope's novels, engagement is often "a bond almost as holy as matrimony itself could be," and breaking an engagement becomes tantamount to divorce.[33] Alice's relatives tell her that a "young lady has no right to change her mind" after "accept[ing] a gentleman" (219), and when Alice tells John she wants to end their engagement, he insists that in effect they are already married: "You are my wife, my own, my dearest, my chosen one" (147).

Alice associates the dissolubility of engagement with the "liberty" that, for better and for worse, pundits attributed to divorce, and she initially sees in George the similarly feminist possibility of an egalitarian union that bypasses sexual difference (59). George considers Alice in a companionable light, describing her as a "partner" (377) and "a dear friend bearing the same name" (244). The fact that Alice would maintain her given surname, Vavasor, were she to marry George symbolizes the hope that she would also be able to retain her political aspirations. Alice feels "none of the love of a woman" for George (490), but is attracted to him because he indulges her love of politics and of London, a place she identifies with masculine aspirations: "Were I a man, no earthly consideration should induce me to live elsewhere" (61). The narrator interprets Alice's inclination to "join her lot to that of her cousin George" as due not to "her love for the man" but her desire to make "herself useful . . . in some sort that might gratify her ambition" (342). Already accused by her relatives of acting more like a "gentleman" than a "girl" when she ends her engagement to John (63), Alice accepts George's invitation to join him on the masculine ground of statesmanship. In a country where, as Alice notes, "Women are not allowed to be politicians," engagement to George allows Alice to identify with a member of the Radical party sympathetic to feminism (258), and George invites Alice to imagine marriage to him as access to manly bravado: "No woman ought to join her lot to mine unless she has within her the courage to be as reckless as I am" (74).

The egalitarian qualities of an individual man cannot alter the inequalities of marriage as a legal state in a novel that envelops marital relations in a rhetoric of obedience. For Alice, however, engagement is not marriage; indeed, she uses marriage promises to defer the act of wedding. Engagements postpone the definitive installation of marital hierarchy, not least because an engaged woman removes herself from the marriage market. When Alice tells John she is breaking their engagement, he responds that they are "already in some sort married" (59) and rejects her attempt to exit their contract: "No, Alice, no; never with my consent. . . . Nothing but your marriage with someone else would convince me" (148). Alice takes John at his word: if he will absolve her of her promise to wed him only if she marries another, then engagement to George is the closest she can come to deflecting marriage to one man without actually marrying the other.

If the marriage ceremony has been taken as an exemplary instance of how to do things with words, Trollope illustrates instead how a woman can use words in order not to do the thing.[34] Alice uses engagements the way a parliamentary agent advises George to use campaign promises: "Of course it won't be done. If it were done, that would be an end of it, and your bread would be taken out of your mouth" (474). George is a perfect choice for a woman who wants to be engaged in order *not* to marry, for he is as ambivalent about wedlock as John is steadfast. Unlike the domestic John, who has already prepared his home for a wife, George cannot think of himself "as a man married" (154) and detaches engagement from any final nuptial result: "How soon after that he might marry her, would be another question" (153). That indifference is congenial to a woman so eager to postpone marriage that her assent to George's epistolary proposal incorporates its own negation: "If it suits you, I will be your wife—but it cannot be quite at once" (355). Soon after she becomes engaged to George, Alice vows to herself never to marry him: "Come what might, she would never stand with him at the altar" (399). That antimarriage promise reinforces that engagements do not necessarily lead to marriage and can even be used to prevent it from taking place.

An engagement that highlights the relative egalitarianism of the affianced state and presumes its own dissolubility becomes contractual when George and Alice conduct their premarital business in writing, as a series of negotiations that lead to painstakingly documented agreements about money. George's marriage proposal is a commercial proposition that arrives in the form of a letter asking Alice to fund his political career. His mercenary interest in Alice's independent income harmonizes with her desire to conceive of their engagement as a financial agreement between equals. By permitting George to use her money, Alice realizes her desire to "run . . . risk" and enter an economy in which promises are credit (350). Her written reply treats George's epistolary proposal as a step in a negotiation: "[I]f you will accept me under such circumstances, I will be your wife" (355). In an act the narrator calls an "offer," George later tells Alice she can "retract" her letter accepting him (378). Alice's engagement to George becomes a literal contract when she signs bills of exchange for him, "four bills, each of five hundred pounds, drawn at fourteen days' date," making her marital pledge a monetary one (628). When George explains, in a letter delivered by a moneylender, that it is "more than ever incumbent on you that you should be true to your pledge to me" (628), he means her pledge to lend him money, not to marry him. Instructing Alice how to sign bills, George explains that her "name must come under the word 'accepted,'" transforming a word that initially had marital connotations into a business term (628–629).

The contractual engagement Alice formulates with George also entails a union between Alice and the woman who mediates his suit. Midway through *Can You Forgive Her?*, Alice refuses to kiss George after having accepted his proposal, and the narrator asks, "Of what marriage had she thought, when she was writing that letter back to George Vavasor?" (397). The question is not rhetorical, since the narrator answers it, explaining that Alice had imagined marriage to George as that of "one friend" with another: "His disgrace should be her disgrace;—his glory her glory;—his pursuits her pursuits. Was not that the marriage to which she had consented?" (398). Alice's reported thoughts equate marriage to George with the biblical tale whose balanced cadences she echoes, the story of Ruth and Naomi. That allusion to a popular motif of female friendship suggests what the novel elsewhere confirms, that the marriage Alice thought of when accepting George was a marriage to his female intercessor.[35] That many of George's encounters with Alice take place in her home on Queen Anne Street, named after the royal figure whom the second volume of Thomas Macaulay's *History of England* (1848) equated with her devotion to a female favorite, further feminizes their projected union.[36]

The novel casts contractual marriage as female marriage even more directly by representing the male suitor as a female one. Although in other respects George is hyperbolically masculine, the anatomical part he offers Alice in marriage, his hand, is remarkable for having a "surface smooth as a woman's," and the hand that orchestrates his engagement to Alice is not merely like a woman's but literally belongs to one—Alice's cousin and George's sister, Kate (177). Critics have explained Kate's zeal in promoting Alice's marriage to George as a displacement of incestuous desire for her brother, an instance of symptomatic reading overpowering what just reading finds on the text's surface.[37] The search for hidden heterosexual meanings has neglected homoerotic ones that are far more obvious, for the bond Kate fosters between Alice and George is embedded in the equally deep one between the two women. George reminds Kate that his love for Alice never originated with him but was his sister's invention: "You have always been under a matchmaking hallucination on that point" (409). George only proposes because, literally and figuratively, Kate makes "room for him between herself and Alice" (91). When he shows little eagerness to court his cousin, Kate complains, "I'm moving heaven and earth to bring you two together" (94), and she later berates herself for having separated Alice from John Grey in order to "allure her into the arms of" George Vavasor (600). The narrative even suggests that Kate and George, who have the same kinship relation to Alice, occupy an equivalent place in her marital projects. When Alice tells herself that "after all she might as well marry her cousin" (397), or remembers herself accepting "her cousin's offer" (373), the neutral kinship term suggests that Kate is as much her prospective spouse as George is.

If grammatical ambiguity suggests that the cousin who offers marriage could be female as well as male, the novel's handling of the formal climax of a marriage plot, the proposal scene, leaves no doubt about who offers marriage to Alice. In "Among the Fells," the chapter Trollope wrote when the Emily Faithfull scandal was revealing how closely a woman might become entangled in another woman's marriage, Alice spends Christmas with her grandfather, father, and Kate, and receives a proposal letter from

George. The previous chapter, written from George's point of view in London, depicts him composing a letter asking Alice to marry him and ends by rapidly projecting into the future: "And before the end of the week the answer came (335)." That cliffhanger ending heightens the narrative stakes of the following chapter, which breaks with linear convention by moving back in time to divulge the outcome that the narrator has announced but not revealed.

"Among the Fells" presents marriage between a man and a woman as a contractual agreement negotiated in writing and female marriage as a passionate encounter between embodied subjects. The manifest resolution to the question posed at the end of the preceding chapter is that Alice accepts George's epistolary proposal, but equally manifest is George's absence from the scene of her assent and Kate's presence as a powerful surrogate suitor. It is Kate who incarnates courtship as she and Alice walk together in an expressionist landscape dominated by trinities, figures of three that symbolize how the engagement between a man and a woman creates a triangle that also includes a female couple. Kate and Alice's destination when they seek a spot to discuss George's letter is a lake "not above three miles long," carved deep into a rock in "the shape of the figure of 3" (344). "The shape of the figure of 3" is a curious phrase that embodies how multiple components can coalesce into single units. The definite singular article appears twice (*the* shape of *the* figure), and Trollope makes the typographically startling choice to use the numeral "3," more compact and unified than its verbal equivalent, "three." As a shape, the numeral "3" consists of two equal parts, a symmetrical form that mirrors the egalitarian couple Alice hopes to form with George and the same-sex couple she forms with Kate. When the narrator strains usage to describe the lake as "embosomed" in the mountains (344), he draws our attention to the femininity of the two identical parts that comprise "the figure of 3," for his metaphor directs the reader to see how the numeral's form resembles the outline of a pair of breasts.

The content of the chapter develops the imagery of female coupling expressed by its setting. By giving Kate George's letter to read, Alice asks her to materialize his proposal, and Kate avidly sets herself to that task, demanding not that Alice promise to accept George but that she say yes instantly—to Kate. Immediately after reading George's letter, Kate uses the words and gestures of a Victorian suitor demanding the hand of the woman he loves: "'Oh, Alice, may I hope? Alice, my own Alice, my darling, my friend! Say that it shall be so!' And Kate knelt at her friend's feet upon the heather, and looked up into her face with eyes full of tears" (345). Only a few pages before, Kate herself explicates the marital connotations of her posture when she conjectures that one of her aunt's eager suitors "kneels there on every occasion . . . and repeats his offer . . . twice a week" (340). When Kate imagines Alice accepting George, she longs to be in his place, saying of "the love-sweet words" she imagines Alice will use, "I know how sweet they will be. Oh, heavens! how I envy him!" (347). Kate identifies so completely with George's desire to marry Alice that after reading his missive, she exults: "[I]s it not a letter of which if you were his brother you would feel proud if another girl had shown it to you?" (345). The choice of sibling term is striking: although she is George's sister, Kate asks Alice to imagine her as a man; as George's brother; or, since George is her only brother, as George himself.

Trollope represents the woman who courts another woman on a man's behalf as going far beyond the role of intermediary. Kate kisses the spot where she has read George's letter (345); she insists to Alice, "I know you will not refuse him; but make me happy by saying so with your own lips" (346); and she requests that Alice "not answer him without speaking to me first" (347). Like all Alice's suitors, Kate seeks to quicken the pace of Alice's response, and as with all her suitors, Alice complains that she does not want to answer quickly: "I knew well . . . that you would strive to hurry me into an immediate promise" (346). Like any canny aspiring husband, Kate responds by saying that she accepts delay, but does not desire it: "No, Alice, I will not hurry you. . . . But you cannot be surprised that I should be very eager. Has it not been the longing of all my life? Have I not passed my time plotting and planning and thinking of it till I have had time to think of nothing else?" (346). Kate repeats throughout the chapter that she is not simply vicariously happy for George and Alice, but that their marriage realizes her own desires: "[C]an you be surprised that I am wild with joy when I begin to see that everything will be as I wish;—for it will be as I wish, Alice" (346).

In the plot of female amity, women's friendships often bring about marriage between a man and a woman, but *Can You Forgive Her?* forgoes that sequential relationship in favor of a total coincidence between one woman's proposal to another and the engagement of a man and a woman. Indeed, Trollope invests Kate's marriage proposal with an ease noticeably absent from the novel's many instances of impeded wooing between women and men. Alice responds to Kate more readily than to either of the men who court her, acknowledging that Kate's enthusiasm makes it "almost impossible for her *now* to say that her answer to George must be a refusal" (345, emphasis added). Alice gives George her acceptance in writing but informs Kate of it in person; Kate takes Alice's arm, asks what she has written to George, and Alice replies obliquely, "I have kept my promise" (348). Kate then claims Alice with a performative utterance and gesture that fix the meaning of Alice's response: "'My sister,—my own sister,' said Kate. And then, as Alice met her embrace, there was no longer any doubt as to the nature of the reply" (348). Kate's reply mimics the marriage ceremony's ability to create new relationships through proprietary renaming ("my own sister") and expressive touch (the embrace). When Alice determines that "Kate should talk to her father" (351), she assigns Kate the suitor's role of asking for a daughter's hand.

Just as the woman proposing marriage to another woman on a man's behalf does so as an extension of her own desires, the woman who accepts her proposal announces an independent interest in her female suitor. Alice avows at several junctures that her love for Kate is independent of what she feels—or does not feel—for George. Although Alice expresses affection for both John and George when she is not engaged to them, after promising to marry each of them, she experiences "dread" (394), "dismay" (376) and "disgust" (376), and responds to George's written marriage proposal by warning him, "There is no . . . passion left to me;—nor, as I think, to you either" (355). If there is no passion left to Alice, it is because Kate has left her side, for when she prepares to write John of her engagement to George, she wishes she had done so when "Kate had been near her, and she had been comforted by Kate's affectionate happiness. . . . The atmosphere of the fells had buoyed her up" (386). Throughout a novel in which she is spectacularly indecisive, Alice retains her fantasy of pledging herself to Kate, even without the mediation of marriage to a man identified with her. Early on, Alice says, "I hope that Kate will always live with me. . . . I don't think she will ever find that I shall separate myself from her" (174–75). She recalls that wish hundreds of pages later, after having broken her engagement with George: "I believe that everything has been done for the best. I am inclined to think that I can live alone, or perhaps with my cousin Kate, more happily than I could with any husband" (716). The narrator has Alice "contemplate . . . a life of spinsterhood with her cousin Kate," an oxymoron that articulates Trollope's awareness that women who did not marry men were not necessarily solitary (313). Even characters outside the female couple recognize the strength of Alice's love for Kate; Glencora Palliser teases Alice about her indifference to male suitors, playfully wondering "whether you ever did care for anybody in your life,—for him, or for that other one, or for anybody. For nobody, I believe;—except your cousin Kate" (728). Despite those pronouncements, in "Among the Fells" one woman proposes to another as the ostensible representative of a male suitor, and it is to the type of marriage that male suitor represents that we must now turn.

MARRIAGE AS FORGIVENESS: PRIMITIVE CONTRACT AND MODERN PUNISHMENT

Can You Forgive Her? gives Victorian debates about marriage narrative form. George is a sign of contract's affinity with modernity and progress early in the novel, but eventually becomes an avatar of "great violence"

(594) who annihilates the basis of contract—writing. Instead of using his hand to pen offers, he deploys it against his proxy suitor Kate, pushing her with so much force that he leaves her "right arm . . . powerless" (594), so that "writing to Alice" becomes "out of the question" (600). The novel punishes Kate for having helped to make marriage a contract, a written form, by retaliating against her as a writer, and it punishes Alice for having chosen contractual marriage by transforming her modern suitor into a raging tyrant. At the novel's outset, George represents Alice's freedom to dissolve marriage promises and her feminist ambition and independence. By the novel's end, he is living proof of the primitive violence conservatives warned would result if divorce were to make marriage a dissoluble agreement between equals.

Contemporary literary critics have long equated both contract and marriage with fixed constraints that consolidate hierarchies. In *Adultery in the Novel*, Tony Tanner defines contract as the laws and distinctions that found society and argues that novels stage a conflict between the form of marriage and the volatile formlessness of adultery, incest, and homosexuality.[38] Tanner's structuralist account of contract cannot explain, however, why a novelist like Trollope aligned contract with a heroine's disruptive fantasies of equality and autonomy. Although Tanner cites Maine's distinction between status and contract, by defining contract as a fixed structure opposed to the anarchic desires embodied in adultery and homosexuality, he actually assigns to contract the rigid, authoritarian valences that Maine assigned to status.[39] Trollope's narrative, by contrast, associates contract with the feminist reform of marriage. Its marriage plot does not stage a battle between form and antiform but between two social structures: hierarchical marriage, which depends on female friendship, and egalitarian marriage, which coexists with female marriage. The contest is a genuine one, for the triumph of hierarchical marriage is never a foregone conclusion in a Trollope novel. Although his narrators uphold male superiority and parental authority as traditional powers that can legitimately limit female autonomy, they also advocate individualism, which mandates romantic love as the basis for marriage and requires that a woman freely choose her mate. Trollope's usual solution to this conflict is to characterize romantic love as its own form of compulsion for women.

Can You Forgive Her? divests its heroine's choice of husband of its connotations of equality and autonomy in two ways: the novel depicts her as repeatedly paralyzed by the act of choosing, and it assimilates the two-suitor plot to a civilizational narrative that casts contractual marriage as primitive. As we saw in the previous chapter, Victorian social thinkers including Henry Sumner Maine, John Stuart Mill, Edith Simcox, and Mona Caird associated contract with modernity, civilization, and progress toward equality between women and men. Trollope, however, represents contract as a primitive form of marriage. In a comic subplot, the widowed Mrs. Greenow, with two determined suitors, flirts with polyandry so seriously that she has to be reminded that in matters of marriage, "there's no crying halves" (220). Trollope based Mrs. Greenow and her multiple suitors on the title character of Fanny Trollope's *The Widow Barnaby* (1839), and he uses her to show that he can outdo his mother's literary skill by bringing his own to bear on the portrait of a woman who is herself a mild satire on matriarchal rule. Mrs. Greenow expertly manipulates her two suitors, always retaining her "authority" as "the mistress of the occasion" and taking "much care in securing the payment of her own income into her own hands" after marriage (802). That contractual approach is portrayed as a carnivalesque guarantee that she will always remain a woman on top, and the novel depicts her contractual marriage to Captain Bellfield as a parodic reversal of primitive marriage by purchase; like a potentate, Mrs. Greenow offers Bellfield "money [and] strength," buys him a "trousseau" (719), and controls his actions (683), suggesting that she arrogates the privileges of a husband who can buy romance and submission.

Where the novel's comic plot associates contractual marriage with a harmless but undesirable vulgarity, its main plot represents contract as a dangerous reversion to violence when George metamorphoses into a wild and savage villain. George's status as Alice's cousin might seem to frame their projected union as a primitive reversion to incest from the very outset, but marriage between first cousins was widely accepted in Victorian society, particularly in royal and aristocratic circles, and other Trollope novels conclude with happy cousin unions. Alice's contractual relationship with George devolves into savagery not because he is her cousin, but because he is, as Glencora calls him, "that dangerous cousin" (248). Indeed, the heroine's contractual project comes under the sign of primitive matriarchy even before the narrator identifies her choice of husband as misguided. The narrator introduces Alice by referring to her "blood," which he identifies with her aristocratic maternal relatives. Alice has inherited her mother's first name and wealth, transmitted directly from mother to daughter in a bequest that bypassed the laws of coverture (40). That independent income allows Alice to exercise a propensity, also inherited from her mother, to give "offence" to her elders by choosing a husband against their wishes (39–40). When Alice engages herself to marry a member of her father's family, she does so in opposition to both maternal and paternal kin. Her prospective marriage of alliance with George positions her not as a passive pawn exchanged between men, but as a self-appointed "messenger" (353) who will be the "the means of reconciling George to his grandfather" (343). By marrying him, Alice "act[s]" as a clan leader who will make "George Vavasor . . . Vavasor of

Vavasor . . . so . . . that future Vavasors might at any rate not be less in the world" (343).

The novel aligns contractual engagement with primitive promiscuity as well as with matriarchy. In *The Small House at Allington*, the narrator compares stories of broken betrothal to bigamy plots, and *Can You Forgive Her?* similarly equates the jilt and the bigamist, both of whom declare love for more than one man.[40] Alice never professes love for George, but what she lacks in romantic avowals she makes up for in promiscuous promises to marry and the guilty shame those promises inspire. When she tells her grandfather of her engagement to George, he exclaims "'Another!'. . . . And by the tone of his voice he accused his granddaughter of having a larger number of favoured suitors than ought to fall to the lot of any young lady" (353). Alice takes his censure to heart, and the narrator echoes it: "She had done very wrong. She knew that she had done wrong. She knew that she had sinned with that sin which specially disgraces a woman. . . . She had thrown off her that wondrous aroma of precious delicacy, which is the greatest treasure of womanhood" (352). Alice's sense of pollution stems from having transgressed the absolute monogamy demanded of women, and she lacerates herself for having committed bigamy of the heart for most of the novel, telling John when he proposes again, "You do not know me . . . how vile I have been! You do not think what it is,—for a woman to have promised herself to one man while she loved another. . . . I am a fallen creature" (770–71). By the novel's end, the aura of bigamy has cast the pall of primitive promiscuity on contractual marriage.

Alice's contractual engagement to George comes to seem even more primitive when the novel intensifies its characterization of George as a "wild man" (56) whom one reviewer described as "savage."[41] The novel initially compares George to a light-hearted polygamist who makes Kate and Alice "joint minister[s]" to his "idle fantasies" and "do[es] his despotism pleasantly" (79–80). There are early hints he will do his despotism less pleasantly as the novel proceeds; the narrator describes George as "uncommonly dark" (191) and as the proud bearer of a facial scar that evokes ethnographic accounts of scarification among primitive tribes. That scar, a "black ravine running through his cheek" (75), symbolizes violence with a semiotic directness that was itself considered a hallmark of primitive sign systems, for when George is angry, it "seem[s] to open itself and to become purple with fresh blood stains" (550). As the novel progresses, George becomes a "wild beast" (596) who makes "assaults upon [Alice's] purse" (490), entertains murderous wishes, and becomes a figure of real violence in three separate attacks on Alice, Kate, and John Grey. Even his speech becomes primitive, issuing from him "with a stigmatizing hiss," and his behavior to Kate and Alice exemplifies what Victorians considered the male savage's tendency to press the advantage of superior strength (496).

The contempt George shows to a former mistress in chapter 71 similarly exhibits the callousness of a polygamist who refuses to abide by marriage laws, and his "hard ferocity" and "hatred, as he called it, of conventional rules" mean that he is "controlled by none of the ordinary bonds of society" (580). The narrator calls George's dislike of convention "Bohemian," a term that marks George's lawlessness as simultaneously primitive and hypermodern (329). An avant-garde belief in "the absurdity of . . . indissoluble ties" (330) makes him like a "heathen," yet also "almost inclined to think that marriage was an old-fashioned custom . . . not adapted to his advanced intelligence" (329). By describing George's "advanced intelligence" as an attempt "to imitate the wisdom of the brutes," the narrator equates the modern idea of dissoluble ties with primitive violence and promiscuity (330). Thus when George confronts John in his lodgings, he presents contract (written agreements) and violence (physical fighting) as two sides of the same coin: "You shall either give me your written promise never to go near [Alice] again, or you shall fight me" (748). Rather than represent an advance over primitivism, contract becomes its counterpart.

Trollope's commitment to hierarchical marriage, however, means that even as he condemns George's violence as the primitive outcome of contract's excessive modernity, he asserts that violence has its proper place in traditional marriage. When George shoves Kate, the narrator comments that men should not strike "women," but adds that since marriage is permanent, a "wife may have to bear [a blow] and . . . return" (600), thus going out of his way to suggest that such violence could be acceptable within an indissoluble marriage. As the prelude to John's final, successful wooing of Alice, George's blatant aggression makes John's milder coercion seem more palatable. John's gentle force comes to seem necessary to preserve Trollope's conservative ideal of innovation without revolution, an ideal rendered even more appealing by contrast to the havoc wreaked by the radical, bohemian George.

The novel's most vivid reduction of the contractual to the primitive takes place when George sends a clerk who asks Alice to sign notes—literal contracts—under nearly Gothic duress. The narrator describes George's emissary as a primitive incursion into Alice's drawing-room: "Mr Levy was certainly not a gentleman of the sort to which [Alice] had been most accustomed. He was a little dark man, with sharp eyes, set very near to each other in his head, with a beaked nose, thick at the bridge, and a black moustache, but no other beard. Alice did not at all like the look of Mr Levy" (627–28). Mr. Levy's looks recall George's—both men are dark and wear moustaches—and the narrator dwells on the taint of his presence and the degrading effect of the bills he makes Alice sign, which make Alice's "name . . . the same as ready money—just the same" (630) and run the risk of being "dishonoured" if they are not paid (642). Like the Jew in the eyes of the anti-Semite, contract becomes in Trollope's narrative the point where modernity becomes primitive. When Alice reluctantly signs the notes, the act of freely making a contract becomes submission to an anonymous market where a potentially limitless series of strangers have the power to trade her bills, and to devalue them, precisely because "ladies' bills never mean . . . business" (633). The self-cancelling structure of a woman transacting business only to learn that ladies' contracts never mean it encapsulates the novel's overarching narrative drive to discredit contract.

George's use of coercion to make Alice enter monetary agreements with him contrasts with another complex financial subplot calculated to absolve hierarchical marriage of similar charges of theft. Feminists accused the law of coverture of allowing husbands to steal their wives' property, but *Can You Forgive Her?* depicts contractual, dissoluble agreements as posing a greater danger to women's wealth. Apprised of Alice's transactions with George, John Grey works to nullify her contracts, colluding with her father so that John, not Alice, pays George the money promised by her signed bills. Although if Alice marries John, he will legally own her assets, he demonstrates indifference to his economic interests by willingly giving up his own money to preserve Alice's wealth even after she has dissolved their engagement. George, in contrast, is one of the only men in the novel to accept money from a woman who is not his wife; he does not acquire wealth through marriage, but through a business transaction in which she is an equal partner. By giving George money before marrying him, Alice advertises that the money is hers to give, not his for the taking.

For George's economy of contractual exchange, John substitutes gift and sacrifice, generously asserting his superior wealth and power by spending his own money, so that Alice can keep hers and be indebted to him. Ultimately, however, the political economy of marriage cancels any gift or debt between husband and wife. John promises Alice's father that he will allow himself to be repaid if he and Alice do not ultimately marry (642), but since he does marry Alice, he finally owns the wealth he had protected. Despite his best intentions, his gift returns to him in a circuit that fulfills the novel's deeper intention: to guarantee that Alice does not contract to give away money of her own free will but instead loses it through subjection to the law. When Alice learns of John's secret plot to pay the notes she had signed, she insists that he "must be paid," but her father reminds her that marriage will automatically cancel her debt in a statement that syntactically effaces any trace of Alice's financial agency: "Paid! . . . he can pay himself now" (798).

The coverture and coercion that feminist contemporaries labeled relics of primitive marriage become necessary elements in *Can You Forgive Her?*, which almost revels in the fact that its heroine must be forced to marry. To make compulsion palatable as such, the narrator represents it as figurative, ethically justified violence, and represents aspects of marriage that Victorian feminists labeled primitive relics as necessary preludes to the modern marriages that conclude the novel. The Pallisers, for example, recapitulate John McLennan's vision in *Primitive Marriage* of marriage by capture leading to patrilineal monogamy and modern civilization. Glencora is initially a polyandrous heroine who oscillates between two men; even after she marries Palliser, she is still "a wife who loved another man better than she loved him" (271). Her match with Palliser is a marriage by purchase, a "matter of sagacious bargaining," as he calls it in the final book of the Palliser series, *The Duke's Children*.[42] It is also a marriage by capture, in which Glencora is subject to family pressure so intense that she and the narrator describe her as married against her will, "sacrificed" (608), "tortured" (701), "forced" (701), "jumped on" (252), "like a beast that is driven as its owner chooses" (288). Although Glencora's marriage fulfills neither of modern marriage's prerequisites (true love and free consent), the narrator glorifies Plantagenet Palliser as the acme of Britain's superior blend of tradition and progress. Palliser is closely associated with the eminently rational dream of converting English currency to a decimal system, and with Parliament, from which the narrator gushes, "flow the waters of the world's progress,—the fullest fountain of advancing civilization" (480). But his political influence depends on lineage and reveals that the state depends on status even when it rewards merit. In contrast to Maine, who argued that blood, status, custom, and patriarchal power were antithetical to modernity, Trollope uses Palliser to argue that status and patriarchal power are the best means of successfully instituting it.

The justness of traditional political privileges extends to those of husbands. Just as the novel deems Palliser's class is "right" to "have kept in their hands, as rewards for their own services to the country, no more than the country is manifestly willing to give them" (721), it supports a husband's right to assert the power his wife gives him when she consents to marriage. The problems that plague the Palliser marriage may stem from its origins in primitive coercion, but the novel does not resolve them by making their marriage more egalitarian. Plantagenet demonstrates his love for his wife when he foregoes a cabinet position to travel with her, but his sacrifice establishes harmony by instituting his superiority more firmly. In giving up his political ambitions, he has "conquered" Glencora (618); in organizing their trip, he has "arranged his plans with his wife . . . or, I should more correctly say . . . given her his orders" (643); and while traveling, "he had his own way in everything. Lady Glencora . . . had her own way in nothing" (707–8). Once Glencora is pregnant, Palliser issues "violent edict[s]" (755) that control her movements so extremely that Glencora jokingly declares they "will kill" her (761).[43] Bigamy, uncertain paternity, and the "idolatry" of baby worship all become tolerable if they promote an untroubled patriarchal inheritance (828). When Glencora gives birth to a boy, "[o]ne might have supposed that it was the Duke's baby, and not the baby of Lady Glencora and Mr. Palliser" (826), but since she has produced the lineage's longed-for male heir, it is acceptable for Glencora to have "two . . . lords and masters" (827–28). Just as status and hierarchy protect civilization from corrosion by contract, marriage by capture and inequality between men and women secure the bloodline and become compatible with marital love.

Alice's acceptance of hierarchical marriage similarly depends on the consolidation of transgenerational patriarchal bonds. Her story begins under the sign of paternal deficiency when the narrator introduces her father, John Vavasor, as a younger son who has repeatedly "failed" and "done nothing to raise the family name to eminence" (39). Mr. Vavasor's dispossession from authority is so complete that his job, one of the novel's several emblems of contract as evacuated agency, consists of "signing his name to accounts which he never read, and at which he was never supposed even to look" (39, 41). Unlike the feckless but endearing fathers who populate Dickens's novels, John Vavasor is charmless, cold, and absent, and though he and Alice live together, they live "apart—quite apart" (44). Alice believes that her father's negligence licenses her own autonomy: she possesses a "firm resolve that her father should not guide her in her path through life" (367) because he "had for many years relieved himself from the burden of a father's care, and now had hardly the right to claim a father's privileges" (354). John Vavasor does not contest her independence, saying to John Grey of her engagement to George, "She's as much her own master as you are yours" (392).

Can You Forgive Her? dramatizes the disaster that results when a woman lacks a father authoritative enough to guide his daughter's choice of lord and master, then presents John Grey as both the husband Alice needs and the father she lacks. The two Johns are doubles in more than name: both are described as handsome, and John Vavasor is introduced as a partial John Grey, with hair beginning to turn "grey" and "eyes . . . bright and grey" (42). John Grey makes John Vavasor whole when they collude to pay George the money Alice has promised him and develop a bond that helps John Vavasor finally approximate paternal authority. With Grey's help, Alice's father finally begins to know more than his daughter and thus know better, and this allows him to comment on her behavior more cuttingly. He has little effect on her when she first breaks with John, but when she later ends her engagement to George and her father says "things of that sort are so often over with you," she experiences his reproach deeply: "The blow struck her with such a force that she staggered under it" (635).

Alice's violent experience of her father's words prepares her for the shift from contract to coverture that takes place when she finally accepts John Grey as a husband. When Alice rejects her father's authority, she "resolved . . . that in this matter she owed her father no obedience. 'There cannot be obedience on one side,' she said to herself, 'without protection and support on the other?'" (366). In echoing the Napoleonic interpretation of coverture, Alice hints at a belief that adequate protection might yield obedience, though by posing that premise as a question she expresses ambivalence about relinquishing contract's equal reciprocities for coverture's asymmetrical exchanges. John Grey has no such ambivalence; he is willing and eager to provide protection and support even if he must resort to violence to do so. Though used to "words" being "sufficient," John throws George down the stairs when, late in the novel, his rival threatens him with a pistol (556). The novel then moves back in time in order to place the account of their battle immediately before the chapter in which John joins Alice at Lucerne. That temporal shuffling underscores that John arrives primed to use any means necessary to compel Alice to accept him.

In Trollope's novel, the space in which one coerces oneself is the space of both contract and guilt, and because Trollope understands that space as sustaining the heroine's will, he insists that she abandon self-laceration for submission to John's forgiveness.[44] Immediately before John's final proposal, the narrator explains that Alice feels too guilty over having previously jilted John to allow herself to take him back: "[A]s far as she could decide at all, she decided against her lover. She had no right of her own to be taken back after the evil she had done, and she did not choose to be taken back as an object of pity and forgiveness" (766). Alice associates her decision not to marry John with her autonomy: she has "no right of *her own*" to marry him and does not "*choose*" to be forgiven by him. John must overcome that autonomy, and he approaches Lucerne "confident that he would, at last, carry his mistress off with him to Nethercoats" (637), an allusion to primitive marriage by capture that adumbrates the violence of his actual proposal. John responds to Alice's belief that her guilt prevents her from marrying him by insisting that his conscience replace hers. His proposal does not ask for her consent but requires it: "And am I to be punished, then, because of your fault? . . . If you love me . . . I have a right to demand your hand. My happiness requires it, and I have a right to expect your compliance. I do demand it. If you love me, Alice, I tell you that you dare not refuse me" (771). By citing love as the premise of his intimidating demand for compliance, John melds compulsion and romance, primitive and companionate marriage. His figures of speech emphasize Alice's physical surrender rather than her verbal assent ("I have a right to *demand* your *hand*"), and his appropriation of her body subsumes the words of the marriage ceremony within his own assertions; John's "I do demand it" contains, anticipates, replaces, and erases Alice's "I do."

Significantly, Alice never does say to John that she will be his wife. Her initial response is wordlessness: "Alice sat silent beneath his gaze, with her eyes turned upon the tombstones beneath her feet" (771). The equivalence between Alice beneath John's gaze and the tombstones beneath her feet underscores that the marriage he proposes is the death of her will. A sentence immediately follows—"Of course she had no choice but to yield"—whose meaning is initially ambiguous because it has two possible sources (771). As an announcement of the narrator's views, it hovers between statement and command; as a report of Alice's thoughts, it is a resigned observation. The ambiguity is resolved when the narrator conveys, several sentences later, Alice's internal acquiescence to John's superiority: "She knew now that she must yield to him,—that his power over her was omnipotent. She was pressed by him as in some countries the prisoner is pressed by the judge" (772). The physicality of the narrator's military and juridical metaphors—"yield," "pressed"—underscores that John's speech has the force of violence and represents Alice's mental discovery ("she now knew") as nothing but an acknowledgment of and submission to her suitor's irresistible force. The marriage that promises to liberate Alice from the circular indecision in which she has trapped herself encloses her even more thoroughly in John's power. Like a prisoner, Alice remains silent: "[T]he word which she had to speak still remained unspoken" (772). John provides the only gesture that signifies agreement to his proposal: "[G]radually he put his arm round her waist. She shrank from him . . . but she could not shrink away from his grasp. She put up her hand to impede his, but his hand, like his character and his words, was full of power. It would not be impeded" (772). Alice's only assent to John's proposal is nothing more than a recognition of his superior strength, which she acknowledges even as she attempts to escape its grip: "'You win everything,—always,' she said, whispering to him, as she still shrank from his embrace" (772).

In order to justify marriage by capture, *Can You Forgive Her?* grafts violence onto an ethics of guilt and forgiveness. Compulsory marriage becomes a matter of conscience—which is not to say that Alice simply marries out of guilt. Rather, the novel requires her to *relinquish* her guilt so that she can marry: John's forgiveness does not establish Alice's guilt but deprives her of it. The novel recasts the marriage plot in terms of injury and forgiveness: first a woman injures a man by breaking her promise to marry him, then she feels guilt, and finally her guilt dissolves when she receives her future husband's forgiveness. To accept forgiveness in the form of the husband who grants it is also to accept the superiority of the one who forgives, since forgiveness is a prerogative of the strong. When Plantagenet Palliser forgives Glencora, the narrator remarks, "He was killing her by his goodness" (616); after subjecting her prospective husband Captain Bellfield to a "cross-examination" in which he confesses all his faults, the formidable Mrs. Greenow "forg[i]ve[s] him all his offences" (674).

Trollope's reduction of contract to violence is surprisingly Nietzschean. We now associate Friedrich Nietzsche with a philosophical conversation in which Victorian novelists had little to say, but *On the Genealogy of Morals* (1887) begins as an attack on "English psychologists," whose anthropological histories of morality equated civilization with contracts that outlawed violent penalties and created equality between the weak and the strong.[45] Nietzsche argues instead that contract merely replaces punishment with promises and trades primitive sacrifice for the bad conscience of guilt. Retaliation for injury becomes the contract between debtor and debtee; just as the primitive culprit's bodily pain repays the injury she has done, the modern wrongdoer honors a contract stipulating that she repair her wrongdoing by suffering from a bad conscience. Guilt becomes a sign of debt and contract because it signifies the painful consequences of not honoring one's promises (65). Nietzsche describes the modern pain of conscience as "imaginative and psychical" (68), a private pain witnessed only by the self observing itself (69), "a madness of the will" in which one punishes oneself "without any possibility of the punishment becoming equal to the guilt" (93).

Nietzsche's account of guilt as an *"instinct for freedom* forcibly made latent" (87) so aptly describes Trollope's self-accusing heroine because both men sought to overturn the received idea that modernity is superior to the past it replaces, although each pursued his critique of modernity along very different lines. Nietzsche's glorification of body over soul and force over weakness attacked the premises of Christianity, while Trollope aimed to integrate force and hierarchy into a Christian framework of conscience, forgiveness, and expiation. *Can You Forgive Her?* effects that integration by condemning the overt violence the narrative associates with George and contract, while at the same time sanctioning the use of force to compel Alice to accept John's right to forgive or punish her. Forgiveness annuls contract's egalitarian possibilities and formalizes the coercion embedded in hierarchical marriage. By compelling Alice to "obey him in that one point, as to which he now required obedience" and accept his forgiveness as authoritative, John forces her to give up her contract with herself to remember the injury she had inflicted on him, a contract that also memorialized her will to power (755). Forgiveness does not end punishment; it simply transfers the punishing agency from the self to others. As Alice wryly notes, "There is a forgiveness which is rather hard to get" (799). The narrator underscores that hardship with lurid figures of violence that describe how Alice must accept the "punishment . . . inflicted on her" and "acknowledge . . . to herself . . . that she deserved all the lashes she received" (822). For Alice to accept forgiveness is to accept that "there was nothing left for her but to do as others wished" (815). The title's invitation to the reader to forgive Alice thus becomes an invitation to participate in her chastisement.

Trollope's novel eliminates its heroine's freedom of contract by replacing it with the violent forgiveness of marriage. Effective as that substitution may be in eliminating contract, it makes for a singularly gloomy marital ending. Few readers could be expected to celebrate Alice's mute acceptance of John in a graveyard, and *Can You Forgive Her?* further suggests that the desire for a marital conclusion does not go without saying by using unusually strained narrative techniques to get there. Well before Alice can acquiesce to John's demand that he forgive her, the reader must submit to a similar order, issued by the narrator: Alice "knew that she could not forgive herself. But can you forgive her, delicate reader? . . . For myself, I have forgiven her. . . . And you also must forgive her before we close the book, or else my story will have been told amiss" (398). Alice's refusal of hierarchical marriage mirrors the "delicate" female reader's resistance to the narrator, and the marriage plot can achieve closure only when all resistance ceases and characters, reader, and narrator agree to absolve Alice. The shift within the narrator's direct address from a question ("can you forgive her?") to an order ("you must forgive her") reproduces at the level of metanarrative the plot of contract giving way to force, autonomous individuals coalescing into one person. For much of the novel, the narrator accompanies his detailed accounts of Alice's thoughts with claims that he does not fully know or understand her. As the plot moves closer to concluding its hierarchical marriage, however, the narrator makes greater use of classic, free-indirect discourse, in which his voice seamlessly incorporates Alice's in order to report her thoughts: "She had left John Grey. . . . Of course she had been wrong. She had been very wrong. . . . She knew that she had been wrong in both, and was undergoing repentance with very bitter inward sackcloth" (718). Once Alice comes to see her situation as the narrator does, his commentary is no longer necessary; her voice can merge perfectly with the narrator's once her conscience is no longer her own but his.

The heroine's submission to the narrator's dictates and her corresponding absorption into his voice poses a problem, however, for the goal the plot seeks to achieve—Alice's complete acceptance of John as her sole guide. The narrator thus makes a startling appearance in the churchyard proposal scene in order to cede Alice to her betrothed. Throughout the novel, the narrator often speaks in the first person but rarely situates himself in the characters' space and time or claims their ontological qualities. The narrator displays his psyche through the medium of his characters; we know him through his descriptions of them, not of himself. Yet just before John demands Alice's hand, the narrator uncharacteristically speaks in the present tense and places himself in the churchyard, which he describes as "one of the prettiest spots in that land of beauty; and its charm is to my feeling enhanced by the sepulchral monuments over which I walk, and by which I am surrounded, as I stand there. Up here, in to these cloisters, Alice and John Grey went together" (767). After compelling Alice to replace her judgments with his own, the narrator leaves her to John's direction and guidance by momentarily becoming a character. Using the more immediate "these" instead of "those," gratuitously repeating "I" three times, and introducing a startling use of the present tense, the narrator claims to occupy the same place as his characters, but not at the same time. That auto-personification disrupts the convention of a disembodied narrator in order, paradoxically, to suggest his separateness from them. The narrator stands apart as a separate presence in the scene by claiming to occupy it in the present ("over which I walk . . . by which I am surrounded"), uncannily close to, yet distinct from, "Alice and John Grey," now designated as a marital unit who exist in the novel's customary past tense ("went together"). Once safely under John's direction, Alice can recede from the narrator's supervision as narratorial coverture makes way for marital coverture. Precisely because *Can You Forgive Her?* exposes the arduous work required to make Alice's wishes coincide with John's and with the narrator's, it does not fully naturalize hierarchical marriage. Narrative technique can veil the paradox of a hierarchical marriage that demands consent, but it cannot dissolve it.

THE PERSISTENCE OF FEMALE RELATIONS

The scene in the graveyard, however, is not the novel's final pronouncement on marriage. Not only does the novel conclude with John fulfilling Alice's fantasy of marrying a man who pursues a career in politics, it also brings the representative of female marriage, Kate Vavasor, back on the scene. *Can You Forgive Her?* elevates the intimacy between erstwhile female suitors above the contractual marriage of man and woman, for the removal of George, who had ostensibly united Kate and Alice, only reaffirms their solidarity. The bond between Kate and Alice becomes even stronger after George's hold on the text frays and he absconds to the United States under a false name. Just as the reader knows of George's proposal only because Alice reads his letter aloud to Kate, the reader knows of the dissolution of their engagement only because Alice confides it to Kate in a letter reproduced in full: "I must tell it to you, but I shall never repeat the story to any one else" (569). Just as Alice asked Kate to make her engagement with George, she asks her to break it: "I do not know whether he understands that everything must be over between us, but, if not, I must ask you to tell him so" (571). The pride of place Alice assigns to Kate in ending the engagement to George preserves the importance Kate acquired in initiating it. Kate's role as Alice's sole addressee underscores that the reader's knowledge of what happens in the heterosexual marriage plot depends on the ongoing communication between two women, and that their communication is not wholly dependent on the man who had been their joint interest.

Can You Forgive Her? allows relationships between men and women to take only one form, hierarchical marriage, but represents women as having multiple forms of relationship at their disposal. When female marriage based on triangulation with a male suitor breaks down, Kate and Alice can reconstruct their solidarity on the basis of their shared rejection of George. They replace their reciprocal adoration of him with an equally mutual revulsion from his violence. After reading Alice's letter, Kate feels "repugnance" toward her brother (591) and wonders if, like Alice, she will need to "abandon him altogether [and] divide herself from him" (600). Even when both women sever their links to George, he continues to strengthen a union now based on shared pain. As Kate tells Alice, "We have both suffered for him; you more than I, perhaps; but I, too, have given up everything for him" (666). Shame isolates, but because Alice and Kate share their humiliating disillusionment in George with each other, even their shame unites rather than separates them. Alice writes Kate that she fears her break with George will cause "a division between us" (571), but Kate responds that even in George's absence, their relationship will retain the sororal, superlative status Kate claimed when Alice first accepted her proposal: "My own Alice—If you will let me, you shall be my sister, and be the nearest to me and the dearest" (574).

As *Can You Forgive Her?* draws to a close, contractual marriage between a man and woman disappears, but the narrative preserves the conjugal connotations of the relationship between Kate and her "nearest . . . and . . . dearest." Kate once again mirrors the actions of a male suitor, this time those of John Grey, when she repays Alice the money George had borrowed. After breaking with George and before embarking on a European trip, Alice visits Kate at Vavasor Hall in a gesture that represents their ongoing pledge to each other. Although Alice's chief characteristic is her difficulty in keeping her word, she assents to "Kate's desire" that she visit her (602) because she is "resolved that she would keep her promise to Kate" (653). In contrast to her engagements to John and George, which she strives to confine to print, Alice seeks direct contact with Kate: "After all that had passed she felt that she owed Kate some sympathy. . . . [T]here are things which can be spoken, but which cannot be written" (653).

The narrator commends the women's loyalty by nominally describing them as a married couple as he wraps up one plot and transitions to another: "Reader, let us wish a happy married life to Captain and Mrs Bellfield! [paragraph break] The day after the ceremony Alice Vavasor and Kate Vavasor started for Matching Priory" (814). The women's destination is the estate where Alice will marry John Grey, but far from implying that marriage requires Alice to relinquish her bond with Kate, the text suggests that they remain wedded to each other. The place-name Matching Priory reinforces the precedence of matches between husbands and wives, but Kate's presence there at Alice's side also underscores the survival of the prior match between two women. The phrase "Alice Vavasor and Kate Vavasor," a reminder of the characters' shared surname that is gratuitous this late in the novel, creates a parallelism that aligns them with the newly minted married couple, "Captain and Mrs. Bellfield," even as Trollope's exact wording subtly distinguishes the female couple from the legally married one. "Captain and Mrs. Bellfield" have only one surname between them, while "Alice Vavasor and Kate Vavasor" have two surnames in common. The first phrase reminds us that legal marriage subsumes even the most powerful woman into her husband, while the second highlights that the female couple consists of linked, equal, self-contained individuals. By the end of the novel, the narrator is referring to "Mr. and Mrs. Grey" (827), but Alice refuses to journey to the site of her wedding without Kate by her side.

Why does the novel eliminate its egalitarian male suitor, but not the woman who proposed for him? One possible answer is that the female suitor has already suffered enough, and indeed one might argue that Kate remains in the text only so we can see her pay for her sins when she breaks her arm in chapter 56, whose title, "Another walk on the Fells," echoes and replaces "Among the Fells." As Kate Flint has shown, one can read Kate as a gender outlaw punished for deviant desires: twice a bridesmaid but never a bride, she has no wish to marry a man (108, 173, 234), is indifferent to masculine beauty (66), and appreciates women's attractions (106). But the novel is not single-minded in the narrative reprisal it inflicts on Kate as an odd woman who rejects marriage and desires women. Kate survives her fall in both physical and narrative terms: as we have seen, the reader sees Alice and Kate together well after Kate's arm has healed, and Kate receives the Victorian novel's ultimate reward, a small independent fortune that enables her to avoid marriage permanently and in comfort.

The novel cannot afford to eliminate the female suitor entirely from its narrative precincts because the intimacy of female marriage so closely resembles the female friendship on which hierarchical marriage itself depends. The role that female amity plays in securing the novel's most valued conjugal form emerges most clearly in Alice's dealings with another cousin, Glencora Palliser. Miming marriage to Alice provides the crucial assistance Glencora needs to resist the temptation offered by a former lover, and thus to stay faithful to Plantagenet Palliser, the imperious husband whom relatives coerced her into marrying. On her first visit to Glencora at Matching Priory, Alice temporarily becomes the loving husband Plantagenet is not: "Lady Glencora was now in the habit of having Alice in what she called the dressing-room every evening, and then they would sit till the small hours came upon them" (286). Alice offers Glencora the complicit looks, whispers, and declarations of love that Plantagenet does not (285, 307, 758). "I love you with all my heart," Alice tells Glencora, who replies, "Some one's love I must have found,—or I could not have remained here" (288). Even after Glencora and Plantagenet strive to become closer, both still require Alice's presence to seal their bond. Plantagenet defers to Glencora by asking her to invite Alice to join them on a trip abroad, and Glencora begs Alice for her company: "Alice, I want you more than I ever wanted you before" (715). The Pallisers's relationship stabilizes after Glencora becomes pregnant and gives birth to a boy, but even in the novel's last pages and final illustration, we see the Palliser heir not with his mother and father, but with the two women (827–28).

Eroticized friendship between women is a necessary lubricant for facilitating marriage between a woman and a man, and the novel finds room for Kate Vavasor because female intimacy is the friend of conjugal happiness, not its foe. Insofar as realism strives to represent the world as it is, Trollope could not ignore the female marriages that he knew existed as recognized social facts. And insofar as realism seeks to represent the world in the image of its values, Trollope can only applaud the loyalty and affection that subtend Kate's proposal to Alice—while at the same time condemning the contractual, egalitarian marriage that Kate promotes between George and Alice. There is even a suggestion that Trollope understands Kate's character as central to the workings of novelistic narrative itself, for in addition to representing female marriage, egalitarian marriage by proxy, and female friendship and kinship, Kate also stands for writing and storytelling throughout the novel. She shares the narrator's ability to tell stories and describe people, and her skillful letters sometimes constitute entire chapters that replace the narrator's voice altogether; indeed, her account of her aunt's two suitors in chapter 14 is almost indistinguishable from the narrator's in other chapters. Like a novelist, Kate receives and transmits information from a privileged point of view and has the power to set characters in motion. When Kate reads in a letter from Alice that marriage to George "cannot follow," she protests: "'But the other thing shall follow,' Kate had said, as she read the words for the second time, and then put the paper into her desk. 'It shall follow'" (165–66). Kate pronounces on the future like an author, reading and arranging papers at a desk, and she ensures her prediction will come to pass by writing letters persuading George and Alice to follow her advice. Throughout the novel, writing is also the form taken by egalitarian marriage, and when George's attack leaves Kate's right arm "powerless" (594) and makes "writing to Alice . . . now out of the question" (600), the reader discerns that Kate suffers for having helped to give marriage a written form. Her punishment at George's hands shows that her sin is his—the crime of contract, executed in writing—and warns readers that those who try to inscribe marriage as contract will either be undone by their own tools or rendered incapable of using them.

Trollope's novel registers the Victorian awareness that marriage as contract, a free agreement between equals, might undo differences between men and women and transform marriage into a union between any two or even any three people. His hectoring title, which challenges readers to rise to the occasion and forgive all the women interpellated by its feminine pronoun, encapsulates the novel's recoding of force as ethics, commands as questions: not "you must forgive her," but "can you forgive her?" Critics have always assumed that insofar as the title refers to Alice, it asks the reader to forgive her for rejecting the right man for the wrong one. But the reader of "Among the Fells" knows that the book also asks us to forgive Alice for assenting to a marriage proposal from Kate, and Kate for proposing to Alice. By construing the reader who cannot forgive as hard-hearted, churlish, even unchristian, Trollope makes it difficult to answer "no" to his title question; but by posing his title as a question, he creates the possibility of a negative response that would leave the women unconstrained by the forgiveness that elsewhere the novel reveals to be violently coercive. Although John does not take no for an answer when he proposes marriage to Alice, Trollope can image a dissenting reply to the question his title poses. To refuse to forgive Alice and Kate for the marriage they willingly contemplate is also to refuse to forget them, to refuse to treat their desire for female marriage as an anomaly, object of pity, or punishable offense. Far from being a disruption of narrative and social forms, the female marriage that contracts to a memory at the novel's end attests to the plasticity of norms perpetually under construction and always subject to reform. Alice can marry only one man, but she ends the novel flanked by two women, Kate and Glencora, in a female figure of three that stands as an emblem of the centrality of female relations in Victorian fiction and fact.

Woolf, Wilde, and Girl Dates

IN MAPPING THE FEMALE WORLD of Victorian England, I have argued that areas that have been conceptualized as utterly distinct, even enemy territories, were in fact intersecting, overlapping, and allied. Conversely, I have shown that regions once thought to constitute a single unit were in fact not one and the same. The female friend turns out to have been the matrix of marriage; the woman's world of fashion and dolls shared with pornography a fascination with looking and display, punishment and humiliation, dominance and submission; and women in female marriages contributed to the legal reform of civil unions between men and women. At the same time, there were important distinctions to be made among female relations: friendship was not identical to family ties, and differed significantly from unrequited love between women and from the reciprocal interdependence of female marriage.

The received wisdom has been that all bonds between women are structured by the opposition between women and men, and therefore that women must either be rivals for men or comrades in the fight against patriarchy. In the latter view, friendship, erotic desire, and sexual relationships between women are interchangeable, since all three are considered subversions of a heterosexual order that requires women to subordinate their bonds with one another to the demands of men. This book has not contested the reach of a heterosexual order, although like much feminist work of the last decades it has suggested that not all husbands were tyrants nor all wives slaves. Rather, each chapter has asked what becomes thinkable if we suspend the assumption that the heterosexual order opposed bonds between women, and then shown that if we dissolve that premise, the differences between various kinds of alliances between women become more significant than their similarities.

The use of lesbian sexuality as the master term for understanding all other bonds between women was one of the defining gestures of twentieth-century feminism, and one that often had the ironic effect of muting explicit discussions of lesbianism. It was a gesture performed in the first half of the century by Virginia Woolf in *A Room of One's Own* (1929). On the verge of quoting a sentence about friendship between women from a recent novel, Woolf's fictional speaker pauses and asks her audience to promise "that behind that red curtain over there the figure of Sir Chartres Biron is not concealed." Only after that dramatic interruption does she read the startling sentence aloud: "Chloe liked Olivia." The phrase "Sir Chartres Biron," which most of us can no longer pronounce, let alone identify, now seems the more enigmatic one, yet Woolf constructs "Chloe liked Olivia" as the scandalous mystery to be discussed only among women. "Do not start. Do not blush," she coyly admonishes her audience. "Let us admit in the privacy of our own society that these things sometimes happen. Sometimes women do like women." To represent such liking in fiction, however, is an "immense . . . change" to a tradition that for centuries depicted women only "in their relation to men."[1]

Great phrases have a life of their own, and Woolf's is no exception. Although Woolf praises Chloe and Olivia for being coworkers, for a friendship "more varied and lasting because . . . less personal" (88), "Chloe liked Olivia" became shorthand for that most personal relationship between women, sexual love. Lillian Faderman justified titling an anthology of lesbian literature *Chloe Plus Olivia* (1994) by explaining that Woolf "surely . . . meant to indicate an emotion far more intense than mere 'liking'. . . . Woolf was predicting what must have seemed all but impossible in her day: a non-medical literature that would unmask the subject of love between women."[2] Faderman's rhetorical insistence on what Woolf "surely" meant only accentuates how her use of the phrase is not licensed by Woolf's text, which states that "Chloe liked Olivia" can only be written by someone who does *not* see a woman as "a lover would see her" (86). Faderman's interpretation is not, however, completely unfounded. If we track down the reference to Sir Chartres Biron with which Woolf nervously prefaced the phrase "Chloe liked Olivia," we see that *A Room of One's Own* is indeed ambiguous about whether "Chloe liked Olivia" refers to impersonal friendship or sexual sentiment, for Sir Chartres Biron was the judge then presiding over the obscenity trial of Radclyffe Hall's lesbian novel, *The Well of Loneliness* (1928). Woolf publicly defended Hall against censorship and was willing to testify on her behalf, but she presents "Chloe liked Olivia" in a deliberately ambiguous way, praising the sentence for its coolness but also associating it with a topic too hot to handle, the lesbian love Woolf will not name directly.[3]

Rather than resolve the true meaning of Woolf's sentence, I offer it as a symptom of exactly the problem she hoped it would correct: our lack of knowledge about women's relationships. That the same sentence can refer to friendship as the antithesis of romance and to romance as the hidden truth of friendship suggests that whether they are lovers, friends, or coworkers, Chloe and Olivia are overworked, and we need more than two proper names and a verb to do justice to the variety and complexity of women's social alliances. Approximately fifty years later, Carroll Smith-Rosenberg contested Woolf's historical account by demonstrating that before the twentieth-century advent of a stigmatized lesbian identity—

epitomized by the negative response to Hall's novel—the fact that women adored women gave rise to a cherished female world. But her influential theory only intensified the belief that Victorians never differentiated among types of relationship between women but assimilated them all to a single model of pastoral romance. Correctives to that theory showed that lesbian deviance could be traced back to the nineteenth century, but a focus on criminal trials and medical discourses of pathology suggested that the history of lesbian sexuality had only a negative relation to the history of women—that lesbians were those who refused or threatened to undo their era's definition of womanhood.

As we have seen, there were many kinds of relationships between women in Victorian England, and the ones examined here were not only tolerated but promoted as necessary elements of middle-class femininity. In 1929, Woolf described female friendship as a relationship that only feminism could bring into being, but in the 1840s, domestic ideologue Sarah Ellis celebrated friendship between women as making the same contribution to society as wifehood or motherhood. Family life incorporated friendship between women; consumer culture was saturated with female homoeroticism; and multiple social networks included women in marital relationships with other women. These forms of conjugality, intimacy, eroticism, and sociability were not policed, forbidden, or stigmatized, but instead were the very stuff of national, imperial, and religious mores. The fact of shared tolerance does not, however, point to any deeper similarity that would make all relationships between women ultimately the same. Indeed, though I have referred throughout to relationships between women, what it meant to be a woman as a friend was quite different from what it meant to be a woman as a spectator of fashion plates, as an agent of maternal discipline, or as another woman's spouse. Each case has also demonstrated that the asexual Victorian woman able only to respond to male advances is a myth—not a Victorian myth, but our own. Victorian novels, children's books, lifewriting, anthropological narratives, and fashion iconography all conceived of women and girls as far more complicated and aggressive agents of desire than they appeared to be in the medical textbooks, household management manuals, or isolated essays that have been mainstays for historians of gender and sexuality.

This book has raised several questions it has left unanswered because only in-depth additional research could address them. One of the most fundamental questions posed here is how to conceptualize those aspects of social relationships that cannot be explained in terms of power differences. What remains to the social when relations of domination, oppression, status, discipline, and governmentality are set aside? One way to answer that question is to explore what theory of the social can be derived from relationships like those between women of the same class and nation—never free from power differentials, but never exhaustively defined by them. A book focused on one country in one century also begs the question of how specific its claims are; to answer that would require a comparative synthesis of existing work and fresh research, since so much of the extant scholarship on sexuality and gender uses assumptions about women's relationships debunked here. There are many more relationships between women to identify and analyze beyond those discussed in this book, and also between women and men. The assumption of female powerlessness has meant that even family history pays very little attention, for example, to relationships between Victorian mothers and sons, and the belief that Victorian men and women who were not kin could only be linked by sex has meant that almost no research has been done on male-female friendship.

Perhaps the most compelling question this book has not had room to answer is whether the variety of relationships nineteenth-century women could have with one another also extended to men. The problem of how to think about friends in relation to same-sex lovers is not unique to women: there is a vast literature on sexual relationships between men in the nineteenth century, and much of it addresses their complex links to male friendship. If Eve Kosofsky Sedgwick helped to inaugurate queer studies by arguing in *Between Men* that the nineteenth century instated a mortal antagonism between men's homosocial bonds and homoerotic desires, more recent work has shown that male friendships could be as directly ardent as those between women, and their love affairs with each other as conjugal. We may be tempted to assume that the latitude permitted to female friends was forbidden to male ones, but the intense romances men had with each other belies that preconception. Byron compared the love he felt for a Cambridge choirboy to that of two famous female spouses, the Ladies of Llangollen.[4] In 1859 the seventeen-year-old John Russell (father of Bertrand Russell) wrote mournfully in his diary of his schoolmate Alexander: "[O]ne thing I have not; & that is the love of him whom I love so very deeply . . . who is ever present in my thoughts. . . . I cannot help still clinging to him with some faint hope of his coming back to me yet; & it is this which fills me with feelings of jealousy which I never, never ought to indulge." Russell did not see his love as impure, but rather condemned himself for the "selfishness" implicit in jealousy. Like many of the religious women whose diaries we explored in chapter 1, he felt a strong need to reconcile his sentimental passion for his friend with his love of God—"may he give me grace to overcome all that is jealous or selfish."[5]

The varied ways that women could incorporate female relationships into married life were also available to men. In France, the marquis Astolphe de Custine and his lover Edward Saint-Barbe lived together as married; like many of the women discussed here, de Custine willed his property to Saint-Barbe.[6] Just as Minnie Benson lived with her husband and her female lover while raising children, men like John Symonds, Oscar Wilde, and Viscount Esher married women, had children with them, and pursued sexual relationships and erotic infatuations with men, sometimes with their wives' knowledge. Oscar Wilde is a particularly telling example of how contemporary scholarship has imposed on the past a strict division between sexual orientations that did not exist, even for the man whom historians now consider the catalyst of modern gay identity. Historians of sexuality have used Oscar Wilde's writings and his trials to show how late in the nineteenth century, an opposition crystallized between normative sexuality (represented by marriage, the family, and men's desire for women) and deviant sexuality (typified by a sexual subculture based on men's desire for men). In the process, they have ignored his important bonds with women, his personal and aesthetic investments in marriage and parenthood, and his preoccupation with relationships between women. As I hope to show in future work, Wilde's role as editor of *Woman's World*, his own social relations, and his plays all evince his interest in female fantasy, the plot of female amity, and erotic desire between women. Far from being the absence that historians of the gay Wilde have made it out to be, the social force of female bonds and their relation to male ones were questions he returned to repeatedly, and are thus at the center of the epochal changes in the history of sexuality that he represents.

The final question this book raises is what, if anything, it can tell us about the present. What was specific to the Victorians, and what has changed since? Does a fresh look at the past affect how we conceptualize the present? The most salient discontinuity is the invention of distinct lesbian identities around 1880, which took firm hold in England by the 1930s. Important as that development has been, its significance should not be overstated, not least because the popularization of lesbian subcultures and stereotypes never expunged earlier ideas. I have shown how anachronistic it is to assume that lesbian marriage was, until quite recently, an oxymoron, and there is evidence that the notion of female marriage survived throughout the twentieth century. A 1913 letter hidden in a picture frame and found decades later attests to the longevity of marital language between women; its author, Margaret, addressed her correspondent, Louise, as "my perfect bride—my pure bride . . . I hold you close—I kiss your breath away—I take you—soon. Your lover, Margaret."[7] In the twentieth century, the commitment to pagan free love among lesbian modernists like Natalie Barney and the socialist-feminist critique of monogamous marriage intensified the cognitive gap between lesbianism and marriage. But if one thinks of Gertrude Stein and Alice B. Toklas as equally important emblems of twentieth-century lesbianism, it is clear that marriage remained a reference point for lesbian couples, and that we need to be aware of not only the sharp break between the Victorians and the moderns but also the continuities between them.

Finally, given how intensely the developed world has monitored the boundaries between homo and hetero in the twentieth century, it is notable how central female relations remain even in societies designed to overwhelm their members with heterosexuality. Sexual relationships between women are, of course, more prominent now than they were in Victorian England, but female friendships have also retained their importance in literature and life. Consumer culture continues to promote multiple permutations of sexual desire, and normative femininity incorporates intimacy between women even as it nervously defends against imputations of lesbianism. Female romance writers explain that they write in order to "make ladies' hearts throb with anticipation," heterosexual romance still requires the assistance of female friendship, and mainstream magazines write about "girl dates" and "girl breakups" that have the thrill of romance "without the complications of sex."[8] At the same time, the vastly more explicit discourse of sex in contemporary media makes it clear that lesbianism and heterosexuality are no longer adequate concepts for describing women's sexual practices and fantasies. A recent survey shows that the number of women who have had at least one sexual experience with another woman and describe themselves as "mostly," rather than "only," attracted to men is on the increase.[9] A female advice columnist for a men's magazine comforts an anxious boyfriend who has found a copy of *Playboy* under his girlfriend's bed by explaining that many straight women are aroused by pornographic images of women.[10]

These are observations too diverse to wrap up in a neat statement about sexuality today, but they bring home what may ultimately be the most surprising commonality this book has found between Victorian society and our own: in the past as in the present, marriage and family, gender and sexuality, are far more intricate, mobile, and malleable than we imagine them to be. We cannot and should not tidy up that complexity, but we can keep developing theories, writing histories, and reading stories that acknowledge its existence.

Notes

INTRODUCTION
The Female Relations of Victorian England

1. Emily Pepys, cited in Harriet Blodgett, *"Capacious Hold-All": An Anthology of Englishwomen's Diary Writings* (Charlottesville: University Press of Virginia, 1991), 79. For a fuller edition of the diary, see Gillian Avery, ed., *The Diary of Emily Pepys* (London: Prospect Books, 1984).

2. The foundational texts are Leonore Davidoff and Catherine Hall, *Family Fortunes: Men and Women of the English Middle Class 1780–1850* (Chicago: University of Chicago Press, 1987); Mary Poovey, *Uneven Developments: The Ideological Work of Gender in Mid-Victorian England* (Chicago: University of Chicago Press, 1988); and Thomas W. Laqueur, *Making Sex: Body and Gender from the Greeks to Freud* (Cambridge, Mass.: Harvard University Press, 1990). For a recent synthetic history that cites these views as standard, see Susan Kingsley Kent, *Gender and Power in Britain, 1640–1990* (London: Routledge, 1999), 179–80.

3. Frances Power Cobbe, *Life of Frances Power Cobbe. By Herself*, vol. 2 (Boston: Houghton, Mifflin, 1894), 361, 645. The letters, which Cobbe wrote in 1865 to Mary Somerville, are cited in Sally Mitchell, *Frances Power Cobbe: Victorian Feminist, Journalist, Reformer* (Charlottesville: University of Virginia Press, 2004), 209, 157, 197.

4. See John Stuart Mill, *Autobiography* (1873; repr., New York: The Liberal Arts Press, 1957), especially the sections in which he discusses his relationship and collaboration with Harriet Taylor, later Harriet Mill, and with his stepdaughter Helen Taylor, 119–23, 154–69.

5. For influential treatments of desire as an antisocial force, see Leo Bersani, *A Future for Astyanax: Character and Desire in Literature* (Boston: Little, Brown, 1976), and Tony Tanner, *Adultery in the Novel: Contract and Transgression* (Baltimore: Johns Hopkins University Press, 1979).

6. Gayle Rubin, "The Traffic in Women: Notes toward a Political Economy of Sex," in *Toward an Anthropology of Women*, ed. Rayna Reiter (New York: Monthly Review Press, 1975), 157–210.

7. For an exception to that rule, see Michael Mason, *The Making of Victorian Sexuality* (Oxford: Oxford University Press, 1994).

8. See Davidoff and Hall, *Family Fortunes*, 155, and the many other works cited in chapter 1. On the increasingly polarized sense of sexual difference in Victorian scientific and medical models, see Laqueur, *Making Sex*. For the class dimensions of the belief in the domestic, self-regulated woman, see Judith Walkowitz, *Prostitution in Victorian Society: Women, Class, and the State* (Cambridge: Cambridge University Press, 1980), and Nancy Armstrong, *Desire and Domestic Fiction: A Political History of the Novel* (New York: Oxford University Press, 1987). Others have shown that beginning in the late eighteenth century, sex itself began to be increasingly defined as penis-centered and procreative. See Rachel P.

Maines, *The Technology of Orgasm: "Hysteria," the Vibrator, and Women's Sexual Satisfaction* (Baltimore: Johns Hopkins University Press, 1999); Henry Abelove's discussion of the history of sexual intercourse in the long eighteenth century, in *Deep Gossip* (Minneapolis: University of Minnesota Press, 2003); and Tim Hitchcock, "Redefining Sex in Eighteenth-Century England," *History Workshop Journal* 41 (1996), 72–90.

9. The most thorough discussion of the Victorian preoccupation with sodomy as a crime is in Harry Cocks, *Nameless Offences: Homosexual Desire in the 19th Century* (I. B. Tauris, 2003).

10. See Randolph Trumbach, "London's Sapphists: From Three Sexes to Four Genders in the Making of Modern Culture," in *Body Guards: The Cultural Politics of Gender Ambiguity*, eds. Julia Epstein and Kristina Straub (New York: Routledge, 1991), 112–41; Elizabeth Wahl, *Invisible Relations: Representations of Female Intimacy in the Age of Enlightenment* (Stanford: Stanford University Press, 1999); and Emma Donoghue, *Passions Between Women: British Lesbian Culture 1688–1801* (New York: HarperCollins, 1993).

11. On the shifts in sexual discourse in the 1880s, see Judith Walkowitz, *City of Dreadful Delight: Narratives of Sexual Danger in Late-Victorian London* (Chicago: University of Chicago Press, 1992), and Elaine Showalter, *Sexual Anarchy: Gender and Culture at the Fin de Siècle* (New York: Viking, 1990). For a vivid illustration of how the increasingly explicit public discourse of sex after the 1880s led to an increasing preoccupation with heterosexuality, see Dora Langlois, *The Child: Its Origin and Development: A Manual Enabling Mothers to Initiate Their Daughters Gradually and Modestly into All the Mysteries of Life* (London: W. Reeves, 1896), a one-shilling pamphlet that reduced sex and marriage to reproduction and therefore to "the union of the sexes," 11.

12. On the late-nineteenth-century invention of heterosexuality as a distinct concept opposed to homosexuality, see Jonathan Ned Katz, *The Invention of Heterosexuality* (New York: Plume, 1995).

13. For women's responses to Carpenter and Ellis, see Liz Stanley, "Romantic Friendship? Some Issues in Researching Lesbian History and Biography," *Women's History Review* 1.2 (1992), 198–209.

14. On Maud Allan, see Judith Walkowitz, "The 'Vision of Salome': Cosmopolitanism and Erotic Dancing in Central London, 1908–1918," in *American Historical Review* 108.2 (April 2003), 337–76. On the Hall trial and its larger context, see Laura Doan, *Fashioning Sapphism: The Origins of a Modern English Lesbian Culture* (New York: Columbia University Press, 2001).

15. On the overtly asexual ideals of women in the 1890s and after, see Susan Pedersen, *Eleanor Rathbone and the Politics of Conscience* (New Haven: Yale University Press, 2004), 151–75, and Sheila Jeffreys, *The Spinster and Her Enemies: Feminism and Sexuality 1880–1930* (London: Pandora Press, 1985). On lesbians and bohemian sexual modernism, see Terry Castle, *The Apparitional Lesbian* (New York: Columbia University Press, 1993); Martha Vicinus, *Intimate Friends: Women Who Loved Women 1778–1928* (Chicago: University of Chicago Press, 2004); Shari Benstock, *Women of the Left Bank: Paris, 1900–1940* (Austin: University of Texas Press, 1986), and Christine Stansell, *American Moderns: Bohemian New York and the Creation of a New Century* (New York: Henry Holt, 2000).

16. [Eliza Lynn Linton], "The Girl of the Period," *Saturday Review* (March 14, 1868), 339–40.

17. Diana Fuss, "Fashion and the Homospectatorial Look," in *On Fashion*, eds. Shari Benstock and Suzanne Ferris (New Brunswick, NJ: Rutgers University Press, 1994), 211–32; Erica Rand, *Barbie's Queer Accessories* (Durham: Duke University Press, 1995). In *Bound to Please: A History of the Victorian Corset* (Oxford: Berg, 2001), Leigh Summers draws on Fuss's work to speculate about whether women derived erotic pleasure from corset advertisements, but she assumes that Victorian women can be divided into "lesbian and heterosexual" ones who would perceive images "quite differently," with the lesbians providing an "oppositional" reading, 185. This view of lesbians as a distinct minority and the only kind of women experiencing erotic desire for women does not hold for the Victorian period, which is defined precisely by the absence of a lesbian minority role and the diffusion of erotic desire for women among all women.

18. On marriage as a social alliance between men that effaced erotic desire between them, see Eve Kosofsky Sedgwick, *Between Men: English Literature and Homosocial Desire* (New York: Columbia University Press, 1985). On marriage as the cancellation of bonds between women, see Castle, *The Apparitional Lesbian*, 73.

19. Davidoff and Hall, *Family Fortunes*, 569, 568, 402.

20. Some of the most sustained work on female friendship has focused on feminist and cross-class alliances between women. See Seth Koven, *Slumming: Sexual and Social Politics in Victorian London* (Princeton: Princeton University Press, 2004), and Philippa Levine, *Feminist Lives in Victorian England: Private Role and Public Commitment* (Oxford: Basil Blackwell, 1990).

21. Carroll Smith-Rosenberg, "The Female World of Love and Ritual," in *Feminism and the Politics of History*, ed. Joan Wallach Scott (Oxford: Oxford University Press, 1996), 367, 385.

22. Adrienne Rich, "Compulsory Heterosexuality and Lesbian Existence," in *The Signs Reader: Women, Gender, and Scholarship*, eds. Elizabeth Abel and Emily K. Abel (Chicago: University of Chicago Press, 1983), 139–68. For an analysis of the political and theoretical contexts in which Rich developed her argument, see Carolyn Dever, *Skeptical Feminism: Activist Theory, Activist Practice* (Minneapolis: University of Minnesota Press, 2004), 141–61.

23. See Lisa Duggan, "The Trials of Alice Mitchell: Sensationalism, Sexology, and the Lesbian Subject in Turn-of-the-Century America," *Signs: Journal of Women in Culture and Society* 18.4 (1993), 791–814; Castle, *The Apparitional Lesbian*; Esther Newton, *Margaret Mead Made Me Gay: Personal Essays, Public Ideas* (Durham, NC: Duke University Press, 2000); and Amber Hollibaugh, *My Dangerous Desires: A Queer Girl Dreaming Her Way Home* (Durham, NC: Duke University Press, 2000). Gayle Rubin, in "Thinking Sex: Notes for a Radical Theory of the Politics of Sexuality," argued that the continuum theory conflates gender and sexuality, in *Pleasure and Danger: Exploring Female Sexuality*, ed. Carole S. Vance (Boston: Routledge & Kegan Paul, 1984), 267–319.

24. See especially Duggan, "The Trials of Alice Mitchell," and Vicinus, *Intimate Friends*.

25. Judith Butler, *Gender Trouble: Feminism and the Subversion of Identity* (New York: Routledge, 1990). The phrase "undoing gender" is the title of one of Butler's recent books (New York: Routledge, 2004). For work in Victorian studies that addresses the issues raised by feminism and queer theory, such as desire, domesticity, and subjectivity, without relying on oppositional concepts of gender and sexuality, see Amanda Anderson, *The Powers of Distance: Cosmopolitanism and the Cultivation of Detachment* (Princeton: Princeton University Press, 2001), esp. 34–62, and Jeff Nunokawa, *Tame Passions of Wilde: The Styles of Manageable Desire* (Princeton: Princeton University Press, 2003). In *Female Masculinity* (Durham, NC: Duke University Press, 1998), Judith Halberstam makes a related argument that female masculinity past and present cannot be fully explained in terms of lesbianism.

26. See Duggan, "The Trials of Alice Mitchell"; Vicinus, *Intimate Friends*; Lisa L. Moore, *Dangerous Intimacies: Toward a Sapphic History of the British Novel* (Durham, NC: Duke University Press, 1997); and Andrew Elfenbein, who uses the concepts of excess, transgression, and gender crossing to link genius to queerness and same-sex eroticism, in *Romantic Genius: The Prehistory of a Homosexual Role* (New York: Columbia University Press, 1999).

27. Lillian Faderman, *Surpassing the Love of Men: Romantic Friendship and Love between Women from the Renaissance to the Present* (New York: William Morrow, 1981). Though Faderman mistakenly insisted on the asexual nature of nineteenth-century romantic friendship, her exhaustive research on female couples provided an agenda for biographical research that continues to thrive. For a seminal discussion of "minoritizing" and "universalizing" views of homosexuality and the ways they intermingle, see Eve Kosofsky Sedgwick, *Epistemology of the Closet* (Berkeley: University of California Press, 1990).

28. Vicinus, *Intimate Friends*, xv. Further references are to this edition and appear in the text. I discuss the notion of female marriage extensively in chapters 1 and 5.

29. On the persistent tendency to discount even the most explicitly sexual representations as evidence of a broader cultural awareness of lesbian sex, see Sarah Toulalan, "Extraordinary Satisfactions: Lesbian Visibility in Seventeenth-Century Pornography in England," *Gender & History* 15.1 (2003), 50–68.

30. Denise Riley, *"Am I That Name?" Feminism and the Category of "Women" in History* (Minneapolis: University of Minnesota Press, 1988); Joan Wallach Scott, *Gender and the Politics of History* (New York: Columbia University Press, 1988); Scott, *Only Paradoxes to Offer: French Feminists and the Rights of Man* (Cambridge, Mass.: Harvard University Press, 1996); Sedgwick, *Epistemology*; Butler, *Gender Trouble* and *Undoing Gender*. I discuss the connections between feminism and queer theory in "Queer Theory for Everyone: A Review Essay," *Signs: Journal of Women in Culture and Society* 31.1 (2005), 191–218.

31. Foucault has had an enormous influence on the conceptualization of the homosexual as an exile from the family seeking to invent radically new social relations, although he also understood the homosexual as an effect of power and as the creation of bourgeois society. See Michel Foucault, *The History of Sexuality. Volume 1: An Introduction*, trans. Robert Hurley (New York: Vintage Books, 1980), and Didier Eribon's commentary in "Michel Foucault's Histories of Sexu-

ality," trans. Michael Lucey, *GLQ* 7.1 (2001), 39–42, 49, 75. For strong defenses of queerness as subversion, see Michael Warner, *The Trouble with Normal: Sex, Politics, and the Ethics of Queer Life* (New York: Free Press, 1999); Leo Bersani, *Homos* (Cambridge, Mass.; Harvard University Press, 1995); and Lee Edelman, *No Future: Queer Theory and the Death Drive* (Durham, NC: Duke University Press, 2004). Butler and Sedgwick argue for a queerness that subverts the priority and primacy of heterosexuality and thus becomes as original or fundamental as the heterosexuality from which it cannot truly be distinguished. See *Gender Trouble*, *Between Men*, and *Epistemology*.

32. On the relationship between gay people and ideas of family, traditional and alternative, see Kath Weston, *Families We Choose: Lesbians, Gays, Kinship* (New York: Columbia University Press, 1997).

33. For details about English reviews of French sapphic texts, see Sharon Marcus, "Comparative Sapphism," in *The Literary Channel: The Inter-National Invention of the Novel*, eds., Margaret Cohen and Carolyn Dever (Princeton: Princeton University Press, 2002), 255–61.

34. Charlotte Brontë, *Jane Eyre* (1847; repr., London: Penguin, 1986), 102. Further references are to this edition and appear in the text.

35. Wilkie Collins, *The Woman in White* (1860; repr., London: Penguin, 1985), 61, 97, 209.

36. Christina Rossetti, *Goblin Market* (1862; repr., New York: Dover, 1983), 46–47.

37. See Lorraine Janzen Kooistra, "*Goblin Market* as a Cross-Audienced Poem: Children's Fairy Tale, Adult Erotic Fantasy," *Children's Literature* 25 (1997), 181–204.

38. Sarah Ellis, *The Daughters of England, Their Position in Society, Character and Responsibilities* (London: Fisher, Son, & Co., n.d.), 277.

39. *Englishwoman's Domestic Magazine* 5.46 (1868), 221.

40. Carolyn Dever, *Death and the Mother from Dickens to Freud: Victorian Fiction and the Anxiety of Origins* (Cambridge: Cambridge University Press, 1998).

41. Annie Besant, *An Autobiography* (1893; repr., Adya Madras: The Theosophical Publishing House, 1939), 22, 51.

42. See Ethel Smyth, *Impressions that Remained: Memories*, vol. 1 (London: Longmans, Green & Co., 1919); Constance M. Fulmer and Margaret E. Barfield, eds., *A Monument to the Memory of George Eliot: Edith J. Simcox's Autobiography of a Shirtmaker* (New York: Garland Publishing, 1998), 234; Cobbe, *Life*, vol. 1 (1894), 29; H. G. Rawlinson, ed., *Personal Reminiscences in India and Europe, 1830–1888 of Augusta Becher* (London: Constable, 1930), 33, 21–22.

43. Julia Maitland, *The Doll and Her Friends, or Memoirs of the Lady Seraphina* (Boston: Ticknor, Reed, and Fields, 1852), 1–2.

44. On Victorian awareness of the role that the clitoris played in women's sexual pleasure, see Thomas W. Laqueur, "Amor Veneris, Vel Dulcedo Appeletur," in *Fragments Toward a History of the Body*, eds. Michel Feher et al. (New York: Zone Books, 1989), 91–131; and Laqueur, *Solitary Sex: A Cultural History of Masturbation* (New York: Zone Books, 2003), 29, 64. Most medical writers associated clitoral arousal with masturbation, but pornographic texts

usually mentioned the clitoris in descriptions of sexual acts between women or between women and men. Although William Acton and others famously asserted that women experienced less sexual desire than men, most Victorians, including Acton himself, did not believe that women experienced no sexual pleasure at all. See Steven Marcus, *The Other Victorians: A Study of Sexuality and Pornography in Mid-Nineteenth-Century England* (New York: Basic Books, 1964), 27–31. For a concentrated sampling of academic and popular medical manuals published between 1831 and 1888, written by men and women, that described what they variously called women's lust, passion, orgasm, sensation of desire, and desire for intercourse, see excerpts collected in Patricia Jalland and John Hooper, eds., *Women from Birth to Death: The Female Life Cycle in Britain 1830–1914* (Brighton: Harvester Press, 1986), 232–34. See also Peter Gay, *The Bourgeois Experience from Victoria to Freud*, vol. 1, *Education of the Senses* (New York: Oxford University Press, 1984) and John Maynard, *Victorian Discourses on Sexuality and Religion* (Cambridge: Cambridge University Press, 1993). In *The Technology of Orgasm*, Maines studies the use of vibrators as a form of medical treatment for women in late-nineteenth-century America. Her work suggests that women, like men, had the option of paying for sexual pleasures they could not obtain from their spouses; where men paid prostitutes, women paid medical practitioners to provide them with vulval massages that were considered a treatment for hysteria and other nervous diseases; see 38, 87, 110.

45. *The Romance of Lust* (n.p., n.d.), 69. For other pornographic texts that represented sex between women, see chapter 3.

46. See Anna Jameson, *Memoirs and Essays* (London: Richard Bentley, 1846), 276–77, and Thomas Laycock, *A Treatise of the Nervous Disorders of Women* (London: Longman and Co., 1840), 141, cited in Alison Oram and Annemarie Turnbull, eds., *The Lesbian History Sourcebook* (London: Routledge, 2001), 97. Laycock is not explicitly worrying about lesbianism in the sense of an exclusive sexual orientation towards women, however, since he sees girls' experience of "novel feelings towards the opposite sex" as the source of their enervating experiments with one another.

47. Detailed discussions of the scholarship in each of these areas appear in individual chapters.

48. Butler, *Gender Trouble*, 37–38.

49. See Castle, *The Apparitional Lesbian*; Vicinus, *Intimate Friends*; Julia Markus, *Across an Untried Sea: Discovering Lives Hidden in the Shadow of Convention and Time* (New York: Alfred A. Knopf, 2000); and Lisa Merrill, *When Romeo Was a Woman: Charlotte Cushman and Her Circle of Female Spectators* (Ann Arbor: University of Michigan Press, 1999). Additional citations appear in individual chapters.

50. Vicinus and Merrill offer thorough documentation of the familial and marital language used by women in female couples; I cite and discuss additional examples in chapters 1, 3, 5, and 6.

51. See Michael Lucey, *The Misfit of the Family* (Durham, NC: Duke University Press, 2003); Butler, *Undoing Gender*; Christopher Nealon, *Foundlings: Lesbian and Gay Historical Emotion before Stonewall* (Durham, NC: Duke University Press, 2001); Michael Moon, *A Small Boy and Others: Imitation and*

Initiation in American Culture from Henry James to Andy Warhol (Durham, NC: Duke University Press, 1998).

CHAPTER 1
Friendship and the Play of the System

1. Sarah Ellis, *The Women of England: Their Social Duties, and Domestic Habits*, 2nd ed. (London: Fisher, Son & Co., [1839]), 47. Further references are to this edition and appear in the text.

2. Sarah Ellis, *The Daughters of England, Their Position in Society, Character, and Responsibilities* (London: Fisher, Son, [1842]), 337, 361. Further references are to this edition and appear in the text.

3. "Friend," in Lesley Brown, ed., *The Shorter Oxford English Dictionary*, vol. 1 (Oxford: Clarendon Press, 1993).

4. Naomi Tadmor, *Family and Friends in Eighteenth-Century England: Household, Kinship, and Patronage* (Cambridge: Cambridge University Press, 2001), 167–69, 192; Alan Bray, *The Friend* (Chicago: University of Chicago Press, 2003).

5. On the contemporary sociology of friendship, see Robert A. Hinde, *Relationships: A Dialectical Perspective* (Hove: Psychology Press, 1997), 409–12.

6. Roland Barthes, *Sade/Fourier/Loyola*, trans. Richard Miller (New York: Hill & Wang, 1976), 109–10.

7. On working-class autobiography, and the paucity of works by women, see David Vincent, *Bread, Knowledge, and Freedom: A Study of Nineteenth-Century Working Class Autobiography* (London: Methuen, 1981), and John Burnett, ed., *The Annals of Labour: Autobiographies of British Working Class People, 1820–1920* (Bloomington: Indiana University Press, 1974).

8. Jacqueline Hope-Nicholson, ed., *Life Amongst the Troubridges* (London: John Murray, 1966), 147–49; Helena Whitbread, ed., *I Know My Own Heart: The Diaries of Anne Lister, 1791–1840* (London: Virago, 1988); and Whitbread, ed. *No Priest But Love: Excerpts from the Diaries of Anne Lister, 1824–1826* (New York: New York University Press, 1992).

9. In her analysis of women's lifewriting just before the Victorian era, Amanda Vickery finds that women placed heterosexual sociability at the center of their lives and related with other women primarily through the exchange of consumer services rather than by forging independent emotional ties with prized female friends. Amanda Vickery, *The Gentleman's Daughter: Women's Lives in Georgian England* (New Haven: Yale University Press, 1998), 242, 283. On friendship and companionate marriage before the nineteenth century, see Lawrence Stone, *The Family, Sex, and Marriage in England 1500–1800* (New York: Harper Books, 1979); Margaret R. Hunt, *The Middling Sort: Commerce, Gender, and the Family in England, 1680–1760* (Berkeley: University of California Press, 1996); Irene Q. Brown, "Domesticity, Feminism, and Friendship: Female Aristocratic Culture and Marriage in England, 1660–1760," *Journal of Family History* 7.4 (1982), 406–24; Elizabeth Wahl, *Invisible Relations: Representations of Female Intimacy in the Age of Enlightenment* (Stanford: Stanford University Press, 1999); Susan Lanser, "Befriending the Body: Female Intimacies as Class Acts," *Eighteenth-Century*

Studies 32.2 (1998–99), 179–98; and Lisa L. Moore, *Dangerous Intimacies: Toward a Sapphic History of the British Novel* (Durham, NC: Duke University Press, 1997).

10. Seth Koven, *Slumming: Sexual and Social Politics in Victorian London* (Princeton: Princeton University Press, 2004).

11. Leonore Davidoff and Catherine Hall, *Family Fortunes: Men and Women of the English Middle Class 1780–1850* (Chicago: University of Chicago Press, 1987), 402–3; John Gillis, *For Better, For Worse: British Marriages, 1600 to the Present* (New York: Oxford University Press, 1985), 14, 136–38, 142; and Bray, 217, 226.

12. Adrienne Rich, "Compulsory Heterosexuality and Lesbian Existence," in *The Signs Reader: Women, Gender, and Scholarship*, eds. Elizabeth Abel and Emily K. Abel (Chicago: University of Chicago Press, 1983), 139–68.

13. Martha Vicinus, *Intimate Friends: Women Who Loved Women, 1778–1928* (Chicago: University of Chicago Press, 2004), 69, 51, xv, 232, 59.

14. Edward Carpenter, ed., *Ioläus: An Anthology of Friendship*, 2nd ed. (London: Swann Sonnenschein, 1906); Magnus Hirschfeld, *The Homosexuality of Men and Women*, trans. Michael A. Lombardi-Nash (1914; repr., New York: Prometheus Books, 2000), 230, 805.

15. Carroll Smith-Rosenberg, "The Female World of Love and Ritual," in *Feminism and History*, ed. Joan Wallach Scott (Oxford: Oxford University Press, 1996), 367, 371. Further references are to this edition and appear in the text.

16. On husbands and wives, see *Pages from the Diary of an Oxford Lady, 1843–1862*, ed. Margaret Jeune Gifford (Oxford: Shakespeare Head Press, 1932), 2, 3. Lady Anne Noel Blunt, diary, British Library Mss. ADD. 53821, entries for February 1857.

17. On the ways in which one married man was able to combine marriage to a woman with a series of erotic and sexual relationships with men, see Morris Kaplan's groundbreaking discussion of Viscount Esher in *Sodom on the Thames: Sex, Love and Scandal in Wilde Times* (Ithaca: Cornell University Press, 2005), 102–65. For an example of a seventeen-year-old boy's romantic love for two other boys at public school, see Bertrand Russell and Patricia Russell, eds., *The Amberley Papers: Bertrand Russell's Family Background* (London: George Allen & Unwin, 1966), 180. H.C.G. Matthew discusses William Gladstone's romantic friendship with Arthur Hallam, "the chief love of Gladstone's schooldays," in *Gladstone: 1809–1874* (Oxford: Clarendon Press, 1986), 11.

18. Smith-Rosenberg's opening examples are, for instance, quite different. She herself notes that the women in her second example were "lovers—emotionally if not physically" (371), unlike the women in her first example—yet both pairs exemplify the "female world."

19. For two examples that cite Smith-Rosenberg to discount the erotic implications of women's relationships, see Patricia Jalland's introduction to *Octavia Wilberforce: The Autobiography of a Pioneer Woman Doctor* (London: Cassell, 1989), xxi–xxii, and Frances Porter and Charlotte Macdonald with Tui Macdonald, eds., *"My Hand Will Write What My Heart Dictates": The Unsettled Lives of Women in Nineteenth-Century New Zealand as Revealed to Sisters, Family, and Friends* (Auckland: Auckland University Press, 1996), 185–87.

20. See Vicinus, *Intimate Friends*, 91–98.

21. Hester Ritchie, ed., *Letters of Anne Thackeray Ritchie* (London: John Murray, 1924), 62, 66.

22. H. G. Rawlinson, ed., *Personal Reminiscences in India and Europe 1830–1888 of Augusta Becher* (London: Constable, 1930), 20. Further references are to this edition and appear in the text.

23. Josiah Gilbert, ed., *Autobiography and Other Memorials of Mrs. Gilbert*, 3rd ed. (London: C. Kegan Paul, 1878), 420, 442. Further references are to this edition and appear in the text.

24. On the heterosexual uses of flower imagery, see Amy King, *Bloom: The Botanical Vernacular in the English Novel* (New York: Oxford University Press, 2003). On the use of images of buds to signify the clitoris in nineteenth-century women's poetry, see Paula Bennett, "Critical Clitoridectomy: Female Sexual Imagery and Feminist Psychoanalytic Theory," *Signs: Journal of Women in Culture and Society* 18.2 (1993), 235–59.

25. [Mary Lundie], *Memoir of Mrs. Mary Lundie Duncan: Being Recollections of a Daughter by Her Mother*, 2nd ed. (Edinburgh: William Oliphant & Son, 1842), 228. Further references are to this edition and appear in the text.

26. Charlotte Hanbury, *Life of Mrs. Albert Head* (London: Marshall Brothers, 1905), 100. Further references are to this edition and appear in the text.

27. Virginia Woolf, *A Room of One's Own* (1929; repr., New York: Harcourt Brace Jovanovich, 1979), 93.

28. Scholars who have used Victorian women's lifewriting to study issues other than friendship include Patricia Jalland, *Women, Marriage and Politics 1860–1914* (Oxford: Clarendon Press, 1986); Harriet Blodgett, *Centuries of Female Days: Englishwomen's Private Diaries* (New Brunswick, NJ: Rutgers University Press, 1988); and Leonore Davidoff, *The Best Circles: Society Etiquette and the Season* (1973; repr., London: The Cresset Library, 1986).

29. In the 1980s, literary critics dismissed Victorian women's autobiographies as documenting only how women lacked the authority to write their own lives; see Estelle C. Jelinek, *The Tradition of Women's Autobiography: From Antiquity to the Present* (Boston: Twayne, 1986), 45–46, and Linda H. Peterson, *Victorian Autobiography: The Tradition of Self-Interpretation* (New Haven: Yale University Press, 1986), 129–30. Regenia Gagnier questioned that model by looking at autobiographies by men and women of all classes in *Subjectivities: A History of Self-Representation in Britain, 1832–1920* (New York: Oxford University Press, 1991). Sidonie Smith's *A Poetics of Women's Autobiography: Marginality and the Fictions of Self-Representation* (Bloomington: Indiana University Press, 1987), paved the way for groundbreaking works that appeared in the 1990s: Mary Jean Corbett, *Representing Femininity: Middle-Class Subjectivity in Victorian and Edwardian Women's Autobiographies* (New York: Oxford University Press, 1992), and Linda H. Peterson, *Traditions of Victorian Women's Autobiography: The Poetics and Politics of Life Writing* (Charlottesville: University Press of Virginia, 1999). Corbett argued that female autobiographies tended not to follow the Romantic model of authorship as the self-authorization of a unique genius. Peterson showed that women's autobiographies drew on the tradition of the domestic memoir, which defined the individual in relation to the family.

30. On the hybridity of the self in women's lifewriting and on lifewriting as a hybrid on genre, see Linda H. Peterson, "Collaborative Life Writing as Ideology: The Auto/biographies of Mary Howitt and Her Family," *Prose Studies* 26.1–2 (2003), 176–95. Alison Booth, *How to Make It as a Woman: Collective Biographical History from Victoria to the Present* (Chicago: University of Chicago Press, 2004), notes that biography is an inherently interpersonal genre, and attests to the plethora of collective biographies of women that "flourished from the 1830s," 4, 29.

31. Christabel Coleridge, *Charlotte Mary Yonge: Her Life and Letters* (London: Macmillan & Co., 1903). Further references are to this edition and appear in the text.

32. See Harriet Blodgett, *"Capacious Hold-All": An Anthology of Englishwomen's Diary Writings* (Charlottesville, University Press of Virginia, 1991).

33. Margaret S. Rolt, ed., *A Great-Niece's Journals: Being Extracts from the Journals of Fanny Anne Burney (Mrs. Wood) from 1830–1842* (London: Constable, 1926), xxxii; Gerardine Macpherson, *Memoirs of the Life of Anna Jameson* (London: Longmans, Green & Co., 1878), xi.

34. For sexually revealing diaries kept by nineteenth-century women, see Whitbread, ed., *I Know My Own Heart*; Whitbread, ed., *No Priest But Love*; and Liz Stanley, ed., *The Diaries of Hannah Cullwick, Victorian Maidservant* (New Brunswick, NJ: Rutgers University Press, 1984).

35. Although preprinted diaries were common, many women kept their diaries in blank books. Lady Louisa Rothschild and Byron's granddaughter Anne Noel King used small, bound blank volumes to keep sporadic, nonuniform diaries, while another woman whose journal spanned twenty years and ten volumes used a large account book to sum up each day in one to three lines. Diaries of Lady Louisa de Rothschild, 1837 to 1907, British Library Mss. ADD. 47949–47962; Lady Anne Noel Blunt, diaries, British Library Mss. Add. 53817 ff.; journal kept by Mrs. M. Palfreyman, 1840 to 1861, British Library Mss. ADD. 49276. On preprinted diary formats, see Cynthia Huff, *British Women's Diaries* (New York: AMS Press, 1985), xiv.

36. On sharing diary entries, see Huff, *British Women's Diaries*, 99. On Smyth's secret childhood diary, see *Impressions that Remained: Memoirs*, vol. 1 (London: Longmans, Green & Co., 1919), 89–90.

37. Julia Cartwright [Mrs. Ady], ed., *The Journals of Lady Knightley of Fawsley 1856–1884* (London: John Murray, 1915), xv. Further references are to this edition and appear in the text. On the publication of Burney's diary and its effects, see Stuart Sherman, *Telling Time: Clocks, Diaries, and English Diurnal Form, 1660–1785* (Chicago: University of Chicago Press, 1996), 270–75.

38. On Waugh, see Patrick Joyce, *Democratic Subjects: The Self and the Social in Nineteenth Century England* (Cambridge: Cambridge University Press, 1994), 41; and S. Sophia Beale, ed., *Recollections of a Spinster Aunt* (London: William Heinemann, 1908), 11.

39. On Lehzen's instruction, see Walter L. Arnstein, *Queen Victoria* (Houndmills: Palgrave Macmillan, 2003), 25; on maternal inspection, see Viscount Esher, ed., *The Girlhood of Queen Victoria. A Selection of Her Majesty's Diaries between the Years 1832 and 1840*, vol. 1 (London: John Murray, 1912), 13–14.

40. Marian Bradley, British Library, Mss. EG. 3766 A–C, and Huff, *British Women's Diaries*, xvi, xxiv.

41. [Jane Budge], *A Beloved Mother: Life of Hannah S. Allen, By Her Daughter* (London: Harris & Co., 1884), 33. Further references are to this edition and appear in the text. Huff identifies other diaries justified as instructions to help the author's children avoid mistakes, *British Women's Diaries*, xxv.

42. Marian Bradley, British Library, Mss. EG. 3766 A, 32.

43. Almost any Victorian woman's diary illustrates this point, but for a particularly representative example, see Gifford, ed., *Diary of an Oxford Lady*.

44. M.R.D. Foot, "Introduction," in *The Gladstone Diaries*, vol. 1 (Oxford: Clarendon Press, 1966), xix.

45. Marian Bradley, Mss. EG. 3766 A, 7. A tension between evangelical and Romantic impulses structures many Victorian diaries; Bradley adopted a lyrical, expressive, and spontaneous persona only when describing nature.

46. Lady Louisa de Rothschild, née Montefiore, British Library Mss. ADD. 47949, 4.

47. "Christian biography" is the term the anonymous author uses to describe her work in *Memorials of Agnes Elizabeth Jones* (London: Strahan & Co., 1871), 1. Further references are to this edition and appear in the text. On the religious aims and ideals that subtended collective biographies of women published during the nineteenth century, see Booth, *How to Make It as a Woman*, 79–80.

48. *Letters of Mary Mathison* (London: Spottiswoode & Co., 1875), 9. Further references are to this edition and appear in the text.

49. Nancy Mitford, ed., *The Ladies of Alderley: Being the Letters between Maria Josepha, Lady Stanley of Alderley, and Her Daughter-in-Law Henrietta Maria Stanley during the Years 1841–1850* (London: Chapman and Hall, 1938), xv; Lucy Masterman, ed., *Mary Gladstone (Mrs. Drew): Her Diaries and Letters* (London: Methuen, 1930), vi.

50. On modernism and the memoir form, see Alex Zwerdling, "Mastering the Memoir: Woolf and the Family Legacy," *Modernism/Modernity* 10.1 (2003), 165–88.

51. Eleanor Acland, *Good-Bye for the Present: The Story of Two Childhoods. Milly: 1878–88 & Ellen: 1913–24* (London: Hodder & Stoughton, 1935), 16.

52. Jane Williams, ed., *The Autobiography of Elizabeth Davis, A Balaclava Nurse*, vol. 1 (London: Hurst and Blackett, 1857), 102–3. On female theatricals, see Beale, *Recollections of a Spinster Aunt*, 22. For other examples of boys dressing as girls, see Constance Battersea, *Reminiscences* (London: Macmillan, 1922), 46, and Rawlinson, ed., *Personal Reminiscences of Augusta Becher*, 34–35.

53. Amanda Vickery, "Introduction," in Vickery, ed., *Women, Privilege, and Power: British Politics, 1750 to the Present* (Stanford University Press, 2001), 20.

54. Katherine Harris, diary, 1847–50, British Library Mss. ADD. 52503; see 95, 152. The diary of Marian Bradley recorded news about the Crimean War in 1854; see British Library, Mss. EG. 3766A, 32–41. Georgiana Bloomfield's collection of letters exchanged among her sisters is an excellent example of open discussion of political events by upper-class women; *My Sisters* (Hertford: Simson, 1892).

55. Beale, ed., *Recollections of a Spinster Aunt*, 74, 140.

56. Hon. E.C.F. Collier, ed., *A Victorian Diarist: Extracts from the Journals of Mary, Lady Monkswell* (London: John Murray, 1944), 163. Further references are to this edition and appear in the text. Monkswell also recorded her open disagreements with her husband over political issues such as home rule for Ireland, which he supported and she opposed.

57. For an example in which the biographer excluded love letters her subject received from a man, see Beale, ed. *Recollections of a Spinster Aunt*, 4.

58. *The Diaries and Correspondence of Anna Catherina Bower* (London: Bickers & Son, 1903).

59. Masterman, ed., *Mary Gladstone*, vi.

60. James T. Covert, *A Victorian Family as Seen through the Letters of Louise Creighton to Her Mother* (Lampeter, Wales: The Edwin Mellen Press, 1998), 66, 123, 265. In letters to her mother, Creighton also often wrote about her daughter's friendship with a neighbor girl, 155, 161.

61. Viscount Esher, ed., *Girlhood*, 175, 318.

62. On Queen Victoria as a model of domesticity, see Arnstein, *Queen Victoria*, 49–65; Margaret Homans, *Royal Representations: Queen Victoria and British Culture, 1837–1876* (Chicago: University of Chicago Press, 1998); and Adrienne Munich, *Queen Victoria's Secrets* (New York: Columbia University Press, 1996).

63. Porter, MacDonald, eds., *My Hand Will Write* 201.

64. See Eleanor L. Sewell, ed., *The Autobiography of Elizabeth M. Sewell* (London: Longmans, Green & Co., 1907); Lady Elizabeth Butler, *An Autobiography* (London: Constable, 1922); and Annie Besant, *An Autobiography* (1893; repr. Adya Madras: The Theosophical Publishing House, 1939).

65. Alice Catherine Miles, *Every Girl's Duty: The Diary of a Victorian Debutante*, ed. Maggy Parsons (London: Deutsch, 1992), 84, 32, 36, 88.

66. On the difficulty of defining the intimacy between Mill and Taylor, see Jo Ellen Jacobs, *The Voice of Harriet Taylor Mill* (Bloomington: Indiana University Press, 2002), xxvi, 112, 113, 114, 122. On the likelihood that Munby and Cullwick never had intercourse, see Stanley, ed., *The Diaries of Hannah Cullwick*, 14.

67. On male reticence about marital and extra-marital sexuality in both deeply private and published lifewriting, see Blodgett, *"Capacious Hold-All,"* 7; Joyce, *Democratic Subjects*, 51; Vincent, *Bread, Knowledge, and Freedom*, 43; and Foot, ed., *The Gladstone Diaries*, 93.

68. Butler, *An Autobiography*, 168.

69. See Vicinus, *Intimate Friends*, 121–26; Rosemarie Bodenheimer, "Autobiography in Fragments: The Elusive Life of Edith Simcox," *Victorian Studies* 44.3 (Spring 2002), 399–422; and Pauline Polkey, "Recuperating the Love-Passions of Edith Simcox," in Pauline Polkey, ed., *Women's Lives into Print: The Theory, Practice and Writing of Feminist Auto/Biography* (London: Macmillan, 1999), 61–79.

70. Constance M. Fulmer and Margaret Barfield, eds., *A Monument to the Memory of George Eliot: Edith J. Simcox's* Autobiography of a Shirtmaker (New York: Garland Publishing, 1998), 184, 26. Further references are to this edition and appear in the text.

71. On Simcox's erotic asceticism, see Vicinus, *Intimate Friends*, 123–4.

72. Margaret Todd, *The Life of Sophia Jex-Blake* (London: Macmillan, 1918), 84. Further references are to this edition and appear in the text.

73. Margaret Leicester Warren, *Diaries*, vol. 2 (printed for private circulation, 1924), 233, 247, 249. Further references are to this edition and volume, unless a different volume number is noted, and appear in the text.

74. See, for example, Emma Stebbins's biography of her spouse, Charlotte Cushman, *Charlotte Cushman: Her Letters and Memories of Her Life* (Boston: Houghton, Osgood and Co., 1879), 65, 138.

75. Hirschfeld, *The Homosexuality of Men and Women*, 805. Hirschfeld noted that such marital arrangements were more common among women because men living together were more likely to arouse suspicion, 806.

76. See Susan E. Gunter and Steven H. Jobe, eds., *Dearly Beloved Friends: Henry James's Letters to Younger Men* (Ann Arbor: University of Michigan Press, 2001); 18, and Ronald Sutherland Gower, *Old Diaries 1881–1901* (London: John Murray, 1902), 323.

77. Frank Hird, *Rosa Bonheur* (London: George Bell & Sons, 1904), 37–38. Further references are to this edition and appear in the text.

78. Theodore Stanton, ed., *Reminiscences of Rosa Bonheur* (London: Andrew Melrose, 1910), 94. Further references are to this edition and appear in the text.

79. *The Halifax Guardian*, October 31, 1840, reprinted in Muriel Green, ed., *Miss Lister of Shibden Hall: Selected Letters (1800–1840)* (Sussex: The Book Guild, 1992), 206. The obituary also advertised the two women's intimacy by noting that Walker brought Lister's remains home (Lister died while traveling) "by way of Constantinople, for interment in the family vault," 206. On Lister and marriage, see Vicinus, *Intimate Friends*, 18–30.

80. Frederick Dolman, "Afternoon Tea with Miss Emily Faithfull," *The Young Woman* 3 (1894–1895), 318.

81. Cited in Martha Vicinus, "Lesbian Perversity and Victorian Marriage: The 1864 Codrington Divorce Trial," *Journal of British Studies* 36 (January 1997), 85.

82. Florence Fenwick Miller, in an 1896 article for the *Woman's Signal*, cited in Sally Mitchell, *Frances Power Cobbe: Victorian Feminist, Journalist, Reformer* (Charlottesville: University of Virginia Press, 2004), 351.

83. See Frances Anne Kemble, *Further Records. 1848–1883*, vol. 2 (London: Richard Bentley, 1890), 41–42, 81, 88. Cobbe was still alive when Kemble published the letters cited.

84. Frances Power Cobbe, *Life of Frances Power Cobbe as Told by Herself* (London: Swann Sonnenschein, 1904), 200, 477.

85. The reference to Lloyd as a friend with whom Cobbe shared housekeeping is from her *Life* (1904), 438; on Cobbe's exchanges with Bonheur, see Mitchell, *Frances Power Cobbe*, 351.

86. Cobbe called Lloyd her "life-friend" in an article entitled "Recollections of James Martineau, the Sage of the Nineteenth Century," *Contemporary Review* 77 (February 1900), 186, cited in Mitchell, *Frances Power Cobbe*, 359. Cobbe called Lloyd "my beloved friend" in *Life of Frances Power Cobbe. By Herself*, vol. 2 (Boston: Houghton, Mifflin, 1894), 645; remaining references are all from

letters written in 1865 to the scientist Mary Somerville, in the Mary Somerville Papers in the Bodleian Library, Oxford, cited in Mitchell, 209, 157, 197.

87. Esther Newton, "The Mythic Mannish Lesbian: Radclyffe Hall and the New Woman," in Newton, *Margaret Mead Me Gay: Personal Essays, Public Ideas* (Durham, NC: Duke University Press, 2000), 176–88.

88. Cobbe, *Life* (1904), 393, 711.

89. Cobbe, *Life* (1904), v, 708.

90. Cobbe, *Life* (1894), vol. 2, 645.

91. Cobbe, *Life* (1904), 393.

92. Cobbe, *Life* (1894), vol. 2, 361, 404, 401.

93. Cobbe, *Life* (1904), 395.

94. Cobbe, *Life* (1904), 711, 708.

95. Cobbe, *Life* (1904), 710.

96. Albert Baillie, ed., *Letters of Lady Augusta Stanley: A Young Lady at Court* (London: Gerald Howe, 1927), 12, 14. Baillie was Stanley's nephew and the Dean of Windsor.

97. G. H. Needler, ed., *Letters of Anna Jameson to Ottilie von Goethe* (London: Oxford University Press, 1939), 53–54.

98. *The Journal of Emily Shore* (London: Kegan Paul, 1891), 201, 232. Further references are to this edition and appear in the text.

99. Nancy Cott, *The Bonds of Womanhood: "Woman's Sphere" in New England, 1780–1835* (New Haven: Yale University Press, 1977), 167–88.

100. Osbert Sitwell, *Two Generations* (London: Macmillan, 1940), 28.

101. Mary Clive, ed., *Caroline Clive: From the Diary and Family Papers of Mrs. Archer Clive (1801–1873)* (London: The Bodley Head, 1949), 55–56. Further references are to this edition and appear in the text.

102. James Anthony Froude, ed., *Letters and Memorials of Jane Welsh Carlyle*, vol. 3 (London: Longman, Green & Co., 1883), 110.

103. Cobbe, *Life*, (1894), vol. 2, 350, 349.

104. Froude, ed., *Letters of Jane Carlyle*, vol. 1, 370–1, 8.

105. Bradley diary, Mss. EG. 3766B, 27.

106. In 1939, Lady Sybil Lubbock defended the "element of romance" in "the deep attachment" that she formed for an older English girl in her youth by calling it a "devotion" that lasted only until she "was really grown-up"; *The Child in the Crystal: Reminiscences of Childhood* (London: Jonathan Cape, 1939), 210. Laura Doan has shown that as late as the 1920s, many in England failed to perceive close attachments between women as deviant; *Fashioning Sapphism: The Origins of a Modern English Lesbian Culture* (New York: Columbia University Press, 2001).

107. Froude, ed., *Letters of Jane Carlyle*, vol. 1, 16–17.

108. Froude, ed., *Letters of Jane Carlyle*, vol. 1, 127.

109. Mrs. Catherine Hutton Beale, ed., *Reminiscences of a Gentlewoman of the Last Century: Letters of Catherine Hutton* (Birmingham: Cornish Brothers, 1891), 162–63, 186.

110. John Bailey, ed., *The Diary of Lady Frederick Cavendish*, vol. 1 (London: John Murray, 1927), 87.

111. Dolly Sherwood, *Harriet Hosmer: American Sculptor 1830–1890* (Columbia: University of Missouri Press, 1991), 135, citing the 1879 New York edition of *Records of Girlhood*, 302.

112. Ethyl Smyth worshipped Jenny Lind, as recounted in *Impressions that Remained*, vol. 1, 92; the painter Elizabeth Butler began her career as "worshiper of Beauty" with a girlhood admiration for Ristori, *An Autobiography*, 7. The woman whose journals are excerpted in Beale, ed., *Recollections of a Spinster Aunt*, wrote to her cousin about her interest in Grisi, Taglioni, Elssler, and Madame Vestris, 11, 22.

113. See Kaplan, *Sodom on the Thames*, 102–65.

114. Esher, ed., *Girlhood*, vol. 1, 74, 114. Victoria was also very sensitive to male beauty and commented on it more freely after she reached eighteen and her mother no longer read her diary. From her first meeting with her future husband, Albert, she wrote of her pleasure in his looks, 262–63.

115. Marvin Spevack, ed., *A Victorian Chronicle: The Diary of Henrietta Halliwell-Phillipps* (Hildesheim: Georg Olms Verlag, 1999), 34.

116. Battersea, *Reminiscences*, 66, 90, 91.

117. The classic statement of this issue remains Walter Houghton, *The Victorian Frame of Mind* (New Haven: Yale University Press), 353–75. On the ways that Victorian women combined infatuation, unrequited passion, and conjugal love for women with religious impulses, see Vicinus, *Intimate Friends*, 85–98.

118. Rebekah H. Taylor, *Letters of Mrs. Herbert Wilbraham Taylor to Members of Her Classes, and Friends. Edited by Her Husband* (London: James E. Hawkins, 1878), 260–61.

119. Important studies of Evangelicalism include Davidoff and Hall, *Family Fortunes*; Geoffrey Best, "Evangelicalism and the Victorians," in Anthony Symondson, ed., *The Victorian Crisis of Faith* (London: Society for Promoting Christian Knowledge, 1970), 37–56; Ian Bradley, *The Call to Seriousness: The Evangelical Impact on the Victorians* (New York: Macmillan, 1976); and D. W. Bebbington, *Evangelicalism in Modern Britain: A History from the 1730s to the 1980s* (London: Unwin Hyman, 1989).

120. Bradley diary, Mss. EG. 3766–B, 11.

121. Porter, Macdonald, eds., *My Hand Will Write*, 193.

122. William Beck, ed., *Family Fragments Respecting the Ancestry, Acquaintance and Marriage of Richard Low Beck and Rachel Lucas* (Gloucester: Privately printed by John Bellows, 1897), 107.

123. E. F. Carritt, ed., *Letters of Courtship, Between John Torr and Maria Jackson* (London: Oxford University Press, 1933), 193, 154, 124.

124. Spevack, ed., *A Victorian Chronicle*, xiii.

125. Desmond MacCarthy and Agatha Russell, eds., *Lady John Russell: A Memoir: With Selections from Her Diaries and Correspondence* (London: Methuen, 1910), 59, 68.

126. Cited in Georgiana Bloomfield, *My Sisters*, 123, referring to Jane, *née* Liddell, married to William Keppel, Viscount Barrington.

127. Lotte Hamburger and Joseph Hamburger, *Contemplating Adultery: The Secret Life of a Victorian Woman* (New York: Fawcett Columbine, 1991), and Mitford, ed., *The Ladies of Alderley*, 178.

128. Porter, Macdonald, eds., *My Hand Will Write*, 200.

129. Porter, Macdonald, eds., *My Hand Will Write*, 192.

130. Janet Bathgate, *Aunt Janet's Legacy to Her Nieces: Recollections of Humble Life in Yarrow in the Beginning of the Century*, 2nd ed. (Selkirk: George Lewis & Co., 1895), 90, 92.

131. Christina Rossetti, *Goblin Market* (1862; repr., New York: Dover, 1983), 53.

132. Susan Lanser makes this point about women's friendships in the previous century in "Befriending the Body."

133. For an example of a starkly affectless diary that shows how little time or space working women had for sentiment or friendship, see the journal kept by a woman known only as Mrs. M. Palfreyman, servant, held with the Stanmore Papers in the British Library, Mss. ADD. 49276. For an example of a published memoir by a working-class woman in which friendships with female peers play a very small role, see Mary Ashford, *Life of a Licensed Victualler's Daughter* (London: Saunders & Otley, 1844). By contrast, the diary kept by Robert Louis Stevenson's nurse Alison Cunningham in 1863 when she traveled with the Stevenson family indicates her strong bond with fellow servant Catharine, to whom she also addressed diary entries: "My dear Cashie, O Woman, I like fine to write in this Journal of yours, but I would like better if I could speak to you." Robert T. Skinner, ed., *Cummy's Diary: A Diary Kept by R. L. Stevenson's Nurse Alison Cunningham While Travelling with Him on the Continent during 1863* (London: Chatto & Windus, 1926), 7. In a few examples of working women's autobiography, female friends fulfill a role similar to middle-class friends by facilitating courtship and marriage and fulfilling needs also met by spouses and kin. See Bathgate, *Aunt Janet's Legacy*, 149.

134. Ellen Ross, "Survival Networks: Women's Neighbourhood Sharing in London before World War I," *History Workshop Journal* 15 (1983), 4–27.

135. Lucy Luck, "A Little of My Life," first published in the *London Mercury* (1926), excerpted in Burnett, ed., *Annals of Labour*, 73, 74.

136. Cornelia Carr, ed. *Harriet Hosmer: Letters and Memories* (London: John Lane, The Bodley Head, 1913), 54, 55, 56.

137. For examples of close ties between mothers-in-law and daughters-in-law, see Beatrix Lister, ed., *Emma, Lady Ribblesdale: Letters and Diaries* (London: Privately printed at the Chiswick Press, 1930), 29; and Rowlinson, ed., *Personal Reminiscences of Augusta Becher*, 56.

138. Beck, ed. *Family Fragments*, 142.

139. Fred Edgcumbe, ed., *Letters of Fanny Brawne to Fanny Keats. 1820–1824* (London: Oxford University Press, 1936), esp. 16, 21, 22, 44.

140. Battersea, *Reminiscences*, 48; see also 51–52.

141. Baillie, ed., *Letters of Lady Augusta Stanley*, 319, 295.

142. Masterman, ed., *Mary Gladstone*, 277, 374.

143. Frances Anne Butler [Kemble], *Journal*, vol. 2 (London: John Murray, 1835), 75–76.

CHAPTER 2
Just Reading: Female Friendship and the Marriage Plot

1. George Eliot, *Middlemarch* (1871–1872; repr., Oxford: Oxford University Press World's Classics, 1996), 762. Further references are to this edition and appear in the text.

2. Anthony Trollope, *Barchester Towers* (1857; repr., London: Penguin Books, 1994), 245; Charlotte Brontë, *Shirley* (1849; repr., London: Penguin Books, 1985), 123. Further references are to these editions and appear in the text.

3. See Joseph Allen Boone, *Tradition Counter Tradition: Love and the Form of Fiction* (Chicago: University of Chicago Press, 1987); Rachel Blau DuPlessis, *Writing beyond the Ending: Narrative Strategies of Twentieth-Century Women Writers* (Bloomington: Indiana University Press, 1984); Roland Barthes, *S/Z: An Essay*, trans. Richard Miller (New York: Hill and Wang, 1974); Peter Brooks, *Reading for the Plot: Design and Intention in Narrative* (New York: Vintage, 1984); Tony Tanner, *Adultery in the Novel: Contract and Transgression* (Baltimore: Johns Hopkins University Press, 1979); Margaret Cohen, *The Sentimental Education of the Novel* (Princeton: Princeton University Press, 1999); Katie Trumpener, *Bardic Nationalism: The Romantic Novel and the British Empire* (Princeton: Princeton University Press, 1997); Catherine Gallagher, *The Industrial Reformation of English Fiction 1832–1867* (Chicago: University of Chicago Press, 1985); Nancy Armstrong, *Desire and Domestic Fiction: A Political History of the Novel* (New York: Oxford University Press, 1987); Nancy Miller, "Emphasis Added: Plots and Plausibilities in Women's Fiction," *PMLA* 96 (1981), 36–48; Bruce Robbins, *Upward Mobility and the Common Good* (Princeton: Princeton University Press, 2007); D. A. Miller, "Body Bildung and Textual Liberation," in *A New History of French Literature*, ed. Denis Hollier (Cambridge, Mass.: Harvard University Press, 1989), 681–87. For recent arguments that the novel is defined not by its marital endings but by the flirtations and promiscuous attachments and detachments that dominate its middle sections, see Richard Kaye, *The Flirt's Tragedy: Desire without End in Victorian and Edwardian Fiction* (Charlottesville: University Press of Virginia, 2002), and David Kurnick, "An Erotics of Detachment: *Middlemarch* and Novel-Reading as a Critical Practice," *ELH* (forthcoming).

4. Terry Castle, *The Apparitional Lesbian: Female Homosexuality and Modern Culture* (New York: Columbia University Press, 1993); Marilyn R. Farwell, "Heterosexual Plots and Lesbian Subtexts: Toward a Theory of Lesbian Narrative Space," in *Lesbian Texts and Contexts: Radical Revisions*, eds. Karla Jay and Joanne Glasgow (New York: New York University Press, 1990), 91–103; Lisa L. Moore, *Dangerous Intimacies: Toward a Sapphic History of the British Novel* (Durham, NC: Duke University Press, 1997); and Judith Roof, *Come As You Are: Sexuality and Narrative* (New York: Columbia University Press, 1996).

5. Eve Kosofsky Sedgwick, *Between Men: English Literature and Male Homosocial Desire* (New York: Columbia University Press, 1985).

6. Fredric Jameson, *The Political Unconscious: Narrative as a Socially Symbolic Act* (Ithaca: Cornell University Press, 1981), 49. Further references are to this edition and appear in the text.

7. In her reading of *Shirley*, Terry Castle equates marriage with the eradication of female same-sex bonds; *The Apparitional Lesbian*, 73. I offer an alternative reading of Brontë's novel later in this chapter. In *Women's Friendship in Literature* (New York: Columbia University Press, 1980), Janet Todd focuses on the pre-Victorian novel and argues, somewhat contradictorily, that female friendship both facilitates heterosexual marriage, and that to focus on female friendship is "to concentrate on a relationship and an ideology often opposing . . . heterosexual romance," 4, 6.

8. Eve Kosofsky Sedgwick offers reparative reading as an alternative to what she terms a "hermeneutics of suspicion" in the introduction to her edited collection of essays, *Novel Gazing: Queer Readings in Fiction* (Durham, NC: Duke University Press, 1997), 1–37, but focuses on reparative reading as an affective relation to the text rather than on questions of interpretation and method.

9. In *Sappho and the Virgin Mary: Same-Sex Love and the English Literary Imagination* (New York: Columbia University Press, 1996), Ruth Vanita notes the omnipresence of intimate connections between women in English literature but defines them as utopian opposition to marriage and the patriarchal family.

10. George Eliot, "Janet's Repentance," in *Scenes of Clerical Life* (1857; repr., London: Penguin, 1998), 290. On Eliot's friendship with Sara Hennell, which in youth Eliot described as a marriage, and on Eliot's representation of female friendship in her novels, see Bonnie Zimmerman, "'The Dark Eye Beaming': Female Friendship in George Eliot's Fictions," in *Lesbian Texts and Contexts*, eds. Jay and Glasgow, 126–144. Zimmerman concludes that female friendship in Eliot's novels is ephemeral because it "ultimately serve[s] a heterosexual world order," 140, but as I show here, the Victorian heterosexual order neither eliminated nor undermined female friendship.

11. Kathryn Bond Stockton argues that the novel ultimately "redomesticate[s]" both Rosamond and Dorothea by ending in marriage, a claim that depends on the assumption I challenge throughout this book: that for Victorians, female homoeroticism was incompatible with marriage between men and women. *God Between Their Lips: Desire Between Women in Irigaray, Brontë, Eliot* (Stanford: Stanford University Press, 1994), 247.

12. Vladimir Propp, *Morphology of the Folktale*, trans. Laurence Scott, ed. Louis A. Wagner, 2nd ed. (1928; repr., Austin: University of Texas Press, 1968), 83.

13. Brooks, *Reading for the Plot*, xiii, 37; D. A. Miller, *Narrative and Its Discontents: Problems of Closure in the Traditional Novel* (Princeton: Princeton University Press, 1981).

14. William Makepeace Thackeray, *Vanity Fair* (London: Penguin, 1978), 65, 147, 504. Further references are to this edition and appear in the text.

15. Claudia Johnson notes that only in the 1960s did the study of British fiction begin to focus on the marriage plot, defined as a narrativization of "the maturing process of heterosexual love"; "The Divine Miss Jane," in *Janeites: Austen's Disci-*

ples and Devotees, ed. Deidre Lynch (Princeton: Princeton University Press, 2000), 36.

xpNotes to Pages 81–89
Notes to Pages 74–81

16. George Eliot, *The Mill on the Floss* (1861; repr. London: Penguin, 1979), 471, 477. Further references are to this edition and appear in the text.

17. Wilkie Collins, *Man and Wife*, (1870; repr., Oxford: Oxford University Press, 1995), 372.

18. Frances Trollope, *The Widow Barnaby* (1839; repr., Phoenix Mill, UK: Alan Sutton Publishing, 1995). References are to this edition and appear in the text.

19. George Meredith, *Diana of the Crossways* (1885; repr., New York: Modern Library, n.d.), 447. In *Sappho and the Virgin Mary*, Ruth Vanita offers a detailed reading of Meredith's novel and its investment in love between women as an ideal toward which heterosexual married love should also aspire, 136–39, but her argument is stymied by adopting exclusively lesbian relationships as the teleology of desire. As a result, Vanita can only interpret heterosexuality as obstructing or compromising love between women, 141–42.

20. Harriet Martineau, *Deerbrook* (1839; repr., Garden City, NY: The Dial Press, 1984), 519.

21. In addition to the works cited in chapter 1, see Regenia Gagnier on public school memoirs in *Subjectivities: A History of Self-Representation in Britain, 1832–1920* (New York: Oxford University Press, 1991), 171–94; William Weaver, "A School-Boy's Story: Writing the Victorian Public Schoolboy Subject," *Victorian Studies* 46.3 (2004), 455–87; and Richard Dellamora, *Friendship's Bonds: Democracy and the Novel in Victorian England* (Philadelphia: University of Pennsylvania Press, 2004), which explores the tensions between Victorian fears of sodomy and their political ideals of male friendship. Sarah Rose Cole demonstrates the importance of intimate male friendship for Victorian fiction in a dissertation in progress at Columbia University.

22. Thomas Hardy, *Far from the Madding Crowd*, ed. Robert C. Schweik (1874; repr., New York: W. W. Norton & Co., 1986). References are to this edition and appear in the text.

23. Linda Shires argues that when Bathsheba confronts the corpses of Fanny and her dead infant, she identifies with Fanny as a victim of Troy; see "Narrative, Gender, and Power in *Far from the Madding Crowd*," in *The Sense of Sex: Feminist Perspectives on Hardy*, ed. Margaret R. Higonnet (Urbana: University of Illinois Press, 1993), 49–65. However, in that scene Bathsheba experiences a painful sense that Fanny has attained "ascendancy" over her by dying, 228. Only in the churchyard scene, which Shires does not discuss, does Bathsheba begin to express sympathy for the dead woman.

24. Charles Dickens, *David Copperfield* (1850; repr., London: Penguin, 1996). References are to this edition and appear in the text.

25. See Susan Schoenbauer Thurin, "The Relationship between Dora and Agnes," *Dickens Studies Newsletter* 12.4 (1981), 102–8; and Rebecca Rodolff, "What David Copperfield Remembers of Dora's Death," *The Dickensian* 77.1 (1981), 32–39.

26. Elizabeth Barrett Browning, *Aurora Leigh*, ed. Margaret Reynolds (1856; repr., New York: W. W. Norton & Company, 1996). References are to this edition and appear in the text.

27. For readings that detect, and attempt to reconcile, a tension between the poem's portrait of a woman writer and its marital ending, see Sandra M. Gilbert and Susan Gubar, *The Madwoman in the Attic: The Woman Writer and the Nineteenth-Century Literary Imagination* (New Haven: Yale University Press, 1979), 575–80, and DuPlessis, *Writing Beyond the Ending*, 84–85.

28. On the antisentimental cynicism of French realism, see Cohen, *The Sentimental Education of the Novel*, and Franco Moretti, *The Way of the World* (1987; repr., London: Verso, 2000).

29. Dorothy Mermin notes how Aurora simultaneously proposes marriage, sororal kinship, and coparenting to Marian in *Elizabeth Barrett Browning: The Origins of a New Poetry* (Chicago: University of Chicago Press, 1989), 193, 207.

30. See Joyce Zonana, "The Embodied Muse: Elizabeth Barrett Browning's *Aurora Leigh* and Feminist Poetics," *Tulsa Studies in Women's Literature* 8.2 (1989), 243.

31. One of the most powerful points Sedgwick makes in *Between Men* is that when two men exchange a woman, they form a homosocial bond. Sedgwick focuses on the patriarchal constraints that make this proposition possible only between men, but texts as politically disparate as Dickens's novel and Barrett Browning's poem demonstrate that Victorians were also able to imagine women exchanging men. For an anthropological account of the social bonds of indebtedness established between those who give and receive gifts, see Marcel Mauss, *The Gift: Forms and Functions of Exchange in Archaic Societies*, trans. Ian Cunnison (1924; repr., New York: Norton, 1967). I return to the relationship between debt and marriage in the final chapter of this book.

32. Sandra M. Gilbert poses the suggestive question, "Is Marian the womb that gives new life to Aurora's and Romney's light?" in "From *Patria* to *Matria*: Elizabeth Barrett Browning's Risorgimento," *PMLA* 99.1 (1984), 207.

33. In addition to Castle's argument, cited above, that the novel's final marriages undo female bonds by replacing them with patriarchal ones, see Linda C. Hunt, "Sustenance and Balm: The Question of Female Friendship in *Shirley* and *Villette*," *Tulsa Studies in Women's Literature* 1.1 (1982), 55, 59; and Pauline Nestor, *Female Friendships and Communities: Charlotte Brontë, George Eliot, Elizabeth Gaskell* (Oxford: Clarendon Press, 1985), which emphasizes the novel's portrayal of female friendship as antipathetic to the male world, 117. In *Charlotte Brontë and Female Desire* (New York: Peter Lang, 2003), Jin-Ok Kim notes that the novel depicts homoeroticism as promoting heterosexual marriage and marriage as sustaining and incorporating homoeroticism, 72, 78, but contradictorily equates homoeroticism with the erasure of men, 83.

34. On the similarities and contrasts between the marriages that conclude the novel and "the world of work" it represents, 186, see John Plotz, *The Crowd: British Literature and Public Politics* (Berkeley: University of California Press, 2000), 154–93.

35. On feminine and feminist modes, see Elaine Showalter, *A Literature of Their Own: British Women Novelists from Brontë to Lessing* (Princeton: Princeton University Press, 1977).

36. See Ellen Moers, *Literary Women* (New York: Doubleday, 1976), 254.

37. Charlotte Brontë, *Villette* (1853; repr., London: Penguin Books, 1979). References are to this edition and appear in the text.

38. On repressed desire, see Gilbert and Gubar, "The Buried Life of Lucy Snowe," in *The Madwoman in the Attic*, 399–440, and Mary Jacobus, "The Buried Letter: Feminism and Romanticism in *Villette*," in *Women Writing and Writing about Women*, ed. Mary Jacobus (London: Croom Helm, 1979), 43–54. On the eroticization of repression itself, see John Kucich, *Repression in Victorian Fiction: Charlotte Brontë, George Eliot, and Charles Dickens*, (Berkeley: University of California Press, 1987). In *Libidinal Currents: Sexuality and the Shaping of Modernism* (Chicago: University of Chicago Press, 1998), Joseph Allen Boone reads the novel's disruption of narrative convention as allegorizing its heroine's destabilizing desires, 33–61. In "The Queerness of Lucy Snowe," *Nineteenth-Century Contexts* 18.4 (1995), Ann Weinstone argues for an "anti-straight" rather than lesbian reading of the novel, 368. Terry Castle excerpts *Villette* in *The Literature of Lesbianism: A Historical Anthology from Ariosto to Stonewall* (New York: Columbia University Press, 2003).

39. The characterization of Lucy as "unamiable" comes from a review of *Villette* in the *Dublin Review* 34 (March 1853), 188. Andrew Lang faulted Lucy Snowe for evincing "the bitterness of personal sarcasm," in "Charlotte Brontë," *Good Words* 30 (1889), 237.

40. See Boone, *Libidinal Currents*, 33–61.

41. Christina Crosby draws attention to Lucy's identification with de Hamal in "Charlotte Brontë's Haunted Text," *Studies in English Literature* 24.4 (1984), 701–15.

CHAPTER 3
Dressing Up and Dressing Down the Feminine Plaything

1. *A Victorian Diarist: Extracts from the Journals of Mary, Lady Monkswell*, ed. Hon. E.C.F. Collier (London: John Murray, 1944), 14; Julia Pardoe, *Lady Arabella: or the Adventures of a Doll* (London: Kerby & Son, 1856), 51; and "A Rejoicer in the Restoration of the Rod," *Englishwoman's Domestic Magazine* 8.63 (1870), 189; hereafter referred to as *EDM*.

2. The classic sites of this argument are John Berger, *Ways of Seeing* (London: British Broadcasting Corporation and Penguin Books, 1972), 47; and Laura Mulvey, "Visual Pleasure and Narrative Cinema," *Screen* 16.3 (1975), 6–18. For a recent attempt to complicate the sexual politics of the gaze for the Victorians, see Ellen Bayuk Rosenman, *Unauthorized Pleasures: Accounts of Victorian Erotic Experience* (Ithaca, NY: Cornell University Press, 2003), which pays special attention to the uncertainties of the male gaze, and to the ways in which women's autoerotic pleasure "rejects heterosexuality" (52, 87). I focus here on female homo-

eroticism as an element of Victorian women's heterosexuality, not as a rebellion against it.

3. Margaret Beetham, *A Magazine of Her Own? Domesticity and Desire in the Woman's Magazine 1800–1914* (London: Routledge, 1996), 78, 39. Abigail Solomon-Godeau similarly writes in "The Other Side of Venus: The Visual Economy of Feminine Display" that "while images of femininity may be consumed by women as well as men—think here of any fashion magazine—their material production and ideological underpinnings are unambiguously patriarchal," 114, in Victoria de Grazia and Ellen Furlough, eds., *The Sex of Things: Gender and Consumption in Historical Perspective* (Berkeley: University of California Press, 1996).

4. On the homoerotics of Barbie dolls, see Erica Rand, *Barbie's Queer Accessories* (Durham, NC: Duke University Press, 1995). For a groundbreaking essay on the homoerotic structure of contemporary fashion photography, see Diana Fuss, "Fashion and the Homospectatorial Look," in *On Fashion*, eds. Shari Benstock and Suzanne Ferris (New Brunswick, NJ: Rutgers University Press, 1994), 211–32.

5. Roland Barthes, *Sade/Fourier/Loyola*, trans. Richard Miller (New York: Hill & Wang, 1976), 3–6, 64.

6. See Jessica Benjamin, *Like Subjects, Love Objects: Essays on Recognition and Sexual Difference* (New Haven: Yale University Press, 1995), 180, 204–7; and Lisa Z. Sigel, *Governing Pleasures: Pornography and Social Change in England, 1815–1914* (New Brunswick, NJ: Rutgers University Press, 2002).

7. On fantasy as the primary aim of nineteenth-century pornography, as opposed to political satire in early modern pornography, see Lynn Hunt, *The Invention of Pornography: Obscenity and the Origins of Modernity, 1500–1800* (New York: Zone Books, 1996), 10, 42. Many contemporary critics identify pornography with fantasy, but there is little consensus about how to theorize fantasy. In *The Other Victorians: A Study of Sexuality and Pornography in Mid-Nineteenth-Century England* (New York: Basic Books, 1966), Steven Marcus equates fantasy with ideology, 1, but also argues that it reveals the truth of Victorian society, 100. Sigel understands fantasy as an expression of what a culture finds possible and thinkable but which its adherents do not necessarily practice, 2, 13, and notes that fantasies recycle what society sexually prohibits, 12–13. Object-relations psychoanalytic theorist Jessica Benjamin defines pornography as deliberately working the disjunction between fantasy and reality; 45, 188, 195–96. She thus asserts that pornographic fantasies appeal precisely because they allow people to be aroused by representations of things they would never really want to do, 175–76. On desire, fantasy, and consumer culture, see Colin Campbell, *The Romantic Ethic and the Spirit of Modern Consumerism* (Oxford: Blackwell, 1987).

8. Werner Sombart, *Luxury and Capitalism*, vol. 1, trans. W. R. Dittmar (New York: Columbia University Department of Social Science, 1939), 90, 143.

9. Diana Fuss offers the best account of how identification depends on difference and cannot be securely distinguished from desire, in *Identification Papers* (New York: Routledge, 1995). In *Barbie's Queer Accessories*, Rand argues that contemporary heterosexuality involves an eroticized identification with one's own gender; girls identify with a voluptuous doll they also desire, "dress, undress, fondle, and obsess over," 195. For critiques of the heterosexual circularity embedded

in the distinction between desire and identification, see Eve Kosofksy Sedgwick, *Epistemology of the Closet* (Berkeley: University of California Press, 1991), 62; Judith Butler, *Bodies that Matter*, 239; Michael Warner, "Homo-Narcissism; or, Heterosexuality," in *Engendering Men: The Question of Male Feminist Criticism*, eds. Joseph A. Boone and Michael Cadden (New York: Routledge, 1990), 190–206; and Tim Dean, "Homosexuality and the Problem of Otherness," in Tim Dean and Christopher Lane, eds., *Homosexuality & Psychoanalysis* (Chicago: University of Chicago Press, 2001), 120–43.

10. See Peter Bailey, "Parasexuality and Glamour: The Victorian Barmaid as Cultural Prototype," on the distance and separation between object and beholder built into the very concept of glamour, which "heightens desire"; *Gender & History* 2.2 (Summer 1990), 152.

11. My definition of the erotic has some affinities with Jean LaPlanche and Jean-Baptiste Pontalis's influential definition of sexuality in "Fantasy and the Origins of Sexuality," *The International Journal of Psycho-Analysis* 49 (1968), 1–18. For LaPlanche and Pontalis, fantasy originates in "auto-erotism" or "the repeated disjunction of sexual desire and non-sexual functions" so that "sexuality is detached from any natural object, and is handed over to fantasy, and, by this very fact, starts existing as sexuality" (17). Sexuality thus is defined by its separation from physical acts or body parts; while some fantasies revolve around the problem of sexual difference, that difference is not itself the source of sexuality.

12. Walter Benjamin, *The Arcades Project*, trans. Howard Eiland and Kevin McLaughlin (Cambridge, Mass.: The Belknap Press of Harvard University Press, 1999), 66.

13. For a representative sampling of feminist essays on fashion, see Benstock and Ferris, eds., *On Fashion*. On fashion and fashion plates as the fetishization, commodification, and objectification of women, see Roland Barthes, *The Fashion System*, trans. Matthew Ward and Richard Howard (New York: Hill and Wang, 1983), 242; and Anne Higonnet, *Berthe Morisot's Images of Women* (Cambridge, Mass.: Harvard University Press, 1992), 86, 91–93, 95. On fashion as a vehicle for women's erotic expression, see Valerie Steele, *Fashion and Eroticism: Ideals of Feminine Beauty from the Victorian Era to the Jazz Age* (New York: Oxford University Press, 1985), 5, 3. See also the special issue of *Victorian Literature and Culture* 30.1 (2002) on "Victorian Fashions." For a Victorian who criticized fashion as irrational and unnatural, see Luke Limner [pseud. John Leighton], *Madre Natura versus the Moloch of Fashion: A Social Essay*, 4th ed. (London: Chatto and Windus, 1874). The Victorian dress-reform movement expressed feminist resistance to fashion; see Stella Mary Newton, *Health, Art and Reason: Dress Reformers of the 19th Century* (London: John Murray, 1974), while antifeminist Eliza Lynn Linton's "The Girl of the Period," *Saturday Review* (March 14, 1868), railed against fashion for making young women less ladylike and more like men.

14. For sociological accounts of fashion, see Steele, Philippe Perrot, *Fashioning the Bourgeoisie: A History of Clothing in the Nineteenth Century*, trans. Richard Bienvenu (Princeton: Princeton University Press, 1994); Gilles Lipovetsky, *The Empire of Fashion: Dressing Modern Democracy*, trans. Catherine Porter (Princeton: Princeton University Press, 1994); and Diana Crane, *Fashion and Its Social Agendas: Class, Gender, and Identity in Clothing* (Chicago: University of Chicago

Press, 2000). On the essence of fashion as variety and innovation, see Benjamin, 99, Barthes, 273, and Lipovetsky, 7–8, 16.

15. See Steele, 19, and Crane, 7.

16. Perrot, 99, 91, 93.

17. On fashion as exemplifying the cyclical nature of history, see Agnes Brooks Young, *Recurring Cycles of Fashion: 1760–1934* (New York: Harper, 1937), ix–8. In *The Painter of Modern Life*, Charles Baudelaire argued that modern fashions embody the ephemeral and the universal; trans. Jonathan Mayne (1863; repr., New York: Da Capo Press, 1964), 1–3. For a book-length exploration of fashion as a "paradigm of modern culture," see Ulrich Lehmann, *Tigersprung: Fashion and Modernity* (Cambridge, Mass.: MIT Press, 2000), xv.

18. On innovation in fashion as a requirement of capitalism, see Benjamin, 77, and Perrot, 25.

19. Barthes, 258. See also James Laver, *Clothes* (New York: Horizon Press, 1953), in which he argues that to be in fashion is "to be at home in the world, or rather . . . at home in one's epoch," xiv.

20. See Christina Walkley, *The Way to Wear 'em: 150 years of Punch on Fashion* (London: Peter Owen, 1985), and Doris Langley Moore, *Fashion through Fashion Plates 1771–1970* (London: Ward Lock Ltd., 1971), 28.

21. For circulation figures for fashion magazines, see Higonnet, *Berthe Morisot's Images of Women*, 91.

22. On the definition and history of fashion plates, see Stella Blum, ed., *Ackermann's Costume Plates: Women's Fashions in England, 1812–1828* (New York: Dover, 1978); Vanda Foster, *A Visual History of Costume: The Nineteenth Century* (London: B. T. Batsford, 1984); Madeleine Ginsburg, *An Introduction to Fashion Illustration* (London: Compton Press, 1980); Vyvyan Holland, *Hand Coloured Fashion Plates 1770 to 1899* (London: B. T. Batsford, 1955); JoAnne Olian, *Full-Color Victorian Fashions: 1870–1893* (Mineola, NY: Dover, 1999); and Moore, *Fashion through Fashion Plates*, 10.

23. According to Elizabeth Ewing, the first English periodical to publish a pattern was *The World of Fashion* in August 1850; *Everyday Dress 1650–1900* (London: B. T. Batsford, 1984), 119. From the 1850s on, the *Englishwoman's Domestic Magazine* regularly included needlework and dress patterns along with fashion plates.

24. Olian makes the connection between newspapers and fashion plates, v, and Ginsburg notes that fashion plates were a form of *rapportage*, 3.

25. Beetham, 17, 37–38, 46, 48–54, 34. On the transition from 1830s Romantic magazines emphasizing secular literature for moral improvement to 1860s magazines that were more practical and political, see Jeffrey Auerbach, "What They Read: Mid-Nineteenth Century English Women's Magazines and the Emergence of a Consumer Culture," *Victorian Periodicals Review* 30.2 (1997),121–22.

26. Beetham, 59, 78, 8, 14. See also Kay Boardman, "'A Material Girl in a Material World': The Fashionable Female Body in Victorian Women's Magazines," *Journal of Victorian Culture* 3.1 (Spring 1998), 96.

27. *EDM* 3.25 (1867), 54. Some steel engravings were hand-colored by anonymous female home workers until lithography became the dominant technique in

the 1880s. See Alexandra Buxton, *Discovering 19th-Century Fashions: A Look at the Changes in Fashion through the Victoria & Albert Museum's Dress Collection* (Cambridge: Hobsons Publishing, 1989), 8, and Elizabeth Wilson and Lou Taylor, *Through the Looking Glass: A History of Dress from 1860 to the Present Day* (London: BBC Books, 1989), 35.

28. See Ginsburg, 10; and Olian, v.

29. On the Colin sisters, see Ginsburg, 10; Holland, 73; Moore, 16–17; and Higonnet, *Berthe Morisot's Images of Women*, 97. Holland lists several other Frenchwomen who produced fashion plates, 152–54.

30. See Anne Schirrmeister, "La Dernière Mode: Berthe Morisot and Costume," in T. J. Edelstein, *Perspectives on Morisot* (New York: Hudson Hills Press, 1990), 105.

31. Moore comments on the absence of blondes and redheads in fashion plates, 88.

32. For men's fashion plates, see Diana de Marly, *Fashion for Men: An Illustrated History* (New York: Holmes & Meier, 1985).

33. Anne Higonnet has noted the "discreetly ambiguous relationship" between female figures in fashion plates; *Berthe Morisot's Images of Women*, 113.

34. On inconstancy as a feature of fashion, see Lipovetsky, 4.

35. On the lorgnette as a fashion accessory associated with the anxieties provoked by new forms of realist spectacle and female vision, see Jann Matlock, "Censoring the Realist Gaze," in *Spectacles of Realism: Gender, Body, Genre*, eds. Margaret Cohen and Christopher Prendergast (Minneapolis: University of Minnesota Press, 1995), 28–65.

36. The convention of posing two women together who touch each other was one that fashion plates shared with erotic photography of the time, in which women were often portrayed arm-in-arm, or seated close together, without engaging in any overtly sexual activity; in erotic photographs, women are either nude or dressed in more revealing clothing than the figures in fashion plates. See, for example, the image of "Paphian Revels," from *The Swell's Night Guide through the Metropolis* (1841), reproduced in Peter Fryer, *Mrs. Grundy: Studies in English Prudery* (London: Dennis Dobson, 1964), 29.

37. Fashion plates lack all the elements that Kate Flint has identified as implanting narrative in images: sequencing, symbolic elements and details, and expressive figures; *The Victorians and the Visual Imagination* (Cambridge: Cambridge University Press, 2000), 207–8, 213.

38. On the blankness of the faces depicted in fashion plates, see Olian, vi; on how blankness promotes projection and fantasy, see Rand, 40.

39. Gilles Néret, *Erotica: 19th Century: From Courbet to Gaugin* (Cologne: Taschen, 2001), reproduces a series of French lithographs that turn children's games into erotic adult ones, including an image of one man and three women playing blindman's bluff, 45.

40. On the eroticization of girlhood, see Pamela Tamarkin Reis, "Victorian Centerfold: Another Look at Millais's *Cherry Ripe*," *Victorian Studies* 35.2 (1992), 201–5. It is difficult to date exactly when fashion imagery began to include girls on a regular basis, but in 1868, every fashion plate published in the *Young Englishwoman* depicted two women and a girl.

41. Annabella Maria Browne's *Live Dolls: A Tale for Children of All Ages* (London: Partridge, 1874), approvingly described children as an adult mother's "live dolls," 67; in another children's book, a mother tells her daughter, "I've got a Dolly," and the daughter replies without hesitation, "Yes, I know. . . . I'm your Dolly"; Russell H. Rutherford, *My Dolly* (London: Marcus Ward, 1877), 74.

42. *Letters Addressed to the Editor of the Englishwoman's Domestic Magazine on the Whipping of Girls, and the General Corporal Punishment of Children* (London: Office, Warwick House, Paternoster Row, April 1870), 4; hereafter referred to as *SC*, for "Supplemental Conversazione."

43. *SC* 1 (April 1870), 1. On the eroticization of corporal punishment in Victorian culture, see James R. Kincaid, *Child-Loving: The Erotic Child and Victorian Culture* (New York: Routledge, 1992), who argues that the scene of punishment ultimately becomes a ludic and theatrical one in which distinctions between adult and child begin to break down and what appears to be a fable of domination becomes one of merger, 261–67. Where Kincaid finds a narrative, I find superimposition; within the correspondence column or within a given letter, conflicting fantasies and stances coexisted without effacing each other. I emphasize the fantasy of domination because it has been so neglected as an element of Victorian women's subjectivity.

44. The *EDM* was advertised in the bible in 1871; see Mary Wilson Carpenter, *Imperial Bibles, Domestic Bodies; Women, Sexuality, and Religion in the Victorian Market* (Athens: Ohio University Press, 2003), 63.

45. For details on the *EDM*'s circulation and price, see Holland, 146–47, 152, and Auerbach, 122. Beetham notes that two pence was "unusually cheap" for a monthly magazine that provided thirty-two pages of double-column type plus illustrations, 62, 64.

46. For an article sympathetic to the Society for the Employment of Women, see *EDM* 2.15 (1866), 128. Marion Diamond notes that the *EDM* often championed feminist causes; see "Maria Rye and *The Englishwoman's Domestic Magazine*," *Victorian Periodicals Review* 30.1 (1997), 5–16.

47. Martha Somerville, *Personal Recollections, from Early Life to Old Age, of Mary Somerville, with Selections from Her Correspondence* (London: John Murray, 1873), 47.

48. *EDM* 6.49 (1869), 55.

49. Samuel Beeton himself sided against corporal punishment as "degrading and indecent"; *EDM* 3.29 (1867), 277.

50. *SC* (April 1870), 4, 7.

51. *SC* (April 1870), 15, 3; *SC* (June 1870), 3.

52. *EDM* 3.26 (1867), 109; responses in 3.27, (1867), 165–66.

53. *EDM* 8.62 (1870), 126–27; 8.63 (1870), 189–90.

54. *EDM* 8.63 (1870), 189.

55. *SC* (July 1870), 3.

56. See *SC* (June 1870), 3; *SC* (April 1870), 1.

57. See Walter Kendrick, *The Secret Museum: Pornography in Modern Culture* (Berkeley: University of California Press, 1987), and Sigel, *Governing Pleasures*, 12.

58. In his introduction to a reprint of the Christmas number of the *Pearl* (1881; repr. Atlanta: Pendulum Books, 1867), Jean Chouart notes that pornography magazines parodied family magazines; the *Pearl* was "a complete mirror-image of the publications it was parodying in story, style, content, structure and format," 10.

59. *SC* (August 1870), n.p.

60. See *Experiences of Flagellation: A Series of Remarkable Instances of Whipping Inflicted on Both Sexes, with Curious Anecdotes of Ladies Fond of Administering Birch Discipline*, compiled by an Amateur Flagellant (London: printed for private circulation, 1885); the author explains that he or she draws on "a remarkable exchange of opinion appearing . . . in our amiable contemporary *The Englishwoman's Domestic Journal*," 14. See also *The Whippingham Papers: A Collection of Contributions in Prose and Verse, Chiefly by the Author of the 'Romance of Chastisement'* (London: 1888), 19–21.

61. Pisanus Fraxi [Henry Spencer Ashbee], *Bibliography of Prohibited Books*, vol. 1 (1877; repr., New York: Jack Brussel, 1962), xli.

62. For assertions that men were the only producers and consumers of nineteenth-century pornography, see Hunt, *The Invention of Pornography*, 36, and Peter Gay, *The Bourgeois Experience: Victoria to Freud*, vol. 1, *Education of the Senses* (New York: Oxford University Press, 1984), 376.

63. Edward J. Bristow, *Vice and Vigilance: Purity Movements in Britain since 1700* (Dublin: Gill and Macmillan, 1977), 49.

64. Since pornography was published illicitly, works were not sent to the British Library for copyright deposit and there is therefore no consistent record of what was published. On the difficulties of obtaining accurate information about Victorian pornography, see Ashbee, *Bibliography*; Sigel, *Governing Pleasures*, 6; and Patrick J. Kearney, *The Private Case: An Annotated Bibliography of the Private Case Erotica in the British (Museum) Library* (London: Jay Landesman Ltd., 1981). For information about men involved in writing, printing, publishing, and circulating Victorian erotic literature, see Sigel, *Governing Pleasures*, and Peter Mendes, *Clandestine Erotic Fiction in English 1800–1930* (Aldershot: Scolar Press, 1993), 3–23. For the urban networks through which pornography was sold, see Lynda Nead, *Victorian Babylon: People, Streets and Images in Nineteenth-Century London* (New Haven: Yale University Press, 2000), 161–97. Made possible by the expansion of print technology, pornography also exposed the contradictions of print culture's democratic potential, since the category of obscenity limited access to pornography, and the increasing cost of pornographic materials made them into exclusive luxury items; see Kendrick, *The Secret Museum*; Hunt, *The Invention of Pornography*, 13; and Sigel, *Governing Pleasures*, 21, 25–26, 56.

65. For examples of British women reading, writing, publishing, and selling pornography, see Steven Marcus, *The Other Victorians*, 110, 281; Bristow, *Vice and Vigilance*, 42; Sigel, 85, 21; and Nead, *Victorian Babylon*, 183, 197. On the female author of *Julie ou j'ai sauvé ma rose*, see Kathryn Norberg, "Making Sex Public: Félicité de Choiseul-Meuse and the Lewd Novel," in *Going Public: Women and Publishing in Early Modern France*, eds. Elizabeth C. Goldsmith and Dena Goodman (Ithaca: Cornell University Press, 1995), 161–75. Choiseul-

Meuse included sex scenes between women in her works, and Norberg argues that Choiseul-Meuse imagined young women as the audience for her sexually explicit tales, 166, 170. She notes that Choiseul-Meuse also wrote a didactic book for girls, yet another example of the overlap between obscene literature and feminine culture, 162.

66. The *Times* also reported that a police officer purchased a book from Cannon after being introduced to him by a female acquaintance. For the police officer's testimony, see the *Times*, December 1, 1830, 6. On Cannon's wife, see Ian McCalman, *Radical Underworld: Prophets, Revolutionaries, and Pornographers in London, 1795–1840* (Cambridge: Cambridge University Press, 1988), 213, 216.

67. *SC* (April 1870), 7.

68. Beetham believes that Beeton himself did not make up the correspondence, as some alleged at the time, and that the letters are significant even if written by fetishists, 84. Mary S. Hartman notes that all letter-writers had to include a separate page with their name and address in order to have a letter published in the *EDM*; "Child Abuse and Self-Abuse: Two Victorian Cases," *History of Childhood Quarterly* 2.2 (1974), 240.

69. "A Lady Signing Experience," *EDM* 8.63 (1870), 190.

70. Lady Anne Noel Blunt, British Library Ms. ADD. 53817, vol. 1, n.p.; closest dated entry is July 19, 1850.

71. For a contemporary discussion of women's spanking fantasies that underscores their theatricality, see Eve Kosofsky Sedgwick, "A Poem is Being Written," in Sedgwick, *Tendencies* (Durham, NC: Duke University Press, 1993), 177–214.

72. No matter what its sex in the text, Steven Marcus declares, the figure being beaten "is originally, finally, and always a boy," and Victorian pornography encodes regressive fantasies that attempt to express forbidden incestuous and homosexual urges. He characterizes flagellation fantasies as "a kind of last-ditch compromise with and defense against homosexuality," a flight from the mature genital heterosexuality that he considers the desired goal of all human development; *The Other Victorians*, 260. For a similar view, see Peter Webb, "Victorian Erotica," in *The Sexual Dimension in Literature*, ed. Alan Bold (New York: Barnes and Noble, 1983), 92. Marcus's interpretation acknowledges, however, that Victorian flagellation literature frequently depicted men and women birching girls. For examples of men birching girls, see *The Cremorne*, no. 1 (1851), color plate; and Mrs. Martinet, *The Quintessence of Birch Discipline* (London: Privately printed, 1870), 22. In addition to the many examples of women whipping women cited throughout this chapter, see *Venus School Mistress* (n.d.; repr., New York: Blue Moon Books 1987), 44; "Seduction Unveiled: Female Boarding Schools," *The Exquisite*, no. 109, 68–69; "On Flagellation and Female Boarding Schools," *The Exquisite*, no. 119, 120; and *The Birchen Bouquet* (Birchington-on-Sea: 1881), which included a description of a woman who whips a girl who "had committed several obscenities with little girls," including being "caught playing at the game of mock husband," 9.

73. *Letters from a Friend in Paris*, vol. 2 (London: 1874), 56; *The New Ladies' Tickler; or, the Adventures of Lady Lovesport and the Audacious Harry* (London: Printed for the Bookseller, 1866), 9. Other Victorian pornographic texts that rep-

resent incest between female relatives, male relatives, and male and female relatives, include: *The Romance of Lust* (n.p., n.d.); *Nunnery Tales* (London: Printed for the Booksellers, n.d.); *Library Illustrative of Social Progress*, no. 1 (London: Printed for G. Peacock, 1[8]77), 16, 24; *The New Epicurean* (London: Printed for Thomas Longtool, Rogerwell Street, 1875). I find no support for Lisa Sigel's claim that incest gained popularity only late in the nineteenth century; *Governing Pleasures*, 3.

74. In addition to examples already cited in reference to the flagellation literature, see various plates in *The Exquisite,* including nos. 46, 47, 48, 102, 103, 114; "The Spirit of the Ring; containing many curious anecdotes of the celebrated Marie Antoinette," in *The Exquisite,* no. 116, 92–94, and no. 117, 103; "The Loves of Sappho," in *The Exquisite,* no. 7, 82–83, which notes that women in the present still feel sapphic love and, unusually for this period, that sapphic love is similar to passion between men, 82; *The New Ladies' Tickler; The Festival of the Passions*, vol. 2 (n.p., 1863); *The Romance of Lust*, 31; "The Secret Life of Linda Brent; A Curious History of Slave Life and Slave Wrongs," *The Cremorne*, no. 2 (1851), 45; *Nunnery Tales*, vol. 1, 12–13, 15–17, 94–100; vol. 2, 122; *Letters from a Friend in Paris*, 24; and *The New Epicurean*, 23–35, 79, which also discusses a man's lust for his wife's male lover, 70. *The Elements of Tuition, and Modes of Punishment* (London: Printed for the Bookseller, n.d.) describes girls being sold dildos by their schoolmistress's maidservant, 24. See also prints collected in Néret, *Erotica*, 84, 85, 112, 113, 119, 131, and entries in Pisanus Fraxi [Henry Spencer Ashbee], *Catena Librorum Tacendorum* (1885), which describe nineteenth-century texts that included sex between women. Texts that describe sex between men, in addition to those cited elsewhere, include "The Secret Life of Linda Brent" in *The Cremorne*, no. 1 (1851), 15; Martinet, *The Quintessence of Birch Discipline*, 30; *Letters from a Friend*, 44, which also shows a woman dressing as a man in order to seduce her husband, 60–61; and James Campbell Reddie, *The Amatory Experiences of a Surgeon*, reprinted in *The Libertine Reader* (North Hollywood: Brandon House, 1968), 192–94, which also discusses Sappho and sex between women, 201.

75. See, for example, the *Pearl* Christmas annual, 22, and *The Birchen Bouquet*, 12, 15.

76. *The Sins of the Cities of the Plain. Or the Recollections of a Mary-Ann with Short Essays on Sodomy and Tribadism* (London: Privately printed, 1881), vol. 1, 30–31, 76. In "Cruising in Queer Street: Streetwalking Men in Late-Victorian London," Mark W. Turner calls *Sins* "one of the few books of exclusively homosexual pornography from the late nineteenth century"; in *In a Queer Place: Sexuality and Belonging in British and European Contexts* eds., Kate Chedgzoy, Emma Francis, Murray Pratt (Aldershot: Ashgate, 2002), 92. For an example of how even a short pornographic tale would combine sex between men, between women, and between men and women, see the *Pearl*, 22–27.

77. See Hunt, *The Invention of Pornography*, on pornography's affinity to empiricism; Kendrick, *The Secret Museum*, on pornography and classification; and Frances Ferguson, *Pornography, the Theory: What Utilitarianism Did to Action* (Chicago: University of Chicago Press, 2004), on merit.

78. Mrs. H. R. [Mary] Haweis, *The Art of Beauty* (New York: Harper & Brothers, 1878), 12, 15; Haweis links dress to individuality, originality, and freedom as opposed to conformity, 15–16.

79. Mary S. Hartman notes that the English began to see corporal punishment of children as less acceptable starting in the 1840s, but it was still widely practiced and considered a parental prerogative; "Child-Abuse and Self-Abuse," 239. Deborah Gorham notes that physical punishment of children was the norm, a legacy of the Puritan belief that children's sinful wills needed to be broken, but that parents believed equally strongly in the Enlightenment credo that those disciplining children should use love and reason; *The Victorian Girl and the Feminine Ideal* (London: Croom Helm, 1982), 76–77. Historian Linda Pollock shows that more parents used strict discipline and physical punishment in the nineteenth century than in earlier ones, but that the majority of children did not experience strict discipline even then; *Forgotten Children: Parent-Child Relations from 1500 to 1900* (Cambridge: Cambridge University Press, 1983), 184–85. James Walvin notes that corporal punishment was common in all classes; *A Child's World: A Social History of English Childhood 1800–1914* (Harmondsworth: Penguin Books, 1982), 47. The literature and imagery of nineteenth-century childhood suggests that physical punishment was a real feature of family life. Susan Lasdun's *Making Victorians: The Drummond Children's World 1827–1832* (London: Victor Gollancz, 1983), a collection of pictures done by the Drummond children, shows two images of a girl about to be birched, in one case by her mother, 46, 48.

80. *EDM* 6.49 (1869), 52–3.

81. *EDM* 5.46 (1868), 221.

82. *EDM* 8.63 (1870), 190.

83. *EDM* 5.46 (1868), 221.

84. *SC* (May 1870), 4; *SC* (April 1870), 3.

85. Margaret Anson, *The Order of the Rod* (1868; repr., London: Senate, 1997), 40; first published as *The Merry Order of St. Bridget*, 40.

86. *The Order of the Rod*, 16, 34.

87. *The Romance of Chastisement* (n.p., 1870), 12, 55, 13.

88. *SC* (April 1870), 1.

89. *SC* (April 1870), 5.

90. *The Order of the Rod*, 78.

91. *EDM* 8.63 (1870), 190.

92. Frances Ferguson connects the importance of rank, reward, and punishment in pornography to its modern preoccupation with the utilitarian project of finding ways to visibly incorporate individuals into a social system; *Pornography, the Theory*, 33, 21, 19.

93. *The Order of the Rod*, 18.

94. *EDM* 5.48 (1868), in a letter describing the effect of whippings at a "strict boarding establishment," 327.

95. *EDM* 4.41 (1868), 278.

96. *EDM* 5.45 (1868), 168; *EDM* 3.27 (1867), 165–66.

97. *EDM* 5.47 (1868), 280; *SC* (August 1870), 2.

98. *Indecent Whipping*, (n.p.: n.d.) 12.

99. *SC* (April 1870), 4.

100. *SC* (October 1870), 4.

101. *The Romance of Chastisement*, 67.

102. Ibid. 27–28.

103. Ibid., 57, 60.

104. *Library Illustrative of Social Progress*, no. 1, 7–8, 31.

105. *The Birchen Bouquet*, 3.

106. *The Boudoir*, 206.

107. "The Charm: A Dialogue for the 'Englishwoman's Conversazione'," in *Venus School Mistress, or Birchen Sports* (New York: Blue Moon Books, 1987), 54, 57. This book reprints a 1917 reprint of a nineteenth-century text originally published with the false date of 1788.

108. Theorists of obscene words argue that they represent attempts to close the gap between representation and action by investing language with substance and agency. See Sandor Ferenczi, "On Obscene Words," in which he argues that obscene words are "invested with motor elements" and become more gestural than representational, more referential than symbolic, so that uttering them seems to be in and of itself a sexual act; in *Sex in Psycho-analysis* (New York: Dover Publications, 1956), 120.

109. *Indecent Whipping*, 8.

110. *The Birchen Bouquet*, 7.

111. Ibid., 42–43.

112. Lilian Whiting, ed., *Anna Elizabeth Klumpke: Memoirs of an Artist* (privately printed, n.d.), 13.

113. Ibid., 44.

114. Clara Bradford, *Ethel's Adventures in Doll Country*, ill. T. Pym (London: John F. Shaw, [1880]), 50. Further references are to this edition and appear in the text.

115. Max von Boehn, *Dolls*, trans. Josephine Nicoll (1929; repr. New York: Dover Publications, 1972), 137. Well after the fashion plate took over the function of the fashion doll, children's dolls continued to be sold in fashionable dress.

116. Julia Maitland, *The Doll and Her Friends, or Memoirs of the Lady Seraphina* (Boston: Ticknor, Reed, and Fields, 1852), 4–5; further references are to this edition and appear in the text.

117. On English, French, and German doll manufacturers, see Jürgen and Marianne Cieslik, *Dolls: European Dolls 1800–1900* (London: Studio Vista, 1979), 100; Marco Tosa, *Dolls*, trans. Wendy Dallas (London: B. T. Batsford, 1987); Mary Hillier, *Dolls and Doll-Makers* (London: Weidenfeld & Nicolson, 1968); and Gwen White, *A Book of Dolls* (London: Adam & Charles Black, 1956), 51. On paper cut-out dolls, see Boehn, 153.

118. Cieslik, 52; Hillier, 140, 164; and Maree Tarnowska, *Fashion Dolls* (London: Souvenir Press, 1986), 14.

119. Tosa, *Dolls*, 23.

120. Some girls' periodicals had articles on proper dress; Ann Trugman Ackerman, "Victorian Ideology and British Children's Literature, 1850–1914," Ph.D. diss., 1984, 237–38. On the rise of children's literacy and literature in the nineteenth century, see Gretchen R. Galbraith, *Reading Lives: Reconstructing Child-*

hood, Books, and Schools in Britain, 1870–1920 (New York: St. Martin's Press, 1997), 2, 5, 32–33; J. S. Bratton, *The Impact of Victorian Children's Fiction* (London: Croom Helm, 1981), 13–14, 63; and Alec Ellis, *Library Services for Young People in England and Wales 1830–1950* (London: 1958). On illustrated children's books, see William Feaver, *When We Were Young: Two Centuries of Children's Book Illustration* (New York: Holt, Rinehart, and Winston, 1977), 16. Picture books cost a shilling; since the average worker made about a pound a week, such books were mainly for the middle class, for whom the increasingly popular practice of gift-giving at birthdays and holidays made books a popular purchase; see Ackerman, 88; and Galbraith, 3.

121. For an example of the doll tale cautioning against fashion, see Mrs. Besset, *Memoirs of a Doll; Written by Herself; A New Year's Gift* (London: George Routledge, 1854), in which the doll's last will and testament warns, "Neither be too fond of dress and fine clothes; if you are, in what are you better than dolls?" 173. Further references are to this edition and appear in the text.

122. Cousin Nelly, *Dolly's Outfit: An Amusing and Instructive Work, Teaching Children How to Dress Their Dolls, Assisted by Cut-Out and Made-Up Patterns of Each Article of Dress* (London: Samuel Miller, 1872), title page. In Brenda [Mrs. G. Castle Smith], *Victoria-Bess or the Ups and Downs of a Doll's Life* (London: John F. Shaw, 1879), a mother approves the taste her daughter exhibits when she requests doll clothes from Paris, 80. Further references are to these editions and appear in the text.

123. *The Well-Bred Doll* (London: David Bogue, 1853), 15, 23; further references are to this edition and appear in the text.

124. *Dolly's Story Book. Her Travels in Doll-Land All over the World* (London: Frederick Warne, 1889), 32. Further references are to this edition and appear in the text.

125. On the adult contours of nineteenth-century female dolls, see Tosa, 22.

126. On the adult appearance of nineteenth-century dolls, see Nicole Savy, *Les petites filles modernes* (Paris: Editions de la Réunion des Musées Nationaux, 1989), 18. Historians agree that the majority of dolls throughout the nineteenth century represented fashionable adult women or girls past infancy, whether they were rag, wooden, wax, or porcelain; see Tosa, 73; White, 84; Lois Rostow Kuznets, *When Toys Come Alive: Narratives of Animation, Metamorphosis, and Development* (New Haven: Yale University Press, 1994), 97, 16; Manfred Bachmann and Claus Hansmann, *Dolls: The Wide World Over* (London: Harrap, 1973). Boehn, 156, 170; and Cieslik, 14. English dolls were called "babies" through the early nineteenth century, but those same dolls were also often called "little ladies"; Boehn, 150; Cieslik, 29. Realistic baby dolls were first produced around 1870; see Cieslik, 104; White, 95; Tarnowska, 7; and Fraser, 63.

127. P. J. Stahl, *La Poupée de Mademoiselle Lili* (Hetzel: Bibliothèque d'Education et de Récréation, [1886]), n.p.; "Auntie Bee" [Bertha Buxton], *More Dolls* (London: George Routledge & Sons, 1879), 24. Further references are to these editions and appear in the text.

128. Browne, *Live Dolls*, 1. All further references are to this edition and appear in the text.

129. On playing hero to the doll's heroine, see Kuznets, 96–97.

130. For scholars who interpret dolls as teaching girls how to be dependent, passive, "little" women valued only as objects of male "exploitation and desire," see Bachmann, 75. Other scholars draw attention to how dolls also enable girls to be active and imaginative; see Boehn, 175; Kuznets, 16; and Miriam Formanek-Brunell, *Made to Play House: Dolls and the Commercialization of American Girlhood, 1830–1930* (1993; repr., Baltimore: Johns Hopkins University Press, 1998), 1–2, 10.

131. I discuss Sigmund Freud's and Otto Fenichel's doll theories in chapter 4.

132. Mott's doll is described in Eleanor St. George, *Dolls of Three Centuries* (New York: Charles Scribner's Sons, 1951), 80; Josiah Gilbert, ed., *Autobiography and Memorials of Mrs. Gilbert, formerly Ann Taylor*, 3rd ed. (London: C. Kegan Paul, 1878), 69. On Princess Victoria's dolls, which also included a few child, baby, and male dolls, see Frances H. Low, *Queen Victoria's Dolls* (London: George Newnes, 1894).

133. On how adult desires define children's fiction, see Jacqueline Rose, *The Case of Peter Pan, or the Impossibility of Children's Fiction* (London: Macmillan, 1984), 10, 1–2.

134. For scholars who view children's literature as shifting from instruction to amusement over the course of the nineteenth century, see Humphrey Carpenter, *Secret Gardens: A Study of the Golden Age of Children's Literature* (London: George Allen and Unwin, 1985), 6; E. M. Field, *The Child and His Book: Some Account of the History and Progress of Children's Literature in England*, 2nd ed. (London: Wells Gardner, Darton, 1892), 341; Bettina Hürlimann, *Three Centuries of Children's Books in Europe*, trans. and ed. Brian W. Alderson (London: Oxford University Press, 1967), xii; and Kimberley Reynolds, *Girls Only? Gender and Popular Children's Fiction in Britain, 1880–1910* (New York: Harvester Wheatsheaf, 1990), 2. More nuanced accounts distinguish between late-eighteenth century Enlightenment rationalism, with its secular emphasis on facts, and the imaginative literature produced by many Evangelical writers; see Penny Brown, *The Captured World: The Child and Childhood in Nineteenth-Century Women's Writing* (New York: St. Martin's Press, 1993), 13–15; Gillian Avery, *Childhood's Pattern: A Study of the Heroes and Heroines of Children's Fiction* (London: Hodder and Stoughton, 1975), 2, 16, 33; and Margaret Nancy Cutt, *Ministering Angels: A Study of Nineteenth-Century Evangelical Writing for Children* (Wormley: Five Owls Press, 1979), xii, 11, 20, 23. Jacqueline Rose points out that children's authors easily blend amusement and instruction because both modes assume that adults know what is proper to and for children, *The Case of Peter Pan*, 55–56.

135. Mrs. Robert O'Reilly, *Doll World; or, Play and Earnest: A Study from Real Life* (London: Bell and Daldy, 1872), 19.

136. Mrs. Gatti, *Florence and Her Doll* (London: William Tegg, 1865), 147. Further references are to this edition and appear in the text.

137. *Rosamond: Dolly's New Picture Book*, trans. Madame de Chatelain (London: A. N. Myers, 1870), n.p. Further references are to this edition and appear in the text.

138. See H. Rutherford Russell, *My Dolly* (London: Marcus Ward, 1877), 39, 46, 48, and *May's Doll: Where Its Dress Came from: A Book for Little Girls* (London: John and Charles Mozley, 1851), 6.

139. Examples of the doll's tale as a narrative of social decline include Richard Henry Horne, *Memoirs of a London Doll* (1846; repr., London: Andre Deutsch, 1967); Pardoe, *Lady Arabella*; and Smith, *Victoria-Bess*.

140. For an argument that situates dolls within modernism by defining them as tropes of the real, models of unobservable consciousness and the "tension between exteriority and interiority," see Daniel Tiffany, *Toy Medium: Materialism and Modern Lyric* (Berkeley: University of California Press, 2000), 2–3, 53–54, 72, 82.

141. "Auntie Bee," [Bertha Buxton], *Rosabella. A Doll's Christmas Story* (London: George Routledge, 1878), 27, 92. Further references are to this edition and appear in the text.

142. Some of the key works historicizing childhood are Philippe Ariès, *Centuries of Childhood: A Social History of Family Life*, trans. Robert Baldick (New York: Vintage Books, 1965); Peter Coveney, *The Image of Childhood* (1957; repr., Harmondsworth: Penguin Books, 1967); Carolyn Steedman, *Strange Dislocations: Childhood and the Idea of Human Interiority, 1780–1930* (Cambridge, Mass.: Harvard University Press, 1995); Claudia Nelson, *Boys Will Be Girls: The Feminine Ethic and British Children's Fiction, 1857–1917* (New Brunswick, NJ: Rutgers University Press, 1991); and Catherine Robson, *Men in Wonderland: The Lost Girlhood of the Victorian Gentleman* (Princeton: Princeton University Press, 2001). A classic text by Ivy Pinchbeck and Margaret Hewitt, *Children in English Society*, vol. 2, *From the Eighteenth Century to the Children Act 1948* (London: Routledge and Kegan Paul, 1973), focuses on the gradual extension of the State's authority over children and the erosion of absolute parental authority, 359–60.

143. See Brown, *The Captured World*, 6–7, 79.

144. On the eroticism of childhood innocence, see Kincaid, *Child-Loving*; Rose, *The Case of Peter Pan*; Steedman, *Strange Dislocations*; and Robson, *Men in Wonderland*.

145. For examples of scholars who assume that father-daughter relationships in Victorian literature express "heterosexual desire" and "power," see Lynda Zwinger, *Daughters, Fathers, and the Novel: The Sentimental Romance of Heterosexuality* (Madison: University of Wisconsin Press, 1991), and Leonore Davidoff and Catherine Hall, *Family Fortunes: Men and Women of the English Middle Class 1780–1850* (Chicago: University of Chicago Press, 1987), 347, 351, 356.

146. Carol Mavor, *Becoming: The Photographs of Clementina, Viscountess Hawarden* (Durham, NC: Duke University Press, 1999), 44. On the eroticism of the mother-child relationship in visual culture, see Anne Higonnet, *Pictures of Innocence: The History and Crisis of Ideal Childhood* (London: Thames and Hudson, 1998), 43, 125–26, 129, 199. On maternal erotics between adult women, see Ruth Vanita, *Sappho and the Virgin Mary: Same-Sex Love and the English Literary Imagination* (New York: Columbia University Press, 1996), and Martha Vicinus, *Intimate Friends: Women Who Loved Women, 1778–1928* (Chicago: University of Chicago Press, 2004).

147. For two examples of many in which a girl calls herself her doll's mother, see *Dolly's Outfit*, 6, and Buxton, *More Dolls*, 25.

148. "The Dolls' Ball," in Harriet Myrtle [Mary Gillies], *More Fun for Our Little Friends* (London: Sampson Low, 1864), 46.

149. O'Reilly, *Doll World*, 13. Maggie Tulliver was not the last word in doll abuse. For an example of a girl who attacks her doll, see Pardoe, *Lady Arabella*, in which a girl throws a doll and fractures its skull, 52. In Besset, *Memoirs of a Doll*, a girl tears off her doll's arm accidentally, 32. See also Caroline Leicester, *Susan and the Doll, or Do Not Be Covetous* (London: James Hogg & Son, [1861]).

150. *Jimmy: Scenes from the Life of a Black Doll. Told by Himself to J. G. Sowerby* (London: George Routledge & Sons, 1888), 7.

151. Janet Burne, *Sybil's Dutch Dolls* (London: Field and Tuer, 1887), 18.

152. Buxton, *More Dolls*, 10.

153. Eleanor Acland, *Goodbye for the Present: The Story of Two Childhoods. Milly: 1878–88 & Ellen: 1913–24*, (London: Hodder & Stoughton, 1935), 62–63.

154. *Dolly and I* (London: Fred Warne, 1883), n.p.

155. Jessie Armstrong, *Celestine and Sallie; Or, Two Dolls and Two Homes* (London: Chas. H. Kelly, 1890), 16–17, 19.

156. Christabel Coleridge, *Charlotte Mary Yonge: Her Life and Letters* (London: Macmillan, 1903), 77.

157. Armstrong, *Celestine and Sallie*, 28; Mrs. George Cupples, *The Story of Our Doll* (London: T. Nelson, 1871), 58; Russell, *My Dolly*, 35; Horne, *Memoirs of a London Doll*, 16.

158. Cupples, *The Story of Our Doll*, 20.

159. Buxton, *Rosabella*, 114.

160. Mrs. Gellie, *Dolly Dear or the Story of a Waxen Beauty* (London: Griffith and Farran, 1883), 101.

161. *Dolly's Story Book*, 35.

CHAPTER 4
The Female Accessory in Great Expectations

1. For foundational statements of this interpretation, see Dorothy Van Ghent, "The Dickens World: The View from Todgers's," *Sewanee Review* 58 (1950), 428–31; Julian Moynahan, "The Hero's Guilt: The Case of *Great Expectations*," *Essays in Criticism* 10.1 (1960), 60–79; and F. R. Leavis and Q. D. Leavis, *Dickens the Novelist* (London: Chatto & Windus, 1970), 288.

2. On the novel's repression of plot in its recounting of a quest for lost origins that repeats the traumatic past, see Peter Brooks, *Reading for the Plot: Design and Intention in Narrative* (Cambridge, Mass.: Harvard University Press, 1984) 113–142. On the refusal of growth and experience, see Franco Moretti, *The Way of the World: The* Bildungsroman *in European Culture*, trans. Albert Sbragia (1987; repr. London: Verso, 2000), 181–228. On the novel's relegation of empire to the periphery, see Edward Said, *Culture and Imperialism* (New York: Vintage

Books, 1993), xiv–xvi. See also Michal Peled Ginsburg, "Dickens and the Uncanny: Repression and Displacement in *Great Expectations*," *Dickens Studies Annual* 13 (1984), 115–24. For an argument that empire and genocide were surprisingly unrepressed in Victorian culture, although often set aside by Victorian literature, see Elaine Freedgood, "Realism, Fetishism, and Genocide: 'Negro Head' Tobacco in and around *Great Expectations*," *Novel: A Forum on Fiction* 36.1 (2002), 26–41.

3. On masochistic and sadistic desire, often in relation to Oedipal desire, see A. L. French, "Beating and Cringing," *Essays in Criticism* 24 (1974), 147–68; Judith Weissman and Steven Cohan, "Dickens' *Great Expectations*: Pip's Arrested Development," *American Imago* 38.1 (1981), 105–26; Carol Siegel, "Postmodern Women Novelists Review Victorian Male Masochism," *Genders* 11 (1991), 1–16; and Douglas Steward, "Anti-Oedipalizing *Great Expectations*: Masochism, Subjectivity, Capitalism," *Literature and Psychology* 45.3 (1999), 29–50. On autoerotic and male homoerotic desire, see William Cohen, *Sex Scandal: The Private Parts of Victorian Fiction* (Durham, NC: Duke University Press, 1996), 26–72.

4. Charles Dickens, *Great Expectations* (1861; repr., Oxford: Oxford University Press, 1993), 235. Further references are to this edition and appear in the text.

5. As an example of how critics fail to keep the female dyad in focus when they discuss Pip's desire, see Alex Woloch, who cites a passage in which the phrase "Miss Havisham and Estella" appears three times, but paraphrases it as an instance of Pip's "desire for Estella"; *The One vs. the Many: Minor Characters and the Space of the Protagonist in the Novel* (Princeton: Princeton University Press, 2003), 206. Although Estella's character is now considered a defining aspect of the novel, it received little attention until Lucille P. Shores published "The Character of Estella in *Great Expectations*," *Massachusetts Studies in English* 3.4 (Fall 1972), 91–99.

6. René Girard, *Deceit, Desire, and the Novel: Self and Other in Literary Structure*, trans. Yvonne Freccero (Baltimore: Johns Hopkins University Press, 1965).

7. See Heather Butler, "What do you call a lesbian with long fingers? The Development of Lesbian and Dyke Pornography," in *Porn Studies*, ed. Linda Williams (Durham, NC: Duke University Press, 2004), 167–97.

8. For the foundational scene, see Marcel Proust, *Du côté du chez Swann* (1913; repr., Paris: Gallimard, 1954), 174–93. For important critical commentaries on the narrator's relationship to what Proust often called "Sodom and Gomorrah," see Eve Kosofsky Sedgwick, *Epistemology of the Closet* (Berkeley: University of California Press, 1990), 213–51; Elisabeth Ladenson, *Proust's Lesbianism* (Ithaca: Cornell University Press, 1999); and Michael Lucey, *Never Say I: Sexuality and the First Person in Colette, Gide, and Proust* (Durham, NC: Duke University Press, 2006).

9. Nor did Victorian readers view Miss Havisham as uniquely grotesque, but one of several examples of oddity in the novel, in the company of other notably eccentric characters who included Mrs. Pocket, Orlick, and Wemmick. For reviews, see *Saturday Review* 12 (July 20, 1861), 69; Margaret Oliphant, "Sensation Novels," *Blackwood's Edinburgh Magazine* 91 (May 1862), 579; "Charles Dickens's *Great Expectations*," *Eclectic Review* 114 (October 1861), 473; and "Belles Lettres," *Westminster Review* 77 (January 1862), 288. Only a few reviews

mentioned Estella at all. L. J. Trotter's anonymous review for the *Dublin University Magazine*, 18 (1861), was alone in hinting at an unspeakable eroticism in the two women's relationship. Trotter dismissed Estella's character as "morally and physically absurd; nor would it be worth our while to discuss the probable fruits of any training that a girl so shadowy as Estella could have received from such a phantom mistress," 692.

10. Naomi Lewis, "Introduction," in *The Silent Playmate: A Collection of Doll Stories* (New York: Macmillan, 1981), 12.

11. Mrs. Gellie, *Dolly Dear or the Story of a Waxen Beauty* (London: Griffith and Farran, 1883), 11.

12. Harry Stone, "Dickens's Woman in White," *Victorian Newsletter* 33 (Spring 1968), 6; the article that inspired Dickens was a "Narrative of Law and Crime" in *Household Narrative of Current Events* (January 1850), the monthly supplement to Dickens's weekly *Household Words*, 6.

13. Sigmund Freud, "Femininity," in *New Introductory Lectures on Psychoanalysis*, ed. James Strachey (1932; repr., New York: Norton, 1965), 139–67. He notes that there are two forms of doll play, and only one is an expression of penis envy; the earliest forms of doll play do *not* express femininity (which Freud defines as passivity and desire for men), but the girl's "identification with her mother with the intention of substituting activity for passivity," 159.

14. Sigmund Freud, "Some Psychological Consequences of the Anatomical Distinction between the Sexes," in *Sexuality and the Psychology of Love*, ed. Philip Rieff (1925; repr., New York: Collier Books, 1963), 177–78. Other psychoanalytic theorists can account more effectively than Freud for Pip's conflation of Estella's phallic omnipotence with hyperfemininity and his own desire to become feminine. In "The Symbolic Equation: Girl = Phallus," Otto Fenichel proposed that men's fascination with girls allows them to identify with mothers and daughters as figures for a penis that men want both to relinquish and preserve; *The Psychoanalytic Quarterly* 18.3 (1949), 303–4.

15. Catherine Robson, *Men in Wonderland: The Lost Girlhood of the Victorian Gentleman* (Princeton: Princeton University Press, 2001), 5.

16. Carolyn Dever, *Death and the Mother from Dickens to Freud: Victorian Fiction and the Anxiety of Origins* (Cambridge: Cambridge University Press, 1998).

17. On Estella as instrument, see Elliot L. Gilbert, " 'In Primal Sympathy': *Great Expectations* and the Secret Life," *Dickens Studies Annual* 11 (1983), 98; and Martin Meisel, "Miss Havisham Brought to Book," *PMLA* 81.3 (1966), 283. For Estella as Miss Havisham's "appendage," see Bruce Robbins, "How to Be a Benefactor without Any Money: The Chill of Welfare in *Great Expectations*," in *Knowing the Past: Victorian Literature and Culture*, ed. Suzy Anger (Ithaca: Cornell University Press, 2001), 181; Robbins sees Estella's role as appendage as *de*sexualizing the older woman mentor. "Ornamental object," "thing to be bartered," and "object of appetite" are from Gail Turley Houston, "'Pip' and 'Property': The (Re)production of the Self in *Great Expectations*," *Studies in the Novel* 24.1 (1992), 15. "Property" is from Joseph A. Hynes, "Image and Symbol in *Great Expectations*," *ELH* 30.3 (1963*)*, 284.

18. Judith Butler, "The Lesbian Phallus and the Morphological Imaginary," in Butler, *Bodies that Matter: On the Discursive Limits of "Sex"* (New York: Routledge, 1993), 88, 63.

19. See, for example, "Monsieur Thing's Origin," in *Secret Sexualities: A Sourcebook of 17th and 18th Century Writing*, ed. Ian McCormick (London: Routledge, 1997), 198–202; and Peter Fryer, ed., *The Man of Pleasure's Companion: A Nineteenth Century Anthology of Amorous Entertainment* (London: Arthur Barker Ltd., 1968), 74. For an argument that in contemporary lesbian sexual practice the dildo stands for crossing from one gender identification to another, see Colleen Lamos, "Taking on the Phallus," in *Lesbian Erotics*, ed. Karla Jay (New York: New York University Press, 1995), 109. For an interpretation of the dildo as a fetish that allows women to simultaneously affirm and deny castration, see Heather Findlay, "Freud's 'Fetishism' and the Lesbian Dildo Debates," in *Feminist Studies* 18.3 (1992), 563–79. I do not use the Freudian framework because it obscures the ways in which Dickens posits masculinity as well as femininity in terms of a primary injury and deficiency.

20. Cohen, *Sex Scandal*, 68. Where other critics have read *Great Expectations* as a tale that visits narrative punishment on a series of strong women, Cohen takes the text's reduction of sexuality to male subjectivity as given: "the novel's sexual architectonics bars [women] from sustaining a position as desiring subjects," 62. Cohen reduces Estella to the "denotative" object of male desire, ignoring how Miss Havisham is as "captivated by her looks" as any of the male characters, 68. He assumes that hands connote an exclusively phallic and male sexuality, and thus misses what his own insight supports: that the novel defines Pip's desire for Estella through Miss Havisham's desire for her. In "The Lesbian Hand," Mandy Merck argues that the nongendered nature of hands makes them particularly useful for challenging phallic definitions of sexuality and for signifying lesbian desire; *In Your Face: 9 Sexual Studies* (New York: New York University Press, 2000), 124–247.

21. See French; Weissman and Cohan; Curt Hartog, "The Rape of Miss Havisham," *Studies in the Novel* 14.3 (1982), 248–65; U. C. Knoepflmacher, "From Outrage to Rage: Dickens's Bruised Femininity," in *Dickens and Other Victorians: Essays in Honour of Philip Collins*, ed. Joanne Shattock (Houndmills: Macmillan, 1988); Kathleen Sell, "The Narrator's Shame: Masculine Identity in *Great Expectations*," *Dickens Studies Annual* 26 (1998), 203–26; Susan Walsh, "Bodies of Capital: *Great Expectations* and the Climacteric Economy," *Victorian Studies* 37.1 (1993), 73–98, 89; and Laurie Langbauer, "Women in White, Men in Feminism," *The Yale Journal of Criticism* 2.2 (1989), 223.

22. Hilary M. Schor notes that "Pip views himself as the woman in the text: Pip has chosen to identify himself with the feminized," and "chooses to be a girl, not a boy," but ultimately understands that move as a man's violent absorption and effacement of a female other; *Dickens and the Daughter of the House* (Cambridge: Cambridge University Press, 1999), 159. What Schor reads as a ruse of masculine power, I interpret as a recognition of the social and erotic power vested in the female dyad.

23. For a different reading of social mobility that sees Pip's relation to Miss Havisham as productively anti-erotic, see Robbins, "How to Be a Benefactor," 172–91.

24. William Cohen interprets Estella's scorn for Pip's hands as displaced scorn for his penis; Pip undergoes "the shaming of physical exposure, having his vulgar, vulnerable members seen by a girl," 37.

25. The novel makes Estella's jewelry an instrument of gender mobility when we learn that Compeyson, the man who betrayed Miss Havisham, wore "a watch and a chain and a ring and a breast-pin and a handsome suit of clothes," 343. Miss Havisham endows her female instrument of revenge with an impressive wardrobe and gem collection similar to the one belonging to the man who betrayed her, just as Pip adopts Estella's look to become an object of desire and distinction.

26. On Estella and jewelry, see Van Ghent, 430, and Schor, 161. For a more detailed discussion of jewelry in Victorian culture, see John Plotz, *Portable Properties, Local Logic: Culture on the Move and in Place in Victorian Greater Britain*, forthcoming.

27. During the Regency, the fop, dandy, swell, and toff were typed as male social climbers defined by their showy dress. On the dandy as arriviste, see David Kuchta, *The Three-Piece Suit and Modern Masculinity: England, 1550–1850* (Berkeley: University of California Press, 2002). In *The Hidden Consumer: Masculinities, Fashion and City Life 1860–1914* (Manchester: Manchester University Press, 1999), Christopher Breward argues that flashy clothing was the fashion for men through the 1840s and that only in the 1860s did a new severity in male dress become the norm, 258. On male fashion as a testing ground for definitions of masculinity, see Colin McDowell, *The Man of Fashion: Peacock Males and Perfect Gentlemen* (London: Thames & Hudson, 1997), and Andrew Elfenbein, "Byron and the Work of Homosexual Performance in Early Victorian England," *Modern Language Quarterly* 54 (1993), 535–66. For a general history of the dandy, see Rhonda K. Garelick, *Rising Star: Dandyism, Gender, and Performance in the Fin de Siècle* (Princeton: Princeton University Press, 1998).

28. On the 1850s and 1860s as moments when men's subdued dress and simple silhouettes were sharply differentiated from women's brightly colored clothing and the complicated forms created by crinolines, see Steven Connor, "Men in Skirts," *Women: A Cultural Review* 13.3 (2002), 258; and Brent Shannon, "Re-Fashioning Men: Fashion, Masculinity, and the Cultivation of the Male Consumer in Britain, 1860–1914," *Victorian Studies* 46.4 (2004), 597–630. Shannon argues that from the 1860s forward, retailers made a concerted effort to develop specifically masculine modes of shopping and made a spectacle of the well-dressed male body. Shannon's examples support the notion that when Dickens wrote *Great Expectations*, an interest in clothes and shopping was still considered effeminate, since almost all of his examples of a masculine consumer date from the 1880s and after.

29. Roland Barthes, *The Fashion System*, trans. Matthew Ward and Richard Howard (1967; repr., New York: Hill and Wang, 1983), 262.

30. As Julian Moynahan notes in "The Hero's Guilt," Pip's "ambition is to be passive," an object in Estella's hands, 110.

31. Several critics have written about the sadomasochistic dynamics in *Great Expectations*, including Steward, French, Cohen, and Weissman and Cohan. Gilles Deleuze argues that masochism makes castration of the father a condition of the son's incestuous merger with his mother; "Coldness and Cruelty," in *Masochism*, trans. Jean McNeil (1967; repr., New York: Zone Books, 1989), 66; see also 93. All of these critics, however, assume a heterosexual and patriarchal social order that equates the father with the law, while *Great Expectations* suggests a social order so identified with women that one can only find a place in it by becoming a mother's daughter. For example, Pip imagines that Estella "could not choose but obey" what he believes is Miss Havisham's desire that Estella marry him, a fantasy that equates the mother with the law of exchange, 297.

32. *Letters Addressed to the Editor of the Englishwoman's Domestic Magazine on the Whipping of Girls, and the General Corporal Punishment of Children* (April 1870), 3.

33. *The New Ladies Tickler; or, the Adventures of Lady Lovesport and the Audacious Harry* (London: Printed for the Bookseller, 1866).

34. *Letters Addressed to the Editor* (May 1870), 8.

35. On the Dickensian daughter, see Schor, *Dickens and the Daughter of the House*.

36. Brenda [Mrs. G. Castle Smith], *Victoria-Bess or the Ups and Downs of a Doll's Life* (London: John F. Shaw, 1879), 133.

CHAPTER 5
The Genealogy of Marriage

1. For the social history of marriage in England, see Lawrence Stone, *The Family, Sex and Marriage in England 1500–1800* (New York: Harper Torchbooks, 1979), and John R. Gillis, *For Better, For Worse: British Marriages, 1600 to the Present* (New York: Oxford University Press, 1985). In *Same-Sex Unions in Premodern Europe* (New York: Vintage Books, 1994), John Boswell argued that medieval Christian churches conducted ceremonies to unite men in relationships that resembled marriage, but his claims did not impact subsequent scholarship on modern marriage.

2. President George W. Bush, February 2004 speech advocating a constitutional amendment to ban same-sex marriage, http://www.cnn.com/2004/ALLPOLITICS/02/24/elec04.prez.bush.transcript/index.html. In France, politicians made similar charges that same-sex unions would destroy the symbolic order of culture. On the French debates, see Didier Eribon, *Échapper à la psychanalyse* (Paris: Editions Léo Scheer, 2005); Michael Lucey, *The Misfit of the Family: Balzac and the Social Forms of Sexuality* (Durham, NC: Duke University Press, 2003), 15; and Judith Butler, *Undoing Gender* (New York: Routledge, 2004), 110–23.

3. Stephanie Coontz, "The Heterosexual Revolution," op-ed, *New York Times*, July 5, 2005, A17. George Chauncey similarly argues that developments in heterosexual culture preceded and enabled the lesbian and gay interest in marriage, and heterosexual "acceptance of sexual relations as a source of pleasure . . . made lesbians, bisexuals, and gay men bolder and more confident"; *Why Mar-*

riage? The History Shaping Today's Debate over Gay Equality (New York: Basic Books, 2004), 34.

4. Michael Lucey develops this definition of sexuality through a synthesis of Pierre Bourdieu and Michel Foucault in *The Misfit of the Family*; see 18, 28, 150.

5. Lucey, *The Misfit of the Family*, xxvii.

6. Hendrik Hertzberg, "Dog Bites Man," *New Yorker*, May 5, 2003, 33.

7. Gayle Rubin, "The Traffic in Women: Notes toward a Political Economy of Sex," in *Toward an Anthropology of Women*, ed. Rayna Reiter (New York: Monthly Review Press, 1975), 180. In *Gender Trouble: Feminism and the Subversion of Identity* (New York: Routledge, 1990), Judith Butler developed Rubin's argument into a groundbreaking critique of the "heterosexual matrix," which charges the incest prohibition with producing gender identity as heterosexuality. In *Antigone's Claim: Kinship Between Life and Death* (New York: Columbia University Press, 2000), Butler reconfigured that insight to argue that one must distinguish between prohibitions on incest and on homosexuality and decouple kinship from heterosexuality, 66.

8. Claude Lévi-Strauss, *The Elementary Structures of Kinship*, trans. James Harle Bell, John Richard von Sturmer, and Rodney Needham (1949; repr. Boston: Beacon Press, 1969), 490. All further references are to this edition and appear in the text.

9. The word in French is "homosexualité"; Claude Lévi-Strauss, *Les Structures élémentaires de la parenté* (1947; repr., Paris: Mouton, 1981), 44.

10. Lisa Merrill, *When Romeo Was a Woman: Charlotte Cushman and Her Circle of Female Spectators* (Ann Arbor: University of Michigan Press, 1999), 150. Further references are to this edition and appear in the text.

11. Emma Stebbins, ed., *Charlotte Cushman: Her Letters and Memories of Her Life* (Boston: Houghton, Osgood and Company; Cambridge: The Riverside Press, 1879), 100. For the description of their shared house, see 114–15; for a discussion of their servants, the other "members of this household," see 116–21; on pets, see 112–31. Merrill interprets Stebbins's elision of references to Cushman's former lovers as a suppression of overt references to lesbianism, 251, but it seems instead a subtle admission of a possessive relationship to her biographical subject.

12. Cited in Stebbins, *Charlotte Cushman*, 126–27.

13. The shared pet was a common trope of female marriages. Katherine Bradley and Edith Cooper, who lived together and wrote under the shared name Michael Field, were devoted to a trinity they formed with their dog Whym Chow, whom they saw as mediating their union; see Frederick S. Roden, *Same-Sex Desire in Victorian Religious Culture* (Houndmills: Palgrave Macmillan, 2002), 191–99. On the affinity between homoerotic love and the love of and for animals, see also Ruth Vanita, *Sappho and the Virgin Mary: Same-Sex Love and the English Literary Imagination* (New York: Columbia University Press, 1996), 215–41.

14. Cited in Julia Markus, *Across an Untried Sea: Discovering Lives Hidden in the Shadow of Convention and Time* (New York: Alfred A. Knopf, 2000), 175.

15. See Merrill, 221, 223, 217, 226, 231, 230.

16. Foucault, *The History of Sexuality. Volume 1: An Introduction*, trans. Robert Hurley (New York: Vintage Books, 1980), 109.

17. Dinah Mulock Craik, *Olive* (1850; repr., New York: Oxford University Press, 1999), 314.

18. Henry James discussed Cushman and Hosmer, whose Italian careers he deemed "likely to lead us into bypaths queer and crooked," in *William Wetmore Story and His Friends: From Friends, Diaries, and Recollections*, vol. 1 (1903; repr., New York: Da Capo Press, 1969), 258. In *Across an Untried Sea*, Markus notes the connection between James's acquaintance with Cushman's circle and the plot of *The Golden Bowl*, 72–73. Markus also notes that Emma Crow Cushman, both while married to Ned and after his death, continued to have female lovers, 231, 282.

19. As a specialist in trouser roles, Cushman was often perceived as masculine; her lover before Emma Stebbins, Matilda Hays, was often called Max or Mathew; Merrill, 160. Their friends Harriet Hosmer, Frances Power Cobbe, and Rosa Bonheur were also often described as boyish or masculine. Merrill notes that reviewers often remarked on Cushman's virility as an actress but did not connect that characteristic to her sexuality, 125.

20. For overt hostility to passing women, see *Sinks of London Laid Open* (London: J. Duncombe, 1848), which described a woman who dressed as a man as a "singular being" and "creature" who "had a wife; and, as if that was not enough for any man, likewise had a mistress," 66, 67.

21. "Gleanings from Dark Annals: Modern Amazons," *Chambers's Journal of Popular Literature, Science and Arts* (May 30, 1863), 348–49. On women who dressed or lived as men in the nineteenth century, see Gretchen van Slyke, "Who Wears the Pants Here? The Policing of Women's Dress in Nineteenth-Century England, Germany and France," *Nineteenth-Century Contexts* 17.1 (1993), 17–33; Camilla Townsend, "'I Am the Woman for Spirit': A Working Woman's Gender Transgression in Victorian London," in *Sexualities in Victorian Britain*, eds. Andrew H. Miller and James Eli Adams (Bloomington: Indiana University Press, 1996), 214–33; Julie Wheelright, *Amazons and Military Maids: Women Who Dressed as Men in Pursuit of Life, Liberty and Happiness* (London: Pandora, 1989); and "Cross-dressing Women," in Alison Oram and Annmarie Turnbull, *The Lesbian History Sourcebook: Love and Sex Between Women in Britain from 1780 to 1970* (London: Routledge, 2001), 11–34.

22. Eleanor Butler cited in Rick Incorvati, "Introduction: Women's Friendships and Lesbian Sexuality," *Nineteenth-Century Contexts* 23.2 (2001), 176.

23. Dolly Sherwood, *Harriet Hosmer: American Sculptor 1830–1908* (Columbia: University of Missouri Press, 1991), 271; Markus, *Across an Untried Sea*, 247; and Martha Vicinus, *Intimate Friends: Women Who Loved Women, 1778–1928* (Chicago: University of Chicago Press, 2004), 51, 50.

24. Jill Liddington, *Female Fortune: Land, Gender and Authority. The Anne Lister Diaries and Other Writings* (London and New York: Rivers Oram Press, 1998), 62, 94.

25. *Chicago Herald*, December 27, 1892, cited in Erna Olafson Hellerstein, Leslie Parker Hume, and Karen M. Offen, eds., *Victorian Women: A Documentary Account of Women's Lives in Nineteenth-Century England, France, and the United States* (Stanford: Stanford University Press, 1981), 188–89.

26. In *Intimate Friends*, Vicinus wavers about the social status of relationships like Hosmer's with Ashburton; on the one hand, she writes that Victorians were "happy to let odd sexual relations flourish as long as no one spoke openly about them," 54, on the other that "Cushman and Hosmer . . . never pretended to be other than women who loved women, and they were accepted as such," 55.

27. Cited in Markus, *Across an Untried Sea*, 65.

28. Cook cited in Merrill, 138; 1849 article cited in Merrill, 163.

29. Cited in Robert Browning, *Dearest Isa: Robert Browning's Letters to Isabella Blagden*, ed. Edward C. McAleer (Austin: University of Texas Press, 1951), 27, n. 12; my attention was drawn to this quotation by its partial citation in Merrill, 160, and in Sherwood, 41. Browning misspelled her acquaintance's name, which was Corkran.

30. Lilian Whiting records Robert Browning's gift to Field in *The Brownings: Their Life and Art* (Boston: Little, Brown & Co., 1911), 153–54. On the Brownings's almost daily contact with Hosmer in 1857, see Cornelia Carr, ed., *Harriet Hosmer: Letters and Memories* (London: John Lane, 1913), 92.

31. See Carr, ed., *Harriet Hosmer: Letters and Memories*, 189; Martha Somerville, *Personal Recollections, from Early Life to Old Age, of Mary Somerville* (London: John Murray, 1873), 305, 359, who noted that Mr. Somerville also knew and liked Cobbe, 326. For instances of Englishwomen who mentioned meeting Hosmer (as well as William Story) while visiting Rome, see *Letters of Mary Mathison* (London: for private circulation only, 1875), 11; Georgiana Baroness Bloomfield, *Reminiscences of Court and Diplomatic Life*, vol. 2 (London: Kegan, Paul, Trench & Co, 1883), 301–2, 310; and Hester Ritchie, ed., *Letters of Anne Thackeray Ritchie* (London: John Murray, 1924), 137.

32. Carroll Smith-Rosenberg, "The Female World of Love and Ritual: Relations between Women in Nineteenth-Century America," in *Feminism and History*, ed. Joan Wallach Scott (Oxford: Oxford University Press, 1996), 366–97; Lillian Faderman, *Surpassing the Love of Men: Romantic Friendship and Love Between Women from the Renaissance to the Present* (New York: William Morrow, 1981).

33. On Hays's "ardent friendship" with Monson, see Lee Holcombe, *Wives and Property: Reform of the Married Women's Property Law in Nineteenth-Century England* (Toronto: University of Toronto Press, 1983), 85, and Nancy Fix Anderson, *Woman against Women in Victorian England: A Life of Eliza Lynn Linton* (Bloomington: Indiana University Press, 1987), 63.

34. Matilda Hays, *Adrienne Hope: The Story of a Life* (London: T. Cautley Newby, 1866), 249–50.

35. Matilda Hays, *Helen Stanley: A Tale* (London: E. Churton, 1846), 324.

36. Lilian Whiting, ed., *Anna Elizabeth Klumpke. Memoirs of an Artist* (Privately printed, 1940), 47.

37. See Barbara Taylor, *Eve and the New Jerusalem: Socialism and Feminism in the Nineteenth Century* (New York: Pantheon Books, 1983).

38. Anna Klumpke, *Rosa Bonheur: The Artist's (Auto)biography*, trans. Gretchen van Slyke (1908; repr., Ann Arbor: University of Michigan Press, 1997), 264.

39. Oliver Wendell Holmes, *The Common Law*, ed. Mark DeWolfe Howe (1881; repr., Cambridge, Mass.: The Belknap Press of Harvard University Press, 1963), 236.

40. See Merrill, 185.

41. See Mary Lyndon Shanley, "A Husband's Right to His Wife's Body: Wife Abuse, the Restitution of Conjugal Rights, and Marital Rape," in *Feminism, Marriage, and the Law in Victorian England* (Princeton: Princeton University Press, 1989); Mary Lyndon Shanley, "'One Must Ride Behind': Married Women's Rights and the Divorce Act of 1857," *Victorian Studies* 25 (1982); Margaret K. Woodhouse, "The Marriage and Divorce Bill of 1857," *The American Journal of Legal History* 3 (1959), 260–75; Dorothy Stetson, *A Woman's Issue: The Politics of Family Law Reform in England* (Westport: Greenwood Press, 1982); and Holcombe, *Wives and Property*.

42. "Divorce a Vinculo; or, the Terrors of Sir Cresswell Cresswell," *Once a Week* 2 (February 25, 1860), 184–87; "The Lady and Her Marriage Settlement," *Englishwoman's Domestic Magazine* 47 (1864), 209.

43. Allen Horstman, *Victorian Divorce* (London: Croom Helm, 1985), 32, 85.

44. Gail Savage, "'Intended Only for the Husband': Gender, Class, and the Provision for Divorce in England, 1858–1868," in *Victorian Scandals: Representations of Gender and Class*, ed. Kristine Ottesen Garrigan (Athens: Ohio University Press, 1992), 26.

45. Bessie Rayner Parkes, *Vignettes: Twelve Biographical Sketches* (London: Alexander Strahan, 1866), 445.

46. See Barbara Leckie, *Culture and Adultery: The Novel, the Newspaper, and the Law, 1857–1914* (Philadelphia: University of Pennsylvania Press, 1999), 68; and Jeanne Fahnestock, "Bigamy: The Rise and Fall of a Convention," *Nineteenth-Century Fiction* 36.1 (1981), 47–71.

47. Leckie draws attention to Lecky's call to censor divorce-court reporting, 97.

48. [Dora Greenwell], "Our Single Women," *The North British Review* 36 (February 1862), 63, 64.

49. "Old Maids," *Dublin University Magazine* 56 (December 1860), 709.

50. John Stuart Mill, "Early Essays on Marriage and Divorce," in *Essays on Sex Equality*, ed. Alice Rossi (Chicago: University of Chicago Press, 1970), 72, 77.

51. Caroline Cornwallis, "The Capabilities and Disabilities of Women," *Westminster Review* 67 (January 1857), 43.

52. "Our Single Women," 62, 65, 77.

53. Anne Thackeray Ritchie, "Toilers and Spinsters," in *Toilers and Spinsters and Other Essays* (London: Smith, Elder, & Co., 1876), 5; first published in *Cornhill Magazine* 3 (1861).

54. W. R. Greg, "Why Are Women Redundant?" in Greg, *Literary and Social Judgements* (Boston: James R. Osgood, 1873), 274–308. Further references are to this edition and appear in the text.

55. Frances Power Cobbe, "What Shall We Do with Our Old Maids?" in *Prose by Victorian Women: An Anthology*, eds. Andrea Broomfield and Sally Mitchell

(New York: Garland, 1996), 236–61; first published in *Fraser's Magazine*, November 1862.

56. John Stuart Mill, "The Subjection of Women," in *Essays on Sex Equality: John Stuart Mill and Harriet Taylor Mill*, ed. Alice S. Rossi (Chicago: University of Chicago Press, 1970), 233.

57. Frances Power Cobbe, "Celibacy *v.* Marriage," *Fraser's Magazine* 65 (February 1862), 233.

58. Frances Power Cobbe, *The Duties of Women: A Course of Lectures* (London: Norgate, 1881), 169–70.

59. Cobbe, "What Shall We Do," 239.

60. Frances Power Cobbe, *Life of Frances Power Cobbe. By Herself*, vol. 2 (Boston: Houghton, Mifflin, 1894), 645.

61. See Cobbe, *Life of Frances Power Cobbe* (London: Swan Sonnenschein, 1904), 456, 468–69, 478; and Constance Battersea, *Reminiscences* (London: Macmillan, 1922), 256, 222–23.

62. Cobbe refers to these acquaintances and cites correspondence with them in her autobiography. For her contact with Greg, see *Life* (1904), 469, 471–72; with John Stuart Mill, see 415. On Cobbe's extensive social networks, see also Sally Mitchell, *Frances Power Cobbe: Victorian Feminist, Journalist, Reformer* (Charlottesville: University of Virginia Press, 2004).

63. Frances Power Cobbe, "Wife-Torture in England," *Contemporary Review* 32 (April 1878), 55–87.

64. Ginger Frost, "Bigamy and Cohabitation in Victorian England," *Journal of Family History* 22.3 (1997), 286, 294, 295.

65. On the contemporary relationship between marriage customs and legal definitions of wedlock, see John Borneman, "Until Death Do Us Part: Marriage/Death in Anthropological Discourse," *American Ethnologist* 23.2 (1996), 230.

66. Mona Caird, "The Morality of Marriage," in *Prose by Victorian Women: An Anthology*, eds. Andrea Broomfield and Sally Mitchell (New York: Garland Publishing, 1996), 646; first published in the *Fortnightly Review*, March 1890.

67. "The Bill for Divorce," *Quarterly Review* 101.203 (1857), 252, 283, 274, 276, 285, 287.

68. [Edwin Hill Handley], "Custody of Infants' Bill," *The British and Foreign Review* 7 (July 1838), 409, 278, 381, 382, 386.

69. Kelly v. Kelly, *Courts of Probate and Divorce*, *Law Reports* 2, December 7, 1869, 37.

70. Margaret Oliphant, "The Laws Concerning Women," *Blackwood's Magazine* 79 (April 1856), 380, 382.

71. Ernst Bloch, *Natural Law and Human Dignity*, trans. Dennis J. Schmidt (1961; repr., Cambridge, Mass.: MIT Press, 1996), 36.

72. See Victoria Kahn, *Wayward Contracts: The Crisis of Political Obligation in England, 1640–1674* (Princeton: Princeton University Press, 2004), 7.

73. Ibid., 198.

74. See, for example, Uday S. Mehta, "Liberal Strategies of Exclusion," in *Tensions of Empire: Colonial Cultures in a Bourgeois World*, eds. Frederick Cooper and Ann Laura Stoler (Berkeley: University of California Press, 1997), 59–86.

75. P. S. Atiyah, *The Rise and Fall of Freedom of Contract* (Oxford: Clarendon Press, 1979), 18. Atiyah cites the abolition of breach-of-promise cases as an example of the nineteenth-century distaste for applying contract law to relationships demarcated as private, but in fact, such cases flourished throughout the century and judges often applied contract law to promises to marry. See Ginger Frost, *Promises Broken: Courtship, Class, and Gender in Victorian England* (Charlottesville: University Press of Virginia, 1995).

76. See Olive Anderson, "State, Civil Society and Separation in Victorian Marriage," *Past and Present* 163.1 (1999), 161–201, on the prevalence of judicial separations, which entailed judicial recognition of private agreements between spouses.

77. Judge Charles Parker Butt, *Scott, falsely called Sebright v. Sebright, Law Reports. Probate Division* 12 (1886), 23.

78. Carole Pateman, *The Sexual Contract* (Stanford: Stanford University Press, 1988), 7–8. Further references are to this edition and appear in the text.

79. Monique Wittig, "On the Social Contract," in *Homosexuality, Which Homosexuality?*, eds. Dennis Altman, Carole Vance, Martha Vicinus, Jeffrey Weeks (London: GMP Publishers, 1989), 239–40, 247, 243, 249.

80. Wilkie Collins, *Man and Wife*, ed. with an introduction by Norman Page (1870; repr., Oxford: Oxford University Press, 1995), 232.

81. Shanley, "A Husband's Right," 187; and Shanley, "'One Must Ride Behind,'" 370–71.

82. See Wendy Jones, "Feminism, Fiction and Contract Theory: Trollope's *He Knew He Was Right*," *Criticism* 36.3 (1994), 401–5.

83. John Stuart Mill, "Early Essays on Marriage and Divorce," in *Essays on Sex Equality*, 83, 73, 74, 83. Further references are to this edition and will be cited in the text as "Early Essays" followed by page number.

84. John Stuart Mill, *The Subjection of Women*, in *Essays on Sex Equality*, 133, 158, 169. Further references are to this edition and will appear in the text as *Subjection* followed by page number.

85. William Lecky, *History of European Morals from Augustus to Charlemagne*, vol. 2 (1869; repr., London: Longmans, Green, 1902), 306. Further references are to this edition and volume and appear in the text.

86. [Caroline Cornwallis], "The Property of Married Women," *Westminster Review* 66 (October 1856), 331. Anna Jameson, "'Woman's Mission,' and Woman's Position," in *Memoirs and Essays* (London: Richard Bentley, 1846), 216.

87. Mill shared this framework with a broad public whose beliefs he otherwise opposed; Jane Rendall, "John Stuart Mill, Liberal Politics, and the Movements for Women's Suffrage, 1865–1873," in *Women, Privilege, and Power: British Politics, 1750 to the Present*, ed. Amanda Vickery (Stanford: Stanford University Press, 2001), 168–200.

88. On anthropology in England, see George W. Stocking, Jr., *Victorian Anthropology* (New York: The Free Press, 1987), and Adam Kuper, *The Invention of Primitive Society: Transformations of an Illusion* (London: Routledge, 1988). The *Anthropological Review*, which began publication in 1863, offers many examples of British anthropologists focused on measuring racial differences.

89. Frederick Engels, *The Origin of the Family, Private Property and the State*, ed. with an introduction by Eleanor Burke Leacock (1884; repr., New York: International Publishers, 1972), 74.

90. Lisa Z. Sigel, *Governing Pleasures: Pornography and Social Change in England, 1815–1914* (New Brunswick: Rutgers University Press, 2002), 50, 52, 53, 57.

91. Henry Sumner Maine, *Ancient Law: Its Connection with the Early History of Society and Its Relation to Modern Ideas*, introduction by Frederick Pollock, preface by Raymond Firth (1861; repr., Boston: Beacon Press, 1963). On Maine's influence on several generations of anthropologists, see Firth, xxix–xxx, and Stocking, 117.

92. John F. McLennan, *Primitive Marriage: An Inquiry into the Origin of the Form of Capture in Marriage Ceremonies* (Edinburgh: Adam and Charles Black, 1865), v. Further references are to this edition and appear in the text.

93. On Darwin's influence on Victorian anthropology, see Stocking, 145–85. Stocking sees Maine as non-Darwinian, 168, but Holcombe calls *Ancient Law* an instance of "Darwinism . . . applied to the study of law"; *Wives and Property*, 5.

94. For an argument that *The Descent of Man* does illustrate Darwin's interest in "a sexually varied natural kingdom," 91, see Richard A. Kaye, *The Flirt's Tragedy: Desire without End in Victorian and Edwardian Fiction* (Charlottesville: University Press of Virginia, 2002), 84–117. Kaye notes that this aspect of Darwin's thought makes him an important, if often neglected, contributor to the history of same-sex desire.

95. Charles Darwin, *The Origin of Species by Means of Natural Selection or the Preservation of Favoured Races in the Struggle for Life* (1859; repr., London: Penguin, 1985), 73, 441, 90, 101, 456, 459. Further references are to this edition and appear in the text. Gillian Beer analyzes Darwin's "emphasis on unlikeness, transformation, and kinship," his insistence on "profusion" "variety," and deviation, and his influence on Victorian anthropology 97, in *Darwin's Plots: Evolutionary Narrative in Darwin, George Eliot and Nineteenth-Century Fiction* (1983; repr., Cambridge: Cambridge University Press, 2000) xviii, 13, 59, 97.

96. Although some scholars have argued that anthropology was a reaction against legal reforms that made husbands and wives more equal, others see a continuity between reformers who encouraged Victorians to imagine marriage differently and writers who recorded the varieties of marriage customs and kinship systems. Elizabeth Fee and Elazar Barkan argue that anthropological texts reacted against feminism by invidiously associating marriage reform with reversion to a promiscuous primitive state. Kathy Psomiades sees anthropology as reinventing heterosexuality at a time when sexual difference was breaking down. George Stocking perceives continuity between the 1850s reformers who encouraged Victorians to imagine marriage differently and the 1860s anthropologists who recorded diversity in marriage customs and kinship systems. See Elizabeth Fee, "The Sexual Politics of Victorian Social Anthropology," in *Clio's Consciousness Raised: New Perspectives on the History of Women*, eds. Mary S. Hartman and Lois Banner (New York: Harper Colophon, 1974), 87, 89, 100; Elazar Barkan, "Victorian Promiscuity: Greek Ethics and Primitive Exemplars," in *Prehistories of the Future: The Primitivist Project and the Culture of Modernism*, eds. Elazar Barkan and Ronald Bush (Stanford: Stanford University Press, 1995), 62;

Kathy Psomiades, "Heterosexual Exchange and Other Victorian Fictions: *The Eustace Diamonds* and Victorian Anthropology," *Novel* 33.1 (1999), 94; and Stocking, *Victorian Anthropology*, 207.

97. Lubbock and Morgan also defined the earliest phase of family organization as communal marriage, in which everyone is married to one another. John Lubbock, *The Origin of Civilisation and the Primitive Condition of Man*, ed. and with an introduction by Pierre Rivière (1870; repr., Chicago: University of Chicago Press, 1978), 67.

98. J. J. Bachofen, *Myth, Religion, and Mother Right: Selected Writings of J. J. Bachofen*, preface by George Boas, introduction by Joseph Campbell, trans. Ralph Mannheim (Princeton: Princeton University Press, 1967), 94. This and all other citations are from *Mother Right*, excerpted in this volume and first published in 1861; further references appear in the text. Bachofen wrote in German and his work is still unavailable in full English translation, but the English anthropologists discussed here were aware of it. McLennan consulted Bachofen's work but claimed that he was not indebted to it because he had not read it completely when he published similar views. See J. F. McLennan, "Kinship in Ancient Greece, Part I," *Fortnightly Review* 4 (April 15, 1866), 582.

99. Lorimer Fison and A[lfred] W. Howitt, *Kamilaroi and Kurnai: Group-Marriage and Relationship, and Marriage by Elopement*, introduction by Lewis H. Morgan (Melbourne: George Robertson, 1880), 102, 96; facsimile edition published by Australian Institute of Aboriginal and Torres Strait Islander Studies, Canberra, Australia, 1991.

100. E[dith] J. Simcox, *Primitive Civilizations or Outlines of the History of Ownership in Archaic Communities* (London: Swan Sonnenschein, 1894), 9.

101. Simcox, *Primitive Civilizations*, 9. Gillian Beer explores Simcox's anti-universal understanding of social structures and law in "Knowing a Life: Edith Simcox—Sat est vixisse?" in *Knowing the Past: Victorian Literature and Culture*, ed. Suzy Anger (Ithaca: Cornell University Press, 2001), 255, 262, 264.

102. W. Robertson Smith, *Kinship and Marriage in Early Arabia* (1885; repr., Boston: Beacon Press, 1963), 166, 146. Further references are to this edition and appear in the text.

103. Engels, *The Origin of the Family*, 128; Lecky, *History of European Morals*, 279.

104. Lecky, *History of European Morals*, 297–98, 277.

105. W. S. Lilly, "Marriage and Modern Civilization," *Nineteenth Century and after* 50.298 (1901), 908, 909–10, 919.

106. "The Loves of Sappho," *The Exquisite*, no. 7, 82, 83.

107. On Cobbe, Lloyd, and Darwin, see Cobbe, *Life* (1894), 445, 447; on Lloyd's loan of a pony, see Cobbe, *Life* (1904), 486. On Darwin's father knowing the Ladies of Llangollen, see Elizabeth Mavor, ed., *Life with the Ladies of Llangollen* (New York: Viking, 1984), 36, 69.

108. Cobbe, *Life* (1894), vol. 2, 436. Maine also gave feminists permission to reprint his 1873 lecture "The Early History of the Property of Married Women" as part of their campaign for legal reform of married women's property laws. See George Feaver, *From Status to Contract: A Biography of Sir Henry Maine 1822–1888* (London: Longmans, Green & Co., 1969), 302, n. 22.

109. Engels also argues that the freedom and respect granted to women in early German societies developed from the pairing family form that preceded "the crying moral contradictions of monogamy," 133. He contrasts that pairing family to the moral deterioration the Germans underwent as they migrated east and "acquired not only equestrian skill but also gross, unnatural vices," 133. Engels conflated the Orient with sodomy and deemed both the products of advancing capitalism.

110. Bachofen, *Myth, Religion, and Mother Right*, 204–5.

CHAPTER 6
Contracting Female Marriage in *Can You Forgive Her?*

1. Margaret King, "'Certain Learned Ladies': Trollope's *Can You Forgive Her?* and the Langham Place Circle," *Victorian Literature and Culture* 21 (1993), 307–26; Kathy Psomiades, "Heterosexual Exchange and Other Victorian Fictions: *The Eustace Diamonds* and Victorian Anthropology," *Novel: A Forum on Fiction* 33.1 (1999), 93–118. Psomiades contends that Trollope and Victorian anthropologists only inadvertently opened up a way to think of sexuality as not exclusively heterosexual, 95, while I argue that both had a more knowing awareness of the plasticity of sexuality and marriage.

2. John Stuart Mill, *The Subjection of Women*, in *Essays on Sex Equality*, ed. Alice Rossi (Chicago: University of Chicago Press, 1970), 233.

3. See Barbara Leckie, *Culture and Adultery: The Novel, the Newspaper, and the Law, 1857–1914* (Philadelphia: University of Pennsylvania Press, 1999).

4. Anthony Trollope, "Mrs General Talboys," in *Early Short Stories*, ed. John Sutherland (Oxford: Oxford University Press, 1994), 212, 220. On the publisher's and readers' reactions, see Sutherland, "Introduction," *Early Short Stories*, ix, xiii, xvii. Later in his career, Trollope published other short pieces that represented female marriage and male homoeroticism. On female marriage in "The Telegraph Girl," a story Trollope first published in *Good Words* in 1877, see Katie-Louise Thomas, "A Queer Job for a Girl: Women Postal Workers, Civic Duty and Sexuality 1870–80," in *In a Queer Place: Sexuality and Belonging in British and European Contexts*, eds. Kate Chedgzoy, Emma Francis, and Murray Pratt (Aldershot: Ashgate, 2002), 50–70. On Trollope's treatment of male homoeroticism in "The Turkish Bath," *The Galaxy* 8.5 (1869), 689–703, see Mark Turner, *Trollope and the Magazines: Gendered Issues in Mid-Victorian Britain* (New York: St. Martin's Press, 2000), 201–7.

5. Adelaide A. Procter, ed., *The Victoria Regia: A Volume of Contributions in Poetry and Prose* (London: Emily Faithfull and Co., Victoria Press for the Employment of Women, 1861), and Procter, ed., *A Welcome: Original Contributions in Poetry and Prose Addressed To Alexandra, Princess of Wales* (London: Emily Faithfull and Co., Victoria Press for the Employment of Women, 1863).

6. N. John Hall notes the resemblance between Kate Field and Ophelia Gledd in *Trollope: A Biography* (Oxford: Clarendon Press, 1991), 340.

7. Hall refers to Trollope's "long-standing romantic attachment to Kate Field"; N. John Hall, ed., with the assistance of Nina Burgis, *The Letters of Anthony*

Trollope, vol. 1 (Stanford: Stanford University Press, 1983), 126, n. 7. Sutherland refers to Field as "the young Boston feminist with whom Trollope had a long platonic affair," "Introduction," *Stories*, xxiii.

8. See chapters 1 and 5; Lisa Merrill, *When Romeo Was a Woman: Charlotte Cushman and Her Circle of Female Spectators* (Ann Arbor: University of Michigan Press); Martha Vicinus, *Intimate Friends: Women Who Loved Women, 1778–1928* (Chicago: University of Chicago Press, 2004), 31–55; and Julia Markus, *Across an Untried Sea: Discovering Lives Hidden in the Shadow of Convention and Time* (New York: Alfred A. Knopf, 2000). On Harriet Hosmer's acquaintance with the Trollopes in Italy, see Harriet Hosmer, *Letters and Memories*, ed. Cornelia Carr (London: John Lane, The Bodley Head, 1913), 57.

9. On Field's term for Blagden, see Merrill, 195. On Ashburton and Hosmer, and Cobbe's present, see Lilian Whiting, *Kate Field: A Record* (Boston: Little, Brown, 1900), 126, 102.

10. On Field's terms for Cushman and Stebbins, see Merrill, 195. On Field's first meeting with Cushman, see Whiting, *Kate Field*, 47. On Field's love for her aunt, see Carolyn J. Moss, ed., *Kate Field: Selected Letters* (Carbondale: Southern Illinois University Press, 1996), 17; and Whiting, *Kate Field*, 46–47, 73–75, 99.

11. On Trollope and Cobbe, see Hall, *Letters*, vol. 1, 359, and Frances Power Cobbe, *Life of Frances Power Cobbe*, 2nd ed. (London: Swan Sonnenschein, 1904), in which Cobbe states that Trollope's brother was a frequent visitor to the house she shared with Isa Blagden in Florence, 381; "Mr. Anthony Trollope I knew but slightly," 558. On Trollope and Blagden, see Hall, *Letters*, vol. 1, 190–91; and Broughton, vol. 1, 434; and Edwards, vol. 1, 448, 476. On Trollope and Faithfull, see below.

12. For the letters to Field and Blagden, see Hall, *Letters*, vol. 1, 127, 190.

13. Lady Monson supported a women's reading-room in Langham Place, a project in which Emily Faithfull also participated; see Frederick Dolman, "Afternoon Tea with Miss Emily Faithfull," *The Young Woman* 3 (1894–1895), 318–19.

14. Hall, *Letters*, vol. 1, 175, 193. For an example of Trollope helping Field professionally while simultaneously admonishing her that women belonged at home, see Hall, *Letters*, vol. 2, 709.

15. Blanche Cox Clegg's entry on Lilian Whiting in John A. Garraty and Mark C. Carnes, eds., *American National Biography* (New York: Oxford University Press, 1999), refers to Whiting and Field as "close friends," 268. Jessie Rittenhouse's biography of Whiting refers to Kate Field as the woman "for whom Miss Whiting cherished the most tender and consecrated friendship"; *Lilian Whiting: Journalist, Essayist, Critic, and Poet: A Sketch* (n.d., n.p.), 7.

16. Whiting wrote a review of Emma Crow Cushman's poetry in which she referred to Cushman's connection with her lover Miss Ludwig as a "relation . . . of singular beauty"; "The Poetry of Mrs. Cushman," cited in Markus, 282.

17. Lilian Whiting, *The Golden Road* (Boston: Little, Brown, 1918), 189.

18. Lilian Whiting, *After Her Death: The Story of a Summer* (Boston: Roberts Brothers, 1898), 18, 25, 131. On the link between lesbian eroticism and spiritualism, see Terry Castle, "Marie Antoinette Obsession," in *The Apparitional Les-*

bian: Female Homosexuality and Modern Culture (New York: Columbia University Press, 1993), 107–49.

19. Whiting, *After Her Death*, 130, 28, 142. Clipping enclosed in Boston Public Library copy of *After Her Death*; this particular quote comes from a review in *The Beacon*.

20. On the close contact between Whiting and Field when Field traveled, see *After Her Death*, 58.

21. For a fuller discussion of those conventions, see chapter 1. So strong was the imperative to biographical discretion that a daughter writing her mother's biography referred to her own birth in the third person; see *A Beloved Mother: Life of Hannah S. Allen, By Her Daughter* (London: Samuel Harris & Co., 1884), 114.

22. See *Kate Field*, 190, 414, and Lilian Whiting, *The Brownings: Their Life and Art* (Boston: Little, Brown, 1911), 153–54.

23. On Whiting's request that Field destroy her letters, see *Kate Field*, 296. Whiting also destroyed many of Field's letters; Moss, *Kate Field*, xi.

24. For examples of Whiting's use of "always" in relation to Field, see *Kate Field*, 32, 281, 552, 55, 572. For Whiting's memories of Field's beauty, see *Kate Field*, 432.

25. Hall, *Trollope: A Biography*, 340. On Trollope's friendship with Faithfull, see also King, 311. King discusses how Faithfull and other feminists sought to provide women with alternatives to heterosexual marriage, but does not elaborate on how Faithfull herself chose female marriage as one such alternative. Victoria Glendinning documents Trollope's familiarity with Faithfull and notes that he attended gatherings at Reverend Llewellyn Davies's rectory in Blandford Square, introduced there either by Faithfull or by her fellow feminist Barbara Bodichon; *Trollope* (London: Hutchinson, 1992), 324–25.

26. On Faithfull's role in the Codrington divorce trial, see Vicinus, 69–75. Faithfull's decision to testify against Helen Codrington saved her reputation, even as she continued to have female lovers. She maintained the Victoria Press, started the *Victoria Magazine* in May 1863 (and published it until June 1880), founded a penny weekly on *Women and Work* in 1865, and founded the *West London Express* in 1877. She was later awarded a Civil List pension for her services on behalf of the education and employment of women. On Faithfull's life, see James S. Stone, *Emily Faithfull, Victorian Champion of Women's Rights* (Ontario: P.D. Meany Publishers, 1994), and William E. Fredeman, "Emily Faithfull and the Victoria Press: An Experiment in Sociological Bibliography," *The Library* fifth series, 29.2 (1974), 139–64. Faithfull left all her property to her final lover, the interior decorator Charlotte Robinson, and spoke openly of living with Robinson in an 1894 interview; see Dolman, "Afternoon Tea," 318–19.

27. Stone notes that Adelaide Procter ended her friendship with Faithfull in 1862 and that Bessie Rayner Parkes canceled Faithfull's contract to publish the *English Woman's Journal* in December 1863. Stone also notes that some of Faithfull's other feminist friends remained loyal, including Matilda Hays, Cushman's former lover, 17.

28. For the June 1863 visit, see Hall, *Letters*, vol. 1, 220. For the 1864 dates, see Martha Westwater, *The Wilson Sisters: A Biographical Study of Upper Middle-Class Victorian Life* (Athens: Ohio University Press, 1984), 117.

29. The details of Faithfull's relationship with Wilson are documented in the diaries of Wilson's sister Eliza, excerpted in Westwater. Emilie Wilson Barrington's obituary in the *Times*, March 11, 1933, 12, referred to Faithfull as her "intimate friend"; cited in Westwater, 139, n. 6.

30. Hall notes that *Can You Forgive Her?* "owes something to Trollope's argument with Kate Field"; *Trollope*, 267. Field and Faithfull were acquainted with each other. The Kate Field collection that Lilian Whiting donated to the Boston Public Library contains a condolence letter Faithfull sent to Field when Field's mother died (Ms. KF 192, n.d.), as well as many notes from Faithfull to Field in 1878 discussing a benefit Field was organizing, whose performers included Faithfull's lover at the time, Kate Pattison (Ms. KF 1081–1087). On Faithfull and Pattison, see Stone, *Emily Faithfull*, 206. In 1872, Field wrote to Whitelaw Reid warning him that Emily Faithfull had a bad reputation in London; Moss, *Kate Field*, 101–2. In 1878, however, Field wrote to Faithfull, declining to write for one of Faithfull's publications but saying she would see her the following Sunday; Moss, *Kate Field*, 140.

31. Anthony Trollope, *Can You Forgive Her?* (1864–1865; repr., London: Penguin Books, 1986), 45. Further references are to this edition and appear in the text.

32. [Henry James], review of *Can You Forgive Her?*, *The Nation* (September 28, 1865), 409. Trollope refused to cut the novel, even at the request of an editor who initially wanted it to fit into a weekly part format; see Hall, *Trollope*, 270. Trollope wrote of his "affection" for *Can You Forgive Her?* in *An Autobiography* (1883; repr., Oxford: Oxford University Press, 1987), 179. On the novel's popularity and earnings, see Juliet McMaster, *Trollope's Palliser Novels: Theme and Pattern* (London: Macmillan, 1978), 20; Hall, *Trollope*, 259; and Hall, *Letters*, vol. 1, 317, 367–68.

33. The reference to engagement as a bond almost as holy as matrimony comes from the final novel in the Palliser series, *The Duke's Children* (1880; repr., Oxford: Oxford University Press, 1983), 35.

34. On the marriage ceremony as a performative, and on performatives in general, see J. L. Austin, *How to Do Things with Words*, ed. J. O. Urmson and Marina Sbisà (Cambridge, Mass.: Harvard University Press, 1975). On the ways that promises to marry inscribe their own failure, see Shoshana Felman, *The Scandal of the Speaking Body: Don Juan with J. L. Austin, or Seduction in Two Languages*, trans. Catherine Porter (1980; repr., Stanford: Stanford University Press, 2002). See also Randall Craig's study of how promises epitomize the inherent contradictions of language, *Promising Language: Betrothal in Victorian Law and Fiction* (Albany: State University of New York Press, 2000), 47–48. Felman uses Don Juan's playful refusal to honor his promises as a figure for the subversion of fixed meaning in language and assumes that promises are defined by their constancy, 20. I argue that Trollope creates that constancy by discrediting a contractual understanding of promises as agreements that can legitimately be broken.

35. On Ruth and Naomi as icons of female friendship, see Deborah Cherry, *Painting Women: Victorian Women Artists* (New York: Routledge, 1993), 51. On

the frequent depiction of the two women in illustrated Victorian family bibles, see Mary Wilson Carpenter, *Imperial Bibles, Domestic Bodies: Women, Sexuality, and Religion in the Victorian Market* (Athens: Ohio University Press, 2003), 58. On the homoerotic connotations of the Ruth and Naomi story, see Ruth Vanita, *Sappho and the Virgin Mary: Same-Sex Love and the English Literary Imagination* (New York: Columbia University Press, 1996), 76, 95, 145; Gene Damon, Jan Watson, and Robin Jordan, *The Lesbian in Literature: A Bibliography* 2nd ed. (Reno, Nevada: The Ladder, 1975), 14; and Terry Castle, ed., *The Literature of Lesbianism: A Historical Anthology from Ariosto to Stonewall* (New York: Columbia University Press, 2003), 108–114.

36. Thomas Macaulay, *The History of England*, vol. 2 (1848; repr., Boston: Houghton, Mifflin and Company, 1901), 249–52. Macaulay's treatment of Anne's "romantic fondness" for Churchill as an undue influence on government matches Trollope's sense of Alice of Queen Anne Street having a misguided eagerness to participate in politics. Edward Carpenter cites the friendship between Queen Anne and Lady Churchill in his study of homoerotic friendship, *Ioläus: An Anthology of Friendship*, 2nd ed. (1902; repr., London: Swann Sonnenschein & Co., 1906), 146–47. See also Rose Collis, *Portraits to the Wall: Historic Lesbian Lives Unveiled* (London: Cassell, 1994), 15–28.

37. See James Kincaid, *The Novels of Anthony Trollope* (Oxford: Clarendon Press, 1977), 186; and Kate Flint, "Introduction: Trollope and Sexual Politics," in *Can You Forgive Her?* (Oxford: Oxford University Press, 1982), xxiv.

38. Tony Tanner, *Adultery in the Novel: Contract and Transgression* (Baltimore: Johns Hopkins University Press, 1979), 6, 12, 13, 15. For his equation of homosexuality with adultery, incest, and primitivism, see 6, 53, 14, 97. For another argument that defines novelistic form in terms of the tension between social institutions and individual desire, see Joseph Allen Boone, *Tradition Counter Tradition: Love and the Form of Fiction* (Chicago: University of Chicago Press, 1987), 59, 66.

39. See Tanner, 6, 9, 15, 368.

40. On *Small House*, see Jeanne Fahnestock, "Bigamy: The Rise and Fall of a Convention," *Nineteenth-Century Fiction* 36 (1981), 70.

41. In his review of the novel, Richard Holt Hutton uses the phrase three times and says George is unusually villainous for a Trollope novel; reprinted in John Charles Olmsted, ed., *A Victorian Art of Fiction* (New York: Garland Publishers, 1979), 507–10; the review first appeared in the *Spectator* (September 2, 1865), 978–79.

42. Trollope, *The Duke's Children*, 90; see also *Can You Forgive Her?*, 252, 270.

43. Significantly, Palliser's commands early in the novel are mostly ineffectual; Glencora obeys them only after she comes to believe that he loves her, showing that Trollope is working very hard to reconcile hierarchical marriage with marriage for love. Other critics have remarked on the violence attached to Glencora and Palliser's marital accommodation; see King, 320; Flint, xxvii; Margaret Hewitt, "Anthony Trollope: Historian and Sociologist," *The British Journal of Sociology* 4.3 (1963), 226–39; and George Levine, "Can You Forgive Him? Trollope's 'Can You Forgive Her?' and the Myth of Realism," *Victorian Studies* 18 (1974), 27.

44. As Kincaid notes, in being asked to forgive Alice, "We are being asked to participate in a very ironic forgiveness, asked, in other words, to assist in the suppression of her will," 187. Kincaid observes that Alice holds on to her guilt and refuses forgiveness because "[a]s long as she can maintain her grip on this guilt, she can, of course, elude Grey," 186.

45. Friedrich Nietzsche, *On the Genealogy of Morals*, trans. Walter Kaufmann and R. J. Hollingdale (New York: Vintage Books, 1967), 24. Further references are to this edition and appear in the text. Nietzsche singles out Henry Thomas Buckle, 28, who wrote a popular *History of Civilization* (London: J. Parker & Son, 1857).

CONCLUSION
Woolf, Wilde, and Girl Dates

1. Virginia Woolf, *A Room of One's Own* (1929; repr., New York: Harcourt Brace Jovanovich, 1979), 86.

2. Lillian Faderman, "Preface," *Chloe Plus Olivia: An Anthology of Lesbian Literature from the Seventeenth Century to the Present* (New York: Penguin, 1994), viii.

3. On Woolf's involvement with Hall's trial and its effect on her own writing at the time, see Hermione Lee, *Virginia Woolf* (New York: Vintage Books, 1996), 519.

4. Cited in Edward Carpenter, ed., *Ioläus: An Anthology of Friendship*, 2nd ed. (London: Swan Sonnenschein & Co., 1906), 160–61.

5. Bertrand Russell and Patricia Russell, eds., *The Amberley Papers: Bertrand Russell's Family Background* (London: George Allen & Unwin, 1966), 181.

6. See Michael Lucey, *The Misfit of the Family: Balzac and the Social Forms of Sexuality* (Durham, NC: Duke University Press, 2003), 97–109; and George Rousseau and Caroline Warman, "Made from the Stuff of Saints: Chateaubriand's *René* and Custine's Search for a Homosexual Identity," *GLQ* 7:1 (2001), 1, 22, n. 2.

7. Kay Turner, ed., *Dear Sappho: A Legacy of Lesbian Love Letters* (London: Thames & Hudson, 1996), 138–39.

8. La Vyrle Spencer, cited in Janice Radway, *Reading the Romance: Women, Patriarchy, and Popular Literature* (Chapel Hill: University of North Carolina Press, 1984), 68; Amy Sohn, "Red Wine and Cigarettes," *New York*, May 23, 2005, 62. The final episode of the television series *Sex and the City* offered an update of the plot of female amity, since it represented the main character's three female friends as crucial to the resolution of its heterosexual romance.

9. Tamar Lewin, "Nationwide Survey Includes Data on Teenage Sex Habits," *New York Times*, September 16, 2005, A12.

10. Nicole Beland, "Girl on Girl-on-Girl," *Men's Health*, June 2005, 28.

Bibliography

PRIMARY SOURCES

Acland, Eleanor. *Good-Bye for the Present: The Story of Two Childhoods. Milly: 1878–88 & Ellen: 1913–24*. London: Hodder & Stoughton, 1935.

Anson, Margaret. *The Merry Order of St. Bridget*. 1868. Reprinted as *The Order of the Rod: A Classic of Victorian Erotica*. London: Senate, 1997.

Armstrong, Jessie. *Celestine and Sallie; Or, Two Dolls and Two Homes*. London: Chas. H. Kelly, 1890.

Ashford, Mary. *Life of a Licensed Victualler's Daughter*. London: Saunders & Otley, 1844.

Auntie Bee [Bertha Buxton]. *More Dolls*. London: George Routledge & Sons, 1879.

Avery, Gillian, ed. *The Diary of Emily Pepys*. London: Prospect Books, 1984.

Bachofen, J. J. *Myth, Religion, and Mother Right: Selected Writings of J. J. Bachofen*. Trans. Ralph Mannheim. Princeton: Princeton University Press, 1967.

Bagot, Mrs. Charles [Sophy Louisa]. *Links with the Past*. London: Edward Arnold, 1901.

Bailey, John, ed. *The Diary of Lady Frederick Cavendish*. London: John Murray, 1927.

Baillie, Albert, ed. *Letters of Lady Augusta Stanley: A Young Lady at Court*. London: Gerald Howe, 1927.

Bathgate, Janet. *Aunt Janet's Legacy to Her Nieces: Recollections of Humble Life in Yarrow in the Beginning of the Century*. 2nd ed. Selkirk: George Lewis & Co., 1895.

Battersea, Constance. *Reminiscences*. London: Macmillan, 1922.

Baudelaire, Charles. *The Painter of Modern Life*. Trans. Jonathan Mayne. 1863. Reprint, New York: Da Capo Press, 1964.

Beale, Mrs. Catherine Hutton, ed. *Reminiscences of a Gentlewoman of the Last Century: Letters of Catherine Hutton*. Birmingham: Cornish Brothers, 1891.

Beale, S. Sophia, ed. *Recollections of a Spinster Aunt*. London: William Heinemann, 1908.

Beck, William, ed. *Family Fragments Respecting the Ancestry, Acquaintance and Marriage of Richard Low Beck and Rachel Lucas*. Gloucester: [privately printed by] John Bellows, 1897.

"Belles Lettres." Review of *Great Expectations*, by Charles Dickens. *Westminster Review* 77 (January 1862): 286–302.

Besant, Annie. *An Autobiography*. 1893. Reprint, Adya Madras, India: The Theosophical Publishing House, 1939.

Besset, Mrs. *Memoirs of a Doll; Written by Herself; A New Year's Gift*. London: George Routledge, 1854.

"The Bill for Divorce." *Quarterly Review* 102.203 (1857): 251–83.

The Birchen Bouquet: or Curious and Original Anecdotes of Ladies fond of administering the Birch Discipline, and published for the amusement, as well as the benefit of those Ladies who have under their tuition sulky, stupid, wanton, lying or idle Young Ladies or Gentleman. Birchington-on-Sea, 1881.

Bloomfield, Georgiana. *My Sisters.* Hertford: Simson, 1892.

Blunt, Lady Anne Noel. Diaries. 1847 to 1917. British Library, Mss. ADD. 53817–54030.

The Boudoir: A Victorian Magazine of Scandal. 1883. Reprint, New York: Grove Press, 1971.

Bradford, Clara. *Ethel's Adventures in Doll Country.* Ill. T. Pym. London: John F. Shaw, n.d. [1880].

Bradley, Marian. Diary. British Library, Mss. EG. 3766 A–B.

Braithwaite, J. Bevan. *Memoirs of Anna Braithwaite.* London: Headley Brothers, 1905.

Brenda [Mrs. G. Castle Smith]. *Victoria-Bess or the Ups and Downs of a Doll's Life.* London: John F. Shaw, 1879.

Brontë, Charlotte. *Jane Eyre.* 1847. Reprint, London: Penguin, 1986.

———. *Shirley.* 1849. Reprint, Penguin Books: London, 1985.

———. *Villette.* 1853. Reprint, London: Penguin Books, 1979.

[Brooke, Stopford]. "Recent Novels." *Dublin University Magazine* 42 (November 1853): 611–27.

Browne, Annabella Maria. *Live Dolls: A Tale for Children of All Ages.* London: Partridge, 1874.

Browning, Elizabeth Barrett. *Aurora Leigh*, ed. Margaret Reynolds. 1856. Reprint, New York: W. W. Norton & Company, 1996.

Browning, Robert. *Dearest Isa: Robert Browning's Letters to Isabella Blagden*, ed. Edward C. McAleer. Austin: University of Texas Press, 1951.

Buckle, Henry Thomas. *History of Civilization.* 2 vols. London: J. W. Parker and Son, 1857.

[Budge, Jane]. *A Beloved Mother: Life of Hannah S. Allen, by Her Daughter.* London: Samuel Harris and Co., 1884.

Burne, Janet. *Sybil's Dutch Dolls.* London: Field and Tuer, 1887.

Butler, Lady Elizabeth. *An Autobiography.* London: Constable, 1922.

Caird, Mona. "The Morality of Marriage." *Fortnightly Review* 53 (March 1890): 310–30. Reprinted in *Prose by Victorian Women: An Anthology*, eds. Andrea Broomfield and Sally Mitchell, 629–54. New York: Garland Publishing, 1996.

Carpenter, Edward. *Intermediate Types among Primitive Folk.* 2nd ed. 1919. Reprint, New York: Arno Press, 1975.

———. *Ioläus: An Anthology of Friendship.* 2nd ed. London: Swann Sonnenschein and Company, 1906.

Carr, Cornelia, ed. *Harriet Hosmer: Letters and Memories.* London: John Lane, The Bodley Head, 1913.

Carritt, E. F., ed. *Letters of Courtship, Between John Torr and Maria Jackson.* London: Oxford University Press, 1933.

Cartwright, Julia [Mrs. Ady], ed. *The Journals of Lady Knightley of Fawsley 1856–1884.* London: John Murray, 1915.

Chapman, Maria Weston, ed. *Harriet Martineau's Autobiography; With Memorials by Maria Weston Chapman.* 2nd ed. London: Smith, Elder & Co., 1877.

"Charles Dickens's *Great Expectations.*" Review of *Great Expectations*, by Charles Dickens. *Eclectic Review* 114 (October 1861): 458–77.

"The Charm: A Dialogue for the Englishwoman's Conversazione." In *Venus School Mistress, or Birchen Sports*, 53–57. N.d. Reprint, New York: Blue Moon Books, 1987.

Chouart, Jean. [Introduction to a reprint of the Christmas number]. *The Pearl* (1881): 5–11.

Clive, Mary, ed. *Caroline Clive: From the Diary and Family Papers of Mrs. Archer Clive (1801–1873).* London: The Bodley Head, 1949.

Cobbe, Frances Power. "Celibacy *v.* Marriage." *Fraser's Magazine* 65 (February 1862): 228–35.

———. *The Duties of Women: A Course of Lectures.* London: Norgate, 1881.

———. *Life of Frances Power Cobbe. By Herself.* 2 volumes. Boston: Houghton, Mifflin, 1894.

———. *Life of Frances Power Cobbe.* 2nd ed. London: Swan Sonnenschein, 1904.

———. "What Shall We Do with Our Old Maids?" 1862. Reprinted in *Prose by Victorian Women: An Anthology*, eds. Andrea Broomfield and Sally Mitchell, 236–61. New York: Garland, 1996.

———. "Wife-Torture in England." *Contemporary Review* 32 (April 1878): 55–87.

Coleridge, Christabel. *Charlotte Mary Yonge: Her Life and Letters.* London: Macmillan & Co., 1903.

Collier, Hon. E.C.F., ed. *A Victorian Diarist: Extracts from the Journals of Mary, Lady Monkswell.* London: John Murray, 1944.

———. *A Victorian Diarist: Later Extracts.* London: John Murray, 1946.

Collins, Wilkie. *Man and Wife.* 1870. Reprint, Oxford: Oxford University Press, 1995.

———. *The Woman in White.* 1860. Reprint, London: Penguin, 1985.

Cornwallis, Caroline Frances. "The Capabilities and Disabilities of Women." *Westminster Review* 67 (January 1857): 42–72.

———. "The Property of Married Women." *Westminster Review* 66 (October 1856): 331–60.

Cousin Nelly. *Dolly's Outfit: An Amusing and Instructive Work, Teaching Children How to Dress Their Dolls, Assisted by Cut-Out and Made-Up Patterns of Each Article of Dress.* London: Samuel Miller, 1872.

Covert, James T. *A Victorian Family as Seen through the Letters of Louise Creighton to Her Mother.* Lampeter, Wales: The Edwin Mellen Press, 1998.

Cupples, Mrs. George. *The Story of Our Doll.* London: T. Nelson, 1871.

Darwin, Charles. *On the Origin of Species by Means of Natural Selection, or the Preservation of Favoured Races in the Struggle for Life.* 1859. Reprint, London: Penguin, 1985.

The Diaries and Correspondence of Anna Catherina Bower. London: Bickers & Son, for private circulation only, 1903.

Dickens, Charles. *David Copperfield.* 1850. Reprint, London: Penguin, 1996.

Dickens, Charles. *Great Expectations*. 1861. Reprint, Oxford: Oxford University Press, 1993.

"Divorce a Vinculo; or, the Terrors of Sir Cresswell Cresswell." *Once a Week* 2 (February 25, 1860): 184–87.

Dolly and I. London: Fred Warne, 1883.

Dolly's Story Book. Her Travels in Doll-Land All over the World, London: Frederick Warne, 1889.

Dolman, Frederick. "Afternoon Tea with Miss Emily Faithfull." *The Young Woman* 3 (1894–1895): 318–19.

Edgcumbe, Fred, ed. *Letters of Fanny Brawne to Fanny Keats. 1820–1824*. London: Oxford University Press, 1936.

The Elements of Tuition, and Modes of Punishment. London: Printed for the Bookseller, n.d.

Eliot, George. "Janet's Repentance." In *Scenes of Clerical Life*. 1857. Reprint, London: Penguin, 1998.

———. *Middlemarch*. 1871–1872. Reprint, Oxford: Oxford University Press, 1996.

———. *The Mill on the Floss*. 1860. Reprint, London: Penguin, 1979.

Ellis, Sarah. *The Daughters of England, Their Position in Society, Character, and Responsibilities*. New York: Appleton, 1842. Reprint, London: Fisher, Son, n.d.

———. *The Women of England: Their Social Duties, and Domestic Habits*. 2nd ed. London: Fisher, Son & Co., [1839].

Engels, Frederick. *The Origin of the Family, Private Property and the State*, ed. Eleanor Burke Leacock. 1884. Reprint, New York: International Publishers, 1972.

Englishwoman's Domestic Magazine, 1866–1870.

Erskine, Mrs. Steuart. *Anna Jameson: Letters and Friendships (1812–1860)*. London: T. Fisher Unwin, 1915.

Esher, Viscount, ed. *The Girlhood of Queen Victoria. A Selection of Her Majesty's Diaries between the Years 1832 and 1840*. Vol. 1. London: John Murray, 1912.

Experiences of Flagellation: A Series of Remarkable Instances of Whipping Inflicted on Both Sexes, with Curious Anecdotes of Ladies Fond of Administering Birch Discipline. Compiled by an Amateur Flagellant. London: Printed for Private Circulation, 1885.

The Festival of the Passions; or, Voluptuous Miscellany. Vol. 2. N.p., 1863.

Field, E. M. *The Child and His Book: Some Account of the History and Progress of Children's Literature in England*. 2nd ed. London: Wells Gardner, Darton, 1892.

Field, Kate. Letters from Emily Faithfull 1878. Mss. KF 192, n.d., 1081–1087. Boston Public Library Collection.

Fison, Lorimer and A[lfred] W. Howitt. *Kamilaroi and Kurnai: Group-Marriage and Relationship, and Marriage by Elopement*. Melbourne: George Robertson, 1880. Reprint, Camberra: Australian Institute of Aboriginal and Torres Strait Islander Studies, 1991.

Foot, M.R.D., ed. *The Gladstone Diaries*. Oxford: Clarendon Press, 1966.

Fraxi, Pisanus [Henry Spencer Ashbee]. *Bibliography of Prohibited Books*. Vol. 1. 1877. Reprint, New York: Jack Brussel, 1962.

————. *Catena Librorum Tacendorum.* N.p., 1885.

Froude, James Anthony, ed. *Letters and Memorials of Jane Welsh Carlyle.* Vol. 2. London: Longman, Green & Co., 1883.

Fulmer, Constance M. and Margaret Barfield, eds. *A Monument to the Memory of George Eliot: Edith J. Simcox's* Autobiography of a Shirtmaker. New York: Garland Publishing, 1998.

Gatti, Mrs. *Florence and Her Doll.* New edition. London: William Tegg, 1865.

Gellie, Mrs. *Dolly Dear or the Story of a Waxen Beauty.* London: Griffith and Farran, 1883.

Gifford, Margaret Jeune, ed. *Pages from the Diary of an Oxford Lady, 1843–1862.* Oxford: The Shakespeare Head Press, 1932.

Gilbert, Josiah, ed. *Autobiography and Other Memorials of Mrs. Gilbert, formerly Ann Taylor.* 3rd ed. London: C. Kegan Paul, 1878.

"Gleanings from Dark Annals: Modern Amazons." *Chambers's Journal of Popular Literature, Science and Arts,* May 30, 1863, 348–51.

Gower, Ronald Sutherland. *Old Diaries 1881–1901.* London: John Murray, 1902.

Green, Muriel, ed. *Miss Lister of Shibden Hall: Selected Letters (1800–1840).* Sussex: The Book Guild, 1992.

[Greenwell, Dora]. "Our Single Women." *The North British Review* 36 (February 1862): 62–87.

Greg, W. R. "Why Are Women Redundant?" 1862. Reprinted in W. R. Greg, *Literary and Social Judgements.* Boston: James R. Osgood, 1873.

Gunter, Susan E., and Steven H. Jobe, eds. *Dearly Beloved Friends: Henry James's Letters to Younger Men.* Ann Arbor: University of Michigan Press, 2001.

Hall, N. John, ed., with the assistance of Nina Burgis. *The Letters of Anthony Trollope.* Vol. 1., 1835–1870. Stanford: Stanford University Press, 1983.

Hanbury, Charlotte. *Life of Mrs. Albert Head.* London: Marshall Brothers, 1905.

[Handley, Edwin Hill]. "Custody of Infants' Bill." *The British and Foreign Review* 7 (July 1838): 269–411.

Hardy, Thomas. *Far from the Madding Crowd.* 1874. Reprint, New York: W. W. Norton & Co., 1986.

Harris, Katherine. Diary. 1847 to 1850. British Library Mss. ADD. 52503.

Haweis, Mrs. H. R. [Mary]. *The Art of Beauty.* New York: Harper & Brothers, 1878.

Hays, Matilda. *Adrienne Hope: The Story of a Life.* London: T. Cautley Newby, 1866.

————. *Helen Stanley: A Tale.* London: E. Churton, 1846.

Hellerstein, Erna Olafson, Leslie Parker Hume, and Karen M. Offen, eds. *Victorian Women: A Documentary Account of Women's Lives in Nineteenth-Century England, France, and the United States.* Stanford: Stanford University Press, 1981.

Hering, Jeanie. *Minnie's Dolls.* London: George Routledge, 1880.

Hird, Frank. *Rosa Bonheur.* London: George Bell & Sons, 1904.

Hirschfeld, Magnus. *The Homosexuality of Men and Women.* Trans. Michael A. Lombardi-Nash. 1914. Reprint, New York: Prometheus Books, 2000.

Holmes, Oliver Wendell. *The Common Law.* Ed. Mark DeWolfe Howe. 1881. Reprint, Cambridge, Mass.: The Belknap Press of Harvard University Press, 1963.

Hope-Nicholson, Jacqueline, ed. *Life Amongst the Troubridges.* London: John Murray, 1966.

Horne, Richard Henry. *Memoirs of a London Doll, Written by Herself.* 1846. Reprint, London: Andre Deutsch, 1967.

Hosmer, Harriet. *Letters and Memories.* Edited by Cornelia Carr. London: John Lane, The Bodley Head, 1913.

Hutton, Richard Holt. Review of *Can You Forgive Her?*, by Anthony Trollope. *Spectator*, September 2, 1865. Reprinted in *A Victorian Art of Fiction*, ed. John Charles Olmsted, 507–10. New York: Garland, 1979.

Indecent Whipping. N.p., n.d.

Ireland, Mrs. Alexander [Annie E.], ed. *Selections from the Letters of Geraldine Endsor Jewsbury to Jane Welsh Carlyle.* London: Longman, Green & Co., 1892.

James, Henry. Review of *Can You Forgive Her? The Nation*, September 28, 1865.
———. *William Wetmore Story and His Friends: From Friends, Diaries, and Recollections.* 1903. Reprint, New York: Da Capo Press, 1969.

Jameson, Anna. *Memoirs and Essays.* London: Richard Bentley, 1846.

Jay, Elisabeth, ed. *The Autobiography of Margaret Oliphant.* 1889. Reprint, Toronto: Broadview Press, 2002.

Jimmy: Scenes from the Life of a Black Doll. Told by Himself to J. G. Sowerby. London: George Routledge & Sons, 1888.

The Journal of Emily Shore. London: Kegan Paul, 1891.

Keary, Eliza. *A Memoir of Annie Keary, By Her Sister.* London: Macmillan and Co., 1883.

Kelly v. Kelly. *Law Reports. Courts of Probate and Divorce* 2 (1869): 37.

Kemble, Frances Anne. *Further Records. 1848–1883.* Vol. 2. London: Richard Bentley, 1890.

[Kemble], Frances Anne Butler. *Journal.* Vol. 1. London: John Murray, 1835.

Klumpke, Anna. *Rosa Bonheur: The Artist's (Auto)biography.* Trans. Gretchen van Slyke. 1908. Reprint, Ann Arbor: University of Michigan Press, 1997.

"The Lady and Her Marriage Settlement." *Englishwoman's Domestic Magazine* 47 (1864): 207–11.

Langlois, Dora. *The Child: Its Origin and Development: A Manual Enabling Mothers to Initiate Their Daughters Gradually and Modestly into All the Mysteries of Life.* London: W. Reeves, 1896.

Laycock, Thomas. *A Treatise of the Nervous Disorders of Women.* London: Longman and Co., 1840.

Lecky, William. *History of European Morals from Augustus to Charlemagne.* 2 vols. 1869. Reprint of the 1877 edition. London: Longmans, Green, 1902.

Leicester, Caroline. *Susan and the Doll, or Do Not Be Covetous.* London: James Hogg & Son, n.d. [1861].

Letters Addressed to the Editor of the Englishwoman's Domestic Magazine on the Whipping of Girls, and the General Corporal Punishment of Children. Nos. 1–7 (April–October 1870).

Letters from a Friend in Paris. Vol. 2. London: 1874.

Library Illustrative of Social Progress: From the Original Editions Collected by the Late Henry Thomas Buckle. London: Printed for G. Peacock, 1[8]77.

Lilly, W. S. "Marriage and Modern Civilization." *Nineteenth Century and after* 50.298 (1901): 905.

Limner, Luke [John Leighton]. *Madre Natura versus the Moloch of Fashion: A Social Essay.* 4th ed. London: Chatto and Windus, 1874.

Linton, Eliza Lynn. "The Girl of the Period." *Saturday Review*, March 14, 1868, 339–40.

Lister, Beatrix, ed. *Emma, Lady Ribblesdale: Letters and Diaries.* London: Privately printed at the Chiswick Press, 1930.

"The Loves of Sappho." *The Exquisite* (no. 7), 82–83.

Low, Frances H. *Queen Victoria's Dolls.* London: George Newnes, 1894.

Lowry, James M. *The Dolls' Garden Party.* London: The Leadenhall Press, 1892.

Lubbock, John. *The Origin of Civilisation and the Primitive Condition of Man,* ed. Pierre Rivière. 1870. Reprint, Chicago: University of Chicago Press, 1978.

Lubbock, Lady Sybil. *The Child in the Crystal: Reminiscences of Childhood.* London: Jonathan Cape, 1939.

[Lundie, Mary]. *Memoir of Mrs. Mary Lundie Duncan: Being Recollections of a Daughter by Her Mother.* 2nd ed. Edinburgh: William Oliphant & Son, 1842.

Macaulay, Thomas. *The History of England.* Vol. 2. 1848. Reprint, Boston: Houghton, Mifflin and Company, 1901.

MacCarthy, Desmond, and Agatha Russell, eds. *Lady John Russell: A Memoir: With Selections from Her Diaries and Correspondence.* London: Methuen, 1910.

Macpherson, Gerardine. *Memoirs of the Life of Anna Jameson.* London: Longmans, Green & Co., 1878.

Maine, Henry Sumner. *Ancient Law: Its Connection with the Early History of Society and Its Relation to Modern Ideas.* 1861. Reprint, Boston: Beacon Press, 1963.

Maitland, Julia. *The Doll and Her Friends, or Memoirs of the Lady Seraphina.* Boston: Ticknor, Reed, and Fields, 1852.

Martineau, Harriet. *Deerbrook.* 1839. Reprint, Garden City, NY: The Dial Press, 1984.

Martinet, Mrs. *The Quintessence of Birch Discipline.* London: Privately printed, 1870.

Masterman, Lucy, ed. *Mary Gladstone (Mrs. Drew): Her Diaries and Letters.* London: Methuen, 1930.

Mathison, Mary. *Letters of Mary Mathison.* London: Spottiswoode & Co., for private circulation only, 1875.

May's Doll: Where Its Dress Came from. A Book for Little Girls. London: John and Charles Mozley, 1851.

McLennan, John F. "Kinship in Ancient Greece, Part I." *Fortnightly Review* 4 (15 April 1866): 569–88.

———. *Primitive Marriage: An Inquiry into the Origin of the Form of Capture in Marriage Ceremonies.* Edinburgh: Adam and Charles Black, 1865.

Memorials of Agnes Elizabeth Jones. London: Strahan & Co., 1871.

Meredith, George. *Diana of the Crossways*. 1885. Reprint, New York: Modern Library, n.d.

Miles, Alice Catherine. *Every Girl's Duty: The Diary of a Victorian Debutante*, ed. Maggy Parsons. London: Deutsch, 1992.

Mill, John Stuart. *Autobiography*. 1873. Reprint, New York: The Liberal Arts Press, 1957.

———. "Early Essays on Marriage and Divorce." 1832. Reprinted in *Essays on Sex Equality*, ed. Alice Rossi. Chicago: University of Chicago Press, 1970.

———. "The Subjection of Women." 1869. Reprinted in *Essays on Sex Equality*, ed. Alice Rossi. Chicago: University of Chicago Press, 1970.

Mitford, Nancy, ed. *The Ladies of Alderley: Being the Letters between Maria Josepha, Lady Stanley of Alderley, and her Daughter-in-Law Henrietta Maria Stanley during the Years 1841–1850*. London: Chapman and Hall, 1938.

Moss, Carolyn J., ed. *Kate Field: Selected Letters*. Carbondale: Southern Illinois University Press, 1996.

"Mrs. Russell Barrington, Author and Artist." *Times*, March 11, 1933.

Myrtle, Harriet [Mary Gillies]. "The Dolls' Ball." In *More Fun for Our Little Friends*. London: Sampson Low, 1864.

Needler, G. H., ed. *Letters of Anna Jameson to Ottilie von Goethe*. London: Oxford University Press, 1939.

The New Epicurean; or the Delights of Sex Facetiously and Philosophically Considered in Graphic Letters Addressed to Young Ladies of Quality. New edition. London: Printed for Thomas Longtool, Rogerwell Street, 1875.

The New Ladies Tickler; or, the Adventures of Lady Lovesport and the Audacious Harry. London: Printed for the Bookseller, 1866.

Nietzsche, Friedrich. *On the Genealogy of Morals*. 1887. Trans. Walter Kaufmann and R. J. Hollingdale. Reprint, New York: Vintage Books, 1967.

Nordau, Max. *Degeneration*. 1892. Reprint, Lincoln: University of Nebraska Press, 1993.

Nunnery Tales; or, Cruising under False Colours: A Tale of Love and Lust. 3 vols. London: Printed for the Booksellers, n.d.

"Old Maids." *Dublin University Magazine* 56 (December 1860): 709.

Oliphant, Margaret. "The Laws Concerning Women." *Blackwood's Magazine* 79 (April 1856): 379–87.

———. "Sensation Novels." Review of *Great Expectations*, by Charles Dickens. *Blackwood Edinburgh's Magazine* 91 (May 1862): 564–84.

"On Flagellation and Female Boarding Schools." *The Exquisite*, no. 119 (n.d.): 120.

Oram, Alison, and Annmarie Turnbull. *The Lesbian History Sourcebook: Love and Sex Between Women in Britain from 1780 to 1970*. London: Routledge, 2001.

O'Reilly, Mrs. Robert. *Doll World; or, Play and Earnest: A Study from Real Life*. London: Bell and Daldy, 1872.

Palfreyman, Mrs. M. Journal. 1840 to 1861. British Library Mss. ADD. 49276.

Pardoe, Julia. *Lady Arabella: or the Adventures of a Doll*. London: Kerby & Son, 1856.

Parkes, Bessie Rayner. *Vignettes: Twelve Biographical Sketches*. London: Alexander Strahan, 1866.

Parkes, Fanny. *Wanderings of a Pilgrim*. London: Pelham Richardson, 1850.

The Pearl. Christmas annual number. 1881. Reprint, Atlanta: Pendulum Books, 1967.

Porter, Frances, Charlotte Macdonald, and Tui Macdonald, eds. *"My Hand Will Write What My Heart Dictates": The Unsettled Lives of Women in Nineteenth-Century New Zealand as Revealed to Sisters, Family, and Friends*. Auckland: Auckland University Press, 1996.

Procter, Adelaide A., ed. *The Victoria Regia: A Volume of Contributions in Poetry and Prose*. London: Emily Faithfull and Co., Victoria Press for the Employment of Women, 1861.

———. *A Welcome: Original Contributions in Poetry and Prose Addressed to Alexandra, Princess of Wales*. London: Printed and Published by Emily Faithfull and Co., Victoria Press for the Employment of Women, 1863.

Proust, Marcel, *Du côté du chez Swann*, eds. Pierre Clarac and André Ferré. 1913. Reprint, Paris: Gallimard, 1954.

Rawlinson, H. G., ed. *Personal Reminiscences in India and Europe 1830–1888 of Augusta Becher*. London: Constable, 1930.

Reddie, James Campbell. *The Amatory Experiences of a Surgeon*. In *The Libertine Reader*. 191–240. North Hollywood: Brandon House, 1968.

Review of *Great Expectations*, by Charles Dickens. *Saturday Review* 12 (July 20, 1861): 69–70.

Ritchie, Anne Thackeray. "Toilers and Spinsters." *Cornhill Magazine* 3 (1861): 318. Reprinted in *Toilers and Spinsters and Other Essays*. London: Smith, Elder, & Co., 1876.

Ritchie, Hester, ed. *Letters of Anne Thackeray Ritchie*. London: John Murray, 1924.

Rittenhouse, Jessie. *Lilian Whiting: Journalist, Essayist, Critic and Poet: A Sketch*. N.p., n.d.

Rolt, Margaret S., ed. *A Great-Niece's Journals: Being Extracts from the Journals of Fanny Anne Burney (Mrs. Wood) from 1830–1842*. London: Constable, 1926.

The Romance of Chastisement, or, Revelations of the School and Bedroom. N.p., 1870.

The Romance of Lust; or, Early Experiences. 4 vols. N.p., n.d.

Rosamond: Dolly's New Picture Book. Trans. Madame de Chatelain. London: A. N. Myers, 1870.

Rossetti, Christina. *Goblin Market*. 1862. Reprint, New York: Dover, 1983.

Rothschild, Lady Louisa de. Diaries. 1837 to 1907. British Library Mss. ADD. 47949–47962.

Russell, Bertrand, and Patricia Russell, eds. *The Amberley Papers: Bertrand Russell's Family Background*. London: George Allen & Unwin, 1966.

[Russell, C. W.]. "Novel-Morality: the Novels of 1853." Review of *Villette*. *Dublin Review* 34 (March 1853): 174–203.

Russell, H. Rutherford. *My Dolly*. London: Marcus Ward, 1877.

Scott, falsely called Sebright v. Sebright. *Law Reports. Probate Division* 12 (1886): 21–31.

"The Secret Life of Linda Brent; A Curious History of Slave Life and Slave Wrongs." *The Cremorne*, no. 2 (February 1851): 45.

"Seduction Unveiled: Female Boarding Schools." *The Exquisite*, no. 109 (n.d.): 68–69.

Sewell, Eleanor L., ed. *The Autobiography of Elizabeth M. Sewell*. London: Longmans, Green & Co., 1907.

Simcox, E[dith] J. *Primitive Civilizations or Outlines of the History of Ownership in Archaic Communities*. London: Swan Sonnenschein, 1894.

Sinks of London Laid Open. London: J. Duncombe, 1848.

The Sins of the Cities of the Plain. Or the Recollections of a Mary-Ann with Short Essays on Sodomy and Tribadism. 2 vols. London: Privately printed, 1881.

Sitwell, Osbert. *Two Generations*. London: Macmillan, 1940.

Skinner, Robert T., ed. *Cummy's Diary: A Diary Kept by R. L. Stevenson's Nurse Alison Cunningham While Travelling with Him on the Continent during 1863*. London: Chatto & Windus, 1926.

Smith, William Robertson. *Kinship and Marriage in Early Arabia*. 1885. Reprint, Boston: Beacon Press, 1963.

Smyth, Ethel. *Impressions that Remained: Memoirs*. Vol. 1. London: Longmans, Green & Co., 1919.

Somerville, Martha. *Personal Recollections, from Early Life to Old Age, of Mary Somerville, with Selections from Her Correspondence*. London: John Murray, 1873.

Spevack, Marvin, ed. *A Victorian Chronicle: The Diary of Henrietta Halliwell-Phillipps*. Hildesheim: Georg Olms Verlag, 1999.

"The Spirit of the Ring; containing many curious anecdotes of the celebrated Marie Antoinette." *The Exquisite*, no. 116 (n.d.): 92–94; no. 117 (n.d.): 103.

Stahl, P. J. *La Poupée de Mademoiselle Lili*. Hetzel: Bibliothèque d'Education et de Récréation. N.p, [1886].

Stanley, Liz, ed. *The Diaries of Hannah Cullwick, Victorian Maidservant*. New Brunswick, NJ: Rutgers University Press, 1984.

Stanton, Theodore, ed. *Reminiscences of Rosa Bonheur*. London: Andrew Melrose, 1910.

Stebbins, Emma. *Charlotte Cushman: Her Letters and Memories of Her Life*. Boston: Houghton, Osgood and Co., 1879.

Taylor, Rebekah H., Mrs. *Letters of Mrs. H. W. Taylor to Members of Her Classes, and Friends*. Edited by Her Husband. London: James E. Hawkins, 1878.

Todd, Margaret. *The Life of Sophia Jex-Blake*. London: Macmillan, 1918.

Trollope, Anthony. *An Autobiography*. 1883. Reprint, Oxford: Oxford University Press, 1987.

———. *Barchester Towers*. 1857. Reprint, London: Penguin Books, 1994.

———. *Can You Forgive Her?* 1865. Reprint, London: Penguin Books, 1986.

———. *The Duke's Children*. 1880. Reprint, Oxford: Oxford University Press, 1983.

———. "Mrs. General Talboys." In *Early Short Stories*. Ed. John Sutherland. Oxford: Oxford University Press, 1994.

————. "The Telegraph Girl." *Good Words.* 1877. Reprint, London: Chatto & Windus, 1892.

————. "The Turkish Bath." *The Galaxy* 8.5 (November 1869): 689–703.

Trollope, Frances. *The Widow Barnaby.* 1839. Repr., Phoenix Mill: Alan Sutton Publishing, 1995.

[Trotter, L. J.]. "Mr. Dicken's Last Novel." Review of *Great Expectations. Dublin University Magazine* 18 (1861): 685–93.

U[niacke], M[ary]. *The Dolls' Pic-Nic.* London: Darton, 1860.

Venus School Mistress. n.d. Reprint, New York: Blue Moon Books, 1987.

von Boehn, Max. *Dolls.* Trans. Josephine Nicoll. 1929. Repr., New York: Dover Publications, 1972.

Warren, Margaret Leicester. *Diaries.* Printed for private circulation, 1924.

The Well-Bred Doll. London: David Bogue, 1853.

The Whippingham Papers: A Collection of Contributions in Prose and Verse, Chiefly by the Author of the 'Romance of Chastisement.' London, 1888.

Whitbread, Helena, ed. *I Know My Own Heart: The Diaries of Anne Lister, 1791–1840.* London: Virago, 1988.

————, ed. *No Priest But Love: Excerpts from the Diaries of Anne Lister, 1824–1826.* New York: New York University Press, 1992.

Whiting, Lilian. *After Her Death: The Story of a Summer.* Boston: Roberts Brothers, 1898.

————. *The Brownings: Their Life and Art.* Boston: Little Brown, 1911.

————. *From Dreamland Sent.* Boston: Roberts Brothers, 1895.

————. *The Golden Road.* Boston: Little Brown, 1918.

————. *Kate Field: A Record.* Boston: Little Brown, 1900.

————, ed. *Anna Elizabeth Klumpke. Memoirs of an Artist.* Privately printed, 1940.

Williams, Jane, ed. *The Autobiography of Elizabeth Davis, A Balaclava Nurse.* London: Hurst and Blackett, 1857.

Woolf, Virginia. *A Room of One's Own.* 1929. Reprint, New York: Harcourt Brace Jovanovich, 1979.

SECONDARY SOURCES

Abelove, Henry. *Deep Gossip.* Minneapolis: University of Minnesota Press, 2003.

Ablow, Rachel. "Labors of Love: The Sympathetic Subjects of *David Copperfield.*" *Dickens Studies Annual* 31 (2002): 23–46.

Ackerman, Ann Trugman. "Victorian Ideology and British Children's Literature, 1850–1914." Ph.D. dissertation. North Texas State University, 1984.

Anderson, Amanda. *The Powers of Distance: Cosmopolitanism and the Cultivation of Detachment.* Princeton: Princeton University Press, 2001.

Anderson, Nancy Fix. *Women against Women in Victorian England: A Life of Eliza Lynn Linton.* Bloomington: Indiana University Press, 1987.

Anderson, Olive. "State, Civil Society and Separation in Victorian Marriage." *Past and Present* 163.1 (1999): 161–201.

Ariès, Philippe. *Centuries of Childhood: A Social History of Family Life.* Trans. Robert Baldick. New York: Vintage Books, 1965.

Armstrong, Nancy. *Desire and Domestic Fiction: A Political History of the Novel.* New York: Oxford University Press, 1987.

Arnstein, Walter L. *Queen Victoria.* Houndmills: Palgrave Macmillan, 2003.

Atiyah, P. S. *The Rise and Fall of Freedom of Contract.* Oxford: Clarendon Press, 1979.

Auerbach, Jeffrey. "What They Read: Mid-Nineteenth Century English Women's Magazines and the Emergence of a Consumer Culture." *Victorian Periodicals Review* 30:2 (1997): 121–40.

Austin, J. L. *How to Do Things with Words,* eds. J. O. Urmson and Marina Sbisà. Cambridge, Mass.: Harvard University Press, 1975.

Avery, Gillian. *Childhood's Pattern: A Study of the Heroes and Heroines of Children's Fiction.* London: Hodder and Stoughton, 1975.

Bachmann, Manfred, and Claus Hansmann. *Dolls: The Wide World Over: An Historical Account.* Trans. Ruth Michaelis-Jena with the collaboration of Patrick Murray. 1971. Reprint, London: Harrap, 1973.

Bailey, Peter. "Parasexuality and Glamour: The Victorian Barmaid as Cultural Prototype." *Gender & History* 2.2 (1990): 148–72.

Barkan, Elazar. "Victorian Promiscuity: Greek Ethics and Primitive Exemplars." In *Prehistories of the Future: The Primitivist Project and the Culture of Modernism.* eds. Elazar Barkan and Ronald Bush, 56–92. Stanford: Stanford University Press, 1995.

Barthes, Roland. *L'aventure sémiologique.* Paris: Editions du Seuil, 1985.

———. *The Fashion System.* Trans. Matthew Ward and Richard Howard. 1967. Reprint, New York: Hill and Wang, 1983.

———. *Sade/Fourier/Loyola.* Trans. Richard Miller. New York: Hill & Wang, 1976.

———. *S/Z: An Essay.* Trans. Richard Miller. New York: Hill and Wang, 1974.

Bebbington, D. W. *Evangelicalism in Modern Britain: A History from the 1730s to the 1980s.* London: Unwin Hyman, 1989.

Beer, Gillian. *Darwin's Plots: Evolutionary Narrative in Darwin, George Eliot and Nineteenth-Century Fiction.* 2nd ed. Cambridge: Cambridge University Press, 2000.

———. "Knowing a Life: Edith Simcox—Sat est vixisse?" In *Knowing the Past: Victorian Literature and Culture.* ed. Suzy Anger, 252–66. Ithaca, NY: Cornell University Press, 2001.

Beetham, Margaret. *A Magazine of Her Own? Domesticity and Desire in the Woman's Magazine 1800–1914.* London: Routledge, 1996.

Beland, Nicole. "Girl on Girl-on-Girl." *Men's Health,* June 2005, 28.

Benjamin, Jessica. *Like Subjects, Love Objects: Essays on Recognition and Sexual Difference.* New Haven: Yale University Press, 1995.

Benjamin, Walter. *The Arcades Project.* Trans. Howard Eiland and Kevin McLaughlin. Cambridge, Mass.: The Belknap Press of Harvard University Press, 1999.

Bennett, Paula. "Critical Clitoridectomy: Female Sexual Imagery and Feminist Psychoanalytic Theory." *Signs: Journal of Women in Culture and Society* 18.2 (1993): 235–59.

Benstock, Shari. *Women of the Left Bank: Paris, 1900–1940.* Austin: University of Texas Press, 1986.

Berger, John. *Ways of Seeing.* London: British Broadcasting Corporation and Penguin Books, 1972.

Bersani, Leo. *A Future for Astyanax: Character and Desire in Literature.* Boston: Little, Brown, 1976.

———. *Homos.* Cambridge, Mass.: Harvard University Press, 1995.

Best, Geoffrey. "Evangelicalism and the Victorians." In *The Victorian Crisis of Faith,* ed. Anthony Symondson, 37–56. London: Society for Promoting Christian Knowledge, 1970.

Bloch, Ernst. *Natural Law and Human Dignity.* Trans. Dennis J. Schmidt. 1961. Reprint, Cambridge, Mass.: The MIT Press, 1996.

Blodgett, Harriet. *'Capacious Hold-All': An Anthology of Englishwomen's Diary Writings.* Charlottesville: University Press of Virginia, 1991.

———. *Centuries of Female Days: Englishwomen's Private Diaries.* New Brunswick, NJ: Rutgers University Press, 1988.

Blum, Stella, ed. *Ackermann's Costume Plates: Women's Fashions in England, 1812–1828.* New York: Dover, 1978.

Boardman, Kay. "'A Material Girl in a Material World': The Fashionable Female Body in Victorian Women's Magazines." *Journal of Victorian Culture* 3.1 (1998): 93–110.

Bodenheimer, Rosemarie. "Autobiography in Fragments: The Elusive Life of Edith Simcox." *Victorian Studies* 44.3 (2002): 399–422.

Boone, Joseph Allen. *Libidinal Currents: Sexuality and the Shaping of Modernism.* Chicago: University of Chicago Press, 1998.

———. *Tradition Counter Tradition: Love and the Form of Fiction.* Chicago: University of Chicago Press, 1987.

Booth, Alison. *How To Make It as a Woman: Collective Biographical History from Victoria to the Present.* Chicago: University of Chicago Press, 2004.

Borneman, John. "Until Death Do Us Part: Marriage/Death in Anthropological Discourse." *American Ethnologist* 23.2 (1996): 215–35.

Boswell, John. *Same-Sex Unions in Premodern Europe.* New York: Villiard Books, 1994.

Bradley, Ian. *The Call to Seriousness: The Evangelical Impact on the Victorians.* New York: Macmillan, 1976.

Bratton, J. S. *The Impact of Victorian Children's Fiction.* London: Croom Helm, 1981.

Bray, Alan. *The Friend.* Chicago: University of Chicago Press, 2003.

Breward, Christopher. *The Hidden Consumer: Masculinities, Fashion and City Life 1860–1914.* Manchester: Manchester University Press, 1999.

Bristow, Edward J. *Vice and Vigilance: Purity Movements in Britain since 1700.* Dublin: Gill and Macmillan, 1977.

Brooks, Peter. *Reading for the Plot: Design and Intention in Narrative.* New York: Vintage, 1984.

Brown, Irene Q. "Domesticity, Feminism, and Friendship: Female Aristocratic Culture and Marriage in England, 1660–1760." *Journal of Family History* 7.4 (1982): 406–24.

Brown, Lesley, ed. *The Shorter Oxford English Dictionary.* Vol. 1. Oxford: Clarendon Press, 1993.

Brown, Penny. *The Captured World: The Child and Childhood in Nineteenth-Century Women's Writing.* New York: St. Martin's Press, 1993.

Burnett, John, ed. *The Annals of Labour: Autobiographies of British Working Class People, 1820–1920.* Bloomington: Indiana University Press, 1974.

Bush, Julia. "Ladylike Lives? Upper Class Women's Autobiographies and the Politics of Late Victorian and Edwardian Britain." *Literature & History* 3rd series 10.2 (2001): 42–61.

Butler, Heather. "What do you call a lesbian with long fingers? The Development of Lesbian and Dyke Pornography." In *Porn Studies.* ed. Linda Williams, 167–97. Durham, NC: Duke University Press, 2004.

Butler, Judith. *Antigone's Claim: Kinship Between Life and Death.* New York: Columbia University Press, 2000.

———. *Bodies that Matter: On the Discursive Limits of "Sex".* New York: Routledge, 1993.

———. *Gender Trouble: Feminism and the Subversion of Identity.* New York: Routledge, 1990.

———. *Undoing Gender.* New York: Routledge, 2004.

Buxton, Alexandra. *Discovering 19th–Century Fashions: A Look at the Changes in Fashion through the Victoria & Albert Museum's Dress Collection.* Cambridge: Hobsons Publishing, 1989.

Campbell, Colin. *The Romantic Ethic and the Spirit of Modern Consumerism.* Oxford: Blackwell, 1987.

Carpenter, Humphrey. *Secret Gardens: A Study of the Golden Age of Children's Literature.* London: George Allen and Unwin, 1985.

Carpenter, Mary Wilson. *Imperial Bibles, Domestic Bodies: Women, Sexuality and Religion in the Victorian Market.* Athens: Ohio University Press, 2003.

Carter, Kathryn. "The Cultural Work of Diaries in Mid-Century Victorian Britain." *Victorian Review* 23.2 (1997): 251–67.

Casteras, Susan P. *Images of Victorian Womanhood in English Art.* Rutherford: Fairleigh Dickinson University Press, 1987.

Castle, Terry. *The Apparitional Lesbian: Female Homosexuality and Modern Culture.* New York: Columbia University Press, 1993.

———, ed. *The Literature of Lesbianism: A Historical Anthology from Ariosto to Stonewall.* New York: Columbia University Press, 2003.

Chauncey, George. *Why Marriage? The History Shaping Today's Debate over Gay Equality.* New York: Basic Books, 2004.

Cherry, Deborah. *Painting Women: Victorian Women Artists.* New York: Routledge, 1993.

Cieslik, Jürgen and Marianne Cieslik. *Dolls: European Dolls 1800–1900.* London: Studio Vista, 1979.

Clarke, Norma. *Ambitious Heights: Writing, Friendship, Love—the Jewsbury Sisters, Felicia Hemans, and Jane Carlyle.* London: Routledge, 1990.

Clegg, Cox. "Lilian Whiting." Entry in *American National Biography*, eds. John A. Garraty and Mark C. Carnes. New York: Oxford University Press, 1999.

Cocks, Harry. *Nameless Offences: Homosexual Desire in the 19th Century*. London: I. B. Tauris, 2003.

Cohen, Ed. *Talk on the Wilde Side*. New York: Routledge, 1993.

Cohen, Margaret. *The Sentimental Education of the Novel*. Princeton: Princeton University Press, 1999.

Cohen, William. *Sex Scandal: The Private Parts of Victorian Fiction*. Durham, NC: Duke University Press, 1996.

Cole, Sarah Rose. Ph.D. dissertation, Columbia University, in progress.

Collis, Rose. *Portraits to the Wall: Historic Lesbian Lives Unveiled*. London: Cassell, 1994.

Connor, Steven. "Men in Skirts." *Women: A Cultural Review* 13.3 (2002): 257–71.

Coontz, Stephanie. "The Heterosexual Revolution." *New York Times*, July 5, 2005, A17.

Corbett, Mary Jean. *Representing Femininity: Middle-Class Subjectivity in Victorian and Edwardian Women's Autobiographies*. New York: Oxford University Press, 1992.

Cott, Nancy. *The Bonds of Womanhood: "Woman's Sphere" in New England, 1780–1835*. New Haven: Yale University Press, 1977.

———. *Public Vows: A History of Marriage and the Nation*. Cambridge, Mass.: Harvard University Press, 2000.

Coveney, Peter. *The Image of Childhood*. 1957. Reprint, Harmondsworth: Penguin Books, 1967.

Coward, Rosalind. *Patriarchal Precedents: Sexuality and Social Relations*. London: Routledge and Kegan Paul, 1983.

Craig, Randall. *Promising Language: Betrothal in Victorian Law and Fiction*. Albany: State University of New York Press, 2000.

Crane, Diana. *Fashion and Its Social Agendas: Class, Gender, and Identity in Clothing*. Chicago: University of Chicago Press, 2000.

Crawford, Julie. "Charlotte Cushman." In *Lesbian Histories and Cultures: An Encyclopedia*, ed. Bonnie Zimmerman, 217. New York: Garland Publishing, 2000.

Crosby, Christina. "Charlotte Brontë's Haunted Text." *Studies in English Literature* 24.4 (1984): 701–15.

Cutt, Margaret Nancy. *Ministering Angels: A Study of Nineteenth-Century Evangelical Writing for Children*. Wormley: Five Owls Press, 1979.

Damon, Gene, Jan Watson, and Robin Jordan. *The Lesbian in Literature: A Bibliography*. 2nd ed. Reno, Nevada: The Ladder, 1975.

Davidoff, Leonore, *The Best Circles: Society Etiquette and the Season*. 1973. Reprint, London: The Cresset Library, 1986.

Davidoff, Leonore and Catherine Hall. *Family Fortunes: Men and Women of the English Middle Class 1780–1850*. Chicago: University of Chicago Press, 1987.

Dean, Tim. "Homosexuality and the Problem of Otherness." In *Homosexuality & Psychoanalysis*, eds. Tim Dean and Christopher Lane, 120–43. Chicago: University of Chicago Press, 2001.

Deitcher, David. *Dear Friends: American Photographs of Men Together, 1840–1918*. New York: Harry N. Abrams, 2001.

Deleuze, Gilles. "Coldness and Cruelty." Trans. Jean McNeil. In *Masochism*, 9–138. 1967. Reprint, New York: Zone Books, 1989.

Dellamora, Richard. *Friendship's Bonds: Democracy and the Novel in Victorian England*. Philadelphia: University of Pennsylvania Press, 2004.

de Marly, Diana. *Fashion for Men: An Illustrated History*. New York: Holmes & Meier, 1985.

Dever, Carolyn. *Death and the Mother from Dickens to Freud: Victorian Fiction and the Anxiety of Origins*. Cambridge: Cambridge University Press, 1998.

———. *Skeptical Feminism: Activist Theory, Activist Practice*. Minneapolis: University of Minnesota Press, 2004.

Diamond, Marion. "Maria Rye and *The Englishwoman's Domestic Magazine*." *Victorian Periodicals Review* 30.1 (1997): 5–16.

Doan, Laura. *Fashioning Sapphism: The Origins of a Modern English Lesbian Culture*. New York: Columbia University Press, 2001.

Donoghue, Emma. *Passions Between Women: British Lesbian Culture 1688–1801*. New York: HarperCollins, 1993.

Dreger, Alice Domurat. *Hermaphrodites and the Medical Invention of Sex*. Cambridge, Mass.: Harvard University Press, 1998.

Duggan, Lisa. "The Trials of Alice Mitchell: Sensationalism, Sexology, and the Lesbian Subject in Turn-of-the-Century America." *Signs: Journal of Women in Culture and Society* 18.4 (1993): 791–814.

DuPlessis, Rachel Blau. *Writing beyond the Ending: Narrative Strategies of Twentieth-Century Women Writers*. Bloomington: Indiana University Press, 1984.

Edelman, Lee. *No Future: Queer Theory and the Death Drive*. Durham, NC: Duke University Press, 2004.

Elfenbein, Andrew. "Byron and the Work of Homosexual Performance in Early Victorian England." *Modern Language Quarterly* 54 (1993): 535–66.

———. *Romantic Genius: The Prehistory of a Homosexual Role*. New York: Columbia University Press, 1999.

Ellis, Alec. *Library Services for Young People in England Wales 1830–1950*. London, 1958.

Eribon, Didier. "Michel Foucault's Histories of Sexuality." Trans. Michael Lucey. *GLQ* 7.1 (2001): 31–86.

———. *Sur cet instant fragile . . . Carnets, janvier-août 2004*. Paris: Fayard, 2004.

Ewing, Elizabeth. *Everyday Dress 1650–1900*. London: B. T. Batsford, 1984.

Faderman, Lillian. *Chloe Plus Olivia: An Anthology of Lesbian Literature from the Seventeenth Century to the Present*. New York: Penguin, 1994.

———. *Surpassing the Love of Men: Romantic Friendship and Love between Women from the Renaissance to the Present*. New York: William Morrow, 1981.

———. *To Believe in Women: What Lesbians Have Done for America—A History*. Boston: Houghton Mifflin, 1999.

Fahnestock, Jeanne. "Bigamy: The Rise and Fall of a Convention." *Nineteenth-Century Fiction* 36.1 (1981): 47–71.

Farwell, Marilyn R. "Heterosexual Plots and Lesbian Subtexts: Toward a Theory of Lesbian Narrative Space." In *Lesbian Texts and Contexts: Radical Revisions*, eds. Karla Jay and Joanne Glasgow, 91–103. New York: New York University Press, 1990.

Feaver, George. *From Status to Contract: A Biography of Sir Henry Maine 1822–1888*. London: Longmans, Green & Co., 1969.

Feaver, William. *When We Were Young: Two Centuries of Children's Book Illustration*. New York: Holt, Rinehart, and Winston, 1977.

Fee, Elizabeth. "The Sexual Politics of Victorian Social Anthropology." In *Clio's Consciousness Raised: New Perspectives on the History of Women*, eds. Mary S. Hartman and Lois Banner, 86–102. New York: Harper Colophon, 1974.

Felman, Shoshana. *The Scandal of the Speaking Body: Don Juan with J. L. Austin, or Seduction in Two Languages*. Trans. Catherine Porter. 1980. Reprint, Stanford: Stanford University Press, 2002.

Fenichel, Otto. "The Symbolic Equation: Girl = Phallus." *The Psychoanalytic Quarterly* 18.3 (1949): 303–24.

Ferenczi, Sandor. "On Obscene Words." In *Sex in Psycho-analysis*. New York: Dover Publications, 1956.

Ferguson, Frances. *Pornography, the Theory: What Utilitarianism Did to Action*. Chicago: University of Chicago Press, 2004.

Findlay, Heather. "Freud's 'Fetishism' and the Lesbian Dildo Debates." *Feminist Studies* 18.3 (1992): 563–79.

Fisher, Margery. Introduction to *Memoirs of a London Doll, Written by Herself*, by Richard Henry Horne. 1846. Reprint, London: Andre Deutsch, 1967.

Flint, Kate. "Introduction: Trollope and Sexual Politics." In *Can You Forgive Her?*, by Anthony Trollope. Oxford: Oxford University Press, 1982.

———. *The Victorians and the Visual Imagination*. Cambridge: Cambridge University Press, 2000.

Formanek-Brunell, Miriam. *Made to Play House: Dolls and the Commercialization of American Girlhood, 1830–1930*. 1993. Reprint, Baltimore: Johns Hopkins University Press, 1998.

Foster, Vanda. *A Visual History of Costume: The Nineteenth Century*. London: B. T. Batsford, 1984.

Foucault, Michel. *The History of Sexuality. Volume 1: An Introduction*. Trans. Robert Hurley. New York: Vintage, 1980.

Fraser, Antonia. *Dolls*. London: Weidenfeld and Nicolson, 1963.

Fredeman, William E. "Emily Faithfull and the Victoria Press: An Experiment in Sociological Biography." *The Library*, 5th ser., 29.2 (1974): 139–64.

Freedgood, Elaine. "Realism, Fetishism, and Genocide: 'Negro Head' Tobacco in and around *Great Expectations*." *Novel: A Forum on Fiction* 36.1 (2002): 26–41.

French, A. L. "Beating and Cringing." *Essays in Criticism* 24 (1974): 147–68.

Freud, Sigmund. "Femininity." 1932. Reprinted in *New Introductory Lectures on Psychoanalysis*, ed. James Strachey, 139–67. New York: Norton, 1965.

Freud, Sigmund. "Some Psychological Consequences of the Anatomical Distinction between the Sexes." 1925. Reprinted in *Sexuality and the Psychology of Love*, ed. Philip Rieff. New York: Collier, 1963.

Frost, Ginger. "Bigamy and Cohabitation in Victorian England." *Journal of Family History* 22.3 (1997): 286–306.

———. *Promises Broken: Courtship, Class, and Gender in Victorian England.* Charlottesville: University Press of Virginia, 1995.

Fryer, Peter, ed. *The Man of Pleasure's Companion: A Nineteenth Century Anthology of Amorous Entertainment.* London: Arthur Barker Ltd., 1968.

———. *Mrs. Grundy: Studies in English Prudery.* London: Dennis Dobson, 1964.

Fuss, Diana. *Identification Papers.* New York: Routledge, 1995.

———. "Fashion and the Homospectatorial Look." In *On Fashion*, eds. Shari Benstock and Suzanne Ferris, 211–32. New Brunswick, NJ: Rutgers University Press, 1994.

Gagnier, Regenia. *Subjectivities: A History of Self-Representation in Britain, 1832–1920.* New York: Oxford University Press, 1991.

Galbraith, Gretchen R. *Reading Lives: Reconstructing Childhood, Books, and Schools in Britain, 1870–1920.* New York: St. Martin's Press, 1997.

Gallagher, Catherine. *The Industrial Reformation of English Fiction 1832–1867.* Chicago: University of Chicago Press, 1985.

Garelick, Rhonda K. *Rising Star: Dandyism, Gender, and Performance in the Fin de Siècle.* Princeton: Princeton University Press, 1998.

Gay, Peter. *The Bourgeois Experience: Victoria to Freud.* Vol. 1, *Education of the Senses.* New York: Oxford University Press, 1984.

Gilbert, Elliot L. "'In Primal Sympathy': *Great Expectations* and the Secret Life." *Dickens Studies Annual* 11 (1983): 89–113.

Gilbert, Sandra M. "From *Patria* to *Matria*: Elizabeth Barrett Browning's Risorgimento." *PMLA* 99.1 (1984): 194–211.

Gilbert, Sandra M., and Susan Gubar. *The Madwoman in the Attic: The Woman Writer and the Nineteenth-Century Literary Imagination.* New Haven: Yale University Press, 1979.

Gillis, John. *For Better, For Worse: British Marriages, 1600 to the Present.* New York: Oxford University Press, 1985.

Ginsburg, Madeleine. *An Introduction to Fashion Illustration.* London: Compton Press, 1980.

Ginsburg, Michal Peled. "Dickens and the Uncanny: Repression and Displacement in *Great Expectations*." *Dickens Studies Annual* 13 (1984): 115–24.

Girard, René. *Deceit, Desire, and the Novel: Self and Other in Literary Structure.* Trans. Yvonne Freccero. 1961. Reprint, Baltimore: Johns Hopkins University Press, 1965.

Glendinning, Victoria. *Trollope.* London: Hutchinson, 1992.

Gorham, Deborah. *The Victorian Girl and the Feminine Ideal.* London: Croom Helm, 1982.

Green, Roger Lancelyn. *Tellers of Tales: Children's Books and Their Authors from 1800 to 1964.* London: Edmund Ward Publishers, 1965.

Halberstam, Judith. *Female Masculinity.* Durham, NC: Duke University Press, 1998.

Hall, N. John. *Trollope: A Biography.* Oxford: Clarendon Press, 1991.

Hamburger, Lotte, and Joseph Hamburger. *Contemplating Adultery: The Secret Life of a Victorian Woman.* New York: Fawcett Columbine, 1991.

Hartman, Mary S. "Child Abuse and Self-Abuse: Two Victorian Cases." *History of Childhood Quarterly* 2.2 (1974): 221–48.

Hartog, Curt. "The Rape of Miss Havisham." *Studies in the Novel* 14.3 (1982): 248–65.

Hertzberg, Hendrik. "Dog Bites Man." *New Yorker,* May 5, 2003, 33.

Hewitt, Margaret. "Anthony Trollope: Historian and Sociologist." *The British Journal of Sociology* 14.3 (1963): 226–39.

Higonnet, Anne. *Berthe Morisot's Images of Women.* Cambridge, Mass.: Harvard University Press, 1992.

———. *Pictures of Innocence: The History and Crisis of Ideal Childhood.* London: Thames and Hudson, 1998.

Hillier, Mary. *Dolls and Doll-Makers.* London: Weidenfeld & Nicolson, 1968.

Hinde, Robert A. *Relationships: A Dialectical Perspective.* Hove: Psychology Press, 1997.

Hitchcock, Tim. "Redefining Sex in Eighteenth-Century England." *History Workshop Journal* 41 (1996): 72–90.

Holcombe, Lee. *Wives and Property: Reform of the Married Women's Property Law in Nineteenth-Century England.* Toronto: University of Toronto Press, 1983.

Holland, Vyvyan. *Hand Coloured Fashion Plates, 1770 to 1899.* London: B. T. Batsford, 1955.

Hollibaugh, Amber. *My Dangerous Desires: A Queer Girl Dreaming Her Way Home.* Durham, NC: Duke University Press, 2000.

Homans, Margaret. *Royal Representations: Queen Victoria and British Culture, 1837–1876.* Chicago: University of Chicago Press, 1998.

Horstman, Allen. *Victorian Divorce.* London: Croom Helm, 1985.

Houghton, Walter. *The Victorian Frame of Mind, 1830–1870.* New Haven: Yale University Press, 1957.

Houston, Gail Turley. "'Pip' and 'Property': The (Re)production of the Self in *Great Expectations.*" *Studies in the Novel* 24.1 (1992): 13–25.

Huff, Cynthia. *British Women's Diaries.* New York: AMS Press, 1985.

Hunt, Linda C. "Sustenance and Balm: The Question of Female Friendship in *Shirley* and *Villette.*" *Tulsa Studies in Women's Literature* 1.1 (1982): 55–66.

Hunt, Lynn. *The Invention of Pornography: Obscenity and the Origins of Modernity, 1500–1800.* New York: Zone Books, 1996.

Hunt, Margaret R. *The Middling Sort: Commerce, Gender, and the Family in England, 1680–1760.* Berkeley: University of California Press, 1996.

Hürlimann, Bettina. *Three Centuries of Children's Books in Europe.* Trans. and ed. Brian W. Alderson. London: Oxford University Press, 1967.

Hynes, Joseph A. "Image and Symbol in *Great Expectations.*" *ELH* 30.3 (1963): 258–92.

Incorvati, Rick. "Introduction: Women's Friendships and Lesbian Sexuality." *Nineteenth-Century Contexts* 23.2 (2001): 176.

Jacobs, Jo Ellen. *The Voice of Harriet Taylor Mill.* Bloomington: Indiana University Press, 2002.

Jacobus, Mary. "The Buried Letter: Feminism and Romanticism in *Villette.*" In *Women Writing and Writing about Women*, ed. Mary Jacobus, 43–54. London: Croom Helm, 1979.

Jalland, Patricia. Introduction to *Octavia Wilberforce: Autobiography of a Pioneer Woman Doctor.* London: Cassell, 1989.

———. *Women, Marriage and Politics 1860–1914.* Oxford: Clarendon Press, 1986.

Jalland, Patricia, and John Hooper, eds. *Women from Birth to Death: The Female Life Cycle in Britain 1830–1914.* Brighton: Harvester Press, 1986.

Jameson, Fredric. *The Political Unconscious: Narrative as a Socially Symbolic Act.* Ithaca: Cornell University Press, 1981.

Jeffreys, Sheila. *The Spinster and Her Enemies: Feminism and Sexuality 1880–1930.* London: Pandora Press, 1985.

Jelinek, Estelle C. *The Tradition of Women's Autobiography: From Antiquity to the Present.* Boston: Twayne, 1986.

Johnson, Claudia. "The Divine Miss Jane." In *Janeites: Austen's Disciples and Devotees*, ed. Deidre Lynch, 25–44. Princeton: Princeton University Press, 2000.

Jones, Wendy. "Feminism, Fiction and Contract Theory: Trollope's *He Knew He Was Right.*" *Criticism* 36.3 (1994): 401–5.

Joyce, Patrick. *Democratic Subjects: The Self and the Social in Nineteenth-Century England.* Cambridge: Cambridge University Press, 1994.

Kahn, Victoria. *Wayward Contracts: The Crisis of Political Obligation in England, 1640–1674.* Princeton: Princeton University Press, 2004.

Kaplan, Morris. *Sodom on the Thames: Sex, Love and Scandal in Wilde Times.* Ithaca: Cornell University Press, 2005.

Katz, Jonathan Ned. *The Invention of Heterosexuality.* New York: Plume, 1996.

———. *Love Stories: Sex Between Men Before Homosexuality.* Chicago: University of Chicago Press, 2001.

Kaye, Richard A. *The Flirt's Tragedy: Desire without End in Victorian and Edwardian Fiction.* Charlottesville: University Press of Virginia, 2002.

Kearney, Patrick J. *The Private Case: An Annotated Bibliography of the Private Case Erotica in the British (Museum) Library.* London: Jay Landesman Ltd., 1981.

Kendrick, Walter. *The Secret Museum: Pornography in Modern Culture.* Berkeley: University of California Press, 1987.

Kent, Susan Kingsley. *Gender and Power in Britain, 1640–1990.* London: Routledge, 1999.

Kim, Jin-Ok. *Charlotte Brontë and Female Desire.* New York: Peter Lang, 2003.

Kincaid, James. *Child-Loving: The Erotic Child and Victorian Culture.* New York: Routledge, 1992.

———. *The Novels of Anthony Trollope.* Oxford: Clarendon Press, 1977.

King, Amy. *Bloom: The Botanical Vernacular in the English Novel.* New York: Oxford University Press, 2003.

King, Margaret. "'Certain Learned Ladies': Trollope's *Can You Forgive Her?* and the Langham Place Circle." *Victorian Literature and Culture* 21 (1993): 307–26.

Kooistra, Lorraine Janzen. "*Goblin Market* as a Cross-Audienced Poem: Children's Fairy Tale, Adult Erotic Fantasy." In *Children's Literature*, vol. 25, 181–204. New Haven: Yale University Press, 1997.

Koven, Seth. *Slumming: Sexual and Social Politics in Victorian London*. Princeton: Princeton University Press, 2004.

Kuchta, David. *The Three-Piece Suit and Modern Masculinity: England, 1550–1850*. Berkeley: University of California Press, 2002.

Kucich, John. *Repression in Victorian Fiction: Charlotte Brontë, George Eliot, and Charles Dickens*. Berkeley: University of California Press, 1987.

Kuper, Adam. *The Invention of Primitive Society: Transformations of an Illusion*. London: Routledge, 1988.

Kurnick, David. "An Erotics of Detachment: *Middlemarch* and Novel-Reading as a Critical Practice," *ELH* (forthcoming).

Kuznets, Lois Rostow. *When Toys Come Alive: Narratives of Animation, Metamorphosis, and Development*. New Haven: Yale University Press, 1994.

Ladenson, Elisabeth. *Proust's Lesbianism*. Ithaca: Cornell University Press, 1999.

Lamos, Colleen. "Taking on the Phallus." In *Lesbian Erotics*, ed. Karla Jay, 101–24. New York: New York University Press, 1995.

Langbauer, Laurie. "Women in White, Men in Feminism." *The Yale Journal of Criticism* 2.2 (1989): 219–43.

Lanser, Susan S. "Befriending the Body: Female Intimacies as Class Acts." *Eighteenth-Century Studies* 32.2 (1998–1999): 179–98.

LaPlanche, Jean, and Jean-Baptiste Pontalis. "Fantasy and the Origins of Sexuality." *The International Journal of Psycho-Analysis* 49 (1968): 1–18.

Laqueur, Thomas. "Amor Veneris, Vel Dulcedo Appeletur." In *Fragments Toward a History of the Body*, ed. Michel Feher et. al., 91–131. New York: Zone Books, 1989.

———. *Making Sex: Body and Gender from the Greeks to Freud*. Cambridge, Mass.: Harvard University Press, 1990.

———. *Solitary Sex: A Cultural History of Masturbation*. New York: Zone Books, 2003.

Lasdun, Susan. *Making Victorians: The Drummond Children's World 1827–1832*. London: Victor Gollancz, 1983.

Laver, James. *Clothes*. New York: Horizon Press, 1953.

Leavis, F. R., and Q. D. Leavis. *Dickens the Novelist*. London: Chatto & Windus, 1970.

Leckie, Barbara. *Culture and Adultery: The Novel, the Newspaper, and the Law, 1857–1914*. Philadelphia: University of Pennsylvania Press, 1999.

Lee, Hermione. *Virginia Woolf*. New York: Vintage Books, 1996.

Lehmann, Ulrich. *Tigersprung: Fashion and Modernity*. Cambridge, Mass.: MIT Press, 2000.

Levine, George. "Can You Forgive Him? Trollope's 'Can You Forgive Her?' and the Myth of Realism." *Victorian Studies* 18 (1974): 5–30.

Levine, Philippa. *Feminist Lives in Victorian England: Private Role and Public Commitment*. Oxford: Basil Blackwell, 1990.

Lévi-Strauss, Claude. *The Elementary Structures of Kinship*. Trans. James Harle Bell, John Richard von Sturmer, and Rodney Needham. 1949. Reprint, Boston: Beacon Press, 1969.

Lewin, Tamar. "Nationwide Survey Includes Data on Teenage Sex Habits." *New York Times*, September 16, 2005, A12.

Lewis, Naomi. Introduction to *The Silent Playmate: A Collection of Doll Stories*. 1979. Reprint, New York: Macmillan, 1981.

Liddington, Jill. *Female Fortune: Land, Gender and Authority. The Anne Lister Diaries and Other Writings*. London: Rivers Oram Press, 1998.

Lipovetsky, Gilles. *The Empire of Fashion: Dressing Modern Democracy*. Trans. Catherine Porter. Princeton: Princeton University Press, 1994.

Lucey, Michael. *The Misfit of the Family: Balzac and the Social Forms of Sexuality*. Durham, NC: Duke University Press, 2003.

———. *Never Say I: Sexuality and the First Person in Colette, Gide, and Proust*. Durham, NC: Duke University Press, 2006.

MacDonald, Susan Peck. *Anthony Trollope*. Boston: Twayne Publishers, 1987.

Maines, Rachel P. *The Technology of Orgasm: "Hysteria," the Vibrator, and Women's Sexual Satisfaction*. Baltimore: Johns Hopkins University Press, 1999.

Marcus, Sharon. "Comparative Sapphism." In *The Literary Channel: The International Invention of the Novel*, eds. Margaret Cohen and Carolyn Dever, 251–85. Princeton: Princeton University Press, 2002.

———. "Queer Theory for Everyone: A Review Essay." *Signs: Journal of Women in Culture and Society* 31.1 (2005): 191–218.

Marcus, Steven. *The Other Victorians: A Study of Sexuality and Pornography in Mid-Nineteenth-Century England*. New York: Basic Books, 1966.

Markus, Julia. *Across an Untried Sea: Discovering Lives Hidden in the Shadow of Convention and Time*. New York: Alfred A. Knopf, 2000.

Mason, Michael. *The Making of Victorian Sexuality*. Oxford: Oxford University Press, 1994.

Matlock, Jann. "Censoring the Realist Gaze." In *Spectacles of Realism: Gender, Body, Genre*, eds. Margaret Cohen and Christopher Prendergast, 28–65. Minneapolis: University of Minnesota Press, 1995.

Matthew, H.C.G. *Gladstone: 1809–1874*. Oxford: Clarendon Press, 1986.

Mauss, Marcel. *The Gift: Forms and Functions of Exchange in Archaic Societies*. Trans. Ian Cunnison. New York: Norton, 1967.

Mavor, Carol. *Becoming: The Photographs of Clementina, Viscountess Hawarden*. Durham, NC: Duke University Press, 1999.

———. *Pleasures Taken: Performances of Sexuality and Loss in Victorian Photographs*. Durham, NC: Duke University Press, 1995.

Maynard, John. *Victorian Discourses on Sexuality and Religion*. Cambridge: Cambridge University Press, 1993.

McCalman, Ian. *Radical Underworld: Prophets, Revolutionaries, and Pornographers in London, 1795–1840*. Cambridge: Cambridge University Press, 1988.

McCormick, Ian, ed. *Secret Sexualities: A Sourcebook of 17th and 18th Century Writing*. London: Routledge, 1997.

McDowell, Colin. *The Man of Fashion: Peacock Males and Perfect Gentlemen.* London: Thames & Hudson, 1997.

McMaster, Juliet. *Trollope's Palliser Novels: Theme and Pattern.* London: Macmillan, 1978.

Mehta, Uday S. "Liberal Strategies of Exclusion." In *Tensions of Empire: Colonial Cultures in a Bourgeois World*, eds. Frederick Cooper and Ann Laura Stoler, 59–86. Berkeley: University of California Press, 1997.

Meisel, Martin. "Miss Havisham Brought to Book." *PMLA* 81.3 (1966): 278–85.

Mendes, Peter. *Clandestine Erotic Fiction in English 1800–1930.* Aldershot: Scolar Press, 1993.

Merck, Mandy. "The Lesbian Hand." In *In Your Face: 9 Sexual Studies*, 124–247. New York: New York University Press, 2000.

Mermin, Dorothy. *Elizabeth Barrett Browning: The Origins of a New Poetry.* Chicago: University of Chicago Press, 1989.

Merrill, Lisa. *When Romeo Was a Woman: Charlotte Cushman and Her Circle of Female Spectators.* Ann Arbor: University of Michigan Press, 1999.

Miller, D. A. "Body Bildung and Textual Liberation." In *A New History of French Literature*, ed. Denis Hollier, 681–87. Cambridge, Mass.: Harvard University Press, 1989.

———. *Narrative and Its Discontents: Problems of Closure in the Traditional Novel.* Princeton: Princeton University Press, 1981.

———. *The Novel and the Police.* Berkeley: University of California Press, 1988.

Miller, Nancy. "Emphasis Added: Plots and Plausibilities in Women's Fiction." *PMLA* 96 (1981): 36–48.

Mitchell, Sally. *Frances Power Cobbe: Victorian Feminist, Journalist, Reformer.* Charlottesville: University of Virginia Press, 2004.

Moers, Ellen. *Literary Women.* New York: Doubleday, 1976.

Moon, Michael. *A Small Boy and Others: Imitation and Initiation in American Culture from Henry James to Andy Warhol.* Durham, NC: Duke University Press, 1998.

Moore, Doris Langley. *Fashion through Fashion Plates 1771–1970.* London: Ward Lock Ltd., 1971.

Moore, Lisa L. *Dangerous Intimacies: Toward a Sapphic History of the British Novel.* Durham, NC: Duke University Press, 1997.

Moretti, Franco. *The Way of the World: The Bildungsroman in European Culture.* Trans. Albert Sbragia. 1987. Reprint, London: Verso, 2000.

Morgan, Thaïs. "Male Lesbian Bodies: The Construction of Alternative Masculinities in Courbet, Baudelaire, and Swinburne." *Genders* 15 (Winter 1992): 37–57.

Moynahan, Julian. "The Hero's Guilt: The Case of *Great Expectations.*" *Essays in Criticism* 10.1 (1960): 60–79.

Mulvey, Laura. "Visual Pleasure and Narrative Cinema." *Screen* 16.3 (1975): 6–18.

Munich, Adrienne. *Queen Victoria's Secrets.* New York: Columbia University Press, 1996.

Nead, Lynda. *Victorian Babylon: People, Streets and Images in Nineteenth-Century London.* New Haven: Yale University Press, 2000.

Nealon, Christopher. *Foundlings: Lesbian and Gay Historical Emotion before Stonewall.* Durham, NC: Duke University Press, 2001.

Nelson, Claudia. *Boys Will Be Girls: The Feminine Ethic and British Children's Fiction, 1857–1917.* New Brunswick, NJ: Rutgers University Press, 1991.

Néret, Gilles. *Erotica: 19th Century: From Courbet to Gaugin.* Cologne: Taschen, 2001.

Nestor, Pauline. *Female Friendships and Communities: Charlotte Brontë, George Eliot, Elizabeth Gaskell.* Oxford: Clarendon Press, 1985.

Newton, Esther. "The Mythic Mannish Lesbian: Radclyffe Hall and the New Woman." Reprinted in *Margaret Mead Me Gay: Personal Essays, Public Ideas*, 176–88. Durham, NC: Duke University Press, 2000.

Newton, Stella Mary. *Health, Art and Reason: Dress Reformers of the 19th Century.* London: John Murray, 1974.

Norberg, Kathryn. "Making Sex Public: Félicité de Choiseul-Meuse and the Lewd Novel." In *Going Public: Women and Publishing in Early Modern France*, eds. Elizabeth C. Goldsmith and Dena Goodman, 161–75. Ithaca: Cornell University Press, 1995.

Nunokawa, Jeff. *Tame Pleasures of Wilde: The Styles of Manageable Desire.* Princeton: Princeton University Press, 2003.

Olian, JoAnne. *Full-Color Victorian Fashions: 1870–1893.* Mineola, NY: Dover, 1999.

Pateman, Carole. *The Sexual Contract.* Stanford: Stanford University Press, 1988.

Pedersen, Susan. *Eleanor Rathbone and the Politics of Conscience.* New Haven: Yale University Press, 2004.

Perrot, Philippe. *Fashioning the Bourgeoisie: A History of Clothing in the Nineteenth Century.* Trans. Richard Bienvenu. Princeton: Princeton University Press, 1994.

Peterson, Linda H. "Collaborative Life Writing as Ideology: The Auto/biographies of Mary Howitt and Her Family." *Prose Studies* 26.1–2 (2003): 176–95.

———. *Traditions of Victorian Women's Autobiography: The Poetics and Politics of Life Writing.* Charlottesville: University Press of Virginia, 1999.

———. *Victorian Autobiography: The Tradition of Self-Interpretation.* New Haven: Yale University Press, 1986.

Pinchbeck, Ivy, and Margaret Hewitt. *Children in English Society.* Vol. 2, *From the Eighteenth Century to the Children Act 1948.* London: Routledge and Kegan Paul, 1973.

Plotz, John. *The Crowd: British Literature and Public Politics.* Berkeley: University of California Press, 2000.

———. *Portable Properties, Local Logic: Culture on the Move and in Place in Victorian Greater Britain.* Forthcoming.

Polhemus, Robert. *The Changing World of Anthony Trollope.* Berkeley: University of California Press, 1968.

Polkey, Pauline. "Recuperating the Love-Passions of Edith Simcox." In *Women's Lives into Print: The Theory, Practice and Writing of Feminist Auto/biography*, ed. Pauline Polkey, 61–79. London: Macmillan, 1999.

Pollock, Linda. *Forgotten Children: Parent-Child Relations from 1500 to 1900.* Cambridge: Cambridge University Press, 1983.

Poovey, Mary. *Uneven Developments: The Ideological Work of Gender in Mid-Victorian England.* Chicago: University of Chicago Press, 1988.

President George W. Bush. Speech announcing support for a constitutional amendment banning same-sex marriage, delivered February 24, 2004. http://www.cnn.com/2004/ALLPOLITICS/02/24/elec04.prez.bush.transcript/index.html

Propp, Vladimir. *Morphology of the Folktale*, ed. Louis A. Wagner. Trans. Laurence Scott. 1928. Reprint, Austin: University of Texas Press, 1968.

Psomiades, Kathy. "Heterosexual Exchange and Other Victorian Fictions: *The Eustace Diamonds* and Victorian Anthropology." *Novel: A Forum on Fiction* 33.1 (1999): 93–118.

Radway, Janice. *Reading the Romance: Women, Patriarchy, and Popular Literature.* Chapel Hill: University of North Carolina Press, 1984.

Rand, Erica. *Barbie's Queer Accessories.* Durham, NC: Duke University Press, 1995.

Reis, Pamela Tamarkin. "Victorian Centerfold: Another Look at Millais's *Cherry Ripe.*" *Victorian Studies* 35.2 (1992): 201–5.

Rendall, Jane. "John Stuart Mill, Liberal Politics, and the Movements for Women's Suffrage, 1865–1873." In *Women, Privilege, and Power: British Politics, 1750 to the Present*, ed. Amanda Vickery, 168–200. Stanford: Stanford University Press, 2001.

Reynolds, Kimberley. *Girls Only? Gender and Popular Children's Fiction in Britain, 1880–1910.* New York: Harvester Wheatsheaf, 1990.

Ribeiro, Aileen. *Dress and Morality.* London: B. T. Batsford, 1986.

Rich, Adrienne. "Compulsory Heterosexuality and Lesbian Existence." In *The Signs Reader: Women, Gender, and Scholarship*, eds. Elizabeth Abel and Emily K. Abel, 139–68. 1980. Reprint, Chicago: University of Chicago Press, 1983.

Riley, Denise. *"Am I That Name?" Feminism and the Category of "Women" in History.* Minneapolis: University of Minnesota Press, 1988.

Robbins, Bruce. "How to Be a Benefactor without Any Money: The Chill of Welfare in *Great Expectations.*" In *Knowing the Past: Victorian Literature and Culture*, ed. Suzy Anger, 172–91. Ithaca: Cornell University Press, 2001.

———. *Upward Mobility and the Common Good.* Princeton: Princeton University Press, 2007.

Robson, Catherine. *Men in Wonderland: The Lost Girlhood of the Victorian Gentleman.* Princeton: Princeton University Press, 2001.

Roden, Frederick S. *Same-Sex Desire in Victorian Religious Culture.* Houndmills: Palgrave Macmillan, 2002.

Rodolff, Rebecca. "What David Copperfield Remembers of Dora's Death." *The Dickensian* 77.1 (Spring 1981): 32–39.

Roof, Judith. *All About Thelma and Eve: Sidekicks and Third Wheels.* Urbana: University of Illinois Press, 2002.

———. *Come As You Are: Sexuality and Narrative.* New York: Columbia University Press, 1996.

Rose, Jacqueline. *The Case of Peter Pan or the Impossibility of Children's Fiction*. London: Macmillan, 1984.

Rosenman, Ellen Bayuk. *Unauthorized Pleasures: Accounts of Victorian Erotic Experience*. Ithaca, NY: Cornell University Press, 2003.

Ross, Ellen. "Survival Networks: Women's Neighbourhood Sharing in London before World War I." *History Workshop Journal* 15 (1983): 4–27.

Rousseau, George, and Caroline Warman. "Made from the Stuff of Saints: Chateaubriand's *René* and Custine's Search for a Homosexual Identity." *GLQ* 7.1 (2001): 1–29.

Rubin, Gayle. "Thinking Sex: Notes for a Radical Theory of the Politics of Sexuality." In *Pleasure and Danger: Exploring Female Sexuality*, ed. Carole S. Vance, 267–319. Boston: Routledge & Kegan Paul, 1984.

———. "The Traffic in Women: Notes toward a Political Economy of Sex." In *Toward an Anthropology of Women*, ed. Rayna Reiter, 157–210. New York: Monthly Review Press, 1975.

Said, Edward. *Culture and Imperialism*. New York: Vintage Books, 1993.

Savage, Gail L. "'Intended Only for the Husband': Gender, Class, and the Provision for Divorce in England, 1858–1868." In *Victorian Scandals: Representations of Gender and Class*, ed. Kristine Ottesen Garrigan, 11–42. Athens: Ohio University Press, 1992.

Savy, Nicole. *Les petites filles modernes*. Paris: Editions de la Réunion des Musées Nationaux, 1989.

Schirrmeister, Anne. "La Dernière Mode: Berthe Morisot and Costume." In *Perspectives on Morisot*, ed. T. J. Edelstein, 103–115. New York: Hudson Hills Press, 1990.

Schor, Hilary. *Dickens and the Daughter of the House*. Cambridge: Cambridge University Press, 1999.

Scott, Joan Wallach. *Gender and the Politics of History*. New York: Columbia University Press, 1988.

———. *Only Paradoxes to Offer: French Feminists and the Rights of Man*. Cambridge, Mass.: Harvard University Press, 1996.

Sedgwick, Eve Kosofsky. *Between Men: English Literature and Male Homosocial Desire*. New York: Columbia University Press, 1985.

———. *Epistemology of the Closet*. Berkeley: University of California Press, 1990.

———. *Tendencies*. Durham: Duke University Press, 1993.

———, ed. *Novel Gazing: Queer Readings in Fiction*. Durham, NC: Duke University Press, 1997.

Sell, Kathleen. "The Narrator's Shame: Masculine Identity in *Great Expectations*." *Dickens Studies Annual* 26 (1988): 203–26.

Shanley, Mary Lyndon. "A Husband's Right to His Wife's Body: Wife Abuse, the Restitution of Conjugal Rights, and Marital Rape," in *Feminism, Marriage, and the Law in Victorian England* (Princeton: Princeton University Press, 1989): 156–88.

———. "'One Must Ride Behind': Married Women's Rights and the Divorce Act of 1857," *Victorian Studies* 25 (1982): 355–76.

Shannon, Brent. "ReFashioning Men: Fashion, Masculinity, and the Cultivation of the Male Consumer in Britain, 1860–1914." *Victorian Studies* 46.4 (2004): 597–630.

Sherman, Stuart. *Telling Time: Clocks, Diaries, and English Diurnal Form, 1660–1785.* Chicago: University of Chicago Press, 1996.

Sherwood, Dolly. *Harriet Hosmer: American Sculptor 1830–1890.* Columbia: University of Missouri Press, 1991.

Shires, Linda. "Narrative, Gender, and Power in *Far from the Madding Crowd.*" In *The Sense of Sex: Feminist Perspectives on Hardy,* ed. Margaret R. Higonnet, 49–65. Urbana: University of Illinois Press, 1993.

Shores, Lucille P. "The Character of Estella in *Great Expectations.*" *Massachusetts Studies in English* 3.4 (1972): 91–99.

Showalter, Elaine. *A Literature of Their Own: British Women Novelists from Brontë to Lessing.* Princeton: Princeton University Press, 1977.

———. *Sexual Anarchy: Gender and Culture at the Fin de Siècle.* New York: Viking, 1990.

Siegel, Carol. "Postmodern Women Novelists Review Victorian Male Masochism." *Genders* 11 (1991): 1–16.

Sigel, Lisa Z. *Governing Pleasures: Pornography and Social Change in England, 1815–1914.* New Brunswick, NJ: Rutgers University Press, 2002.

Sinfield, Alan. "Lesbian and Gay Taxonomies." *Critical Inquiry* 29 (Autumn 2002): 120–38.

Slater, Michael. *Dickens and Women.* London: J. M. Dent, 1983.

Smith, Sidonie. *A Poetics of Women's Autobiography: Marginality and the Fictions of Self-Representation.* Bloomington: Indiana University Press, 1987.

Smith-Rosenberg, Carroll. "The Female World of Love and Ritual." In *Feminism and History,* ed. Joan Scott, 366–97. Oxford: Oxford University Press, 1996.

Solomon-Godeau, Abigail. "The Other Side of Venus: The Visual Economy of Feminine Display." In *The Sex of Things: Gender and Consumption in Historical Perspective,* eds. Victoria de Grazia and Ellen Furlough, 113–50. Berkeley: University of California Press, 1996.

Sombart, Werner. *Luxury and Capitalism.* Vol. 1. Trans. W. R. Dittmar. New York: Columbia University Department of Social Science, 1939.

Somerville, Siobhan. *Queering the Color Line: Race and the Invention of Homosexuality in American Culture.* Durham, NC: Duke University Press, 2000.

Spain, Nancy. *The Beeton Story.* London: Ward, Lock & Co., 1956.

St. George, Eleanor. *Dolls of Three Centuries.* New York: Charles Scribner's Sons, 1951.

Stansell, Christine. *American Moderns: Bohemian New York and the Creation of a New Century.* New York: Henry Holt, 2000.

Steedman, Carolyn. *Strange Dislocations: Childhood and the Idea of Human Interiority, 1780–1930.* Cambridge, Mass.: Harvard University Press, 1995.

Steele, Valerie. *Fashion and Eroticism: Ideals of Feminine Beauty from the Victorian Era to the Jazz Age.* New York: Oxford University Press, 1985.

Stein, Edward. "Past and Present Proposed Amendments to the United States Constitution Regarding Marriage." *Washington University Law Quarterly* 82.3 (2004): 611–85.

Stetson, Dorothy. *A Woman's Issue: The Politics of Family Law Reform in England*. Westport, CT: Greenwood Press, 1982.

Steward, Douglas. "Anti-Oedipalizing *Great Expectations*: Masochism, Subjectivity, Capitalism." *Literature and Psychology* 45.3 (1999): 29–50.

Stocking, George. W. Jr. *Victorian Anthropology*. New York: The Free Press, 1987.

Stockton, Kathryn Bond. *God Between Their Lips: Desire Between Women in Irigaray, Brontë, Eliot*. Stanford: Stanford University Press, 1994.

Stone, Harry. "Dickens's Woman in White." *Victorian Newsletter* 33 (Spring 1968): 5–8.

Stone, James S. *Emily Faithfull, Victorian Champion of Women's Rights*. Ontario: P. D. Meany Publishers, 1994.

Stone, Lawrence. *The Family, Sex, and Marriage in England 1500–1800*. New York: Harper Books, 1979.

Summers, Leigh. *Bound to Please: A History of the Victorian Corset*. Oxford: Berg, 2001.

Tadmor, Naomi. *Family and Friends in Eighteenth-Century England: Household, Kinship, and Patronage*. Cambridge: Cambridge University Press, 2001.

Tanner, Tony. *Adultery in the Novel: Contract and Transgression*. Baltimore: Johns Hopkins Press, 1979.

Tarnowska, Maree. *Fashion Dolls*. London: Souvenir Press, 1986.

Taylor, Barbara. *Eve and the New Jerusalem: Socialism and Feminism in the Nineteenth Century*. New York: Pantheon Books, 1983.

Terry, Jennifer. *An American Obsession: Science, Medicine, and Homosexuality in Modern Society*. Chicago: University of Chicago Press, 1999.

Thomas, Katie-Louise. "A Queer Job for a Girl: Women Postal Workers, Civic Duty and Sexuality 1870–80." In *In A Queer Place: Sexuality and Belonging in British and European Contexts*, eds. Kate Chedgzoy, Emma Francis, and Murray Pratt, 50–70. Aldershot, UK: Ashgate, 2002.

Thurin, Susan Schoenbauer. "The Relationship between Dora and Agnes." *Dickens Studies Newsletter* 12.4 (1981): 102–8.

Tiffany, Daniel. *Toy Medium: Materialism and Modern Lyric*. Berkeley: University of California Press, 2000.

Todd, Janet. *Women's Friendship in Literature*. New York: Columbia University Press, 1980.

Tosa, Marco. *Dolls*. Trans. Wendy Dallas. London: B. T. Batsford, 1987.

Toulalan, Sarah. "Extraordinary Satisfactions: Lesbian Visibility in Seventeenth-Century Pornography in England." *Gender & History* 15.1 (2003): 50–68.

Townsend, Camilla. "'I Am the Woman for Spirit': A Working Woman's Gender Transgression in Victorian London." In *Sexualities in Victorian Britain*, eds. Andrew H. Miller and James Eli Adams, 214–33. Bloomington: Indiana University Press, 1996.

Trumbach, Randolph. "London's Sapphists: From Three Sexes to Four Genders in the Making of Modern Culture." In *Body Guards: The Cultural Politics of Gender Ambiguity*, eds. Julia Epstein and Kristina Straub, 112–41. New York: Routledge, 1991.

Trumpener, Katie. *Bardic Nationalism: The Romantic Novel and the British Empire.* Princeton: Princeton University Press, 1997.

Turner, Kay, ed. *Dear Sappho: A Legacy of Lesbian Love Letters.* London: Thames & Hudson, 1996.

Turner, Mark. "Cruising in Queer Street: Streetwalking Men in Late-Victorian London." In *In a Queer Place: Sexuality and Belonging in British and European Contexts*, eds. Kate Chedgzoy, Emma Francis, and Murray Pratt, 89–109. Aldershot, UK: Ashgate, 2002.

———. *Trollope and the Magazines: Gendered Issues in Mid-Victorian Britain.* New York: St. Martin's Press, 2000.

Vanita, Ruth. *Sappho and the Virgin Mary: Same-Sex Love and the English Literary Imagination.* New York: Columbia University Press, 1996.

Van Arsdel, Rosemary T. *Florence Fenwick Miller: Victorian Feminist, Journalist, and Educator.* Aldershot: Ashgate, 2001.

Van Ghent, Dorothy. "The Dickens World: The View from Todgers's." *Sewanee Review* 58 (1950): 419–38.

van Slyke, Gretchen. "Who Wears the Pants Here? The Policing of Women's Dress in Nineteenth-Century England, Germany and France." *Nineteenth-Century Contexts* 17.1 (1993): 17–33.

Vicinus, Martha. "Lesbian Perversity and Victorian Marriage: The 1864 Codrington Divorce Trial." *Journal of British Studies* 36 (January 1997): 70–98.

———. *Intimate Friends: Women Who Loved Women, 1778–1928.* Chicago: University of Chicago Press, 2004.

Vickery, Amanda. *The Gentleman's Daughter: Women's Lives in Georgian England.* New Haven: Yale University Press, 1998.

———, ed. *Women, Privilege, and Power: British Politics, 1750 to the Present.* Stanford: Stanford University Press, 2001.

Vincent, David. *Bread, Knowledge, and Freedom: A Study of Nineteenth-Century Working-Class Autobiography.* London: Methuen, 1981.

Wahl, Elizabeth. *Invisible Relations: Representations of Female Intimacy in the Age of Enlightenment.* Stanford: Stanford University Press, 1999.

Walkley, Christina. *The Way to Wear 'em: 150 Years of Punch on Fashion.* London: Peter Owen, 1985.

Walkowitz, Judith. *City of Dreadful Delight: Narratives of Sexual Danger in Late-Victorian London.* Chicago: University of Chicago Press, 1992.

———. *Prostitution in Victorian Society: Women, Class, and the State.* Cambridge: Cambridge University Press, 1980.

———. "The 'Vision of Salome': Cosmopolitanism and Erotic Dancing in Central London, 1908–1918." *American Historical Review* 108.2 (2003): 337–76.

Walsh, Susan. "Bodies of Capital: *Great Expectations* and the Climacteric Economy." *Victorian Studies* 37.1 (1993): 73–98.

Walvin, James. *A Child's World: A Social History of English Childhood 1800–1914.* Harmondsworth: Penguin Books, 1982.

Warner, Michael. "Homo-Narcissism; or, Heterosexuality." In *Engendering Men: The Question of Male Feminist Criticism*, eds. Joseph A. Boone and Michael Cadden, 190–206. New York: Routledge, 1990.

———. *The Trouble with Normal: Sex, Politics, and the Ethics of Queer Life.* New York: Free Press, 1999.

Weaver, William. "'A School-Boy's Story': Writing the Victorian Public Schoolboy Subject." *Victorian Studies* 46.3 (2004): 455–87.

Webb, Peter. "Victorian Erotica." In *The Sexual Dimension in Literature*, ed. Alan Bold, 90–121. New York: Barnes and Noble, 1983.

Weinstone, Ann. "The Queerness of Lucy Snowe." *Nineteenth-Century Contexts* 18.4 (1995): 367–84.

Weissman, Judith, and Steven Cohan. "Dickens's *Great Expectations*: Pip's Arrested Development." *American Imago* 38.1 (1981): 105–26.

Weston, Kath. *Families We Choose: Lesbians, Gays, Kinship.* New York: Columbia University Press, 1997.

Westwater, Martha. *The Wilson Sisters: A Biographical Study of Upper Middle-Class Victorian Life.* Athens: Ohio University Press, 1984.

Wheelright, Julie. *Amazons and Military Maids: Women Who Dressed as Men in Pursuit of Life, Liberty and Happiness.* London: Pandora, 1989.

White, Gwen. *A Book of Dolls.* London: Adam & Charles Black, 1956.

Wilson, Anita Carol. "Literary Criticism of Children's Literature in Mid-Victorian England." Ph.D. dissertation. SUNY Stonybrook, 1981.

Wilson, Elizabeth, and Lou Taylor. *Through the Looking Glass: A History of Dress from 1860 to the Present Day.* London: BBC Books, 1989.

Wittig, Monique. "On the Social Contract." In *Homosexuality, Which Homosexuality?*, eds. Dennis Altman, Carole Vance, Martha Vicinus, and Jeffrey Weeks, 239–49. London: GMP Publishers, 1989.

Woloch, Alex. *The One vs. the Many: Minor Characters and the Space of the Protagonist in the Novel.* Princeton: Princeton University Press, 2003.

Woodhouse, Margaret K. "The Marriage and Divorce Bill of 1857." *The American Journal of Legal History* 3 (1959): 260–75.

Young, Agnes Brooks. *Recurring Cycles of Fashion: 1760–1934.* New York: Harper, 1937.

Zimmerman, Bonnie. "'The Dark Eye Beaming': Female Friendship in George Eliot's Fictions." In *Lesbian Texts and Contexts: Radical Revisions*, eds. Karla Jay and Joanne Glasgow, 126–44. New York: New York University Press, 1990.

Zonana, Joyce. "The Embodied Muse: Elizabeth Barrett Browning's *Aurora Leigh* and Feminist Poetics." *Tulsa Studies in Women's Literature* 8.2 (1989): 240–62.

Zwerdling, Alex. "Mastering the Memoir: Woolf and the Family Legacy." *Modernism/Modernity* 10.1 (2003): 165–88.

Zwinger, Lynda. *Daughters, Fathers, and the Novel: The Sentimental Romance of Heterosexuality.* Madison: University of Wisconsin Press, 1991.

Illustration Credits

Permission to reprint figures 6, 9, 12, 14, and 15 from JoAnne Olian, *Full Color Victorian Fashions 1870–1893* (Mineola, NY: Dover Publications, 1999), kindly granted by Dover Publications.

Permission to reprint figure 2 from Christina Walkley, *The Way to Wear 'em: 150 Years of* Punch *on Fashion* (London: Peter Owen, 1985), kindly granted by Peter Owen Ltd.

Permission to reprint figure 20 from Margaret Whitton, *The Jumeau Doll* (Toronto: Dover Publications, in association with the Margaret Woodbury Strong Museum, 1980), kindly granted by Dover Publications.

Index